Asia Rising

Asia Rising

Growth and Resilience in an Uncertain
Global Economy

Edited by

Hal Hill

*H.W. Arndt Professor of Southeast Asian Economies,
Australian National University*

Maria Socorro Gochoco-Bautista

*Senior Economic Advisor, Asian Development Bank, on leave
as Professor of Economics, University of the Philippines*

CO-PUBLICATION OF THE ASIAN DEVELOPMENT BANK AND
EDWARD ELGAR PUBLISHING

Edward Elgar
Cheltenham, UK • Northampton, MA, USA

ADB

Published by
Edward Elgar Publishing Limited
The Lypiatts
15 Lansdown Road
Cheltenham
Glos GL50 2JA
UK

Edward Elgar Publishing, Inc.
William Pratt House
9 Dewey Court
Northampton
Massachusetts 01060
USA

The views expressed in this book are those of the authors and do not necessarily reflect the views and policies of the Asian Development Bank (ADB), its Board of Governors or the governments they represent.

ADB does not guarantee the accuracy of the data included in this publication and accepts no responsibility for any consequences of their use.

By making any designation of or reference to a particular territory or geographic area, or by using the term "country" in this document, ADB does not intend to make any judgments as to the legal or other status of any territory or area.

Asian Development Bank

6 ADB Avenue, Mandaluyong City
1550 Metro Manila, Philippines
Tel +63 2 632 4444
Fax +63 2 636 2444
www.adb.org

A catalogue record for this book
is available from the British Library

Library of Congress Control Number: 2012943191

MIX
Paper from
responsible sources
FSC
www.fsc.org   FSC® C018575

ISBN 978 1 78100 797 6

Typeset by Servis Filmsetting Ltd, Stockport, Cheshire
Printed and bound by MPG Books Group, UK

Contents

List of contributors   vii
Foreword by Changyong Rhee   ix
Preface   xi
List of abbreviations   xiv

PART I OVERVIEW

1 Perspectives and issues   3
Hal Hill and Maria Socorro Gochoco-Bautista

PART II ASIAN DEVELOPMENT CHALLENGES

2 Institutions and governance   49
Emmanuel S. de Dios and Geoffrey M. Ducanes

3 Infrastructure   76
Douglas H. Brooks and Eugenia C. Go

4 Productivity and capital accumulation   104
Kyoji Fukao

5 Savings and investment   137
Charles Yuji Horioka and Akiko Terada-Hagiwara

6 Finance   154
Shin-ichi Fukuda

7 Investment treaties: ASEAN   184
Diane A. Desierto

PART III COUNTRY STUDIES

8 Malaysia   213
Tham Siew Yean

9 Indonesia   246
Ari Kuncoro

10   India   285
     Rajendra R. Vaidya

11   People's Republic of China   313
     Siow Yue Chia

12   Thailand   345
     Bhanupong Nidhiprabha

13   Philippines   385
     Desiree A. Desierto and Geoffrey M. Ducanes

Index   409

Contributors

Douglas H. Brooks is Assistant Chief Economist, Economics and Research Department, Asian Development Bank, Manila.

Siow Yue Chia is Senior Research Fellow, Singapore Institute of International Affairs, and formerly Executive Director, Institute of Southeast Asian Studies, and Professor of Economics, National University of Singapore.

Emmanuel S. de Dios is Professor of Economics, School of Economics, University of the Philippines, Diliman.

Desiree A. Desierto is Assistant Professor of Economics, School of Economics, University of the Philippines, Diliman.

Diane A. Desierto is Assistant Professor (international economic law and international human rights) at Peking University School of Transnational Law, Shenzhen, People's Republic of China.

Geoffrey M. Ducanes is Assistant Professor of Economics, School of Economics, University of the Philippines, Diliman.

Kyoji Fukao is Professor, Institute of Economic Research, Hitotsubashi University, Tokyo and Program Director of the Research Institute of Economy, Trade and Industry in Japan.

Shin-ichi Fukuda is Professor of Economics, University of Tokyo.

Eugenia C. Go is Economics and Statistics Officer, Economics and Research Department, Asian Development Bank, Manila.

Maria Socorro Gochoco-Bautista is Senior Economic Advisor, Economics and Research Department, Asian Development Bank, Manila and Professor of Economics (on leave), University of the Philippines.

Hal Hill is the H.W. Arndt Professor of Southeast Asian Economies, Arndt-Corden Department of Economics, Crawford School, College of Asia and the Pacific, Australian National University, Canberra.

Charles Yuji Horioka is Professor, Institute of Social and Economic Research, Osaka University, Osaka, Japan and Research Associate,

National Bureau of Economic Research, Cambridge, Massachusetts, USA.

Ari Kuncoro is Professor of Economics, University of Indonesia, Jakarta, Visiting Research Fellow at Large, Brown University and Visiting Fellow, Australian National University.

Bhanupong Nidhiprabha is Associate Professor of Economics, and Dean, Faculty of Economics, Thammasat University, Bangkok.

Akiko Terada-Hagiwara is Economist, Economics and Research Department, Asian Development Bank, Manila.

Tham Siew Yean is Professor of International Trade and Principal Research Fellow and former Director, Institute of Malaysian and International Studies, National University of Malaysia, Kuala Lumpur.

Rajendra R. Vaidya is Professor of Economics, Indira Gandhi Institute of Development Research, Mumbai, India.

Foreword

This book is about sustaining Asia's growth and prosperity in an increasingly uncertain global economy. The goal of attaining sustainable and inclusive growth in the region underpins ADB's vision for Asia's economic development and this book hopefully provides valuable knowledge for the region's current and future policy makers and leaders.

Asia Rising: Growth and Resilience in an Uncertain Global Economy presents a timely, relevant, and in-depth treatise of issues confronting Asia, the challenges Asia has to surpass, and the available policy options, given an environment of depressed aggregate demand from the advanced economies in the West. Confronted with the threat of chronic and persistent weakness in global demand, Asia needs to rethink its economic policies and strategies for sustained economic growth and development.

The book presents a comprehensive discourse on the region's past and prospective economic performance in relation to its growth dynamics, the development of key sectors and institutions, savings and investment behavior, and the aspects of country level idiosyncrasies and regional coordination and integration. It presents thematic cross-cutting analyses and country-level studies that provide the reader an immersive view of current development issues in Asia.

While Asia has enjoyed rapid economic growth since the 1980s and has successfully hurdled the effects of several financial crises, its ability to sustain growth and eradicate poverty necessitates continued productive investment in the region. Ironically, despite the region's vast savings, investment growth in many countries in Asia has been anemic since the end of the Asian Financial Crisis of 1997–98. The various possible reasons for this – inefficient financial intermediation in the region, low productivity, poor governance, and a weak regulatory framework, among others – are discussed in this volume.

The book is a result of close collaboration by a team of economists from the region. This effort provides a broad and collective view of current development issues and policy options for Asia to sustain its high growth trajectory despite a weaker global economy fraught with uncertainty.

Changyong Rhee
Chief Economist, Asian Development Bank

Preface

The economic recession that commenced in late 2008 in several rich countries has been a defining event for the global economy and Asia's role in it. World economic growth slowed sharply, but the large Asian developing economies, notably the People's Republic of China, India, and Indonesia, continued to grow strongly. This uneven growth dynamic has accelerated Asia's rising global prominence. But it also raised important new challenges for the region.

The first and most important is to maintain the growth momentum. The lower middle-income countries still have a sizeable proportion of the population living precariously just above the poverty line. For the upper middle-income economies, for example Malaysia, a key issue is the elusive goal of 'upgrading' to the ranks of developed economies within the next decade or so. The second challenge is to remove the existing bottlenecks to growth with the provision of efficient infrastructure, still a major problem for several countries, including India, Indonesia and the Philippines. In some cases, this is symptomatic of a broader problem of sluggish investment levels. Third, some countries, such as the People's Republic of China and Malaysia, continue to run sizeable current account surpluses, resulting in exceptionally large foreign exchange reserves being invested in low-return assets and creating international commercial tensions. Fourth, in the wake of the global recession, which had its origins in financial malpractice in several western economies, there is the imperative of further strengthening financial development and regulation, to guard against a recurrence of these difficulties. Fifth, there is the challenge of developing high-quality institutions that underpin and sustain the continuing economic transformation.

To address these issues, an expert team of writers was commissioned. We wanted both country studies for key developing middle-income Asian economies, and cross-cutting thematic papers. The countries chosen were the People's Republic of China, India, Indonesia, Malaysia, the Philippines, and Thailand. The thematic issues focused on governance and institutions, infrastructure, investment and productivity, savings and investment, and financial development. The resulting papers and our overview constitute the chapters of this volume.

Three workshops were held at the ADB headquarters to present and discuss drafts. These were held in June 2010, January 2011, and May 2011.

It is a pleasure to thank the many individuals without whom this volume would not have seen the light of day. Our major debt is to the contributors, who participated in all three workshops, who diligently met our deadlines and who responded to our numerous requests.

At the ADB, Mary Ann Magadia was with us throughout the project. She expertly organized all three workshops, oversaw all the correspondence, and assisted in many other ways.

Several ADB colleagues kindly commented on the draft presentations at the three workshops.

They include:

Akiko Terada-Hagiwara	Asian Development Bank
Amado Mendoza	University of the Philippines
Arief Ramayandi	Asian Development Bank
Ashok Sharma	Asian Development Bank
Benno Ferrarini	Asian Development Bank
Cyn-Young Park	Asian Development Bank
Donghyun Park	Asian Development Bank
Fan Zhai	China Investment Corporation
Guanghua Wan	Asian Development Bank
Hiranya Mukhopadhyay	Asian Development Bank
Hyun Hwa Son	Asian Development Bank
Jayant Menon	Asian Development Bank
Jorn Brommelhorster	Asian Development Bank
Kelly Bird	Asian Development Bank
Kiseok Hong	Ewha Women's University
Niny Khor	Asian Development Bank
Norio Usui	Asian Development Bank
Purnima Rajapakse	Asian Development Bank
Shikha Jha	Asian Development Bank
Tadateru Hayashi	Asian Development Bank
Yi Jiang	Asian Development Bank

Marc Lerner edited the papers, corresponded with the contributors, and prepared the manuscript according to ADB and Edward Elgar style.

Several other ADB staff assisted us. Junray Bautista and Anthony Baluga assisted us with data preparation. Mercedita Cabaneros did the graphics and layout of the manuscript. Maria Guia de Guzman helped prepare the final manuscript for the publisher.

Successive Chief Economists at the ADB, Jong-Wha Lee and Changyong Rhee, provided helpful advice and support throughout the project.

We are especially grateful to Robert Davis of ADB's Department of External Relations and to Emily Neukomm and staff at Edward Elgar for their interest in the project, and their helpful support throughout the publication process.

HH and MSGB
31 May 2012

Abbreviations

ACIA	ASEAN Comprehensive Investment Agreement
AEM	ASEAN Economic Ministers
AFC	Asian financial crisis
AFTA	ASEAN Free Trade Area
AIA	ASEAN Investment Area
APO	Asian Productivity Organization
ASEAN	Association of Southeast Asian Nations
ASEAN IGA	ASEAN Investment Guarantee Agreement
BI	Bank Indonesia
BPO	business process outsourcing
BSP	Bangko Sentral ng Pilipinas
CCI	coordinating committee on investment
CDOs	collateralized debt obligations
CIC	China Investment Corporation
CMI	Chiang Mai Initiative
CPI	consumer price index
EKC	Environmental Kuznets Curve
EMU	Economic and Monetary Union of the European Union
EPF	employee provident fund
EPU	economic planning unit
EU	European Union
FAI	fixed asset investment
FDI	foreign direct investment
FTA	free trade agreement
GCR	Global Competitiveness Report
GER	global economic recession
GFCF	gross fixed capital formation
GLCs	government-linked companies
GDP	gross domestic product
GNI	gross national income
HDN	Human Development Network
HRS	household registration system
ICSID	International Centre for Settlement of Investment Disputes

IEA	International Energy Agency
IFS	International Financial Statistics
IIA	international investment agreements
IMF	International Monetary Fund
IRF	International Road Federation
KWh	kilowatt-hour
Ktoe	kilo tons of oil equivalent
LPI	Logistics Performance Index
MFN	most-favored nation
MNC	multinational corporations
NEDA	National Economic Development Authority
NEM	New Economic Model
NEP	New Economic Policy
NFA	National Food Authority
NIEs	newly industrialized economies
NPL	nonperforming loans
ODI	outward direct investment
OECD	Organisation for Economic Co-operation and Development
OFW	overseas foreign workers
OLS	ordinary least squares
PBC	People's Bank of China
PMG	pooled mean group
PPI	private participation in infrastructure
PPPs	private–public partnerships
PPP	purchasing power parity
PRC	People's Republic of China
PWT	Penn World Tables
RBI	Reserve Bank of India
REER	real effective exchange rate
RORO	roll-on, roll-off
SBIs	Bank Indonesia Certificates
SDP	state domestic product
SEBI	Securities and Exchange Board of India
SEZs	special economic zones
SMEs	medium-sized enterprises
SOE	state-owned enterprise
TAC	Treaty of Amity and Cooperation
TFP	total factor productivity
TMB	Telekom Malaysia Berhad
TRIMS	trade-related investment measures
TRIPS	trade-related aspects of intellectual property rights

UK	United Kingdom
UNCITRAL	United Nations Commission on International Trade Law
UNCTAD	United Nations Conference on Trade and Development
UNIDO	United Nations Industrial Development Organization
US	United States
VAT	value-added tax
WDI	World Development Indicators
WTO	World Trade Organization

PART I

Overview

1. Perspectives and issues

Hal Hill and Maria Socorro Gochoco-Bautista

INTRODUCTION

This may be the Asian Century, but it is also a period of deep global uncertainty. If the global economy is characterized as consisting of five dominant pillars – Europe, North America, Japan, the People's Republic of China (PRC), and a group of major emerging economies – then only the latter two are vibrant and dynamic. The first two dominated the world economy during most of the 20th century, and together with Japan they were the key engines of growth in the post-war period. Now, however, all three are beset by serious problems of low growth, high debt, and a political economy environment that renders growth-oriented economic reform very difficult.

The developing Asian economies therefore have to sustain growth in an exceptionally difficult environment, and one in which they will have to assume increasing responsibility for the maintenance of global economic growth. Their export dynamism is threatened by slow growth in most rich economies, compounded by attendant rising protectionism. As major savers, they also have a stake in the construction of global and regional economic and financial architectures that both hasten recovery and reduce the likelihood of further crises. And yet there is the paradox that rich countries are looking to much poorer countries both as sources of needed capital and as global economic locomotives. After all, in spite of the economic vitality, many millions of people in these developing Asian countries exist in precarious circumstances, at best living only marginally above very modest national poverty thresholds. Moreover, even before the recent global economic recession (GER), some appeared to be in danger of losing their economic dynamism, with investment levels well below those achieved prior to the Asian financial crisis (AFC) of 1997–98.

The central question of this volume is how developing middle-income Asian countries maintain their economic dynamism and navigate through deep economic crises against the backdrop of continuing global uncertainty and instability. At least four broad sets of issues are pertinent in addressing this question. The first is growth dynamics, including long-term growth performance, resilience in response to exogenous shocks, recovery from crises, and the special challenges of upgrading for upper middle-income economies. The second is savings and financial development, with lessons learned from recent events, especially the AFC and the GER. The third is investment behavior after the AFC, including in some countries the challenges of sluggish investment levels and difficulties in funding long-term infrastructure projects. The fourth concerns international and regional dimensions, including uneven recovery patterns, large current account imbalances, and the special problems of coordination and provision of global "public goods."

These questions can be answered only with reference to both broad thematic studies and detailed country-level analyses. This volume therefore includes both. Consistent with our analytical framework and questions, the volume includes studies of investment and productivity, savings behavior, financial development and reform, infrastructure, investment agreements, and institutions and governance. These cross-cutting chapters are combined with six developing-country studies, comprising Asia's two very large developing economies, the PRC and India; the world's fourth most populous nation, Indonesia; and three important mid-sized economies: Malaysia, the Philippines and Thailand.[1] These countries share common membership of the middle-income developing group, geographic proximity, and generally strong economic performance. But there is considerable diversity among them, which provides an analytical and policy richness in addressing the major issues. For example, they vary significantly in their growth rates, size, crises experiences, savings–investment levels and balances, openness, financial development, infrastructure levels, and institutional quality.

Deep crises of the sort that occurred in 2008–09 during the GER are generally defining and unsettling events, which have significant analytical and policy implications. They shake up – and sometimes overturn – complacent governments, and may push them to undertake major reforms. As one comparative political economy study concluded, "Turning points [in economic policy] are invariably associated with macroeconomic crises" (Lal and Myint 1996: 288). Crises also force scholars to reevaluate scholarly orthodoxy, to understand these events, and to develop new ways of forestalling them. The resulting academic debates may continue for a decade or more, as was the experience following the 1930s Great Depression, and is clearly likely in contemporary debates.

The next section of this chapter provides the context for the study, investigating in particular the historic shifts in the global economy occasioned by the rise of middle-income developing Asia, the longer-term growth dynamics of the six economies, and the special challenges of graduation for the more advanced economies in this group. The section that follows examines the impact of, response to, and lessons learned from crises in the six economies, focusing mainly on the events of 2008–09, but referring also to the AFC, which for three of the economies (Indonesia, Malaysia, and Thailand) was a far more serious event. The chapter then analyzes the patterns and determinants of savings and investment behavior and balances in the six economies, including a reference to the special challenge of infrastructure investments. Following that analysis is a section that considers some of the key economic policy issues in the wake of the crises, including the development of an efficient and resilient financial sector, some major macroeconomic policy challenges, nurturing institutions and structures of governance that support durable growth, and the potential for regional and international policy coordination. The final section provides some summary observations.

THE CONTEXT

The Rise of Asia

Most of the six economies have grown quickly since 1980. This observation is subject to four main caveats that will be developed below. First, the high-growth momentum took root in India from the early 1990s and in countries such as Viet Nam from late 1980s. Second, the major exception was the Philippines from 1980 to 2000 when there was no net increase in real per capita gross domestic product (GDP). Third, the AFC and GER slowed growth significantly in all but the two largest economies. Fourth, the three Southeast Asian economies that were severely affected by the AFC recovered quite quickly from the crisis, but for the following decade their growth and investment trajectories remained substantially lower than before the crisis.

The very high growth of the PRC since the late 1970s and India since the late 1990s is one of the most important global economic events of the past four decades. The share of global GDP of the PRC and India declined from 1960 to 1980 as both disengaged from world commerce and accorded a low priority to economic development. But the increases in the share of global GDP have been dramatic since then, especially for the PRC, from 1.7 per cent to 8.6 per cent, while the Indian share rose from 1.8 per cent to 2.4 per cent. Propelled by these increases, over the same period the share of developing Asia also rose very quickly, from 1.8 per cent to 19.9 per cent. The shares of trade and foreign direct investment (FDI) have also risen

*Table 1.1   People's Republic of China (PRC), India and emerging Asia in
the global economy*

	Share of global GDP (%)		
	PRC	India	Asia ex. Japan
1960	4.5	2.7	10.8
1982	1.8	1.8	11.5
2000	3.7	1.4	12.7
2009	8.6	2.4	19.9
2015f	11.8	2.9	27.0
2050	21.5	13.8	47.8
	Share of global trade (%)		
1982	1	0.7	17.1
2000	3.4	0.8	22.1
2009	7.9	1.8	28.3
	Share of global FDI (%)		
1982	0.6	0.1	21.7
2000	1.6	0.2	9.2
2009	6.5	2.2	21.8
	Share of global GDP increment (%)		
1990–2009	16.1	4.0	32.6
2000–09	23.0	5.6	42.3
2005–09	36.4	8.5	59.2
	Share of global trade increment (%)		
1990–2009	10.4	2.3	32.9
2000–09	12.6	2.9	34.8
2005–09	17.2	4.4	43.5

Sources: ADB staff calculations, based on data from World Bank, World Development
Indicators; IMF, World Economic Outlook; and UNCTAD, World Investment Report,
various issues.

very quickly, especially for the PRC where the increase has been about
eightfold. According to various projections these two countries, together
with the rest of emerging Asia, may well constitute about half of the global
economy by the middle of the 21st century (see Table 1.1). Asian economic
prominence is not however a new phenomenon. According to the path-
breaking estimates of the late Angus Maddison (2007), the PRC and India
together accounted for a similar ratio prior to the onset of the European
industrial revolution and the rise of the United States (US).

The rise of emerging Asia was under way in the last quarter of the 20th

GDP Growth
Annual Percentage Change

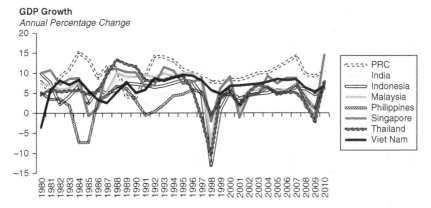

Source: IMF World Economic Outlook Database.

Figure 1.1   Economic growth, 1980–2010

century as growth rates in several of these economies began to exceed that of global GDP by a large margin. But two events began to have a major impact: the spread of high growth from the smaller economies to the giants, and the onset of the GER, which resulted in sluggish growth in the major rich economies. Since the PRC and India – and also Indonesia – have maintained their growth momentum in recent years, their share of the increment to global economic activity in 2008 and 2009 was very large. That is, they have become major global economic locomotives, with all the geopolitical ramifications associated with this historic relocation of the center of global economic gravity. Over the past two decades, the PRC alone has accounted for 16 per cent of the increase in global GDP, and Asia (with the exception of Japan) for almost one-third (see Table 1.1). In the past decade the incremental shares rose to 23 per cent and 42 per cent respectively, while since 2005 the emerging Asia share has been dominant at almost 60 per cent. The shares for trade and FDI have been similarly large and rising.

The Six Economies and their Growth Dynamics

As noted, the six economies are diverse in most respects apart from geographical location, middle-income status, and generally strong economic growth. Several features stand out in the economic growth record since 1980 (see Figure 1.1). The PRC's growth is consistently very high, while India's growth is rising and begins to join the very high-growth group from the late 1990s. Another latecomer, Viet Nam, has been growing very fast for most of the period. There are some synchronized growth variations, especially during the two crises. But there are differences too, with the PRC and India – and Viet Nam to some extent – being much less affected. Indonesia, Malaysia, and Thailand were deeply affected in 1997–98, while in 2008–09 Indonesia continued to register moderately strong growth, whereas Malaysia and Thailand slid into slightly negative growth. The Philippines is something of an outlier, experiencing a deep crisis in the mid-1980s while the rest of the neighborhood prospered. However, it was not deeply affected in either the AFC or the GER, and its growth since the early 1990s has been better than is generally recognized.

Growth has been episodic in most of the countries and quite volatile in the very open economies and commodity exporters that are more exposed to international shocks. Domestic political factors have also affected the growth paths, with political instability an occasional factor in Indonesia, the Philippines, and Thailand. The period under examination is generally not long enough to observe significant turning points in economic fortunes, particularly those associated with major, growth-enhancing economic reforms. These are typically dated at around 1978 for the PRC (Naughton 2007), 1991 for India (Panagariya 2008), 1966 for Indonesia (Hill 2000), and the mid-1980s for Viet Nam. The Philippines experienced a "lost decade" of economic crisis in the transition to democracy (Balisacan and Hill 2003). These turning points are much less relevant for Malaysia and Thailand, where the major policy settings have been broadly consistent since the 1960s.

The decomposition of the sources of economic growth, in particular the contribution of net exports to growth, also underlines the region's diversity (see Table 1.2, column 7). The range is very large, in our sample from 20 per cent (for the Philippines) to −4.2 per cent (for India). The median for emerging Asia is 10.8 per cent, and 9.1 per cent for all six countries in this study. However, this figure is pulled up by the much higher percentages for the three more advanced economies, Hong Kong, China; the Republic of Korea; and Singapore. The ratio for our six economies is much less than that of the two powerful advanced-country exporters, Germany and Japan. Therefore the conclusion that these middle-income Asian countries, as a group, are behaving in a mercantilist fashion, relative to current international norms, is not sustainable.

Table 1.3 further illustrates the diversity of the six economies with reference to some key (and admittedly highly simplified) "stylized facts" for each one, focusing on variables of relevance to this study. These include growth dynamics and the impact of the two major economic crises, fiscal policy and debt, monetary policy and exchange rates, savings, investment, current account balances, infrastructure, and finance development. We return to these stylized facts in the country analysis below.

Table 1.2 Contribution to economic growth, 2000–08

GDP economy	Average GDP growth	GDP growth contributions					Net export's share of contribution to growth	Net exports as per cent of GDP, 2008
		Total	Consumption		Investment	Net exports		
			Private	Government				
	(1)	(2)	(3)	(4)	(5)	(6)	(7)=(6)/(1)	(8)
People's Republic of China (PRC)	10.2	4.1	2.8	1.3	5.0	1.1	10.8	7.9
Hong Kong, China	5.0	2.3	2.1	0.2	1.3	1.7	34.0	12.2
India	7.2	4.1	3.5	0.5	3.6	–0.3	–4.2	–4.3
Indonesia	5.2	3.1	2.5	0.6	1.4	0.4	7.7	9.6
Republic of Korea	4.9	2.5	1.9	0.6	1.0	1.4	28.6	4.4
Malaysia	5.1	4.6	3.5	1.1	0.4	0.1	2.0	13.1
Philippines	5.0	3.9	3.8	0.2	0.7	1.0	20.0	1.4
Singapore	5.5	2.8	2.1	0.6	1.5	1.5	27.3	20.4
Thailand	4.8	2.7	2.4	0.4	1.5	0.5	10.4	15.4
Median								
All Countries	5.1	3.1	2.5	0.6	1.4	1.0	10.8	9.6
All ex. PRC	5.1	3.0	2.5	0.6	1.4	0.8	15.2	10.9
International comparisons								
Germany	1.4	0.5	0.3	0.2	0.1	0.9	64.3	6.8
Japan	1.5	1	0.6	0.4	0.2	0.5	33.3	4.9
United States	2.3	2.3	2	0.3	0.1	–0.1	–0.1	–3.3

Source: Authors' estimates.

9

Asia rising

Table 1.3   The economies – some key stylized facts (I)

Variable	People's Republic of China	India	Indonesia	Viet Nam
Growth dynamics	Extremely high growth	Accelerating growth from the 1980s	High growth slower since 1998	Very high growth since Doi Moi
Crisis effects	Little impact of AFC and GFC	Little impact of AFC and GFC	Deep crisis in 1998, resilient in 2008	Slower growth in AFC and GFC
Fiscal policy and debt	Soft budget constraints challenge fiscal balances	Large deficits and debt, but mainly domestic	Debt explosion in 1998, quickly contained	Soft budget constraints challenge fiscal balances
Monetary policy and exchange rate	Generally fairly prudent, gradually rising RMB	RBI a credible institution, inflation contained	BI independent, struggles to curb inflation	Challenge of multiple targeting
Savings rate	Extremely high savings	Rapid increase in savings since 1970s	Moderately high savings, recovered in 1998	Rapid increase in savings since Doi Moi
CA balance	Large surpluses, a major internat issue	Modest deficits	Modest deficits or surpluses	Sizable deficits, rising ST funding
Infrastructure	Major investments, high quality	Struggles to keep up	Struggles to keep up since 1998	Major investments, overcoming backlog
Finance sector	State dominated vulnerable	Well established and supervised	Gradual recovery from 1998 collapse	State dominated, vulnerable

Notes: AFC = Asian financial crisis; GFC = global financial crisis; RBI = Reserve Bank of India; ST = Short term; BNM = Bank Negara Malaysia; BSP = Bangko Sentral ng Pilipinas; BOT = Bank of Thailand.

Source: Authors' compilation.

Table 1.3   The economies – some key stylized facts (II)

Variable	Malaysia	Philippines	Thailand
Growth dynamics	Very fast but slowing since 1998	Historic under-performer but solid since 1992	Very fast but slowing since 1998
Crisis effects	Negative growth in both AFC and GFC	Maintained weak positive growth in both	Negative growth in both AFC and GFC
Fiscal policy and debt	Consistent deficits, but domestically financed	Continuous fiscal policy struggle	Historical prudence, recovered from AFC debt
Monetary policy and exchange rate	BNM a creditable institution, low inflation	BSP a credible institution, inflation contained	Low inflation, BOT a credible institution
Savings rate	Consistently high savings	Rapid increase in savings since 1970s	Moderately high savings, recovered since 1998
CA balance	Very large surpluses since 1998	General modest deficits	Switch from deficits to surpluses after AFC
Infrastructure	Effective infra provider, though politicized	Struggles to keep up	Effective infra provider, though politicized
Finance sector	Well developed, prudent since 1998	Cautious, well supervised since 1980s collapse	A major rebuilding after 1998 collapse

According to two strands of literature, these generally high growth rates are either misleading because they are primarily input driven, or they are the fortuitous result of exceptionally favorable but temporary demographic dividends. Fukao (Chapter 4) comprehensively examines the productivity record in these economies finding that, as expected, the growth of total factor productivity (TFP) closely follows that of GDP and the business cycle. He also finds little evidence in support of the notion that growth has been achieved primarily through "perspiration," that is, input growth. The story is a mixed one across countries: TFP increased quite strongly in the Republic of Korea after the AFC, the Philippines continues to be an outlier with its consistently slow growth, while both Indonesia and Thailand experienced a sharp drop during the AFC. In both these economies it took about a decade to recover to pre-crisis levels, a finding similar to that of Latin American economies after their crisis episodes. A factor in the decline and slow growth in TFP in some crisis-affected economies has been slowing structural change, with the result that resources have remained locked in the low-productivity agricultural sector. Clearly, the balance sheet effects of crises are serious and long lasting, and it takes time for investment levels and the financial sectors to recover.

Fukao (Chapter 4) also cautions that there are considerable differences in the TFP estimates depending on the methodologies and databases employed. The measurement of labor quality and capital stock has its limitations, while intra-sector TFP is not well measured.

Demographic issues are discussed below with reference to the savings rate. Suffice it to note here that these economies are currently in a development phase characterized by a "demographic bonus," that is with a high proportion of their population of working age. This bonus will progressively come to end for the six, very soon in the case of the PRC and Thailand, and growth rates are therefore likely to decline. But these demographic factors are not the primary explanation of the region's high growth, and thus the transition from "bonus" to "burden" will not lead to a growth collapse (Bloom and Finlay 2009).

The Challenge of Upgrading

With the partial exception of the Philippines, which along with Malaysia had the highest per capita income of the six in the 1950s, these economies have effectively managed the transition from low- to middle-income developing economy status, very recently in the case of India and Viet Nam, owing to their high growth. The richer ones among them – primarily Malaysia, but increasingly also the PRC and Thailand – have now set their goals to achieve developed-country status quite soon, 2020 in the case of Malaysia. A more or less linear projection of past growth rates would suggest that such a goal is readily achievable, that countries are on track to achieve the arbitrarily defined threshold of gross national income (GNI) per capita of $12,000, although later than most official projections indicate.

Is there anything more to the issue than simply a projection forward of the past growth momentum? An emerging body of literature suggests there might be. Illustrative of some of the thinking is the following observation of the World Bank (2007, 1):

> History shows that while many countries have been able to make it from low income to middle income, relatively few have carried on to high income. . . . A lot of complex challenges have to be met, from raising the skills and innovativeness of the labor force to creating sophisticated financial systems, to maintaining social cohesion, to greatly reducing corruption. Without these sorts of tough policy and institutional changes, countries stay where they are, unable to bust out of middle income.

Conventional growth theory, built on the assumption of "convergence," provides little guidance, as it rests uncomfortably alongside the empirical observation that the gap between high- and low-income countries over the past two centuries has widened rather than narrowed. Almost all of the catch-up exceptions have been the high-growth developing economies of East Asia, with Chile in Latin America and Botswana and Mauritius in Africa the only exceptions in the other major developing regions (Collier 2007; Edwards 2010).

One informative body of literature on these issues is that of evolutionary economics, developed by Richard Nelson and others; see for example Nelson (2008), who is the source of the quotes in this paragraph. According to this thesis, the key to catch-up is innovation, "learning to do effectively what countries at the frontier have been doing, often for some time" (2008, 16). Compared to the earlier success stories of the Republic of Korea and Taipei,China, the contemporary challenges are both easier and harder, Nelson argues. They are easier in the sense that the body of codified knowledge underlying most technologies has become much stronger than was the case 30 years ago, and it can also be accessed through training in advanced sciences at leading universities through the world. But in some ways they are also harder. There is arguably a greater need to build up indigenous skills and capacity in engineering and science. Institutional and political economy factors are central. First, "catch-up will be impossible unless a country builds up its education system from bottom to top" (2008, 16). Second, the process of catch up entails rapid structural change, including sometimes a painful process of creative destruction as older firms and technologies are swept away. This may be difficult in view of the "political power of old firms. . . . For comfortable, politically well-connected old firms, creative destruction is not a welcome thing" (2008, 17).

This evolutionary economics literature is indicative of the sorts of policy reforms that are required to facilitate the structural adjustment that sustains the growth momentum beyond the middle-income range. These include a commitment to high-quality education through to the tertiary level; investments in research and development facilities and innovation; regulatory, financial and legal institutions that underpin an advanced market economy; competitive market structures that support the process of rapid structural change and "creative destruction"; and credible, prudent macroeconomic management.

The country in our sample for which this literature is most relevant is Malaysia, which has clearly lost comparative advantage in labor-intensive activities and whose government's pronouncements focus heavily on the graduation objective. As Tham (Chapter 8) observes, "Malaysia is facing increasing pressure on the external front. . . . Internally, the country is at the crossroads politically, economically, and socially." Its slower growth since the late 1990s does provide some prima facie support for the hypothesis that graduation is difficult. However, on closer inspection (see Hill et al. 2012), its recent record provides mixed support for the thesis. The major problems appear to be homegrown: a dominant party in continuous rule for over half a century, displaying all the symptoms of a long period in government – arrogance, complacence, and corruption. An additional factor has been the country's long-running affirmative action program which, while introduced for commendable reasons to preserve social harmony in an ethnically diverse country, has been captured by an elite intent on enriching itself. Thus the country's polity is not able to undertake the requisite institutional and policy reforms for the economy to manage the transition, or at least finds it very difficult to do so.

NAVIGATING CRISES

A detailed study of the economic crises of 1997–98 and 2008–09 is beyond the scope of this volume, but these two events are central to the issues under examination. That is, the crises are both the key to understanding the countries' growth dynamics, and more than any other event over the past two decades they have set the economic policy agendas at the country, regional and international levels. We therefore briefly consider their impacts on the six economies.

The major point to observe is again diversity. Figure 1.2 presents quarterly GDP data for the six for the relevant years, 1997–99 and

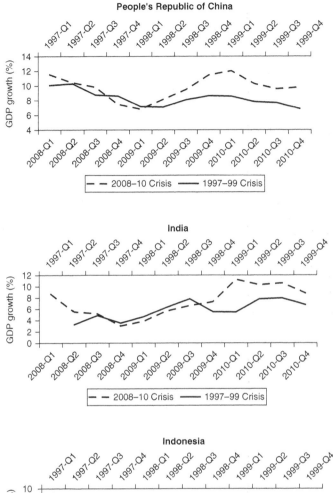

Figure 1.2   Crisis impacts: 1997–98 and 2008–09 compared

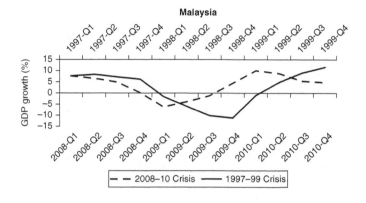

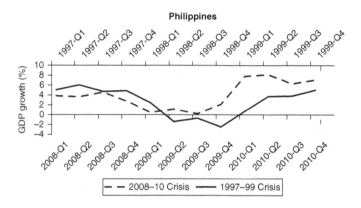

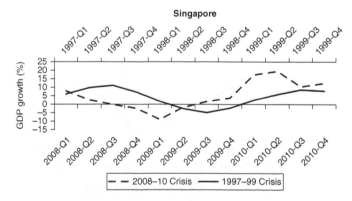

Figure 1.2   (continued)

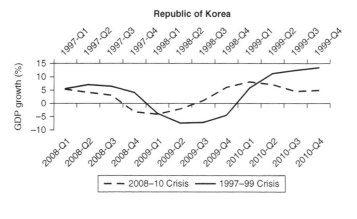

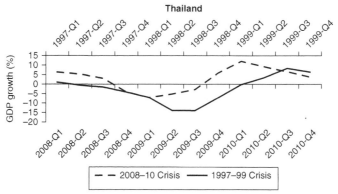

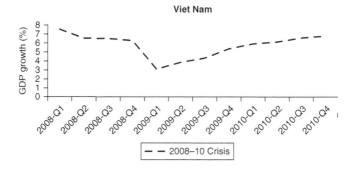

Figure 1.2   (continued)

2008–10. As noted above, economic growth in the PRC and India was little affected on either occasion. In the Philippines and Viet Nam growth slowed markedly but in neither case would it be accurate to characterize the event as an economic crisis. In the case of the Philippines, growth was close to zero in the most affected year, while for Viet Nam growth fell to about half the trend rate. Malaysia and Thailand experienced a year of negative growth on both occasions, but the magnitudes of the growth reversals in the later period were much smaller, around 8 percentage points from peak to trough compared to 15–18 per cent in 1997–98. The capital flight out of these economies in 2008 was smaller, and consequently there was no generalized exchange rate and financial sector collapse. The most interesting case of difference was Indonesia, where the peak-to-trough growth collapse was a spectacular 20 percentage points in 1997–98, but only 2 per cent in 2008–09. Like its higher-income neighbors in the Association of Southeast Asian Nations (ASEAN), in the latter period there was no financial and exchange rate crisis – and for similar reasons.

In comparing the two crises, the global context is of course crucial. Since the global economy was robust in the late 1990s, the large exchange rate depreciations in these open economies were a major boost to their competitiveness, and largely explained their "V-shaped" recoveries, albeit to a somewhat slower trend growth rate. By contrast, such an export-led recovery strategy in the more subdued global environment of the later part of the first decade of this century has not been possible, although the more open economies have recovered quite quickly, the more so if they are closely connected to the Chinese economy.

It is beyond the scope of this chapter to analyze these outcomes in any detail, but some general observations are pertinent. At least four major analytical and policy issues arise in thinking about crises. The first are measures to anticipate them, or at least to mitigate their impact. Much of this discussion focuses on the search for "vulnerability indicators," that is, a rigorous set of indicators that can forewarn policy makers of potential dangers. Discussion of vulnerability indicators also involves the interaction with "trigger" events, such as the collapse of the Thai baht on 2 July 1997, which sparked the AFC, and the US subprime difficulties presaging the GER in 2007–08. The second is the development of resilient systems of macroeconomic management and financial supervision since these are at the heart of crises and their management. We discuss these issues in the section on policy issues, below. The third concerns protection for the vulnerable, which in turn entails the development of quick and effective social safety networks. Finally, there is the issue of a coordinated international response to crises. This is required most obviously when crises have global impact. But even for single-country crises, the international community is likely to be involved, at least through the International Monetary Fund (IMF) and other agencies.

Crises of course vary enormously in their origins and duration. Some are single-country events, entirely homegrown (e.g., Indonesia in the mid-1960s and the Philippines in the mid-1980s). Others are almost entirely external, such as for most developing economies in 2008–09. In some crises, a mix of external and domestic factors is at work, such as in the AFC. Moreover, recoveries range across the stylized letters of the alphabet, including the "V," "L," and "W" outcomes. But there are common elements too. As Krugman and Wells (2010) note, crises have their origins in excessive debt: "Too much debt is always dangerous. It's dangerous when a government borrows heavily from foreigners, but it's equally dangerous when a government borrows heavily from its own citizens. It's dangerous too when the private sector borrows heavily . . ."

There is a general presumption that the country impacts of a crisis will be milder to the extent that:

- A country has historically conservative macroeconomic management, so markets are less likely to mark down its debt, and the government has ample scope for short-run Keynesian macroeconomic policy.
- The international economy is buoyant, offering the scope for export-led recovery following the boost to competitiveness from an exchange rate depreciation. The V-shaped recoveries in the Republic of Korea and most of Southeast Asia after 1998 are good examples of this proposition. Conversely, the US has not had this lifeline in the current crisis; in fact the value of its currency rose for a period during 2008–09 owing to the "safe-haven" effect.
- A resilient financial sector, so that financial institutions do not have to be bailed out – hence leading to fiscal stress – and firms may trade through the crisis, taking advantage of the lower exchange rate.
- A swift and coordinated response from major economies (e.g., of the G20 variety in 2009), and the IMF and donors for country crises.
- Domestic institutional capacity to respond to corporate and social distress in the form of credible central banks, financial regulators, and social providers.
- A strong, effective, decisive, and "legitimate" government able to make quick and tough decisions. This is contrary to the cases of the Marcos regime in the Philippines in 1986 and the Suharto regime in Indonesia in 1998, where economic and political crises interacted and aggravated the situation. More recently, there is also some

concern that Thai policy capacity has been partially incapacitated
by ongoing political uncertainty.

With these general observations in mind, why were the country outcomes
different in the two periods? We focus initially on the country of greatest
difference, Indonesia, drawing on Kuncoro (Chapter 9) and Basri and
Hill (2011). It is convenient to classify the explanatory factors as "good
management," "good luck," and other factors. Among the former – and
central to the explanation – was a more effective response to the crisis,
based in part on the lessons learned from 1997–99. The financial sector
was more cautious, somewhat better regulated, and little connected to the
imploding sectors in the US and the United Kingdom (UK). The exchange
rate regime had become more flexible and was able to operate as a shock
absorber in response to external events. Macroeconomic policy was also
improved. Bank Indonesia, the central bank, had greater autonomy, and it
was able to quickly adopt looser policy. There was room to move in fiscal
policy, too, thanks to the decade of effective fiscal consolidation after the
earlier crisis. Underpinning these policies was a greatly reformed political
system, with a legitimate government able to respond effectively and draw
upon a community consensus that the origins of the crisis were primarily
external and not of the government's making. The international community was also moderately helpful, and there was not the disastrous standoff
between the IMF (and hence also the major donors) and the government.

Good luck also played a role. In Indonesia's case, three such factors
were at work. First, apart from the financial contagion, the international
transmission mechanism of the 2008–09 crisis came through declining
export demand, and Indonesia is not as trade-connected as some of its
ASEAN neighbors. Also, in particular, it is much less plugged into that
part of global trade that fell the fastest, namely the electronics and automotive industries, where consumers quickly deferred expenditures on
durable consumer goods. Another helpful international connection was
the Chinese locomotive factor, and the two countries' strong complementarity in the natural resource trade. Although commodity prices fell briefly
in late 2008 and early 2009, they recovered quickly, and so Indonesia's
terms of trade remained buoyant. A third fortuitous factor was that the
agricultural sector, which still employs almost 40 per cent of the workforce, remained quite resilient thanks to good rainfall, generally strong
prices, and the modest exchange rate depreciation.

Some of these factors were also present in the other Southeast Asian
economies. But there were differences too. Malaysia especially and also
Thailand are much more trade-dependent economies, with electronics
alone comprising over half of merchandise exports. They were therefore

more adversely affected by the global trade slowdown (Bhanupong, Chapter 12; Tham, Chapter 8). The Philippines is also a participant in the global electronics production chains, but on a smaller scale, and its primary international connection is increasingly through remittances (Desierto and Ducanes, Chapter 13), which held up better than other forms of capital flows. These countries had also restored the credibility of their macroeconomic policy institutions after the crises. In the Philippines this had occurred earlier, in the wake of its mid-1980s crisis. Malaysia derived special credibility from the fact that in 1998 the government had eschewed the orthodox IMF approach and instead successfully pursued an alternative strategy of a fixed exchange rate and controls over short-term capital movements. Viet Nam was the one country in the group that in 2008–09 might have experienced a reenactment of the AFC, and for largely similar reasons. That is, the government was attempting to hold on to a fixed nominal exchange rate, in the context of large capital flows and a fragile state-dominated banking sector (Leung et al. 2010). However, in its favor, it had tremendous growth momentum, it is not yet as internationally connected as its more advanced ASEAN neighbors, and agriculture is relatively more important.

In fact, the lower-middle income developing Asian story broadly resembled that of low-income economies in general. The IMF (2010) concluded that real per capita GDP growth stayed positive in two-thirds of these countries. The main effects of the GER were transmitted not so much through movements in terms of trade and interest rates, as in previous occasions, as through a sharp contraction in export demand, FDI, and remittances. Growth was supported by countercyclical fiscal policy, an unusual outcome for these economies, and a response that was facilitated by prudent macroeconomic policy over the preceding decade. While most of the fiscal stimulus occurred through automatic stabilizers, some additional spending was directed to the social sectors and infrastructure.

SAVINGS AND INVESTMENT BEHAVIOR

The high-growth Asian economies have invariably also been high savers and investors. Until the AFC, they typically ran current account deficits, that is, their abundant investment opportunities attracted savings from abroad to supplement their own savings. Nevertheless, until the 1990s and the emergence of some very large current account deficits, their growth was primarily funded from domestic resources. Since the late 1990s, however, some very large savings–investment imbalances have arisen, resulting in historically large foreign exchange reserves and, where the

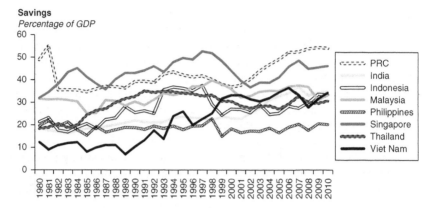

Savings
Percentage of GDP

Legend: PRC, India, Indonesia, Malaysia, Philippines, Singapore, Thailand, Viet Nam

Source: IMF World Economic Outlook Database.

Figure 1.3   Savings/GDP, 1980–2010

economies are large – most notably the PRC – serious global imbalances, with capital flowing from poor to rich economies. We now consider each element of the savings–investment interaction.

Savings

In spite of the dramatic increase in savings rates since the 1960s and the high overall savings record, the patterns among the six economies are diverse (see Figure 1.3). The PRC stands out for its extraordinarily high savings rate, akin to that of Singapore's in recent decades. These are argu-ably cases of "over-saving" in some sense. Savings rates have risen rapidly from very low levels in the once very poor economies of India, Indonesia, and Viet Nam, more than doubling since the 1970s. Savings rates also appear to be resilient in times of economic slowdowns, in the sense that there was no prolonged dip during either the AFC or the GER. The one major outlier among the Asian economies is the Philippines. Its savings rates were broadly comparable to regional norms prior to its deep crisis of the mid-1980s. Savings levels then declined, and they have remained very low ever since, around 20 per cent of GDP, even when moderately strong growth has been restored.

   The general presumption is that these outcomes are explained primarily by the virtuous circle of high growth and savings. Additional factors men-tioned in the literature include favorable demographics, positive financial wealth effects, reasonably effective financial intermediation, mandatory savings programs in some countries (e.g., Malaysia and Singapore), and the absence of social safety nets and financial security provisions. In the aggregate picture, public sector savings sometimes also make a net contribution.

Horioka and Terada-Hagiwara (Chapter 5) provide an authoritative analysis of these savings patterns. They conclude that aging (the age–dependency ratio) has a negative effect, as expected. GDP per capita is negative, but GDP per capita squared is positive. So there is a nonlinear relationship, such that by the late 1970s per capita incomes were generally high enough to exert an impact on savings rates. Credit (credit–GDP) is positive, significant and also nonlinear, the fiscal balance ratio relative to GDP is positive, while social security provisions appear to be negative and significant. Most other variables are generally not significant, including – and perhaps surprisingly – inflation.

Looking forward, the authors conclude: "A shortage of domestic saving will not be a binding constraint on growth and investment in developing Asia, at least for the next two decades." Moreover, "Government policies to stimulate investment and growth are more necessary than government policies to stimulate saving." Demographics are central to their modeling, with the demographic bonus having been completed in Japan around 1990 (hence its savings rate is likely to decline), and progressively for the others from around 2010. They conclude that savings and investment in developing Asia will continue to be highly correlated. That is, following Feldstein-Horioka (1980), investment will still be predominantly domestically financed. But the correlation will gradually weaken over time, as capital accounts become more open.

Investment

The high-growth Asian economies have also been high investors, with a similar story of positive growth–investment interactions (Fukao, Chapter 4). However, the investment picture is more varied, particularly since the AFC (see Figure 1.4). The PRC is again distinguished by its very high level of investment: at 40–45 per cent of GDP, there is the question as to whether it is "overinvesting" in projects with diminishing marginal returns (Chia, Chapter 11). Investment in India and Viet Nam has also risen rapidly since the 1980s. Investment in the three Southeast Asian economies most adversely affected by the AFC fell sharply at that time and has yet to fully recover. The fact that savings has remained buoyant provides a proximate explanation for the large current account surpluses observed in some of them, particularly Malaysia. The Philippines is again an outlier, with very low investment, itself an indicator of the economy's current upper growth limits.

Investment
Percentage of GDP

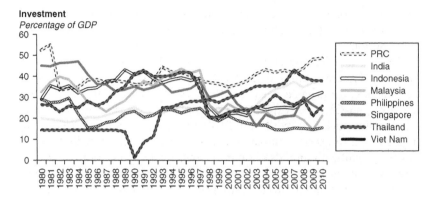

Source: IMF World Economic Outlook Database.

Figure 1.4   Investment/GDP, 1980–2010

Conventional explanations for this investment record emphasize the growth–investment interactions, the generally stable and favorable investment climate (especially compared to alternative country destinations in a world of mobile capital), the readily available pool of investible funds (both domestic and foreign), and the provision of essential supply-side and growth-enhancing inputs such as infrastructure and education. Thus, departures from the high-investment trajectory are generally explained in similarly conventional terms. For example, the World Bank (2009, 53) explained the continuously sluggish investment rate in Malaysia since the AFC as follows: "Malaysia's large private surplus on the current account suggests that investors find it more attractive to invest overseas than domestically."

The evidence as to whether public investment "crowds in" or "crowds out" private investment is mixed, and depends on country circumstances. As a generalization, other things being equal, "productive" public investment such as infrastructure and education will be conducive to private investment by overcoming key bottlenecks to expansion. This appears to be the case for both Indonesia and the Philippines. But in Viet Nam, fears of crowding out appear justifiable given the still extensive public investment levels and its call on scarce savings, together with the uneven playing field for private (especially domestic private) firms.

Concerns about the sluggish investment levels are essentially confined to these three Southeast Asian economies. Several points warrant emphasis. First, their investment levels do appear to be below the norms of very high-growth economies, for example Japan and the newly industrialized economies (NIEs) during their periods of exceptional growth. Second, investment levels have fallen sharply since the late 1990s, but that was from an exceptionally high base. A more relevant comparison is with the levels prevailing in the 1980s, and in this case the decline has been much less pronounced. Third, at issue is not just the level of investment but its composition, with investors showing a preference for short-term, quick-yielding projects such as real estate, as compared to longer-term, more uncertain activities such as infrastructure and mining. This is particularly the case for Indonesia. Fourth, the decline in investment appears to have occurred for all three main investment sources, that is, private domestic, foreign, and public. With increasingly open capital accounts, foreign and domestic investors are evidently responding to a similar set of commercial calculations. Fifth, the fact that the decline has been mostly concentrated in the three crisis-affected economies – and also the Philippines after 1986 – underlines the deep and long-lasting impact of the crisis. That is, the crisis caused a growth slowdown that, combined with the resultant excess capacity, obviated the need for investment for several years. The process of financial restructuring and corporate workouts extended for longer than is commonly realized, and resulted in greater commercial caution. Sixth, Kuncoro (Chapter 9) points to an issue that appears to be unique to Indonesia, namely that monetary policy has provided perverse incentives for investment. This arises because Bank Indonesia, in an effort to mop up excess liquidity resulting from its attempt to stem the appreciation of the rupiah, offers attractive risk-free securities, known as SBIs, that channel savings into its reserves – which in turn are invested abroad in very low-yield securities – and away from much-needed investment projects.

Savings–Investment Imbalances

These varied savings and investment patterns in turn explain the mixed picture on current account balances (see Figure 1.5). Prior to the AFC, there were no significant surplus economies in emerging Asia, apart from Singapore. But then there was a generalized transition to surplus in several: the Southeast Asian economies for the reasons noted, the PRC based on its ever-rising savings rates, and the other NIEs. However, India and Viet Nam continued to behave as traditional developing economy capital importers. Most of these current account balances have been within conventional bounds of up to 5 per cent of GDP. Importantly, the unusual feature of the PRC's large surpluses is not their size relative to GDP but the aggregate size of the economy. The principal outliers have been Malaysia (and Singapore) with exceptionally large surpluses, regu-larly in excess of 10 per cent, and Viet Nam with its investment boom and very large deficits.

26   *Asia rising*

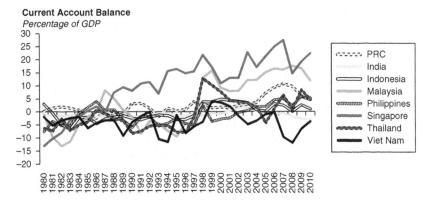

Source: IMF World Economic Outlook Database.

Figure 1.5   Current account balances, 1980–2010

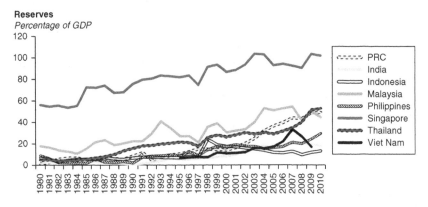

Source: Staff calculation using data from WB World Development Indicators and CEIC Database.

Figure 1.6   Foreign exchange reserves/GDP, 1980–2010

These surpluses have had two results. First, there has been a large increase in foreign exchange reserves (see Figure 1.6). Governments have regarded this as a means of self-insurance in the wake of the AFC, owing to their diminished trust in global institutions, particularly the IMF, and global economic architecture. An exacerbating factor in recent years has also been the attempts to ameliorate exchange rate appreciations in response to rising capital inflows and terms of trade, resulting in greater reserve accumulation than would otherwise have been the case.

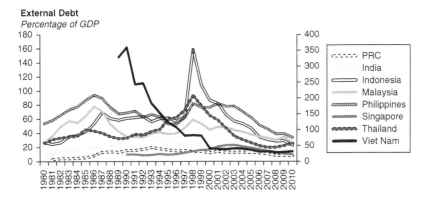

External Debt
Percentage of GDP

Source: Staff calculation using data from WB World Development Indicators and CEIC Database.

Figure 1.7   External debt/GDP, 1980–2010

The second consequence of the surpluses is, obviously, more comfortable external debt positions (see Figure 1.7). Debt–GDP ratios have generally declined since the 1990s, after rising sharply in the late 1990s in the crisis economies. The blip in the latter period was as much the result of plunging currencies, owing to the fact that the debt was typically denominated in foreign currencies. The stabilization and then partial recovery of currencies, combined with current account surpluses and the implementation of debt–equity swaps, quickly pushed down debt ratios. In the countries that continued to run current account deficits, that is India and Viet Nam, the orders of magnitude relative to GDP were typically less than the GDP growth rate, so the overall ratio did not rise.

In global terms, therefore, emerging Asia has switched from being a significant net borrower from the rest of the world to a major net saver (see Figures 1.8 and 1.9). The switch occurred in 1997, and the surpluses have risen continuously since then. The PRC has been by far the dominant contributor, in aggregate overshadowing the smaller Southeast Asian economies, even though in relative terms some of the latter's surpluses are larger.

Investment: The Infrastructure Challenge

Returning to investment levels, two frequently debated issues are infrastructure investment, and why it lags in certain countries, and whether regional and bilateral investment agreements have an impact. We consider

Source: Staff calculation using data from Economist Intelligence Unit.

Figure 1.8   Global savings and investment/GDP, 1980–2010

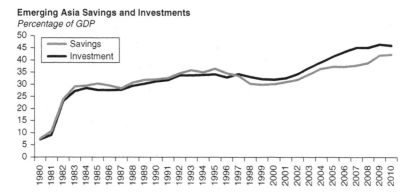

Source: Staff calculation using data from Economist Intelligence Unit. Countries included are the PRC, India, Indonesia, Malaysia, the Philippines, Singapore, Thailand, and Viet Nam.

Figure 1.9   Emerging Asia savings and investment/GDP, 1980–2010

the first in this subsection and the second below in the context of measures to support regional cooperation.

The provision of high-quality physical infrastructure is a key development policy issue that connects to all the main themes of the volume: it constitutes a major supply-side constraint to growth for several countries, including India, Indonesia, and the Philippines in our sample; its underprovision presumably reflects to an important extent the underdeveloped state of the financial sector, particularly the provision of long-term financing; the sector is regarded as a vehicle for recycling current account surpluses; and its highly uneven provision across the group of countries raises important questions about governance and institutional quality.

Brooks and Go (Chapter 3) provide a detailed analysis of the issues. They note the "public good" characteristics of infrastructure, and contrast its diverse state among Asian developing countries. Comparative rankings are generally similar to those of per capita GDP, although the PRC's infrastructure ranking is considerably higher. They affirm the empirical relationship between growth and infrastructure, and also the empirical challenges, including causality, establishing reliable proxies for infrastructure quality and data constraints. Different types of infrastructure are arguably more relevant for certain economies. In more open economies, for example, international ports and airports are critical. At low levels of per capita income, the international financial institutions are typically more important providers. Pricing and long-term funding issues are often significant constraints.

Five main factors appear to account for the inadequate infrastructure provision, although not all of these are present in all cases.

First, to the extent that infrastructure is a public good, at least in the sense that it is not always possible to charge for its use (e.g., much of the road system), infrastructure provision depends on the government's fiscal capacity. Where a government is fiscally constrained – as is often the case in the wake of crises – capital works are typically accorded a low priority as compared to routine expenditures. Moreover, governments may be unable or unwilling to borrow, even for apparently profitable public sector projects. This was clearly evident in post-crisis Indonesia and the Philippines.

Second, governments are often reluctant to allow private sector participation, at least on terms that would attract private sector providers. Infrastructure projects typically have long time horizons, with commensurate funding requirements. Private providers attach a high premium to certainty. They will therefore tend to avoid jurisdictions where there is price uncertainty, as is often the case with roads, power, and water, where there may be strong political pressure to cap prices. Third, and related, governments are sometimes reluctant to liberalize the provision of infrastructure services. This may be partly for ideological reasons, based on the view that these are properly government functions. Or it may be an exaggerated belief in the notion of natural monopolies. In some cases, the reluctance may result from a desire to protect inefficient state-owned enterprise (SOE) providers. Whatever the case, the results of deregulation in sectors such as telecommunications and civil aviation have invariably been dramatic.

Fourth, owing to the scale and time horizons involved, infrastructure projects often attract serious governance problems. Their scale introduces the possibility of high-level corruption and thus reluctance on the part of senior officials to sign off on such projects for fear of possible retribution. This is especially true as trade barriers have fallen, and thus rent-seeking behavior has shifted to non-tradable sectors, of which infrastructure projects are often the most lucrative. Where government is diffused – e.g., between the executive and the legislature, or between central and local governments – coordination and "ownership" problems may exacerbate the under-provision of infrastructure. This problem is present in the three countries mentioned above. Low levels of trust in public institutions and the judiciary may also result in widespread land claims that stymie progress. Public–private partnerships (PPPs) often encounter similar sets of problems, owing to a weak separation of responsibilities.

Fifth, there are often constraints to the funding of long-term projects. Bond markets are still underdeveloped in much of developing Asia. For example, the region has one-quarter of global GDP but only 8 per cent of outstanding bonds. Local currency bonds are still not widely used in middle-income developing economies. There is also the reluctance of some countries to borrow abroad, especially in foreign currencies, in the wake of the AFC.

SOME MAJOR POLICY ISSUES

What Sort of Financial System?

As Fukuda (Chapter 6) emphasizes, building an efficient and robust financial sector is essential for long-run economic development. Moreover, he notes that the "failure of traditional financial development might be responsible for persistent stagnation of capital accumulation after the AFC." The structure and regulation of equity markets may also be inimical to economic development. He reminds us that, as Claessens et al. (2000) showed, before the AFC, governance structures in most East Asian conglomerates were based heavily on family ownership and control, and minority stockholders had few rights. Collusion with government officials often resulted in a kind of "crony capitalism." In addition, in economies such as the PRC and Viet Nam, there is still the problem of a large state-owned banking sector making command loans with soft-budget constraints (Chia, Chapter 11).

Financial crises have been central to virtually every major crisis episode. Here there is a tension between the need for a responsive, competitive, and open financial sector, alongside recognition of the fact that information asymmetries and moral hazard increase the likelihood that such a system will be more crisis prone. The proposition pedaled by powerful vested interests – that "this time is different" and that more elaborate financial instruments, more sophisticated techniques of assessment, and greater risk spreading alleviate the need for tighter regulation – has been shown to be self-serving and illusory, as Reinhart and Rogoff (2009) remind us. But one wants a system that encourages innovation and risk taking.

As Paul Volcker, one of the world's most experienced central bankers, has observed, for policy makers the greatest structural challenge is how to deal with extremely large international banks, which in turn has at least three dimensions (Volcker 2011). First, the risk of the failure of large international banks must be minimized by reducing their size, curtailing their connectedness, or limiting their activities. Second, ways have to be found to promptly manage the orderly process of debt workouts, including minimizing the potential impact on markets and the real economy. Third, these procedures have to be broadly consistent across all the major global financial centers in which the banks operate. Most important, these measures have to adopt ". . . a truly convincing approach to deal with the 'moral hazard' posed by official rescue efforts."

The challenge is how to insulate the general economy and fiscal policy from the sometimes undesirable consequences of highly competitive financial systems. The solution is obviously tighter regulation, a reversal of the post-war trend toward lighter regulation. While this general proposition is widely accepted, the debate over the substance is unresolved. Presumably reforms entail measures to force banks to behave more conservatively than they would otherwise. But how, and is it politically achievable? Higher capital adequacy ratios, greater liquidity, less leverage, less exposure to risky sectors, stricter policing of balance sheets, and greater restrictions on foreign borrowing are the most commonly mentioned. More controversial is the proposition that there should be a return to a two-tier banking system, comprising the "utilities" that are low-risk, low-return entities with government guarantees, alongside a more adventurous set of entities with no government guarantees and presumably restricted in scale so that their collapse would not set off a generalized fiscal and economic crisis. This was the spirit behind the US Glass–Steagall Act, but pressure from Wall Street brought about its repeal in 1999. The US Dodd–Frank Act is an attempt to address this problem, but it does not cover international bank operations, and the separation of propriety trading of the banks has not progressed.

Finally, there is the question of whether the financial sector has become so powerful that it is able to effectively prevent major reform of the financial sector. Reviewing the interim report from Britain's Independent Commission on Banking (the Vickers Report), the former Deputy Governor of the Reserve Bank of Australia opined that since 2008, the "mergers and failures in the US have left the largest banks even larger, more complex, more conglomerated, and probably more unmanageable." Similarly, the issue of bailouts has also become more difficult as banks have become larger, and more international, interconnected, and complex.

This is an area where most developing Asian economies have made significant progress since the late 1990s, with the AFC providing a salutary lesson (see Lee and Park, 2011). As Bhanupong (Chapter 12) observes in the case of Thailand, the financial sector is now ". . . stronger and resilient, thanks to foreign capital injection, good governance, and strengthened financial rules." The bond and stock markets and other non-bank financing may remain underdeveloped. But it is striking that, during even the depths of the GER, as shown above, there was not a single major bank failure in any of the six countries.

Macroeconomic Policy in an Interdependent World

Major economic crises result in a reevaluation of the central tenets of macroeconomic policy, including the institutions and conduct of fiscal and monetary policy, exchange rate regimes, and how to manage volatile capital flows. We consider each one briefly, on the basis of these country studies.

Fiscal policy

Crises typically lead to large increases in public debt as governments resort to deficit financing owing to the effects of automatic stabilizers, the need to expand social safety nets, and as a result of the socialization of corporate and banking debt. This is arguably the most important macroeconomic impact of the GER in economies of the Organisation for Economic Co-operation and Development (OECD). US general government debt (federal, state, and local) has now surpassed the post-war record of 120 per cent of GDP. Japan is more than 200 per cent, while several other OECD economies are approaching 150 per cent (Reinhart and Rogoff 2011). Moreover, this is in peacetime, and low interest rates are restraining debt service costs. What happens when rates begin to rise, as they must? As Reinhart and Rogoff observe, "Debt crises tend to come out of the blue, hitting countries whose debt trajectories simply have no room for error or unplanned adversity."

Public debt levels certainly rose sharply in the economies affected by the AFC (see Figure 1.10). However, apart from this episode, most but not all the countries in the study have run reasonably prudent fiscal policy,

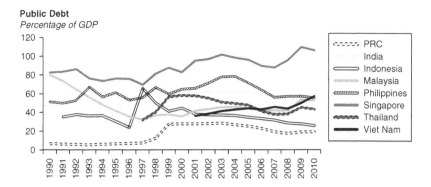

Sources: WB World Development Indicators, Economist Intelligence Unit, and IMF World Economic Outlook.

Figure 1.10 Public debt/GDP, 1980–2010

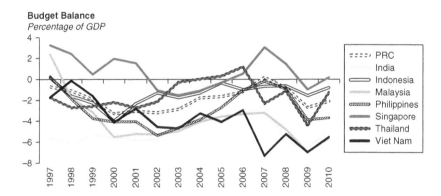

Source: Economist Intelligence Unit.

Figure 1.11 Budget balance/GDP, 1980–2010

in some cases reinforced by legislated restrictions on the size of deficits, so they had room at the onset of the GER to adopt fiscal stimulus measures (see Figure 1.11). This was a particularly important option in those countries where monetary policy was in some sense incapacitated either because interest rates were already very low or because the financial sector was partially frozen. Moreover, some governments in the region have been able to carry higher levels of debt where there are high savings rates and the community is willing – or sometimes forced – to fund these deficits. Japan is the classic case in recent times; the Malaysian government has

also been able to run quite large deficits owing to the cushion of buoyant
– and partially forced – domestic savings (Narayanan 2012). Hence the
medium-term fiscal consolidation challenges for most of developing Asia
are not nearly as serious as in most OECD economies.

Nevertheless, much fiscal policy reform is required. In most of the economies under study, fiscal policy has been at best mildly countercyclical and
often pro-cyclical. Traditionally, the explanation in developing economies
has been that when hit by a crisis, they did not have alternative fiscal
financing means at their disposal: they could not borrow internationally,
there was not a domestic bond market, and printing money would be inflationary and would be prohibited by an IMF program, if operative. Vaidya
(Chapter 10) notes this problem in the Indian context and explains it as
follows: "Given that India is a federation, running surpluses in good times
seems to be difficult because of pressures from states for larger shares of
revenues of the central government." Bhanupong (Chapter 12) attributes
the absence of countercyclical fiscal policy in Thailand during the past
decade to weak institutions and a highly politicized environment.

Governments have also frequently lacked the administrative capacity
to push up expenditures quickly, especially in much-needed infrastructure, and thus the crisis response was more commonly on the revenue
side, which was less effective as tax cuts are more likely to be saved in
times of uncertainty. Moreover, the medium-term fiscal policy agenda
is substantial in many countries: the revenue effort is often weak; there
are low levels of public sector efficiency; more cost-effective social safety
nets are required, in place of large, poorly targeted subsidies; the fiscal
implications of a rapidly aging population are yet to be addressed; large
public sector projects are often corruption prone; SOE sector reform is
slow; and the facilities for longer-term debt markets for infrastructure are
underdeveloped.

One reform that is gaining currency in the wake of the GER is to establish
independent fiscal advisory councils to elevate public understanding of the
issues, to force governments to acknowledge hidden costs of their guarantees and off-balance sheet costs, and to help overcome the very strong deficit
bias inherent in the political cycle. Several countries already have independent fiscal watchdogs, such as the US Congressional Budget Office, but these
typically have limited analytical capacity and they generally accept official
budget documents at face value. More powerful bodies might be created,
with independence analogous to that of many central banks.

Monetary policy and exchange rate regimes

This has generally been an area of policy success over the past decade.
In the wake of the AFC, most countries gradually adopted a regime of

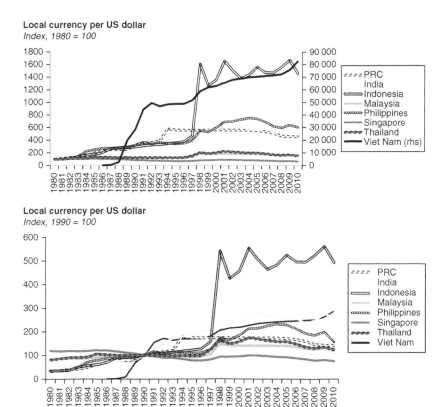

Local currency per US dollar
Index, 1980 = 100

Local currency per US dollar
Index, 1990 = 100

Note: Base year for Viet Nam is 1986. PRC = People's Republic of China.

Source: International Monetary Fund, International Financial Statistics.

Figure 1.12 Comparative exchange rates

independent central banks, inflation targeting, and greater exchange rate flexibility. That is, there has been recognition that "fixed but adjustable" crawling peg regimes do not work in the case of large and sometimes volatile capital flows (and terms of trade movements) in which private borrowers assume no exchange rate risk. Exchange rates fell steeply during the AFC as central banks found they could no longer defend their fixed rates. But after this sharp adjustment, over the past decade and including during the GER, they have generally remained quite stable (see Figure 1.12). Financial markets and corporations are becoming more comfortable with flexible exchange rates. This flexibility also acts as a discipline on government excesses. Hence serious inflation problems are now comparatively

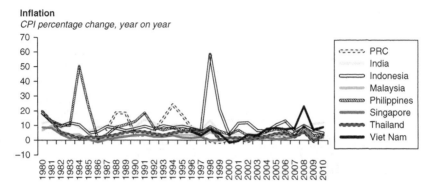

Source: Economist Intelligence Unit.

Figure 1.13   Inflation rates, 1980–2010

rare (see Figure 1.13), and there was scope for running looser monetary policy during the GER.

Flexible exchange rates only work, of course, if the overall policy settings are conducive. This proposition is clearly evident in the case of the PRC (Chia, Chapter 11). That country's large current account surplus can only be addressed with a comprehensive package of measures that includes not just further exchange rate appreciation but also the removal of distortions in the labor, land and capital markets. Moreover, to the extent that exchange rate fluctuations introduce greater food price volatility, especially for poorer countries where 30–50 per cent of the population is clustered very close to the poverty line, cost-effective social safety nets are required to protect the poor.

There were certainly monetary policy lessons from the crisis. Mishkin (2010) provides a convenient survey, mainly with reference to OECD economies, that reaffirms the constants and highlights some lessons learned and new challenges:

> The bad news is that we have just been through a once-in-a-hundred-year credit tsunami that has had a devastating impact on the economy that will last for years to come. The good news is that macro/monetary economists and central bankers do not have to go back to the drawing board and throw out all that they have learned over the past forty years.

What essentially remains unchanged is the recognition that inflation is fundamentally a monetary phenomenon, that there is no necessary long-term trade-off between unemployment and inflation, that expectations play a crucial role in determining inflation, that increased real interest rates are needed to deal with higher inflation, and that central bank independence and commitment to a strong nominal anchor are crucial. What has changed, according to Mishkin (2010), is the need to pay much more attention to the financial sector, and its occasional nonlinear behavior, owing to the extremely high cost of severe financial crises. Therefore there is a stronger case for leaning against credit (but not necessarily asset price) bubbles, and for focusing on the close interdependence between monetary and financial stability policy.

Returning to exchange rates, a major challenge for policy makers in some high-growth developing Asian economies in the wake of the GER has been how to adjust to upward exchange rate pressures. These originate from three sources. First, the US dollar has been depreciating progressively. This is a necessary requirement for that country to work its way through its twin deficits, and it is in the global community's interest that there be international coordination to facilitate this. In the buoyant Asian economies, this inevitably means exchange rate appreciation relative to the US. Second, the region's strong economic growth and higher interest rates have attracted large capital inflows. Gross capital flows to emerging markets are now running at about 6 per cent of their GDP, similar to levels immediately prior to the AFC and GER. Third, an additional factor for some commodity exporters has been strong terms of trade, adding further to the exchange rate pressures.

How should governments respond? Central banks understandably worry that the appreciating rates exacerbate competitiveness concerns in tradable sectors and that the mobile capital that enters the country can just as quickly exit. Ideally, as noted, there needs to be international coordination to facilitate exchange rate adjustment, and reform of international institutions and architecture, so countries do not feel compelled to self-insure with large foreign exchange reserves. But in the absence of these major reforms, or at least while that coordination is being developed, countries need to develop a policy response. There is no simple solution. As the following policy menu illustrates, each option has advantages and disadvantages.

First, central banks could let the currency appreciate, perhaps with smoothing interventions. But this accentuates competitiveness problems, necessitating a major adjustment in tradable goods industries. The problems will be more severe if a major economy, for example, the PRC, does not allow its currency to appreciate. Alternatively, these capital inflows could be viewed as an opportunity to build productive capacity and raise productivity on the premise that a well-managed economy is likely to continue to attract capital inflows and use them productively. That is, the exchange rate movements signal a likely permanent change in relative prices and there is a need for an adjustment.

A second option is to attempt to hold the fixed rate in the face of these capital inflows through central bank market operations in the hope that the inflows are temporary. This is unlikely to be a credible option as it will exacerbate the overheating that the capital inflows are causing. This will result in rising inflation, which with a fixed nominal rate will cause a loss of competitiveness.

Third, the flows could be sterilized by keeping the funds offshore and building up international reserves. This is also an attractive option if there is limited trust of the international financial institutions and other crisis-resolution facilities. However, it entails locking up these funds in low (often negative) return assets, as several authors note. For larger countries, especially the PRC, the scale of the reserves is likely to attract international criticism.

Fourth, the government could respond by instituting a compensatory fiscal contraction, so that there is no net increase in domestic demand. However, this might be a difficult option: fiscal policy is typically not quick acting, especially if it gets held up in the legislature. And there is, in any case, political pressure to spend at a time of buoyant resource inflows.

A fifth policy option would be the introduction of tighter restrictions on bank lending to restrain credit growth and thereby take pressure off asset prices. This is on the premise that the banking sector is a key conduit for capital inflows. Such a measure would generally be worthwhile but it would not necessarily prevent an exchange rate appreciation.

Finally, there is the option of deliberately discouraging inflows, at least those that are considered short term or speculative, through some form of capital controls. This option is theoretically appealing, but in practice not necessarily easy to implement, especially in countries that have recently adopted open capital accounts to escape the corruption and mismanagement often associated with these controls (Gochoco-Bautista et al. 2012). A high-quality central bank is obviously an essential prerequisite for such a strategy.

The extensive international literature regarding the effectiveness of these controls is also ambiguous and cautious. If they are to be implemented, this historical evidence suggests that they are likely to be more effective when they take the form of market-based mechanisms, such as unremunerated reserve requirements, "analogue" measures that can be more easily altered to adjust to flows, and they are not "over-engineered" and too detailed. Obviously, also, they should not be employed to prop up a fundamental disequilibrium in the exchange rate. There needs to be a clearly communicated exit strategy, and there needs to be a distinction between short- and long-term capital flows. Moreover, in the context of any globally coordinated measures, it is important to focus on the "push" factors, principally the extremely loose monetary policy in the rich economies (especially the US) as much as these "pull" factors.

An additional lesson from the AFC is that countries need to introduce accompanying reforms in the process of opening their capital accounts. Bhanupong (Chapter 12) concludes that, in the case of Thailand, "The major deviation from the long-term [growth] trend can be attributed to the premature liberalization of the capital account."

Governance and Institutional Reform

Systems of governance and institutional quality vary widely in the sample of countries (de Dios and Ducanes, Chapter 2), and it is therefore difficult to be too prescriptive. Different governance issues seem to matter at different levels of development. For example, modern economies tend to need more formal institutions, since commercial transactions are more likely to involve "contracting with strangers." Levels of institutional quality typically change very slowly, and they tend to correlate with per capita income across countries. The measurement of governance is highly subjective and empirically elusive, and sometimes the various indicators may diverge. For example, historically much of developing East Asia ranked well with regard to bureaucratic quality and government effectiveness, but rather poorly on democracy. Informal institutions may be just as effective as formal institutions, for example in the case of legal and judicial systems.

We do learn about the political economy of economic policy making, and building institutions more generally, from crises and their aftermath. Crises also test the quality of governance: the speed of response to a crisis is often a critical determinant of the severity and longevity of a crisis. Examples include how quickly governments can respond to ensure that the banking system remains viable, the effectiveness of fiscal stimulus packages, and the ability to protect the poor through social protection measures. Bhanupong (Chapter 12) considers institutional quality to be crucial in understanding the Thai response to crises: "The low quality of institutions impaired the timely response to shocks." Desierto and Ducanes (Chapter 13) have similar observations for the Philippines, noting the highly politicized policy environment, perverse agricultural interventions, and the difficulty of managing major infrastructure projects.

With these observations in mind, a few general observations appear relevant. First, as noted above, a large literature posits that crises may be good for reform to the extent that they embolden governments and force them to push aside vested interests. Crises also typically empower reform-minded ministries of finance, and the resultant weaker currencies may facilitate trade policy reform. There is some evidence for these hypotheses in Indonesia in the mid-1980s, India in 1991, and some of the reforms introduced in Southeast Asia after the AFC. However, crises can be a two-edged sword, to the extent that they weaken governments and create a divided polity, as for example in Indonesia and the Philippines after their crises. The GER does not appear to have led to any significant reforms in the countries represented in this volume, although it may lead to more effective financial sector regulation in some OECD economies.

Second, externally imposed crisis-response programs are rarely successful unless they have a domestic constituency. This was one of the central lessons of the AFC, and it explains the region's continuing reservations about the IMF.

Third, it is desirable to insulate or delink key institutions and policies from political pressures so they may effectively implement objectives prescribed by the executive and legislature. Examples include independent central banks, limits on fiscal deficits, independent regulatory agencies (for example competition commissions), and perhaps even free-trade zones (although they are very much second-best reforms). Judicial and civil service reform appear to be the most difficult areas of progress, and in several countries they constitute a key obstacle to reforming the investment climate.

Fourth, competitive reforms and liberalization can be helpful drivers of policy. This can be achieved through arms-length benchmarking of key performance indicators between countries. As countries decentralize government administration, inter-jurisdictional competition on governance quality can also be a spur to improved policy at the local level.

Regional Cooperation and Coordination

As noted, many of the major policy reforms have regional and global "public good" attributes and therefore require intergovernmental coordination. Progress on the development of durable regional and global institutional structures for economic policy coordination is mixed. The major achievement since 2008 is that governments have not adopted "beggar-thy-neighbor" trade and exchange rate policies, at least not on any significant scale. The G20 has also emerged as the preeminent forum for the discussion of major international economic issues, and it contributed to the adoption of coordinated fiscal stimulus measures in the major economies (Drysdale 2011).

However, the pressure for unilateral action among the major economies and blocs, regardless of the broader consequences, is very powerful. For example, the very loose monetary policy in these economies, the US in particular through successive rounds of "quantitative easing," has greatly increased global liquidity. With traditional stock market options increasingly unattractive, this liquidity has resulted in the increased "financialization" of commodity markets. In turn, this has contributed to their price volatility, with potentially serious social consequences for the poor. The world's most significant example of deep economic integration, the European Union (EU) and the Economic and Monetary Union (EMU) of the EU, is deeply troubled and the future of the latter is highly uncertain. The possible implosion of the EMU is already shaking global financial markets, and the resolution of the euro impasse will certainly involve the major East Asian surplus economies.

Moreover, in many other respects, coordinated international economic governance seems to be getting more difficult. Although markets have not been closed, at least to any significant degree, there is still no resolution of the ailing Doha Round. International financial governance has progressed little, notwithstanding the adoption of Basel 3. "Financial protectionism" reared its ugly head during the GER, perversely, as capital flowed back to the fiscally more powerful jurisdictions from where the crisis emanated. There is still a nontrivial prospect of some sort of a G2 "currency war" between the PRC and the US. Key international institutions, most notably the IMF, are still regarded with suspicion in the developing world. Most currency-swap and fiscal-standby agreements during the GER were organized on a bilateral basis. The current crisis in the euro zone is likely to deter any attempts at currency regions for the foreseeable future, except those of the voluntary variety (for example, currencies voluntarily pegged to the US dollar). There is also very little progress on other major global issues, such as climate change, counterterrorism, and nuclear proliferation

In the Asia Pacific region, it is possible that initiatives with an open international agenda can move faster than reform at the global level (Drysdale 2011). But the evidence to date is mixed. Although ASEAN remains a highly effective diplomatic community, the economic initiatives centered around and involving it, for example, the ASEAN Economic Community, the East Asian Summit, and the Enhanced Chiang Mai Initiative, are variable in impact and still evolving. The mooted "Asian G6" caucus within the G20 appears to have made little progress. It is therefore important to avoid unrealistic expectations about these regional initiatives, and to keep in mind that unilateral reform at home is always going to be the key reform building block.

A special subset of regional cooperation concerns various kinds of international, regional, and bilateral investment agreements that at the margin may improve the overall investment environment. Investors look for certainty and protection, so the argument goes, and these agreements may assist in providing it, especially where the investors are venturing abroad into less familiar legal environments. Desierto (Chapter 7) examines this issue through a detailed examination of ASEAN investment treaties. This is relevant to the volume because four of the countries are ASEAN members and because the issue is evidently being approached more seriously than it has been in the past, as part of its ASEAN Economic Community timetable.

Desierto maintains that the ASEAN Charter of 2008 "transformed ASEAN into an official international legal organization, with a distinct legal personality and capable of binding all 10 states under new treaty organizations." This is in preparation for the full ASEAN Economic Community, which is scheduled to be realized by 2015. Since the Charter was announced, three new agreements have incorporated various clauses and protections into investment treaties, the most important being the 2009 ASEAN Comprehensive Investment Agreement (ACIA). There is no doubt that ASEAN is serious about these initiatives. Whether they are effective remains to be seen. Other ASEAN programs – mostly notably the concessions under the ASEAN Free Trade Area (AFTA) – have been little used to date, and so the test will come if and when investors have recourse to the ACIA. Moreover, legal guarantees of this kind work only in partnership with broader reforms of the commercial climate, and as noted the record has been mixed in this regard in several of the signatory countries.

CONCLUSION

Five main conclusions emerge from our analysis.

First, these economies emerged from the GER in relatively good shape. Thus far, they have been either little affected by the global slowdown, as in the case of the three largest economies, or they have recovered quite quickly. The traditional macroeconomic prudence of these countries has been rewarded, and it has been reinforced in the case of the AFC-affected economies by their reforms over the past decade.

Second, an immediate effect of the GER has been to accelerate the reorientation of global economic activity toward Asian developing economies. However, the global economy is likely to remain subdued for several years, since three major parts of it – the US, the EU, and Japan – are likely to grow slowly as they resolve their debt problems. As a result, domestic demand and regional trade will become relatively more important engines of growth. As a corollary, running large current account surpluses on the basis of undervalued exchange rates will not be a viable strategy going forward. The rich crisis-affected economies have to be allowed to depreciate their currencies, just as they have to be constrained from taking unilateral action (for example, very loose monetary policy) that has the effect of "exporting" the costs of their macroeconomic adjustment to the rest of the world.

Third, the large fraction of global current account imbalances that has its origins in East Asia is unlikely to disappear quickly based on current trends. On plausible assumptions, future savings rates are likely to continue to be high for a decade or more in emerging Asia (that is, excluding Japan, where they are likely to start falling significantly), at least until demographic factors begin to exert a major depressing influence, while investment could well remain subdued.

Fourth, there has been some progress on the reform of macroeconomic and financial regulation policies, but the unresolved agenda is also substantial. For example, there is a consensus on the desirability of conservative fiscal policy, except during periods of crisis, on independent central banks, and on some flexibility in exchange rates – though how much is an issue. But there is less consensus on how to manage volatile capital flows and on the technicalities of enhanced financial supervision. Regional and international cooperation has progressed somewhat, but it is not clear how durable that progress will be in the event of a significant global economic recovery.

Finally, it is crucial to keep in mind the heterogeneity of country experiences, including the countries in this study, and consequently the fact that there is no one-size-fits-all approach. There is no single "Asian model of development" for this group, or for the region as a whole. For example, the country sample includes those running current account surpluses and deficits. Some have generally prudent, conservative macroeconomic policy settings, while others are somewhat more adventurous. Some countries have fragile, underdeveloped financial sectors that are vulnerable to exogenous shocks, while others are resilient and well supervised. Some are highly open, trade-dependent economies, while others are much less internationally engaged. Some countries have a well-developed infrastructure stock, and a seemingly in-built propensity to anticipate future requirements, while others are barely able to keep up with demand.

Thus, for example, the issue of "rebalancing" is really only relevant to those economies running large current account surpluses, and any case for "reassessment" of an export-led strategy will apply only to these economies, which in addition are also highly trade dependent. Similarly, concerns about low investment levels, both in general and specifically in key growth-enhancing sectors such as infrastructure, are relevant only for certain countries.

NOTE

1. Discussions on Viet Nam in this chapter as well as in several of the thematic chapters are drawn in part from Huong (2011).

REFERENCES

Balisacan, A.M., and H. Hill (eds) (2003), *The Philippine Economy: Development, Policies and Challenges*, New York: Oxford University Press.

Basri, M.C., and H. Hill (2011), 'Indonesian growth dynamics', *Asian Economic Policy Review*, **6**, 90–107.

Bloom, D.E., and J.E. Finlay (2009), 'Demographic change and economic growth in Asia', *Asian Economic Policy Review*, **4**, 45–64.

Claessens, S., S. Djankov, and L. Lang (2000), 'The separation of ownership and control in East Asian corporations', *Journal of Financial Economics*, **77**, 57–116.

Collier, P. (2007), *The Bottom Billion*, Oxford: Oxford University Press.

Drysdale, P. (2011), 'Asia's global responsibilities and regional and international cooperation', *Asian Economic Journal*, **25**, 99–112.

Edwards, S. (2010), *Left Behind: Latin America and the False Promise of Populism*, Chicago: University of Chicago Press.

Feldstein, M.S., and C.Y. Horioka (1980), 'Domestic saving and international capital flows', *Economic Journal*, **90**, 314–29.

Gochoco-Bautista, M.S., J. Jongwanich, and J.-W. Lee (2012), 'How effective are capital controls in Asia?', *Asian Economic Papers*, Summer, **11**(2), 122–43.

Hill, H. (2000), *The Indonesian Economy*, second edition, Cambridge: Cambridge University Press.

Hill, H., S.Y. Tham, and H.M.B. Ragayah (eds) (2012), *Malaysia's Development Challenges: Graduating from the Middle*, London: Routledge.

Huong, P.L. (2011), 'Reassessing the role of investment to sustain Viet Nam's growth', unpublished paper, December.

International Monetary Fund (IMF) (2010), *Emerging from the Global Crisis: Macroeconomic Challenges facing Low Income Countries*, Washington, DC: October.

Krugman, P., and R. Wells (2010), 'Our giant banking crisis: what to expect?', *New York Review of Books*, 13 May.

Lal, D., and H. Myint (1996), *The Political Economy of Poverty, Equity and Growth*, Oxford: Oxford University Press.

Lee, J.-W., and C.Y. Park (2011), 'Financial integration in emerging Asia: challenges and prospects', *Asian Economic Policy Review*, **6**, 176–98.

Leung, S., B. Bingham, and M. Davies (eds) (2010), *Globalization and Development in the Mekong Economies*, Cheltenham, UK and Northampton, MA, USA: Edward Elgar.

Maddison, A. (2007), *Contours of the World Economy, 1-2030*, Oxford: Oxford University Press.

Mishkin, F.S. (2010), 'Monetary policy strategy: lessons from the crisis', Paper presented to the ECB Central Banking Conference, Monetary Policy Revisited: Lessons from the Crisis Frankfurt, November 18–19.

Narayanan, S. (2012), 'Public sector resource management', in II. Hill, S.Y. Tham, and H.M.B. Ragayah (eds), *Malaysia's Development Challenges: Graduating from the Middle*, London: Routledge, pp. 131–54.

Naughton, B. (2007), *The Chinese Economy: Transition and Growth*, Cambridge, MA: MIT Press.

Nelson, R.R. (2008), 'Economic development from the perspective of evolutionary economic theory', *Oxford Development Studies*, **36**, 9–21.

Panagariya, A. (2008), *India: The Emerging Giant*, Oxford: Oxford University Press.

Reinhart, C.M., and K.S. Rogoff (2009), *This Time is Different: Eight Centuries of Financial Folly*, Princeton: Princeton University Press.

Reinhart, C.M., and K.S. Rogoff (2011), 'A decade of debt', NBER Working Paper No. w16827, February.

Volcker, P. (2011), 'Financial reform: unfinished business', *The New York Review of Books*, **58** (18), 24 November.

World Bank (2007), *East Asia and Pacific Update: Ten Years after the Crisis*, April, Washington, DC: World Bank.

World Bank (2009), *Malaysia Economic Monitor: Repositioning for Growth*, Washington, DC: World Bank.

PART II

Asian Development Challenges

2. Institutions and governance

Emmanuel S. de Dios and Geoffrey M. Ducanes

INTRODUCTION

From one viewpoint, it appears misplaced to pose the question of raising investment and growth in Asia. After all, in the midst of the recent global economic recession (GER) it is mostly countries in Asia that have shown the greatest resilience and maintained comparatively high investment ratios. All this is relative, however, and when viewed in relation to the Asian financial crisis (AFC), investment ratios in Asia have actually declined.

Table 2.1 shows that this decline has been most pronounced in East Asia, where the average investment ratio fell from 30 per cent in the 5-year period immediately preceding the AFC (1992–96) to 24 per cent in the succeeding period (2002–06), before the GER hit. Declines were particularly marked in countries that were severely affected by the AFC (e.g., Indonesia, the Republic of Korea, Malaysia, the Philippines, Singapore, and Thailand). A decline on average is also notable in Central Asia, from 25 per cent to 21 per cent of gross domestic product (GDP). By contrast, South Asian countries as a group appear to have been less affected; in fact the average investment ratio rose slightly between the two periods. Levels for Oceania (i.e., for countries where comparable data are available) on the other hand, have been more or less constant between the two periods.

Notwithstanding such broad generalizations, there are notable exceptions. For example, investment ratios have continued to rise in the People's Republic of China (PRC), Mongolia, and Viet Nam, despite a general decline for the subregion. Pakistan and Sri Lanka, where investment ratios have declined, are the exceptions in a subregion where investment activity has generally increased since the AFC.

This chapter examines whether considerations of institutions and governance can shed any additional light on this pattern. We examine global patterns, but special attention will be paid to Asia and the countries that are the specific focus of this volume: the PRC, India, Indonesia, Malaysia, the Philippines, Thailand, and Viet Nam.

Asia rising

*Table 2.1   Investment ratios (averages for 1992–96 and 2002–06; selected
            Asian countries)*

Subregion and country	1992–96	2002–06
East Asia[a]	30.1	24.1
Brunei Darussalam[a]	31.9	14.3
Cambodia	12.0	18.4
PRC	34.7	39.3
Hong Kong, China[a]	28.8	22.2
Indonesia[a]	27.5	21.5
Korea, Rep.of[a]	36.9	28.9
Lao PDR	n.a.	29.6
Macao, China	30.0	18.8
Malaysia[a]	40.4	22.2
Mongolia	25.5	28.5
Philippines[a]	22.8	16.2
Singapore[a]	35.6	24.3
Thailand[a]	40.2	25.9
Viet Nam	25.3	32.2
South Asia[b]	26.0	28.5
Afghanistan	n.a.	21.9
Bangladesh	18.6	23.8
Bhutan	45.6	56.0
India	22.7	27.4
Maldives	31.0	33.9
Nepal	21.2	19.9
Pakistan	18.1	16.5
Sri Lanka	25.0	22.2
Central Asia	25.1	20.7
Kazakhstan	24.9	25.7
Kyrgyz Republic	16.7	16.6
Tajikistan	16.2	12.0
Turkmenistan	38.1	26.1
Uzbekistan	29.5	23.1
Oceania[c]	18.4	18.8
Fiji	15.1	18.4
Papua New Guinea	19.1	18.8
Solomon Islands	n.a.	9.4
Tonga	18.1	17.3
Vanuatu	21.3	20.8

Table 2.1 (continued)

Notes:
PRC = People's Republic of China. Lao PDR = Lao People's Democratic Republic.
a. Countries severely affected by the Asian financial crisis.
b. Excludes Afghanistan for comparability.
c. Excludes Solomon Islands for comparability.

Source: Authors' computations based on data from the World Bank World Development Indicators, the World Bank World Governance Indicators 2010, and the Penn World Table Version 7.0.

COMPLICATIONS AND QUALIFICATIONS

Any attempt to draw broad generalizations regarding the post-AFC investment decline will be fraught with difficulties and qualifications. Asian economies are themselves extremely heterogeneous in terms of their investment record, levels of income, and past growth performance, as well as the institutions surrounding their economic performance. Even the most basic growth theories will suggest that an economy's level of maturity, as captured for example by per capita income, will affect its rate of investment.[1] Wide differences in investment outcomes have been noted in Table 2.1. Such growth potential and trajectories also will differ depending on resource endowments, the size of internal markets, and other factors.

Beyond this, however, the nature of investing actors themselves will differ across countries, as will the factors, both narrowly economic and financial as well as institutional, that influence them. Important distinctions can be made between relatively open and closed investment regimes, as well as between those where the public sector plays a large role in financial and industrial policy decisions. Countries with a history of central planning, such as the PRC and Viet Nam, are obvious cases in point. Even exogenous shocks, for example, will not be reflected in a similar manner in different economies, such as those where a significant amount of credit is allocated among state-owned enterprises and those where the private sector is largely free to make decisions.

Finally, one needs to consider the lingering effects of the AFC and the more recent GER. Three of the countries given particular treatment in this volume were heavily affected by the AFC. It is a persuasive argument that the AFC exhibited many of the aspects of a "balance-sheet recession."[2] This implies that investment, especially private investment, may not revive until corporate balance sheets have recovered from the post-recession regime of working off debt. This in itself suggests an *a priori* reason why the investment recovery in affected countries may be delayed. Aside from purely economic factors arising from the AFC, political and institutional changes arising directly from or influenced by that crisis are also undeniable. For example, Indonesia underwent an historic and sometimes violent political and social regime shift. Thailand experimented with successive and occasionally violent electoral and military-supported political changes. In Malaysia new opposition political forces waxed and waned. Even at a preliminary and superficial level, therefore, myriad explanations of the pattern of investment ratios across countries can be advanced.

As for the influence of institutions, an extensive body of literature generally associates institutional factors and measures of governance with economic performance.[3] However, some controversy remains regarding the causality involved and empirical significance of the relationship. On the issue of causality, debate still rages as to whether good economic performance follows upon the adoption of "good" institutions or whether such institutions are in fact the result of the former. As for significance, different empirical studies have found instances suggesting that measures of good institutions, or institutional outcomes, are not uniformly associated with improved economic performance. This may be seen even from Barro's earliest growth investigations (Barro and Sala-i-Martin 1995), which showed that measures of the rule of law and of political instability mattered for growth, while no strong relationship existed with other outcomes of *ex ante* good institutions such as civil liberties, corruption, quality of the bureaucracy, expropriation risk, etc.

Here we follow North (1990) in defining institutions as "humanly devised constraints" on human behavior. These come in two forms, the first being formal institutions that refer to codified or explicit constraints on action, such as constitutions, laws, and rules and regulations promulgated in society. The second is informal institutions that take the form of norms and customs that also regulate behavior but are not codified, making them difficult to measure directly. The conceptual relationship between institutions and governance has not always been clear (see e.g., Zhuang et al. 2010). But here we follow Kaufmann et al. (2003) and define governance as "the traditions and institutions by which authority in a country is exercised." In this way we can conceive of governance as the result of both formal and informal institutions. Indirectly, therefore, the quality of institutions may be judged by governance outcomes.

This chapter pursues the hypothesis that different institutions and measures of governance will matter to countries at different levels of development. Therefore, we take issue with the idea that all *a priori* desirable institutional aspects will matter and represent equally relevant constraints to growth. The latter idea is at least implicit in all empirical attempts to find relationships between measures of governance/institutional outcomes on the one hand and various measures of economic performance on the other.

This issue is especially relevant for Asia, given the political and academic interest surrounding the supposed exceptionalism of Asian institutions and their role in development, as well as the inherent heterogeneity of the countries involved. Many years ago, scholars such as Chang (1990) and more recently Chang and Lin (2009) have argued that – contrary to orthodox advice and representation – deliberate protectionist industrial policy by an activist state was an important factor in the rapid industrial advance of the Republic of Korea.[4] In a somewhat simpler form, this discussion manifested itself in the "Asian values" debate of the 1980s, famously associated with Malaysia's Mahathir bin Mohamad and Singapore's Lee Kuan Yew, during which some Asian leaders defended existing authoritarian political systems and the restriction of civil liberties as necessary components for a state seeking to safeguard social stability or direct industrial priorities, or both. This view was subsequently echoed and given an analytical scaffolding by some scholars, for example, Khan and Jomo (2000), who proposed that we understand the existence of rents, including corruption rents, as at times – though not always – necessary concomitants of the social stability that allows economic development to occur. It was argued, for example, that Malaysia's patently discriminatory and at times confiscatory race-based economic policy was historically necessary in order to purchase the social stability that allowed economic development to occur (Jomo 2000). In a similar vein, Chang (1990) has long argued that the privileges allowed *chaebols* early in the economic history of the Republic of Korea were needed as an enticement for their investment in what the leadership had decided were strategic industries.

More recently, these lines of argument received support in a more general form and a mainstream source. In their ambitious typology of social orders, North et al. (2009) suggest that at a country's initial stages of development (i.e., in "natural" or slightly better "limited-access" orders) the need to control social violence is paramount and is typically achieved through elites reaching a *modus vivendi* among themselves to monopolize or share power and to extract rents. Such arrangements are fundamentally different from the ideal associated with the most developed Western countries (North et al.'s "open-access orders"), where contestable political power and democracy prevail. Necessary conditions for the transition are the acceptance of the rule of law for elites, the existence of impersonal and long-lived social organizations, and control of the military.

The implications of the above framework are too rich to be fully discussed here. For this chapter's purposes, it is sufficient to point out some stark empirical possibilities, namely, the possibility that a poor country with formal institutions appearing to guarantee democracy and civil liberties, or even having a sophisticated bureaucracy, may still perform poorly in pure economic terms if it is threatened by violence and lawlessness. In this case, the absence of political stability or a breakdown in the rule of law may be more important for investment decisions, and hence for growth, than the presence of formal democracy, a related point made recently by Fukuyama (2008). This also raises the possibility that countries with high levels of corruption may nonetheless perform satisfactorily if corruption rents are a concomitant for the elitist control of social violence. Arguments of this type may also rely on some version of the Shleifer and Vishny (1993) argument that decentralized (contestable and duplicative) corruption may yield more inefficient results than the centralized kind.[5]

Indeed at lower levels of development, the shape of higher political arrangements (e.g., at the national level) may matter little since market transactions may be mostly localized and limited in scale to begin with. Whatever formal or legal difficulties are imposed on private contracting can typically be moderated through informal arrangements, as suggested by Acemoglu and Johnson (2005), the latter possibly including corruption, to the extent that such informal arrangements do not conform or even violate the letter of formal rules. In such cases, local institutions, including norms and lower-level accountabilities, may provide enough workable bases for contracting at smaller scales. Possible mechanisms that may mediate such transactions may include informal institutions associated with Confucian values, local trust, and relational contracting (*guanxi*).[6] This may partly explain why single-party systems arising from socialist mass movements (such as those in the PRC and Viet Nam) can nevertheless accommodate high investment and growth over longer periods. Even severe restrictions on civil liberties, as they relate to national politics and decisions, may continue to be compatible with a tradition for greater transactional flexibility and responsiveness with respect to local issues, and in this way, not hinder growth of a certain scale and sophistication. See, for example, Xu Wang (1997) for a hopeful view and Thornton (2008) for a more pessimistic view of Chinese developments.

As the scale of markets widens and anonymous exchange becomes more prevalent and necessary, such small-scale arrangements may prove increasingly inadequate, and one can anticipate a greater need for uniformity in the application of rules and laws over wider geographical areas and more varied transactions. At higher levels of income and development, as the "threshold conditions" described by North et al. (2009) come to be met, the larger scale and greater variety of projects bump up against the capacity and interest of state apparatuses to intervene. The growing number of and differentiation among non-state economic actors can be expected to create a greater demand for better policies and regulation and a more nondiscriminatory application of rules based on objective criteria. At this point, concerns among investors – now more numerous and heterogeneous – for the quality of regulation may grow and threats to investments from capricious decisions are bound to make corruption a more pronounced concern. The inability of the status quo to make such changes may create a demand for civil liberties and accountability at higher national levels.

In purely economic terms, another way to view the matter is to imagine that at initial levels of development a country operates well below its production-possibilities frontier.[7] At that point, the environment will be "forgiving" of small mistakes, since movement in almost any direction is likely to represent some form of improvement. At higher levels of resource utilization (e.g., at points at or close to the frontier), however, information requirements are bound to be more stringent, investment commitments larger, and the risk of mistakes greater. In such conditions, not only the correctness of decisions but also their social legitimacy is bound to represent a constraint on investment choices. At even higher levels of development, when societies seek to push the frontier of possibilities outward rather than merely approach it, innovation and creativity are likely to be compatible only with the freedom of inquiry and expression associated with full-blown formal democracy.[8]

Depending on its level of development and historical circumstances, therefore, each country may face a different binding constraint. Governance, then, is not one thing but many; it is not a real number but a vector.

If at all, this discussion only qualifies the instrumental value of individual freedoms, civil liberties, and democracy for economic performance and does not touch upon what Sen (1999) has termed their intrinsic and constructive values. Each society, however, is left to determine among its own members exactly how far and when civil liberties and democratic institutions should be introduced in its own development path, the inherent dilemma for nondemocratic regimes being how any putative "social choice" is to be legitimized.

TESTS AND RESULTS

To recapitulate, this chapter advances the simple observation that different dimensions of governance may matter for countries at different levels of development. At low levels of income and with large reserves of unused resources, binding constraints may take the form of government effectiveness, the rule of law, and political stability. At early stages of development, the more immediate deterrent to growth may be the fundamental insecurity of investments against the threat of violence, confiscation, and seizure by contending elites. Ultimately, however, as per capita incomes increase and both the scale and variety of potential transactions expand, other governance factors such as controlling corruption, permitting voice and accountability, and providing an intelligent scheme of regulation, may figure more prominently for sustaining high rates of investment.

Empirically, we build upon the results reported by Quibria (2006), which failed to find a strong relationship between growth in a set of developing Asian countries and a constructed general measure of governance using the measures developed in 2003 by Kaufmann, Kraay, and Mastruzzi, referred to as the KKM measures. These measures, which have since become widely used, are constructed indices of six dimensions of governance: voice and accountability; political stability; rule of law; government effectiveness; regulatory quality; and control of corruption.[9] Subsequently, Zhuang et al. (2010) decomposed these general "governance measures" into various components and related these separately to growth performance for a global set of countries and for developing Asian countries in particular. Asian countries were then classified according to whether they manifested a surplus or a deficit with respect to one or the other governance measure, depending on whether they fell above or below the value predicted by the global regression on income. They found that a loose enumeration of Asian countries' subsequent growth performance is more closely associated with earlier "governance surpluses or deficits" with respect to the so-called KKM measures of government effectiveness, regulatory quality, and the rule of law. By contrast, dimensions such as control of corruption, voice and accountability, and political stability appear to have less predictive power.

While this earlier work represents a definite advance, it still suffers from the implicit presumption that the same relevant governance measures potentially affect all countries uniformly on average. The governance measures have, if anything, only restricted the set of variables that might matter on average. Left unelaborated, it may also leave the impression of an unwarranted Asian exceptionalism, which argues that the institutions and conditions required for growth in Asia are inherently different from those required elsewhere.

If our hypothesis holds, however, what is really needed is an allowance for the possibility that different governance outcomes actually matter for countries at different levels of development, a fact that will be hidden by the estimation of average relationships – even those conditioned upon per capita income. Therefore, we build upon this previous empirical work and test the hypothesis of differentiated governance influence by first partitioning the sample of countries based on their per capita GDP in 1991–95, then estimating the effect on the change in investment ratios between 1991–95 and 2002–06 as these relate to changes in measures of governance that are salient to each country's level of development.

Let the sample of countries be partitioned into mutually exclusive categories, say quantiles, Q_1, Q_2, . . ., Q_H and the various governance dimensions (e.g., voice and accountability, political stability, and so on) be indexed by G_i ($i = 1, 2, \ldots, 6$). Each G_i is then mapped into the country categories for which we hypothesize it to be relevant. This then yields the set of categories $Q(G_i) = \{Q_h, h\{1,2,\ldots,H\}|\ G_i$ is an *a priori* binding governance constraint$\}$. Hence, for example, we may hypothesize that voice and accountability is a binding constraint only for countries in the second to fourth quartile; this means $Q(G_1) = \{Q_2, Q_3, Q_4\}$. The value of governance measure i for country k is denoted as G_{ik} so that its change between the two periods is ΔG_{ik}. We then define the dummy variable, D_{ik} such that $D_{ik} = 1$ if country k belongs to $Q(G_i)$, and 0 otherwise. The governance regressors for the change in investment for country k are then specified to be:

$$D_{ik}\Delta G_{ik} \text{ for all } i, k.$$

Denoting the change in the current investment ratio of country k as ΔA_k, the specification for the regressions therefore takes the following general form:

$$\Delta A_k = a_0 + \sum_i a_i D_{ik}\Delta G_{ik} + \sum_j b_j Z_{jk} + \varepsilon_k \qquad (2.1)$$

where the Z_{jk} denote control variables that include, among others: (a) the country's previous level of GDP per capita; or alternatively (b) the change in GDP per capita in the previous period; (c) the previous level of A; and (d) regional dummies. The use of GDP per capita, as well as the change in that variable, is based alternatively on the Solow model and a Keynesian accelerator. A negative coefficient is expected in the case of the Solow model, while a positive sign is expected if accelerator-related factors are taken into account.

The specification in (2.1) is to be contrasted with the notion that governance factors are equally binding so that a common relationship exists that relates changes in any governance variable to some change in the investment ratio, which would be written as:

$$\Delta A_k = a_0 + \sum_i a_i \Delta G_{ik} + \sum_j b_j Z_{jk} + \varepsilon_k. \qquad (2.2)$$

A benchmark is provided by the "naive" equation that seeks to explain the change in the rate of investment, excluding all consideration of any institutional and governance variables. This is shown as Equation 1 in Table 2.2. Here, the only significant variables are the average investment previous period, the Asian crisis dummy, and the sub-Saharan Africa dummy, with the equation itself explaining about one-third of the variation. The only variable of interest to Asia here is then the AFC.

The estimated Equation 2 in Table 2.2, on the other hand, includes governance variables but without differentiating their saliency according to countries' levels of development. This is essentially the implementation of the average relationship (2.2) above. The result is that only two governance variables appear to matter on average: rule of law and regulatory quality. In hindsight, this is a result similar to Barro's earliest findings, reported in Barro and Sala-i-Martin (1995) showing the rule of law – but not democratic institutions – to be an influence on growth and investment. This also essentially reproduces the Zhuang et al. (2010) exercise showing only factors associated with rule-of-law and regulatory-quality variables mattering for growth in Asia. Given the nature of the sample involved, however, it is evident – contrary to what may be suggested by earlier work – that the phenomenon is not peculiarly Asian at all but rather a global one, thus undermining any case for Asian exceptionalism.

Our hypothesis, instead, is that the lack of the apparent influence of other effects of governance variables is due to the failure to account for levels of development. Our first attempt to test the hypothesis in (2.1) above is shown as Equation 3 in Table 2.2, but with no restrictions imposed on the applicable governance variables; rather the full set of variables (G_1 to G_6) is regressed for each income quartile, a procedure that is tantamount to allowing a differential impact of governance variables within each group, conditional upon regional dummies. The results plainly show that different governance measures do matter in different ways for investment in countries in different quartiles, bolstering this chapter's main hypothesis. The governance variable that proves most relevant for the poorest quartile (Q_1) is the rule of law. Meanwhile, voice and accountability, as well as regulatory quality, are significant and of the expected sign for the second quartile; corruption control is significant and of the expected sign for the third quartile, while regulatory quality again appears significant for the richest quartile.

In line with our hypothesis that higher-order governance variables such as voice and accountability and corruption control are less significant in

Table 2.2   *Change in gross investment ratio (relative to GDP; 2002–06 versus 1991–95)*

Variable	1	2	3	4	5	6
Constant	**20.492**	**24.040**	**23.787**	**22.877**	**21.972**	**14.771**
Ln of GDP per capita in 1991–95	−0.905	**−1.190**	−0.930	−0.978	−0.874	
Change in GDP per capita in 1991–95						0.000
Investment ratio in 1991–95	**−0.481**	**−0.488**	**−0.540**	**−0.502**	**−0.507**	**−0.085**
Change in openness	0.021	0.020		0.015	0.014	0.007
Asian Crisis dummy	**−5.492**	**−4.751**		**−5.223**	**−5.069**	**−5.017**
East Asia Pacific dummy	−1.672	−1.618	−0.449	−2.321	−2.356	−2.460
East Europe–Central Asia dummy	−0.048	−0.958	−2.388	−2.221	−2.039	−2.114
Middle East and North Africa dummy	−2.703	**−3.964**	**−5.163**	**−4.456**	**−4.357**	**4.883**
South Asia dummy	2.130	1.111	0.290	0.472	0.029	1.335
Western Europe dummy	−1.305	**−3.027**	−4.705	**−4.262**	**−4.275**	**−7.027**
North America dummy	−0.970	−2.580	−3.934	−3.877	−3.922	−7.003
Sub-Saharan Africa dummy	**−4.038**	**−5.239**	**−5.821**	**−5.303**	**−5.219**	**−3.854**
Improvement in rule of law		2.631				
× Q1 dummy			7.338	**5.838**	**6.899**	**7.153**
× Q2 dummy			−0.065			
× Q3 dummy			3.295			
× Q4 dummy			−0.946			
Improvement in control of corruption						
× Q1 dummy			**−3.621**		**−3.774**	**−4.024**
× Q2 dummy			−1.410			
× Q3 dummy			3.417	3.302	3.262	3.408
× Q4 dummy			−0.124			
Improvement in voice and accountability						
× Q_1 dummy			1.072			
× Q_2 dummy			**5.699**	4.333	4.309	**4.445**
× Q_3 dummy			−1.117			

Table 2.2   (continued)

Variable	1	2	3	4	5	6
× Q_4 dummy			4.189			
Improvement in regulatory quality		**2.604**				
× Q_1 dummy			1.697			
× Q_2 dummy			**3.851**	**3.188**	**3.062**	**2.598**
× Q_3 dummy			**2.889**	**3.205**	**3.149**	**2.768**
× Q_4 dummy			**2.863**	**3.739**	**3.700**	**3.070**
Improvement in political stability						
× Q_1 dummy			−0.199			
× Q_2 dummy			−1.665			
× Q_3 dummy			−1.092			
× Q_4 dummy			0.845			
Change in government effectiveness						
× Q_1 dummy			0.846			
× Q_2 dummy			0.827			
× Q_3 dummy			−1.567			
× Q_4 dummy			0.766			
N	164.000	164.000	164.000	164.000	164.000	164.000
Adjusted R^2	0.337	0.398	0.377	0.410	0.417	0.424
Root mean square error	6.113	5.829	5.958	5.766	5.734	5.700

Notes:
GDP = gross domestic product.
Coefficients in boldface are significant at the 10% level or better. Ln = natural logarithm.

Source: Authors' computations based on data from the World Bank World Development Indicators, the World Bank World Governance Indicators 2010, and the Penn World Table Version 7.0.

the instrumental sense for poorer countries with large unused resources, we proceed to test more restricted sets of governance variables that are *a priori* regarded as more relevant to each quartile. Our favored specifications are Equations 5 and 6, which include a dummy variable identifying countries severely affected by the AFC, which turns out to be negative and highly significant, as well as changes in openness, though insignificant. Equation 5 uses initial per capita GDP (i.e., its natural logarithm) and the previous change in investment as controls, and both have negative and significant coefficients, as the neoclassical theory suggests. On the other hand, Equation 6 replaces the level of GDP per capita with the change in per capita GDP, as accelerator models of investment suggest. The coefficient of that variable is positive and significant, again consistent with theory.

Regional dummies for the Middle East and North Africa, Western Europe, North America, and sub-Saharan Africa are also all significant with negative coefficients.[10] Initially puzzling but ultimately important in both Equations 5 and 6 is the perverse and significant coefficient of the anti-corruption variable in the first quartile, signifying that controlling corruption may have an adverse impact on investment for countries at that level of income. This is entirely consistent with the hypothesis, however. Given the pervasiveness and systemic nature of corruption in some of the poorest countries, significant efforts to combat corruption may unsettle vested interests that are already responsible to a large degree for investment under the existing equilibrium, so that at least initially, investment ratios may fall. Eliminating this variable from the set of regressors (e.g., Equation 4) leads to a significantly weaker performance of the equation, strongly suggesting that this effect cannot be ignored.

When corruption control alone is regressed on changes in investment ratios conditioned on quartiles (not displayed), it shows a negative and significant effect only for Q_1 and the expected positive ones for Q_2–Q_4, although it is significant only for Q_3. This suggests its influence in the other quartiles may be confounded by a correlation with other variables.

The above results are robust in showing the rule of law to be the only variable that matters for countries in the poorest quartile; voice and accountability matter for the next poorest; the quality of regulation is significant for the second, third, and even the richest quartiles; while improvements in the control of corruption appear to matter in the conventional sense only for the third quartile.

In purely statistical terms, the inclusion of governance indicators (i.e., moving from Equation 1 to Equation 6 in Table 2.2) raises the explanatory power of the equation (as represented by the adjusted-R^2 statistic) by some 25 per cent.[11] As one moves from a specification that relates governance indicators to investment that disregards levels of development to one that does (i.e., from Equation 2 to Equation 5 in Table 2.2), adjusted-R^2 increases from 0.3975 to 0.4237, a further 5 per cent increase.

Accounting for both demographic variables and the degree of sophistication of a country's financial system contributes little to the explanation. Table 2.3 shows specifications that involve past-period dependency ratios and the past-period ratio of bank credit to GDP (Equations 5A, 5B, 6A, and 6B), and neither proves significant. The incompleteness of data for these additional variables, moreover, reduces the sample size from 164 to 156 countries, which causes a loss in the significance of regulatory quality

Table 2.3   Change in gross domestic investment ratio (relative to GDP; 2002–06 versus 1991–95)

Variable	5A	5B	6A	6B
Constant	23.875	24.136	14.552	15.257
Ln of GDP per capita in 1991–95	−1.137	−1.207		
Change in GDP per capita in 1991–95			0.000	0.000
Investment ratio in 1991–95	−0.572	−0.573	0.625	−0.622
Change in openness	0.042	0.042	0.036	0.036
Asian crisis dummy	−4.973	−4.848	−5.070	−5.200
Dependency ratio in 1991–95		0.042		−0.075
Bank credit, ratio to GDP, 1992–96		−0.001		−0.001
East Asia Pacific dummy	−1.009	−1.029	−0.888	−0.843
East Europe–Central Asia dummy	−0.125	−0.367	−0.456	−0.094
Middle East and North Africa dummy	−2.455	−2.374	2.761	−2.868
South Asia dummy	1.731	1.761	3.178	2.958
Western Europe dummy	−2.783	−3.280	−4.714	−3.699
North America dummy	−2.099	−2.388	−4.499	−3.727
Sub-Saharan Africa dummy	−4.003	−3.961	2.397	−2.687
Improvement in rule of law				
× Q1 dummy	7.939	7.123	7.701	7.663
× Q2 dummy				
× Q3 dummy				
× Q4 dummy				
Improvement in control of corruption				
× Q1 dummy	−3.894	−3.884	−4.317	−4.241
× Q2 dummy				
× Q3 dummy	3.109	3.006	3.246	3.443
× Q4 dummy				
Improvement in voice/ accountability				
× Q_1 dummy				
× Q_2 dummy	5.366	5.362	5.413	5.329
× Q_3 dummy				
× Q_4 dummy				
Improvement in regulatory quality				
× Q_1 dummy				
× Q_2 dummy	3.305	3.284	2.839	2.884

Table 2.3   (continued)

Variable	5A	5B	6A	6B
× Q$_3$ dummy	**2.332**	**2.377**	**2.102**	**2.067**
× Q$_4$ dummy	3.617	3.812	0.573	0.379
N	156.000	156.000	156.000	156.000
Adjusted R^2	0.546	0.539	0.549	0.544
Root mean square error	4.885	4.919	4.869	4.896

Notes:
GDP = gross domestic product.
Coefficients in boldface are significant at the 10% level or better. Ln = natural logarithm.

Source: Authors' computations based on data from the World Bank World Development Indicators, the World Bank World Governance Indicators 2010, and the Penn World Table Version 7.0.

only in the richest quartile and improves the showing by the openness variable, as well as showing an improved fit. The direction and significance of all other governance variables are as before. In what follows, therefore, we revert to estimates involving the full sample.

Equations 5 and 6 in Table 2.2 involving the full sample correctly predict the change in investment ratios for 24 out of 31 included developing Asian countries, with mean squared errors of 24 and 25.1 respectively.[12] By contrast, Equations 1 and 2 correctly predict 20 and 22 of these investment ratio differences in Asia, with respective mean squared errors of 34.3 and 30.8.

More generally, the relative contribution of differentiated governance variables to the explanation of investment rate changes is detailed in Table 2.4, which breaks down the contribution of each variable to the explanatory power of Equations 2, 5, and 6, following Fields (2004), with the sum totaling unity, including the unexplained residual. Without accounting for development levels, governance variables contribute about 6 per cent to explaining the variation of changing investment levels (Column 1). A consideration of development levels, however, raises the contribution to almost 9 per cent. It may be said, therefore, that differentiating countries by development levels increases by 50 per cent the capacity of governance variables to explain investment rate changes. The table also provides a sense of the significance of changing governance. Changing governance certainly cannot claim to explain, exclusively or even primarily, the bulk of the changes in global investment ratios. The most important variable appears to be the momentum of previous investment. Governance variables, on the other hand, account for as much as 17–18 per cent[13] of the

Table 2.4   Decomposition of contribution to explanatory power[a]
           (governance variables in general versus governance
           differentiated by countries' level of development)

Explanatory variable	1	2	3
	Equation 2	Equation 5	Equation 6
Ln of GDP per capita in 1992–96	0.028	0.021	
Change in GDP per capita 1996–2002			−0.004
Investment ratio in 1992–96	0.295	0.306	0.336
Change in openness 1996–2002	0.002	0.001	0.001
Asian Crisis dummy	0.036	0.039	0.038
Regional dummies	0.034	0.032	0.036
Improvement in			
Rule of law (general)	0.017		
Regulatory quality (general)	0.040		
Rule of law: Q1		0.015	0.015
Control of corruption: Q1		0.009	0.009
Voice and accountability: Q2		0.013	0.013
Regulatory quality: Q2		0.019	0.016
Regulatory quality: Q3		0.007	0.006
Control of corruption: Q3		0.015	0.016
Regulatory quality: Q4		0.013	0.011
Sum governance variables	**0.057**	**0.089**	**0.086**
Residual	0.547	0.512	0.507
Total	1.000	1.000	1.000

Note: a.   Following the method developed in Fields (2004). Ln = natural logarithm.

Source: Authors' computations based on data from the World Bank World Development Indicators, the World Bank World Governance Indicators 2010, and the Penn World Table Version 7.0.

total variation explained by the best specifications and trump the contributions of changing per capita GDP, economic openness, and the AFC itself.

RELEVANCE FOR ASIA

Beyond statistical fit, the more important gain is the increase and differentiation in the number of significant variables and their potentially richer implications for theory and policy. To assess the relevance of these results for Asia, we classify countries according to per capita income quartiles and then examine to what extent changes in the salient

*Table 2.5   Asia and Pacific countries by real per capita GDP quartile
(1992–96)*

Q_1	Q_2	Q_3	Q_4
Afghanistan	**PRC**	**PRC** (2007)	Australia
Bangladesh	Fiji	Marshall Islands	Brunei Darussalam
Bhutan	Micronesia, Fed.	**Malaysia**	Hong Kong, China
India	States	**Thailand**	Japan
Cambodia	**India** (2007)	Tonga	Korea, Republic of
Kiribati	**Indonesia**		Macao, China
Lao PDR	Sri Lanka		New Zealand
Mongolia	Maldives		Palau
Nepal	Pakistan		Singapore
Solomon Islands	**Philippines**		Taipei,China
Viet Nam	Papua New Guinea		
	Viet Nam (2007)		
	Samoa		
	Vanuatu		
Salient variables			
Rule of law	Voice and	Regulatory	Regulatory quality
Control of	accountability	quality	
corruption	Regulatory quality	Control of	
		corruption	

Notes:
PRC = People's Republic of China. Lao PDR = the Lao People's Democratic Republic.
Quartiles based on all countries that have data on real per capita GDP in the Penn World
Table.

Source: Authors' computations based on data from the World Bank World Governance
Indicators 2010 and the Penn World Table Version 7.0.

governance variables relate to changes in investment (Table 2.5). The
countries of specific interest in this volume happen to be neatly distrib-
uted, with India and Viet Nam in the first quartile; the PRC, Indonesia,
and the Philippines in the second; and Malaysia and Thailand in the
third. By 2007, however, India and Viet Nam had transited from the first
to the second quartile, while the PRC leapt from the second to the third
quartile to join Malaysia and Thailand. Effectively, therefore, by the end
of the period under consideration, all seven Asian countries were in the
second or third quartiles.

Among Q_1 countries during the period, Viet Nam, along with Bangladesh
and Mongolia, was an obvious example that conformed to the predicted
average pattern, with investment rising with the rule-of-law measure. In

the said countries, even the incidental slippage in the control of corruption is in line with the trend. India, on the other hand, showed a deteriorating performance in terms of the rule of law, which may itself have been associated with lax control of corruption, but nonetheless showed a markedly higher investment rate.

Among Q_2 countries, the results predict that improvements in voice and accountability and in regulatory quality should matter on average. In the case of the PRC, the perceived fall in regulatory quality during the period appeared not to have had a negative effect, although improving voice and accountability contributed positively. Indonesia, on the other hand, showed a marked improvement in voice and accountability measures, obviously reflecting regime change to a more functional elective democracy in 1999, following three decades of Suharto's New Order. The improved investment ratio is consistent with this change, but this has occurred despite a significant deterioration in regulatory quality. For the Philippines, the deterioration in perceived regulatory quality and in voice and accountability is consistent with the fall in investment ratio during the period. For other countries in this group, as well, model predictions run true on all counts, so that in these countries, deteriorating governance is augmented by other factors to cause falling investment ratios.

The two countries of interest in Q_3, Malaysia and Thailand, both showed a deterioration in the two salient dimensions – control of corruption and regulatory quality – so that institutional and governance factors seem to contribute to an explanation of declining investment performance. The above also suggests that rapid performers, such as the PRC, India, and Viet Nam, that have since crossed categories during the period under study, may soon confront new constraints for which they may be more or less adapted. In the case of the PRC, for example, new circumstances may compel it to confront problems of corruption more aggressively, while India and Viet Nam are obviously differently situated in their ability to respond to possible concerns for regulatory quality and voice and accountability, where these are applicable.[14]

THE NEED FOR CLOSER COUNTRY HISTORICAL STUDIES

The above considerations based on average global relationships are significant. But it is important to emphasize that at the level of individual countries, these are suggestive at best, and it remains to be seen whether the principal factors suggested by this empirical analysis find confirmation in the experience of a specific country. While we are in no doubt that this framework is a helpful guide, there should be no illusion that it can substitute for in-depth and historical approaches to the conditions of individual countries.[15] Two points should be particularly noted. The first is that there is no claim that institutional factors alone are responsible for changes in a country's investment performance, although they have been shown to be significant factors that must be considered. Our own position is that "institutions matter at some point" rather than that "institutions rule" without qualification. The second point, in the same vein, is that a country may progress from or regress into one development category to another without necessarily having resolved all institutional issues of a previous stage – some of which may come back to bite it. This can be seen from significant, albeit non-Asian, examples of Middle East countries caught up in the so-called "Arab Spring." Given the fairly high levels of per capita income of such countries, one might have expected them to have been pre-occupied by "higher order" governance issues such as regulatory quality and control of corruption, just like the Asian countries covered here.[16] Recent events, however, make it evident that more fundamental "first-order" issues pertaining to democracy and accountability remained unresolved in those countries, with the process of their resolution leading to radical regime changes that threaten political stability and the rule of law.

Keeping this in mind, it is notable that on the whole, most governance issues relevant to the Asian countries studied in this volume now pertain – subject to important qualifications discussed further below – only to the two broad issues of regulatory quality and control of corruption. This is so, since India and Viet Nam have since transited into Q_2, while the PRC has moved into Q_3. Table 2.6 provides the values of the World Governance Indicators for the relevant countries.

In one sense, the countries in question appear to have passed over or outgrown most of the first-order governance issues that typically afflict poorer or failing states, especially problems related to the maintenance of order, basic contract enforcement, and the maintenance of regime legitimacy and stability. An issue such as regulatory quality is, after all, ultimately a higher-order issue relating to the direction of policy rather than the capacity to formulate and implement policy itself. These include such issues as nationality restrictions, trade policies, industrial priorities and incentives, and financial regulations, which Kaufmann et al. (2008) sum up as "sound policies and regulations that permit and promote private sector development." Likewise, that corruption issues should become prominent already presupposes that broad and formally impartial laws and rules are in place and a civil society or business community exists

Table 2.6   Governance indicators for selected countries (2007; percentile rankings in parentheses)

	Rule of law	Voice and accountability	Control of corruption	Regulatory Quality
PRC	−0.45 (41.0)	−1.72 (4.8)	−0.60 (33.8)	−0.18 (49.5)
India	+0.14 (56.7)	+0.47 (60.2)	−0.37 (44.4)	−0.21 (47.1)
Indonesia	−0.64 (30.0)	−0.15 (43.3)	−0.60 (33.3)	−0.25 (44.2)
Malaysia	+0.57 (65.2)	−0.57 (32.2)	+0.35 (67.6)	+0.57 (67.5)
Philippines	−0.47 (40.5)	−0.16 (42.8)	−0.67 (29.0)	−0.06 (51.9)
Thailand	−0.02 (53.3)	−0.61 (30.3)	−0.29 (48.3)	+0.16 (57.3)
Viet Nam	−0.41 (43.9)	−1.60 (7.2)	−0.61 (32.4)	−0.43 (35.4)

Note: PRC = People's Republic of China.

Source: Kaufmann, Kraay, and Mastruzzi (2003) accessed from: http://info.worldbank.org/governance/wgi/index.asp.

that expects such rules to be adhered to. The saliency of the problem itself reflects the inadequacy or failure of informal institutions and modes of relational contracting to resolve transactional issues relating to business.

These issues are evident in the experiences of some individual countries. In Malaysia, for example, a major regulatory issue affecting investment has been the continuation of the preferential ethnic ownership quotas for large enterprises under the nation's long-standing *bumiputera* policy. It has been pointed out, among others by Hill (2010), that this policy has an obvious disincentive effect for non-Malays, particularly ethnic Chinese, to expand their businesses. It imposes a real penalty for entrepreneurs in so-called "Ali Baba" accommodations,[17] as well as reinforcing the continuation of the large role of government-linked companies in the economy, which have been important vehicles of patronage. While the ethnic quota pre-dates the AFC, its deleterious effects on investment may have been exacerbated in the period of lower global growth. Moreover, the very uncertainty of the continuation of that policy – with the prime minister himself moving towards its reconsideration and given the ruling party's weakening political hold on power – may paradoxically contribute to the observed investment decline. The same post-crisis weakening of the dominant United Malays National Organisation political party may lead to shorter horizons and paradoxically lead to demands for larger side-payments to create or maintain Ali Baba arrangements.

The institutional factors affecting Thailand's recent economic performance are admittedly more complex than the scheme laid out above. A short discussion of the situation is still instructive, nonetheless, if only to prove the point that unresolved institutional issues may yet return to haunt a country. The average model predicts that for its level of income, Thailand should have outgrown questions of regime legitimacy and accountability. Yet it is evident that part of the dramatic deterioration in the Thai economy's investment performance must be due to the uncertainty wrought by deep and unresolved political divisions that have persisted since 2005 and which have resulted in nullified elections, actual or threatened coups d'état, violent mass demonstrations and their equally violent suppression – in short, concerns of regime legitimacy and accountability more typical of a Q_2 country.[18] This strongly suggests, in the language of North et al. (2009), a failure among the country's elites – civilian politicians, the military, and monarchic circles – to agree on the process for a normal succession and sharing of power. But it also points to the deeper problem of social cohesion and the wide gulf between the urban middle classes and the rural population, which past economic growth has failed to bridge.

In this sense, Indonesia provides a contemporary contrast in that it continues to ride the wave of its having resolved legitimacy and accountability questions following the AFC, an issue that conforms to its level of development. The decline in Indonesia's post-crisis investment rate is notably far less than that seen in Thailand. It must be remembered, of course, that the current stability has been purchased at the cost of dealing with serious ethnic violence and separatist challenges in the period during and immediately after the AFC. In any event, the successful operation of regular electoral processes and the meeting of regional demands with greater local autonomy – or, in the extreme, independence as was the case of Timor-Leste, a former Portuguese colony and Indonesian territory – of some provinces have for now resolved questions of stability, legitimacy, and accountability and prevented these factors from interfering with the recovery of accumulation rates.

The Philippines, likewise, experienced a comparatively smaller decline in the investment ratio compared to Malaysia and Thailand after the AFC. But unlike Indonesia, its investment ratio was already low to begin with. The Philippines has continued to be afflicted by issues of political stability and contract enforcement, even if its income level predicts it should have moved on to higher-order governance issues. Again, like Indonesia, it went through acute problems of regime legitimacy soon after the AFC – first with the extra-constitutional deposition of President Joseph Estrada in 2001, and then with the disputed election victory of President Gloria Macapagal-Arroyo in 2004 – that appeared to have further dented investor confidence. A credible transition occurred in 2010 with the election of President Benigno Aquino III, who has put anticorruption at the forefront of his reform efforts, but so far with no perceptible

impact on investment demand.[19] In fact, the anticorruption efforts of the
new government are sometimes judged to be in conflict with bolstering
contract enforcement, particularly as they have led to the cancellation
of contracts with some foreign enterprises (see Chapter 12). Regardless,
other institutional barriers serve to hamper investment demand, such as
a weak bureaucracy – partly due to the extraordinary power of appointment of the president and constitutional provisions that are not conducive
to foreign investments, such as a limit on foreign ownership of land and
equity in firms. The country has recently made notable gains in tax collections, which are largely responsible for the credit-rating upgrade it has
received from various credit rating agencies. It will be interesting to see if
such gains can be sustained and what the impact will be on the investment
rate in the country.

In the meantime, a growing concern with corruption has pervaded
most countries considered in this study, apart from the Philippines, most
notably the PRC, India, and Indonesia. The PRC's prime minister has
been quoted as saying that "corruption is the greatest threat to the PRC."[20]
Official media has also been more forthcoming regarding the existence
and scale of corruption, reporting for example on recent crackdowns on
corrupt officials and almost casually mentioning a remarkable Ministry
of Commerce estimate that more than $30 billion has been illicitly taken
overseas by some 4000 corrupt officials over three decades.[21] It is difficult
to judge the seriousness of such pronouncements and whether they will
ultimately lead to effective action; nor is corruption by any means a novel
phenomenon. The government's express concern and greater official
media frankness about the issue at this time, however, demonstrate its
anticipation of a next-generation problem that resonates with a more sensitive civil society and a more demanding domestic and foreign business
community. It is incidentally also in line with the simple sequence outlined
here (i.e., the PRC's rapid transit from Q_2 to Q_3). By portraying corruption
as a serious issue that could "destabilize social stability," the government
there is clearly aware of the possibility that the issue might otherwise spill
over into questions of regime legitimacy.[22] The government, therefore,
implicitly believes that addressing the corruption issue is a vital factor –
and indeed possibly a substitute – for the other salient Q_2 variable, voice
and accountability, where the PRC's low indicator placed it in the 4.8
percentile of countries in 2007 (see Table 2.6). In particular, the government may believe that the demand for pluralism, democratic processes,
and civil liberties might be staved off – at least in the short-term – by a
prompt response to the corruption issue and improved regulatory quality.
At the very least, however, this is an untested theory, and it remains to
be seen whether a substitution in historical practice is possible between

mechanisms of social accountability even at higher levels of economic development, i.e., as between traditional institutions of liberal democracy, on the one hand, and the ability of a massive state bureaucracy to reform itself from within, on the other, or even whether a gradual transition from one to the other is possible. For a pessimistic outlook, see Pei (2007).

In the future but not the near term, such considerations are also likely to confront Viet Nam, which shares the same features of party- and state-dominated economic decision making as the PRC. Viet Nam actually ranks slightly worse, in the 32nd percentile, in terms of corruption than the PRC, in the 34th percentile (see Table 2.6). The reason that corruption has not become more urgent in Viet Nam, as follows from our framework, lies in the various economic levels that exist in the two countries. In other words, the large number of various exploitable market opportunities and untapped resources at several levels allow sufficient returns to be earned by both large and small economic actors, even in the presence of corruption. It may be anticipated, however, that, as in the PRC, once the scale and sophistication of transactions reaches a certain level, margins will no longer be generous enough to accommodate grand corruption by officials. Especially relevant is a specific characteristic of recent Vietnamese growth, namely its high dependence on foreign savings and foreign capital, as contrasted with the PRC's primary reliance on home investment.[23] This means, among other things, that Viet Nam is likely to confront a tougher and more fickle audience, since a large part of it is foreign, when the need to make palpable headway against corruption finally becomes urgent. In the short term, however, the lure of unused resources and a tolerable rule-of-law environment may be sufficient to sustain the rapid pace of investment in Viet Nam.

The significance of corruption in the other countries treated here is also unlikely to be as potentially dramatic as in the PRC, or in Viet Nam in the future. While media and politicians have also reflected the serious public concern over corruption in India and Indonesia, for example, that concern is far less likely to spill over into questions of regime legitimacy in the future, although it might matter for the fate of particular governments. This is because unlike the PRC, India, and Indonesia already have existing political processes that allow for the orderly change of ruling elites (e.g., as a rough indicator India was in the 60th percentile and Indonesia was in the 40th percentile of the voice-and-accountability index, while the PRC was in the 5th percentile and Viet Nam was in the 7th percentile).

This country-by-country discussion illustrates our point: that the importance of various governance factors will manifest at different times depending on a country's level of development. Even this treatment, however, is suggestive at best, although we believe it represents a systematic improvement over other discussions of institutional factors that generally tend to be ad hoc and impressionistic. Further work can be undertaken to refine the relevant concept of a "development level" (we have used only the crudest form, which is a grouping according to per capita income), as well as its empirical specification. More importantly, there can be no substitute for in-depth, single-country studies through time in order to test the validity of results hidden behind the veil of averages.

CONCLUSION

We have advanced the hypothesis – straightforward but apparently novel in the formal literature – that the specific governance factors affecting a country's economic performance, taken here to mean investment, hinge on a country's level of development. This idea has been tested empirically, and the results of that test have been examined against the specific situations of selected Asian countries.

On the whole, we conclude that governance and institutional factors do exert an influence on investment in Asia and that they form part of the explanation of the observed investment behavior in the region. Governance factors such as the rule of law, the control of corruption, and regulatory quality have been identified as being particularly relevant. Countries such as Indonesia, Malaysia, and Thailand have manifested lower investment ratios partly owing to the purely economic consequences of the AFC, but also because of the changed relevance of existing institutions that that crisis has provoked. Changes in political institutions and practices have been adequate to clear the way for an eventual rebound of investment rates in some cases, but less so in others. Even countries such as the PRC, India, and Viet Nam, which have not experienced an investment slowdown during the period under study, will need to be concerned about taking the next appropriate steps to reform aspects of governance relevant to their histories and levels of economic and social development if they are to sustain the momentum they thus far have enjoyed.

NOTES

1. The Solow growth model, for example, represents this as an economy's distance from its steady state.
2. The phrase is associated with Koo (2008), who used it to explain the Japanese recession of the 1990s. We owe to discussions with Felipe Medalla and Victor Valdepeñas many years ago the insight that this might apply to the AFC as well. Insights along these lines

were, of course, provided much earlier by Minsky (1975), whose ideas have enjoyed a revival since the onset of the recent GER.

3. A recent survey is found in Zhuang et al. (2010).
4. Chang and other writers were concerned to correct the representation of the success of East Asian tigers as a triumph of fairly liberal economic policies, as asserted, e.g., by the World Bank (1990).
5. Indeed, these authors use the post-Marcos experience in the Philippines as a negative example.
6. Zhuang et al. (2010) noted that a number of high-performing Asian countries, such as the PRC and Viet Nam, manifested high levels of "trust" or social capital.
7. We thank Juzhong Zhuang for this observation, which came up in earlier discussions.
8. This is by no means a novel idea; the discouragement of freedom of inquiry and thought was J.S. Mill's primary apprehension regarding a hypothetical collectivist society, which he thought would be inconsistent with the "diversity of tastes and talents, and variety of intellectual points of view" that are "the mainspring of mental and moral progression" (J.S. Mill [1848], *Principles of Political Economy*, Book 2, Chapter 1). Knowing what we now do regarding the continuing importance of creativity in a knowledge-based economy, we might well have added "material progression" to Mill's list.
9. Strictly speaking, these governance indicators cannot be aggregated, as Kaufmann, Kraay, and Mastruzzi have cautioned.
10. The comparator is Central and South America.
11. Note that $0.4237/0.3373 = 1.256$.
12. These mean squared errors (MSEs) are computed only for predictions for included Asian countries and are distinct from the global sample MSEs reported in Tables 2.2 and 2.3.
13. Referring to the last three rows of Table 2.4, that is $0.089/(1 - 0.512)$ and $0.086/(1 - 0.507)$, respectively.
14. Indeed, the authorities may already have become sensitized to this given central measures recently announced, which are designed to strengthen the government's corruption efforts.
15. In a study one of us undertook of the Philippines, for example, it was found that while the country's categorization suggests that voice and accountability and regulatory quality may be the relevant factors, a closer look indicates that corruption and political instability may have been the historically significant deterrents to investment (de Dios 2009).
16. Egypt and Tunisia are in Q_3, while Libya is in Q_4.
17. That is, arrangements in which Malays, in exchange for fees or directorships, front as majority shareholders for non-Malays to fulfill ethnic requirements and gain access to contracts.
18. See also Chapter 12.
19. It is probably too soon to judge the economic impact of the reform efforts of Aquino. At the time of the writing of this chapter, Arroyo is under arrest charged with electoral fraud, while the Chief Justice of the Supreme Court, who was appointed by Arroyo, is facing impeachment charges for alleged partiality to Arroyo.
20. Wen Jiabao at the National People's Congress on 3 March 2011.
21. See *Xinhua* (China Daily) at http://www.chinadaily.com.cn/china/2010-02/26/content_9506256.htm.
22. Wen Jiabao on 25 March 2011, see http://news.xinhuanet.com/english2010/china/2011-03/25/c_13798577.htm.
23. Vietnamese growth has been based on perennial current-account deficits, which have been largely offset by foreign direct investment. As much as 25–30 per cent of total investment in Viet Nam is foreign-owned.

REFERENCES

Acemoglu, D., and S. Johnson (2005), 'Unbundling institutions', *Journal of Political Economy*, **114** (5), 949–95.

Barro, R., and X. Sala-i-Martin (1995), *Economic Growth*, New York: McGraw-Hill.

Chang, H.-J. (1990), *Industrial Policy in [the Republic of] Korea*, Cambridge: Cambridge University Press.

Chang, H.-J., and J. Lin (2009), 'Should industrial policy in developing countries conform to comparative advantage or defy it? A debate between Justin Lin and Ha-Joon Chang', *Development Policy Review*, **27** (5), 483–502.

de Dios, E. (2009), 'Governance, institutions, and political economy', in D. Canlas, M.E. Khan, and J. Zhuang (eds), *Diagnosing the Philippine Economy*, London, New York, Delhi: Anthem Press, and the Asian Development Bank, pp. 295–336.

Fields, G. (2004), 'Regression-based decompositions: a new tool for managerial decision making', http://www.ilr.cornell.edu/directory/downloads/fields/Author_decomposingRegressions_mar04.pdf.

Fukuyama, F. (2008), 'What do we know about the relationship between the political and economic dimensions of development?', in World Bank (ed.), *Governance, Growth, and Development Decision-making – reflections* by Douglass North, Daron Acemoglu, Francis Fukuyama, Dani Rodrik, Washington, DC: World Bank.

Hill, H. (2010), 'Malaysian economic development: looking backwards and forward', Australian National University Working Papers in Trade and Development, November, No. 2010/13.

Jomo, K. (2000), 'The Malaysian development dilemma', in M. Khan and K. Jomo (eds), *Rents, Rent-seeking, and Economic Development: Theory and Evidence in Asia*, Cambridge: Cambridge University Press, pp. 274–303.

Kaufmann, D., A. Kraay, and M. Mastruzzi (2003), 'Governance Matters III: governance indicators for 1996–2002', World Bank Policy Research Working Papers No. 3106, World Bank, Washington, DC.

Kaufmann, D., A. Kraay, and M. Mastruzzi (2008) 'Governance Matter VII: Aggregate and individual governance indicators 1996–2007', World Bank Policy Research Working Paper No. 4654, World Bank, Washington, DC.

Khan, M., and K. Jomo (eds), (2000), *Rents, Rent-seeking, and Economic Development: Theory and Evidence in Asia*, Cambridge: Cambridge University Press.

Koo, R. (2008), *The Holy Grail of Macroeconomics: Lessons from Japan's Great Recession*, Singapore: Wiley and Sons.

Minsky, H. (1975), *John Maynard Keynes*, New York: McGraw-Hill.

North, D. (1990), *Institutions, Institutional Change, and Economic Growth*, Cambridge: Cambridge University Press.

North, D., J. Wallis, and B. Weingast (2009), *Violence and Social Orders: A Conceptual Framework for Interpreting Recorded Human History*, Cambridge: Cambridge University Press.

Pei, M. (2007), *[People's Republic of] China's Trapped Transition: The Limits of Developmental Autocracy*, Cambridge: Harvard University Press.

Quibria, M. (2006), 'Does governance matter? Yes, no, or maybe: some evidence from developing Asia', *Kyklos*, **59**, 99–114.

Sen, A. (1999), 'Democracy as a universal value', *Journal of Democracy*, **10**, 3–17.

Shleifer, A., and R. Vishny (1993), 'Corruption', *Quarterly Journal of Economics*, **108**, 599–617.

Thornton, J. (2008), 'Long time coming: the prospects for democracy in [the People's Republic of] China', *Foreign Affairs*, Council on Foreign Relations, January–February,1–22.

World Bank (1990), *The Miracle of East Asia,*. Washington, DC: World Bank.

World Bank (2008), *Governance, Growth, and Development Decision-Making – Reflections by: Douglass North, Daron Acemoglu, Francis Fukuyama, Dani Rodrik*, Washington, DC: World Bank.

Xu Wang (1997), 'Mutual empowerment of state and peasantry: grassroots democracy in rural [People's Republic of] China', *World Development*, **25**, 1431–42.

Zhuang, J., E. de Dios, and A. Lagman-Martin (2010), 'Governance and institutional quality and the links with growth and inequality: how Asia fares', in J. Zhuang (ed.), *Poverty and Inclusive Growth in Asia: Measurement, Policy Issues, and Country Studies*, London, New York, Delhi: Anthem Press, and Asian Development Bank, pp.268–315.

3. Infrastructure

Douglas H. Brooks and Eugenia C. Go

INTRODUCTION

Asia's high investment rates in recent decades have supported the rapid expansion of infrastructure, which in turn has supported the region's rapid growth. The processes by which investments in physical infrastructure are planned and financed and by which they generate useful services, as well as the manner in which those services are allocated to producers and consumers, can be complex. Focusing on infrastructure assets, services, and markets – and the environment in which infrastructure makes its contributions to economic growth and development – helps in analyzing effective infrastructure investment and related policies.

Infrastructure consists of physical assets such as power generation, transmission, and distribution systems, transportation or communications networks, and water and sanitation systems. By some definitions, social, organizational, or regulatory institutions can also be considered as infrastructure – often referred to as "soft" infrastructure to differentiate it from "hard" (physical) infrastructure. This chapter focuses primarily on the role of hard infrastructure in sustaining Asia's growth. Even so, the scope is too broad to permit much more than an overview of relevant issues.

Infrastructure has been widely characterized by theory and empirical studies as a source and facilitator of economic growth. Infrastructure contributes to growth directly through its fiscal stimulus effects and through the services it provides, which can serve as inputs to other economic activities. Indirectly, it contributes to growth through externalities, or spillover effects, that improve productivity, such as facilitating technology dissemination, prolonging the longevity of complementary capital goods, etc. For a region as dependent upon trade as Asia, infrastructure that facilitates regional trade can also lead to cross-country growth spillovers.

While Asian economies in general have grown at unprecedented rates in recent decades, sustained growth is imperative if the 1.8 billion people living below $2 a day (in terms of purchasing power parity) in the region are to be lifted out of poverty, and if the Millennium Development Goal

Table 3.1   Challenges in access to infrastructure services in Asia

Infrastructure	Issues
Energy	800 million people in Asia have no access to basic electric service; 1.8 billion people still rely on traditional biomass for cooking and heating
Water	1.8 billion people lack basic sanitation; 600 million people lack safe drinking water. Region at high risk due to climate change
Transport	Half of roads are unpaved; in some countries 30–40% of villages are without all-weather road access. Tens of millions of people have no access to affordable and convenient transport services
Urban	505 million slum dwellers in Asia; significant increase of urban poor without access to urban services

Source: 'Key challenges and role of ADB in infrastructure', presentation by Gil-Hong Kim, ADB, 14 April 2011.

of halving by 2015 the proportion of the population living below $1 a day is to be achieved in the region.[1] At present, the need for greater infrastructure remains substantial (Table 3.1).

Moreover, the rest of the world is looking to Asia to play an even more important role in shaping the world economy in the aftermath of the recent global economic recession (GER), which has made economic restructuring inevitable. While this may mean opportunities for high- and upper-middle-income countries in the region to consolidate their economic and social gains, it also implies opportunities for lower-middle and low-income economies to catch up with their higher-income counterparts in the region and the rest of the world.

In this context, it is important to understand how infrastructure can help sustain growth in Asian economies. In particular, it would be useful to know the parameters and variables related to infrastructure at different stages of development that policy makers have to consider over the medium and long term to ensure that Asian economies are well positioned to exploit the opportunities that global economic restructuring may offer. This chapter intends to contribute to this important discussion through (i) a comprehensive overview of the issues and policies involved in infrastructure investment, post-construction asset management, and the political economy of these activities; (ii) reexamining the empirical findings and underpinnings of the nexus between growth and infrastructure;

(iii) an empirical analysis on the kinds of infrastructure that are critical in supporting growth for economies at different stages of development; and (iv) policy recommendations for infrastructure development in the region based on the preceding analyses.

The chapter is structured as follows. The first section discusses some key characteristics of infrastructure that make it a special sector in terms of demand (consumption of infrastructure services) and supply (investment). The next section discusses the political economy of infrastructure investment, and is followed by a review of the empirical literature on the interaction between infrastructure and growth. Finally, we discuss the empirical methodology employed in this chapter and analyze the estimation results before concluding with considerations on further challenges and issues in infrastructure investment, and policy recommendations for infrastructure development in the region.

KEY CHARACTERISTICS OF INFRASTRUCTURE

According to Underhill (2010, 163), infrastructure is "a broad mix of large scale public systems, services, and facilities . . . necessary for economic activity to function." While it is apparent from this definition that infrastructure can refer to a vast array of large-scale structures and attendant services, this chapter focuses on the physical infrastructure of telecommunications, energy, and transportation. Infrastructure assets often require large investments and lengthy construction periods, delaying realization of the potential for cost recovery. Such assets usually cover particular geographic areas with the services they generate and may be natural monopoly providers of their services within those areas.

Public Goods Characteristics

Infrastructure investments usually generate externalities that can be either positive or negative, or both depending on who is affected. This may make it difficult to exclude users who are unwilling to pay for the services, to set prices that accurately reflect economic effects, or to collect payments that are proportional to usage. These characteristics mean that infrastructure services are usually at least partly public goods, and the public sector has a role to play. That infrastructure services often benefit the poor, in turn generating positive externalities, strengthens the public sector role.

Externalities and poverty among service consumers make implementation of user fees difficult. The public sector should be substantially involved in most infrastructure sectors, but poor countries face weak revenue-raising capacity and limited access to financial markets, suggesting a domestic dilemma. Network effects and coverage characteristics also make it difficult to delimit an appropriate role for public infrastructure policy.

The scale and long time horizon typical of infrastructure projects also lead toward public sector involvement. These characteristics raise particular issues in financing infrastructure investments and for the importance of financial market development in supporting infrastructure investment. In particular, bond markets with long-term bonds in local currency ease foreign exchange risk in international financial intermediation. Limited capacity in the public sector budget highlights the importance of crowding in the private sector, which is easier in some infrastructure sectors, such as telecommunications, than in others. Where pure private sector investment is unlikely, public–private partnerships (PPPs) offer a possible financing modality. Success in PPPs depends on reaching appropriate risk-sharing agreements and reliable institutional structures. Political risk coverage or risk sharing helps to mitigate risks of potential political turmoil to private sector investors over a lengthy horizon.

The large scale and long time horizon also mean that infrastructure projects are usually bulky investments, which are more likely to be undertaken by powerful agents in the local economy, especially when foreign investment is discouraged. The domestic political or economic power of the investors leads in turn to threats of possible market dominance and/or regulatory capture. Good governance then plays a critical role in providing an adequate level of comfort for private sector investors to participate in infrastructure investment. The complementarity of physical and institutional infrastructure has its own dynamic in the development process, with development of quality institutional infrastructure often playing catch-up to physical infrastructure in the early stages of development.

Infrastructure–Industry–Growth Nexus

As a bulky expenditure in the economy, infrastructure is widely recognized to directly contribute to growth as stimulus spending. This is what Roland-Holst (2006) termed as the Keynesian aspect of infrastructure spending. As a rule of thumb, total investment needs appear to vary from well over 7 per cent of gross domestic product (GDP) in low-income countries to around 3.1 per cent of GDP in upper-middle-income countries (Estache and Fay 2007).

Another direct channel by which infrastructure and its concomitant services contribute to growth comes from their intrinsic property as intermediate inputs to nearly if not all forms of economic activity. In the standard production function context, infrastructure is an input that improves general productivity and the productivity of other inputs (Straub 2008). Empirically, the presumed link between infrastructure and growth stems from the idea that cross-country disparities in productivity can be explained by differences in the availability and quality of infrastructure.

From the demand side, the nexus between firm productivity and infrastructure can perhaps be substantiated by firm experience as captured by the World Bank Enterprise Surveys (2010) where firms identified electricity and transportation as significant constraints to doing business (East Asia 24 per cent and 16.4 per cent; East Europe and Central Asia 35.1 per cent and 19 per cent; Latin America and Caribbean 39 per cent and 19 per cent; Middle East and North Africa 42.9 per cent and 21.5 per cent; member countries of the Organisation for Economic Development and Co-operation (OECD) 6.1 per cent and 7.4 per cent).[2] From the supply side, investment-climate surveys and empirical evidence also reveal that infrastructure is one of the major determinants in attracting investments to an economy, thereby promoting growth (Estache and Fay 2007; Nabar and Syed 2011).

The facilitating properties of infrastructure also reduce cost and distribution margins in an economy, thus promoting market integration, domestic and international trade, and enhancing comparative advantage.

Finally, infrastructure contributes to growth through indirect channels. Agénor and Moreno-Dodson (2006) explained that infrastructure can extend the longevity of private capital through mitigation of wear and tear, reducing adjustment costs by making possible quick responses to economic opportunities, and improving access to health and education services by providing means to use these social services. The first two improvements make efficiency gains possible, while the last is important not only because of its social benefits but also because education and health are ways by which human capital improvement is achieved, which in turn accounts for total factor productivity (TFP) improvements in growth models. Finally, Estache and Fay (2007) add that reliability and access to infrastructure also promote technology adoption by firms.

Moreover, a study by Roberts and Deichmann (2009) points to evidence that infrastructure capital enables an economy to benefit substantially from growth spillovers of neighboring economies. These effects were shown to be particularly relevant and substantial for landlocked countries.

While the focus is on positive interactions between infrastructure and growth, there are also cases when infrastructure can dampen growth and/or exacerbate income inequality in an economy. First, the spatial character of infrastructure services means that the geographical location of infrastructure assets affects the access to those services. Second, their public investment aspect also means that they compete with other essential investments, such as those on health and education, which may or may not be more important than infrastructure at certain income levels. Third, the opportunity costs associated with infrastructure investment may also be substantial, especially when they are provided over their growth-maximizing levels (Canning and Pedroni 2004). Finally, infrastructure investment may lead to crowding out of other investment activities if its manner of financing is unsustainable, such as through increases in distortionary taxes (Agénor and Moreno-Dodson 2006). It is therefore important for policy makers to realize that different infrastructure sectors have different characteristics and interact with different industries in different ways. The complexities of these relationships limit the efficacy of public planning for infrastructure and contribute to the dynamics of structural transformation and comparative advantage, with alternative environmental impacts. They also influence the spatial development of the host economy with far-reaching consequences.

Infrastructure in Asia and the Pacific

The infrastructure performance of Asia and the Pacific economies varies widely. Table 3.2 shows that on the one hand, high-income economies in the region, such as the People's Republic of China (PRC); Hong Kong, China; Japan; the Republic of Korea; Singapore; and Taipei,China, have infrastructure ranked as among the best in the world, while, on the other hand, countries in the region such as Afghanistan, Bhutan, and Nepal have infrastructures that are among the poorest globally.

On a regional and economic group basis, the World Bank's Logistics Performance Index (LPI) ranks infrastructure in Asia and Pacific next to that of the OECD countries (Figure 3.1). However, the average scores between the two groups (3.71 and 2.55) reveal that there is a considerable gap to fill if the region is to achieve an infrastructure level comparable to that of the OECD countries. An even larger gap is to be filled in some Asia and the Pacific economies if the infrastructure level of Singapore, which has the highest score, is a good indication of the ideal levels and quality of infrastructure in an economy.

The World Economic Forum's Global Competitiveness Report (GCR) also provides scores for an economy's infrastructure based on the responses of firms to its Executive Opinion Survey. Table 3.3 provides resulting scores that indicate the quality and sufficiency of roads, rail, ports, and electricity for Asian economies included in the survey, and the average number of mobile and fixed-line phone subscriptions per 100 people. Once

Table 3.2   Infrastructure scores based on the logistics performance index

Rank	Economy	Infrastructure
4	Singapore	4.22
5	Japan	4.19
13	Hong Kong, China	4.0
22	Taipei,China	3.62
23	Korea, Rep.of	3.62
27	PRC	3.54
28	Malaysia	3.5
36	Thailand	3.16
47	India	2.91
57	Kazakhstan	2.66
64	Philippines	2.57
66	Viet Nam	2.56
69	Indonesia	2.54
72	Bangladesh	2.49
92	Armenia	2.32
104	Azerbaijan	2.23
109	Georgia	2.17
111	Maldives	2.16
114	Cambodia	2.12
118	Kyrgyz Rep.	2.09
120	Pakistan	2.08
128	Tajikistan	2.0
132	Lao PDR	1.95
133	Mongolia	1.94
134	Myanmar	1.92
135	PNG	1.91
138	Sri Lanka	1.88
139	Afghanistan	1.87
141	Bhutan	1.83
143	Nepal	1.8

Notes:
PRC = People's Republic of China; Lao PDR = Lao People's Democratic Republic; PNG =
Papua New Guinea.
Scores from 1 to 5, with 1 as the lowest score and 5 as the maximum score.

Source: Logistics Performance Index, World Bank (2010).

again, it is apparent that the high-income economies in the region dominate in the scores for these essential forms of infrastructure.

Upon reviewing the figures presented in the table, one is prompted to
ask whether the high incomes of some of the economies in the region were

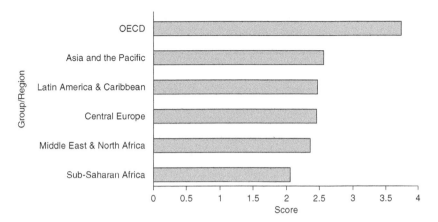

Note: OECD = Organisation for Economic Co-operation and Development. Japan, the Republic of Korea, and Mexico were not included as OECD in the computation.

Source: Computed by the authors based on the Logistics Performance Index, World Bank (2010).

Figure 3.1   Average infrastructure score by region

in a significant way caused by investing in the right types and appropriate levels of infrastructure. The next section examines this question through a brief review of related empirical literature on the nexus between growth and infrastructure.

POLITICAL ECONOMY OF INFRASTRUCTURE

The characteristics of infrastructure described above make the political economy of infrastructure investment difficult, with political considerations often outweighing economic ones. The large scale and large cost of most infrastructure projects mean that the political stakes associated with their success or failure are high. Similarly, their long-term nature, with much time taken to negotiate, implement, and build – while public interest typically has a much shorter time horizon – means that potential political gains are likely to be front-loaded, while costs are more likely to arise in the more distant future, when current incumbents may have left office. In addition, the fact that a politician typically gets more media attention for equal spending on new infrastructure as compared with maintenance of existing assets skews the balance of interest against maintenance.

The public goods nature of many infrastructure projects, along with the

Table 3.3   Infrastructure scores of Asian economies based on the Global Competitiveness Report

Economy	GCR Scores				Phones per 100 people[a]
	Road	Rail	Ports	Electricity	
Hong Kong, China	6.5	6.7	6.8	6.9	116.7
Singapore	6.6	5.8	6.8	6.7	89.8
Japan	5.6	6.6	5.2	6.8	62.7
Korea, Rep. of	5.8	5.7	5.5	6.3	69.6
Taipei,China	5.8	5.7	5.4	6.2	90.0
Malaysia	5.7	4.7	5.6	5.7	63.1
Brunei Darussalam	5.3	N.A.	4.5	5.2	63.5
Thailand	5.1	3.0	5.0	5.7	66.5
PRC	4.3	4.3	4.3	5.3	39.4
Sri Lanka	4.2	3.6	4.9	4.6	43.3
Georgia	3.9	3.6	4.0	5.1	40.6
Azerbaijan	3.8	3.9	4.2	4.1	51.8
India	3.8	4.6	3.9	3.1	23.5
Kazakhstan	2.4	4.0	3.3	4.1	60.0
Indonesia	3.5	3.0	3.6	3.6	42.0
Pakistan	3.8	3.1	4.0	2.1	29.6
Armenia	3.4	2.2	2.9	4.4	52.7
Viet Nam	2.7	2.9	3.6	3.6	67.8
Cambodia	3.8	1.6	3.9	3.1	19.1
Tajikistan	3.0	3.2	1.9	2.6	37.4
Philippines	2.8	1.7	2.8	3.4	42.8
Mongolia	1.7	2.5	3.3	3.1	45.7
Bangladesh	3.0	2.5	3.4	1.6	16.0
Kyrgyz Republic	2.7	2.8	1.4	2.3	45.5
Timor-Leste	2.2	N.A.	2.5	1.6	5.2
Nepal	2.3	1.2	2.9	1.2	14.4

Notes:
PRC = People's Republic of China.
a.   Data is as of 2008 and calculated by the authors based on Global Competitiveness Report (2010–2011), World Economic Forum GCR 2010–2011, WEF.
For road, rail, ports, and electricity, scoring is from 1 to 7, with 1 as the lowest score and 7 the highest.

Sources: Global Competitiveness Report (2010–2011), World Economic Forum GCR 2010–2011.

potential local monopoly characteristics of projects, also ensures attention to these issues in political debates. The largely local nature of benefits raises the potential for differences of interest between central and local authorities. In this context, a country's system of fiscal decentralization or revenue sharing can have a strong influence, and unfortunately fiscal systems with perverse incentives are not rare.

The potential monopoly gains and the importance of infrastructure services as inputs to other production or sales processes, including transportation, similarly raise the stakes for private sector enterprises to influence the design and investment process. The strategic importance to public well-being of some infrastructure services, notably power, transportation, and water, make them easy targets for suppressing prices below market levels. Price suppression may be politically popular, but it encourages overconsumption and waste by consumers and discourages suppliers from providing expanded services.

Concerns about strategic importance, including for communications, may also be used to limit foreign investment. Conversely, some foreign investors may be able to exert undue influence through their much greater size and more developed human resources, particularly in smaller and poorer economies. Poorly developed local bond markets may give foreign investors with easier access to international markets an advantage over local investors in financing infrastructure projects.

When some or all of these factors come together in designing and implementing PPPs for large, high-stakes projects, there is tremendous temptation for one or more participants to try to resort to side or informal payments to influence the negotiation process. Good governance becomes critical in maintaining efficiency of investment. A policy environment that aims to be conducive to infrastructure investment will have policies that are long term (to match the investment horizon), certain (to mitigate risks for investors), and transparent (to promote competition, where feasible).

REVIEW OF EMPIRICAL EVIDENCE ON INFRASTRUCTURE'S CONTRIBUTION TO GROWTH

Growth Accounting Framework

The predominant approach to the empirical study of the relationship between growth and infrastructure has been through the growth accounting framework. Infrastructure is normally included as a factor of production together with non-infrastructure capital, labor, and human capital. A pioneer of this approach is Aschauer (1989) who arguably spurred the widespread and controversial interest now given to the subject because of his findings that the contribution of public expenditures – as a proxy for the contribution of infrastructure – to growth and productivity can be much higher than those from private investment (Egert et al. 2009). However, his findings were later disputed because of their failure to deal with important estimation issues arising from the model.

First, public expenditures were observed to be poor proxies for infrastructure. Expenditure figures tend to overestimate infrastructure capital because of inefficiencies and rent seeking. Moreover, broad public capital can be different from public expenditure on infrastructure because of the heavy involvement of some government bodies in non-infrastructure commercial and industrial activities. Calderón et al. (2011) point out that using expenditure figures as proxies for infrastructure also ignores the increasing private participation in infrastructure investment and management. Many studies following Aschauer have continued to use public expenditures as proxies, but the assembly of data sets on infrastructure stocks has led to the predominant use of the latter in more recent empirical studies.

Second, in a study dealing with subjects across time, one has to deal with the time-series properties of the data. Numerous studies have found that many of the variables included in infrastructure-augmented growth models tend to exhibit non-stationarity in their levels, which may lead to spurious regressions if simply ignored. This is particularly true for variables such as GDP per capita (Egert et al. 2009).

Third, aside from the stationarity, one also has to deal with issues of heterogeneity of the subjects in a cross-country and panel analysis. The issue may be particularly severe when members of a panel are diverse (Hurlin 2006), as is the case in our study.

Fourth, in an analysis that attempts to examine the effect of different types of infrastructure on growth, it is important to deal with multicollinearity among the infrastructure variables. Indeed, Calderón and Servén (2005) find a correlation of 0.94 between telephone density and power-generating capacity and a 0.6 correlation between roads and power-generating capacity.

Fifth, endogeneity is an aspect of infrastructure-growth analysis that should be examined. Infrastructure can contribute to growth, but infrastructure stocks may also be increasing because more prosperous economies, those growing faster, have a tendency to increase investments in infrastructure (Hurlin 2006).

While there is much empirical work on the subject, few are comprehensive enough to deal with all the complications arising from the nature of the investigation. Seethepalli et al. (2008) employed a panel of East Asian economies but did not confront the heterogeneity of the subjects in the study, reasoning that the issue is less relevant because of the small number of observations.

Straub and Terada-Hagiwara (2010), on the other hand, conducted three types of empirical analyses. Their cross-section analysis of 102 countries collapsed the data set through averaging over the period.[3] While averaging is an accepted smoothing technique and regularly applied in growth accounting framework-based studies, the scale of averaging involved in this exercise is such that it can at best only give tentative indications of the relationship between infrastructure and growth. The second set of the Straub and Terada-Hagiwara analyses attempted to capture the growth externalities arising from infrastructure investment by performing individual time-series regressions for 14 developing countries in Asia, employing total factor productivity (TFP) as a dependent variable and infrastructure stocks as control variables. However, this procedure did not adequately take into account the time-series properties of the data. Finally, the third set of analyses involved panel data using the same approach as the second set of analyses.

Canning and Pedroni (2004) dealt adequately with the time series properties, heterogeneity and endogeneity issues of the data in their panel of countries but examined only the direction of the net impact of infrastructure on growth, not its extent.

Hurlin (2006) focused his investigation of OECD countries on the network aspect of infrastructure through a panel threshold regression framework. The premise of his specification is that the network characteristic of infrastructure implies non-linearity in the contribution of these structures, depending on the extent of "completeness" of the network. The paper addressed the methodological issues through assumptions that: (i) reverse causation is a consequence of threshold effects; (ii) the non-stationarity of the data series implies that the true data-generating model is a threshold model; and (iii) cross-country heterogeneity is a consequence of threshold effects (Hurlin 2006). The validity of these assumptions, however, still needs to be verified empirically.

Calderón et al. (2011) employed the pooled mean group (PMG) estimation technique in their study covering 88 countries. This method allows for short-term parameter heterogeneity while imposing long-run homogeneity by assuming that the presence of a single co-integrating vector among the variables implies a common long-run production function for the countries. Some, however, are skeptical of the validity of imposing a single long-run production function across a very diverse set of countries (Straub and Terada-Hagiwara 2010).

Fernald (1999) used industry-level analyses emphasizing the network and geographic location aspects of infrastructure to examine how road building in the United States (US) impacted on the productivity of 29 industries. His findings indicate that road building in the US prior to 1973 did improve productivity of US industries, albeit benefiting vehicle-intensive industries disproportionately. After 1973, when the road network had already been completed, the findings do not indicate any abnormal rate of return from road construction (Fernald, 1999).

Overall, the majority of growth-accounting-based frameworks have found empirical support for a positive link between infrastructure and growth (Straub 2008). All the studies mentioned in the preceding paragraphs find positive and significant contributions of infrastructure to growth. In particular, telecommunications infrastructure is consistently found to be a significant growth factor.

Cost–Function Approach

Aside from the growth accounting framework, the other mainstream approach to examining the infrastructure–growth nexus is through a cost–function framework, which assumes that a firm maximizes profit given the price of its product and a cost function that takes infrastructure into account (Egert et al. 2009).

Using this approach, Iimi (2008) employed a business environment survey and estimated substantial cost savings from improved electricity, telecommunications and water supply for firms in selected European and Central Asian countries. Demetriades and Mamuneas (2000) found positive contributions of public infrastructure capital to the supply of products in an economy and its demand for inputs of production.

Other than the two general frameworks mentioned above, there remain a number of imaginative yet pragmatic ways to study the growth–infrastructure nexus. Straub (2008) has pointed out the importance of studying the spatial characteristics of infrastructure and incorporating advances in the field of economics of agglomeration to make empirical literature more relevant and informative for policy makers. Hulten (1996) stressed that the effectiveness with which infrastructure is used or maintained can be more important than green infrastructure investments. Agénor and Moreno-Dodson (2006) provide a survey of empirical studies of how infrastructure contributes to growth through indirect channels, such as labor productivity improvements, reduced adjustment costs, extended durability of other capital, and improved access to education and health services. Calderón and Servén (2005) also explored the links between infrastructure and income distribution, while that of Jalilian and Weiss (2006) and Menon and Warr (2008) examine the effects of infrastructure provision on poverty.

AN EMPIRICAL APPROACH TO INFRASTRUCTURE AND STAGES OF GROWTH

The theoretical framework of this chapter adopts a Cobb–Douglas infrastructure-augmented aggregate production function as a starting point for the analysis.

$$Y = AK^{\alpha}H^{\beta}Z^{\gamma}L^{1-\alpha-\beta-\gamma}Y \qquad (3.1)$$

Y is output, K is (physical) capital stock, H is human capital stock, Z is infrastructure stock, L is labor, and A denotes total factor productivity. As is common in the literature, constant returns to scale are assumed.

Expressing the variables in per worker terms and taking their logs gives the estimation function described by equation (3.2).[4]

$$y_{it} = \mu_i + \alpha k_{it} + \beta h_{it} + \gamma z_{it} + \varepsilon_{it} \qquad (3.2)$$

Parameters, α, β, and γ, denote the elasticities with respect to output and ε is a disturbance term. μ_i captures the time invariant fixed effects of total factor productivity in the economy. The lower-case variables y, k, and z represent the per worker and log values of the variables in equation (3.1). h is the average years of schooling of the working population and is not expressed in log values in accordance with the specification adopted by Barro and Lee (2010). The subscript *it* denotes the panel nature of the data set, where i denotes individual economies and t denotes the time.

Infrastructure appears twice in the function above: once lumped together with other capital, and then once again by itself. γ therefore cannot be directly interpreted as the elasticity of infrastructure. Instead, it merely represents the extent to which the output contribution of infrastructure capital surpasses or falls below the output contribution of total capital (Calderón and Servén 2004). It can be interpreted as the impact of redirecting resources invested in other types of capital to investments in infrastructure (Canning and Bennathan 2000). On the other hand, insignificant coefficients imply that infrastructure has the same return as that associated with other capital (Estache and Fay 2007). The implication is that the elasticity associated with infrastructure depends on its ratio to capital stocks (Hurlin 2006).

The data in this study cover 123 economies from 1971 to 2005. While data pertaining to output, capital, and labor are complete, data on infrastructure have gaps, making the panel unbalanced. The problem of data gaps was mitigated by collapsing the data into intervals of five-year averages.

The proxy variables used for the chapter's estimation, including their sources, are detailed below. Like other recent studies on growth and infrastructure, we used stocks rather than flows to mitigate the problem of reverse causation. We also avoided using public expenditures as a proxy for infrastructure for reasons explained earlier.

Dependent variable   The dependent variable in the model is real GDP per worker sourced from the Penn World Tables (PWT) (Heston et al. 2009).

Infrastructure variables[5]
The data on the number of workers used to derive the per worker variables were sourced from the World Development Indicators (WDI).[6]

- Telecommunications
  All telecommunications data were sourced from the World Databank.
  (i)   Internet – number of Internet users
  (ii)   Mobile phones – number of mobile cellular subscriptions
  (iii)   Fixed phone lines – number of fixed-line phones connected to the public switched telephone network.
- Transportation
  All transport infrastructure data were sourced from the World Databank and were complemented with data from the International Road Federation (IRF) in the case of road networks.
  (i)   Air freight – the "volume of freight ... carried on each flight stage ... measured in metric tons times kilometers traveled"
  (ii)   Air carriers – domestic and international takeoffs of air carriers registered in the country
  (iii)   Rail network – total rail route in kilometers[7]
  (iv)   Rail goods – "the volume of goods transported by railway, measured in metric tons times kilometers traveled"
  (v)   Road networks – total road network in kilometers, which includes "motorways, highways, and main or national roads, secondary or regional roads, and all other roads in a country."[8]
- Energy
  All energy infrastructure data were sourced from the World Databank.
  (i)   Electricity consumption – electricity production net of transmission, distribution and transformation losses, measured in kilowatt-hour (KWh)
  (ii)   Electricity production – electricity production in KWh

(iii) Energy production or generation – production of "forms of primary energy . . . and combustible renewables and waste, all converted into oil equivalents" measured in kilo tons of oil equivalent (Ktoe)

(iv) Energy consumption – the "use of primary energy before transformation to other end-use fuels" in Ktoe. This figure includes energy imports and stock changes.

Other control variables

- Capital stock
  There are no direct data pertaining to capital stock. They were derived using the perpetual inventory method. A uniform depreciation rate was assumed to be 0.07, while the initial capital stock was derived using the approach of Bernanke and Gurkaynak (2001), which used the 10-year forward average growth rate of output to approximate an economy's steady state growth rate. The investment and real GDP used for the computation were sourced from the Penn World Table 6.3.

- Human capital stock – the average years of schooling of an economy's population aged 15 and above were from Barro and Lee (2010).

Methodology

Two models were employed to estimate the effects of infrastructure on growth. Model 1 employs ordinary least squares (OLS), while Model 2 employs instrumental variables through two-stage least squares (2-SLS). Model 2 is employed to take into account possible endogeneity in the model, which cannot be completely addressed by simply using stocks rather than flow values. Indeed, Hausman specification tests confirm simultaneity between the log values of different infrastructure stocks and GDP. Instrumental variables (IV) were therefore employed by using the lag of the explanatory variables as instruments except for education, which uses parental education as instrument.[9]

Fixed effects were used in both Models 1 and 2 to account for the unobserved heterogeneity of the economies. This allows the model to account for varying definitions of similarly termed variables across economies to the extent that they are time invariant. The same principle applies to institutional qualities such as governance and regulatory environment. Furthermore, a Hausman test strongly rejects a random specification in favor of fixed effects.

Finally, infrastructure variables were introduced into the estimation separately to avoid multicollinearity. Estimations were first run on the entire set of economies, followed by estimations on subgroups of economies currently classified as low income, lower middle income, upper middle income and high income by the World Bank to explore possible variations in the relationships between infrastructure and economies in different levels or stages of growth.[10] A set of estimations were also performed for Asian economies to examine if the relationship between growth and infrastructure that is observed for the world economies is confirmed for Asia.

Results[11]

Telecommunications

There is considerable empirical evidence on how access to telecommunication infrastructure has improved the income of the poor and thus promotes growth. Jensen (2007) documented how fishermen in Kerala state in India increased their income by using mobile phones for price arbitration and information coordination. These benefits translated to reduced waste and spoilage, higher income for fishermen, and a significant reduction in price variation for fishery products. Bhavani et al. (2008) likewise documented various studies demonstrating how mobile telephony has aided job searching and entrepreneurship for housekeepers, porters, and hairdressers in the PRC, Pakistan, and Thailand.

The results for the full set of the panel suggest that consistent with previous studies, telecommunication infrastructure supports growth. This is true for the different proxies of telecommunications that were used (telephone fixed lines; total fixed lines and mobiles; and fixed lines, mobiles, and the Internet).

The sub-panels of Asia and high-income economies likewise confirm the positive relationship between growth and telecommunications infrastructure. Fixed phone lines do not exhibit influence on the growth in low-income economies. The relationship, however, changes once mobile phones and the Internet are taken into account. Meanwhile, there appears to be overinvestment in telecommunications infrastructure in upper-middle-income economies. Finally, a significant link between growth and telecommunications is not established for lower-middle-income economies.

Transportation

This chapter has attempted to capture the growth contributions of transport infrastructure using different variables. For the full panel, air transport, proxied by air carriers and airfreight, as means of moving people as well as goods, is supportive of growth. So are roads and rail networks. But rail as a means of transporting goods did not prove to support growth as much as other capital. The same conclusion applies to the combined length of roads and rail networks. This perhaps reflects a general substitution effect between the two forms of transport.

In Asia, only roads were found to be more productive than other forms of capital. The relationship between air transport and growth observed in the full panel is not detected for Asia. Meanwhile, we refrain from drawing conclusions on variables involving rail due to the smaller sample sizes involved in the analyses. Instrumental variables procedures tend to yield biased estimates when sample sizes are not sufficiently large.[12]

For the income subgroups, air transport as a means for trade is only significantly associated with growth for upper-middle-income economies, perhaps reflecting the importance of trade in goods with high-value-to-bulk ratios in such economies. Meanwhile, the number of air carrier take-offs supports growth in lower-middle and high-income economies.

Rail networks appear to be important to growth only in middle-income economies, though the same cannot be said of the volume of goods carried by rail. Roads yield significant growth effects only in lower-middle-income economies. However, the combined effect of roads and rail support growth for upper-middle-income economies. The positive relationship for the same infrastructure variable cannot be confirmed for low-income economies due to insufficient sample size. Finally, results suggest a possible overinvestment in land-related transport for high-income economies.

The results herein are supportive of evidence found in other studies, such as Banerjee et al. (2009), which shows proximity to transportation networks in the PRC has led to increases in growth of per capita income. Moreover, these increases reflect the expansion of aggregate output rather than just effects of productive firms replacing less productive ones near the network.

Energy
Electricity consumption is only significantly associated with growth for the high-income group. On the other hand, electricity production does not seem to be supportive of growth for any group of economies. In fact, upper-middle-income economies appear to have overinvested in electricity consumption and production, implying that investments in other forms of capital might support growth better.

However, estimations with energy generation and consumption, which are broader variables than electricity, indicate that energy generation supports growth in the full panel of economies in Asia and in upper-middle-income and high-income economies. Energy consumption also supports

Asia rising

Table 3.4   Infrastructure and stages of growth

Income group	Infrastructure
Low	Combined phone mainlines and mobile phones
Lower middle income	Roads
Upper middle income	Combined road and rail network
Middle income	Rail network
High income	Energy consumption

Source: Compiled by the authors.

growth in high-income economies, while the same does not appear true for upper middle-income economies.

To account for possible biases in energy generation results arising from the status of an economy as an exporter of energy, an estimation excluding all major crude oil exporting economies was performed. The results suggest that energy production, albeit with lower coefficients, and energy use contribute to growth in non-oil exporting economies. It is interesting to note that energy consumption, while insignificant in the panel including oil-exporting economies, becomes significant once these economies are taken out of the estimation.

General results

In general, the results of infrastructure's ability to explain growth differences across economies vary with the type of infrastructure. An examination of the subsets of economies classified according to income levels also reveals that infrastructure needs in each group may vary. Table 3.4 summarizes the empirical findings by income category of economy, showing which types of infrastructure offer the greatest contribution to growth.

Since the different forms of infrastructure have been measured in terms of their stocks rather than value, the marginal cost of a 1 per cent increase in the infrastructure stock is not equivalent across infrastructure types, thus the findings should not be taken as directly relevant for policy prescriptions. Moreover, the small sample sizes of infrastructure data in some subgroups and some categories of infrastructure did not permit complete assessment under the method employed. Nonetheless, the general findings can be taken as evidence that infrastructure does contribute to growth and individual countries can consider their current stocks and likely contributions to growth of additional investment in different infrastructure assets. In general, the findings suggest a rough hierarchy for investment priorities, from communications for low-income economies, through transportation in middle-income economies, and to greater emphasis on energy for high-income economies.

In the case of Asia, the findings of positive contributions to growth from infrastructure can perhaps be validated by the private sector pouring substantial investments into infrastructure projects. The World Bank Private Participation in Infrastructure (PPI) Project Database reveals that from 2000 to 2009, the private sector poured $131 billion into the telecommunications sector. This accounts for 37 per cent of total PPI projects in South Asia and in East Asia and the Pacific (2010).[13] The corresponding figure for the energy sector is $129.9 billion for the same time frame. Finally, the transport sector received $63.5 billion in the form of completed projects from 2000 to 2008 (World Development Indicators 2010).

It is noteworthy that aside from combined mobile and main phone lines and the Internet, the results for the low-income group do not definitively identify any infrastructure as especially important to growth. A plausible explanation might be the relative importance of other investments in basic services, such as health and quality education. Limitations on data availability and quality that are more severe than for the other groups have also been observed.

Another aspect of the results worth noting is the insignificance of education in a number of the estimations. This runs counter to common perceptions. Such observations may arise from the limitation of average years of schooling as a proxy for human capital. Hanushek and Wößmann (2007) pointed out that growth returns from education will vary across countries not only on the basis of years of schooling, but perhaps more importantly because of variations in the quality of education, which captures the cognitive skills of a population better. Moreover, schooling alone does not capture other important aspects of human capital, such as health. Including basic water and sanitation facilities might have been a satisfactory way to account for this. However, the limited data availability did not permit meaningful analysis.[14]

In the final analysis, the extent and nature of infrastructure's role in growth must be interpreted in light of the other variables included in the estimation and existing conditions in an economy. According to Ascher and Krupp (2010), high returns on infrastructure variables tend to be observed when investment in them has been lagging behind those of other factors of growth. Moreover, the marginal returns from additional infrastructure investments crucially depend on the extent to which additional investments address existing bottlenecks in the network (Romp and de Haan 2007), and the extent to which they create synergies with human capital and other investments to realize the potential for growth in an economy (Canning and Bennathan 2000).

MAJOR ISSUES AND CHALLENGES IN INFRASTRUCTURE INVESTMENT

What and Where to Build?

The question of what infrastructure to build can generally be answered by the results of the estimations. Economies should invest in infrastructure that yields high returns to growth. The results of the estimations above should be interpreted in the context of a panel of data. The types of infrastructure and the optimal levels are expected to vary in an economy according to the levels of other inputs to production and the particular infrastructure bottlenecks that need attention.

The question of where to build is harder, if not impossible, to answer using the framework of this study. The aggregate level of our data does not allow for the full spatial nature of infrastructure to be taken into account or for a proper assessment of the full potential of regional coop-eration. This is one of the weaknesses of macro-level empirical studies that is often pointed out. While analysis of aggregate figures may imply that returns to a certain type of infrastructure are high, it does not take into account that the infrastructure may already be over-provided in some areas, while there remains a strong need for the same infrastructure in other areas. This can potentially be addressed if more disaggregated data on infrastructure provision can be used. This scenario is, however, more feasible in a study dealing with a single economy rather than a panel of economies.

These basic guides to what needs to be built and where are, however, rarely the only considerations in deciding what infrastructure will be constructed. Legitimate considerations pertaining to maximization of social returns through means such as equitable access, physical and social integration, and possibly less legitimate considerations pertaining to maxi-mization of political returns, often come into play and define the contours of policy making in infrastructure.

Obviously the decision-making process and structure will be crucial in allocating scarce infrastructure investments. Public sector budget limita-tions in most countries, as well as technical and managerial expertise in the private sector, argue strongly for involving private investment in infrastructure. At the same time, for the reasons described earlier in this chapter, the public sector generally also has a role to play. To address these dual sets of concerns, PPPs are commonly advocated. PPPs work most effectively when public and private sectors each work to manage the types of risk for which they are best suited. For example, political risk may best be borne by the public sector, while credit risk can be more effectively hedged in the private sector, assuming private financial markets and institutions are sufficiently developed.

To encourage and support private sector involvement in the development of infrastructure assets and the provision of infrastructure services over an extended time horizon requires an enabling environment of property rights, guarantees, and good governance. This is why, for more developed economies, complementary soft infrastructure becomes increasingly important. Reside and Mendoza (2010) suggest that the type of political stability that comes from a form of government with commanding authority may encourage investment and when combined with a more flexible regulatory regime may lead to better project outcomes. This could in part explain why infrastructure investment in Indonesia during the Soeharto era appears to have outperformed that in the Philippines. However, the authors also note that the expectation of high future growth, which was common in much of Southeast Asia before the Asian financial crisis (AFC), can lead to a moral hazard in which unviable projects get approved after passing through less rigorous screening processes.

As mentioned earlier, success in PPPs depends on reaching appropriate risk-sharing agreements and reliable institutional structures. In much of Asia, PPPs have become increasingly subject to renegotiation, particularly where there have been currency mismatches between the investment financing and service-generated revenue, or guaranteed service (demand) offtakes that were not supported by macroeconomic developments. Divestment or buyouts have also become common, in effect shortening the implicit investment time horizon. Long-term, stable, and transparent investment climate policies should help to reverse this trend.

In most countries, the technological frontier is advanced primarily through the private sector. At the same time, this perhaps relies on public sector support for research and development, as well as social services that support the development of human capital and innovation. The public sector also has a critical role to play in planning the development of infrastructure where industrial policy is a priority, rather than merely reacting to bottlenecks.

The Way Ahead

Infrastructure plays an important role in the growth of an economy and in the distribution of the benefits from that growth. The public goods nature of infrastructure services, the bulkiness and lengthy time horizon of investing in infrastructure assets, and the potential local monopoly character of markets for infrastructure services all justify at least some public sector involvement in investment in infrastructure assets, the provision of infrastructure services, and the regulation of the markets for those services.

Limitations on public sector budgets, as well as private sector advantages in infrastructure technology, financing, management, and marketing, strongly suggest a role for private sector infrastructure investment and management. To realize private sector potential in infrastructure investment, regional debt markets to mobilize and allocate regional savings are a priority. McCawley (2010) notes that two significant factors underpinning the reluctance of private sector firms to invest in infrastructure have been regulatory uncertainty and price suppression. Major reforms in the policy environment, including better and more reliable policies and regulatory arrangements, as well as improved contract enforcement procedures, are likely to be needed to attract private investors. But the complementarity of public and private sector risk and risk management capabilities highlights the potential for PPPs in infrastructure. When the private investors are foreign, additional benefits and complications are possible and good governance becomes even more essential.

As economies grow and develop, their demands for infrastructure services evolve over time. The analysis here has shown that for lower-income economies, where it is likely that all forms of infrastructure can raise productivity, the ability to communicate through telecommunications services may be most important. Fortunately, modern communications technology allows large geographic regions to be covered by such services at relatively low cost, with sufficient cost recovery to entice private sector investment. The spatial distribution of other infrastructure investments in these economies may be critical for poverty reduction and ensuring inclusiveness of growth, while avoiding severe congestion, particularly in transport infrastructure.

In middle-income economies, road infrastructure – and as incomes rise, railway networks – may be most significant. For high-income economies, the results become more difficult to interpret beyond increasing energy consumption, but suggest that human capital may be most important. This most likely reflects the already high levels of physical infrastructure assets, more sophisticated production processes, and the dominance of knowledge-based industries. In this case, more attention may be needed for maintenance of existing assets and the connectivity of network infrastructure, both in single sectors, such as telecommunications or transportation networks, and in more complex logistics chains.

Better understanding of the dynamics of infrastructure's contributions to growth will assist planning over the lengthy lifetimes of infrastructure assets. As urbanization is closely correlated with rising incomes, development of urban infrastructure must balance benefits for existing urban residents with the potential costs of encouraging rapid rural urban migration, and should be undertaken with a view of the overall system of cities in an economy.

Allocating scarce resources for efficient infrastructure investment currently relies on imperfect measurement and assessment of both costs and benefits. For example, at present we cannot adequately reflect the benefits of low-carbon transportation systems designed for road safety and fuel savings through public transport options. The issue of climate change mitigation and adaptation further complicates such evaluations.

Costs are also difficult to assess, particularly where there are sizable externalities and poor governance. It is often possible to raise the provision of infrastructure services without investing in new infrastructure assets simply through efficiency gains in public utilities, such as reducing piped water losses or increasing meterage of electricity. Various empirical studies show that in some instances returns from infrastructure maintenance outweigh returns from new infrastructure investments (Hulten 1996; Heggie 1995). The greater visibility and probable political returns of new infrastructure, however, tend to create bias against maintenance (Ascher and Krupp 2010). Better regulation of markets for public utilities, and particularly price regulation, can often yield substantial efficiency improvements.

Regional cooperation is particularly important for infrastructure supporting international trade and investment (Brooks and Stone 2010; Hummels 2009). In the Asian context, where international production networks are essential, parts of many supply chains and exports have accounted for such a large share of growth, international public sector agreements offer a critical framework for regional integration to capitalize on growth spillovers.

Although beyond the scope of the current chapter, the financing of infrastructure investments may also limit their scale, frequency, location, and technical efficiency. To reduce risks of foreign currency transactions, long-term local currency bond markets can play a key role in infrastructure development. Particularly for poorer countries, foreign sources of finance, including multilateral financial institutions, can be important contributors of capital, technology, and governance practices. Their involvement may be dependent on opportunities for cost recovery, as well as alternative modalities and innovative instruments for financing. Also, particularly for poorer countries, the size of infrastructure projects can be disproportionately large, with macroeconomic implications suggesting the need for careful attention to financing modalities (Brooks and Zhai 2008).

The rapid economic growth of Asia has benefited billions of people. It has also strained its infrastructure resources, its physical environment, and in some cases, social justice. For infrastructure to contribute effectively and sustainably to Asia's future growth will require that it be cost effective, technologically efficient, environmentally benign, and socially inclusive. To accomplish this, better understanding of how infrastructure contributes to growth will be essential.

NOTES

1. The $1-a-day poverty threshold was recently revised to $1.25. However, the target is still referred to by its old name for convenience (ADB 2010).
2. First figures refer to electricity and second figures refer to transportation in each region.
3. The period covered by the analyses varied according to data availability of infrastructure variables.
4. Representing the aggregate relationship in per worker terms implies ignoring scale effects which may be important in estimating the effects between growth and infrastructure. Such an approach, however, allows for a simple way to account for reverse causation, which has been a major challenge to the integrity of aggregate production functions (Canning and Bennathan 2000).
5. Infrastructure data for Taipei,China were sourced from the Directorate General of Budget, Accounting and Statistics.
6. The WDI series started in 1980. Imputations using the size of the population aged 15 to 65, less the average difference between this number and the number of labor force for years where data are available, were utilized to derive the labor figures from 1971 to 1979. The demographic data were also sourced from the WDI.
7. One must, however, note that only 62 per cent of the economies included in the study have data on rail. Rail is simply nonexistent in some economies, especially those that have small land areas.
8. The series on road data had many gaps. There were also cases where suspected changes in the definition of roads in a particular country – sources of IRF data – led to drastic increases or decreases in road statistics, which are highly unrealistic. Such observations are of limited instances and data like these were removed from the series. In cases where the data of percentage of paved roads and kilometers of road networks in the IRF matches those of the WDI, the values for the kilometers of roads were imputed from the existing values.
9. Parental education was derived from Barro and Lee (2010) using years of schooling of population aged 40 and above.
10. A category of middle-income economies, which is the sum of economies classified as lower-middle and upper-middle-income economies, is also introduced to exploit the asymptotic properties of instrumental variable regressions.
11. Estimation results can be accessed in the working papers version of this chapter, http://www.adb.org/publications/infrastructures-role-sustaining-asias-growth.
12. The literature does not define exactly what constitutes a sufficiently large sample size for instrumental variables procedures. It has been the authors' decision to limit interpretations to estimations that have at least 100 observations.
13. Private investments in East Asia and the Pacific were concentrated in the PRC, Indonesia, Malaysia, and the Philippines, while those in South Asia were primarily in India and Pakistan. The figures reported account for 24 economies in the region.
14. Estimations on sanitation infrastructure using the same methodology were also performed. However, the results were not very meaningful (erratic behavior of coefficients) in view of large data gaps. Moreover, since the direct contribution of sanitation is supposed to affect growth or productivity through human capital, there might be a need

to model the effects of sanitation through its relationship to human capital instead of treating it in the same way as other infrastructure.

REFERENCES

Agénor, P., and B. Moreno-Dodson (2006), 'Public infrastructure and growth: new channels and policy implications', World Bank Policy Research Working Paper No. 4064.

Aschauer, D. (1989), 'Is public expenditure productive?', *Journal of Monetary Economics*, March.

Ascher, W., and C. Krupp (2010), *Physical Infrastructure Development: Balancing Growth, Equity, and Environmental Imperatives*, New York: Palgrave Macmillan.

Asian Development Bank (ADB) (2010), *Key Indicators for Asia and the Pacific 2009*, Manila, Philippines.

Banerjee, A., E. Duflo, and N. Qian (2009), 'On the road: access to transportation infrastructure and economic growth in [the People's Republic of] China', (preliminary version).

Barro, R., and J. Lee (2010), 'A new dataset of educational attainment in the world, 1950–2010', National Bureau of Economic Research Working Paper 15902.

Bernanke, B.S., and R.S. Gurkaynak (2001), 'Is growth exogenous? Taking Mankiw, Romer and Weil seriously', *NBER Macroeconomics Annual*, **16**, 11–57.

Bhavani, A., R. Won-Wai Chiu, S. Janakiram, and P. Silarszky (2008), 'The role of mobile phones in sustainable rural poverty reduction', World Bank ICT Policy Division Report.

Brooks, D.H., and F. Zhai (2008), 'The macroeconomic effects of infrastructure financing: a tale of two countries', *Integration and Trade Journal*, **28**, 297–323.

Brooks, D.H., and S.F. Stone (2010), *Trade Facilitation and Regional Cooperation in Asia*, Cheltenham, UK and Northampton, MA, USA: Edward Elgar.

Calderón, C., and L. Servén (2004), 'Trends in infrastructure in Latin America 1980–2001', Policy Research Working Paper 340, World Bank.

Calderón, C., and L. Servén (2005), 'The effects of infrastructure on growth and income distribution', Working Papers Central Bank of Chile 270.

Calderón, C., E. Moral-Benito, and L. Servén (2011), 'Is infrastructure capital productive? A dynamic heterogenous approach', Policy Research Working Paper 5682, World Bank.

Canning, D., and E. Bennathan, (2000), 'The social rate of return on infrastructure investment', World Bank Policy Research Working Paper No. 2390.

Canning, D., and P. Pedroni (2004), 'The effect of infrastructure on long run economic growth', CAER Discussion Paper.

Demetriades, P.O., and T. Mamuneas (2000), 'Intertemporal output and employment effects of public infrastructure capital', *Economic Journal*, **110**, (465), 687–712.

Egert, B., T. Kozluk, and D. Sutherland (2009), 'Infrastructure and growth: empirical evidence', William Davidson Institute Working Paper No. 957.

Estache, A., and M. Fay (2007), 'Current debates on infrastructure policy', World Bank Policy Research Working Paper No. 4410.

Fernald, J (1999), 'Roads to prosperity? Assessing the link between public capital and productivity', *American Economic Review*, **89**, (3), 619–38.

Hanushek, E., and L. Wößmann (2007), 'The role of education quality in economic growth', Policy Research Working Paper 4122, World Bank.

Heggie, I. (1995), 'Management and financing of roads: an agenda for reform', World Bank Technical Report 275, Washington, DC, World Bank.

Heston, A., R. Summers, and B. Aten, (2009), *Penn World Table Version 6.3*, Center for International Comparisons of Production, Income and Prices, Philadelphia: The University of Pennsylvania.

Hulten, C. (1996), 'Infrastructure capital and economic growth: how well you use it may be more important than how much you have', NBER Working Paper Series.

Hummels, D. (2009), 'Trends in Asian trade: implications for transport infrastructure and trade costs', in D.H. Brooks and D. Hummels (eds), *Infrastructure's Role in Lowering Asia's Trade Costs: Building for Trade*, Cheltenham, UK and Northampton, MA, USA: Edward Elgar, pp. 17–36.

Hurlin, C. (2006), 'Network effects of the productivity of infrastructure in developing countries', World Bank Policy Research Working Paper 3808.

Iimi, A. (2008), 'Effects of improving infrastructure quality on business costs: evidence from firm-level data', World Bank Policy Research Working Paper No. 4581.

Jalilian, H., and J. Weiss (2006), 'Infrastructure, growth and poverty: some cross country evidence', in J. Weiss and H. Khan (eds), *Poverty Strategies in Asia: A Growth Plus Approach*, Cheltenham, UK and Northampton, MA, USA: Edward Elgar.

Jensen, R. (2007), 'The digital provide: information (technology), market performance, and welfare in the South Indian fisheries sector', *Quarterly Journal of Economics*, **122**, 879–924.

McCawley, P. (2010), 'Infrastructure policy in Asian developing countries', *Asian-Pacific Economic Literature*, **24**, 9–25.

Menon, J., and P. Warr (2008), 'Roads and poverty: a general equilibrium analysis for Lao PDR', in D.H. Brooks and J. Menon (eds), *Infrastructure and Trade in Asia*, Cheltenham, UK and Northampton, MA, USA: Edward Elgar.

Nabar, M., and M. Syed (2011), 'The great rebalancing act: can investment be a lever in Asia?', IMF Working Paper WP/11/35.

Reside, R.E., Jr., and A.M. Mendoza Jr. (2010), 'Determinants of outcomes of public–private partnerships in infrastructure in Asia', University of the Philippines School of Economics Discussion Paper No. 2010-03.

Roberts, M., and U. Deichmann (2009), 'International growth spillovers, geography and infrastructure', World Bank Policy Research Working Paper No. 5153.

Roland-Holst, D. (2006), 'Infrastructure as a catalyst for regional integration, growth, and economic convergence: scenario analysis for Asia', ADB Economics Working Paper No. 91.

Romp, W., and J. de Haan (2007), 'Public capital and economic growth: a critical survey', *Perspektiven der Wirtschaftspolitik*, **8** (1), 6–52.

Seethepalli, K., M. Bramati, and D. Veredas (2008), 'How relevant is infrastructure to growth in East Asia?', World Bank Policy Research Working Paper No. 4597.

Straub, S. (2008), 'Infrastructure and growth in developing countries: recent advances and research challenges', World Bank Policy Research Working Paper No. 4460.

Straub, S., and A. Terada-Hagiwara (2010), 'Infrastructure and growth in developing Asia', ADB Economics Working Paper No. 231.

Underhill, M. (2010), 'What is listed infrastructure?', in *The Handbook of Infrastructure Investing*, Hoboken, NJ: John Wiley & Sons.

World Bank Business Enterprise Surveys. Accessed on 11 November 2010. Available at: http://www.enterprisesurveys.org/CustomQuery/ViewCustomReport.aspx.

World Bank Logistics Performance Indicators (2010). Accessed 2 November 2010. Available at: http://info.worldbank.org/etools/tradesurvey/mode1b.asp.

4. Productivity and capital accumulation

Kyoji Fukao

INTRODUCTION

It has been well documented that the major countries of the Association of Southeast Asian Nations (ASEAN) – Indonesia, Malaysia, the Philippines, and Thailand – as well as the Republic of Korea have experienced sharp declines in the ratio between gross fixed capital formation and gross domestic product (GDP) following the Asian financial crisis (AFC) of 1997–98 (Figure 4.1). Many studies have tried to answer why capital accumulation declined in crisis-hit Asia.

The Asian Development Bank's *Asian Development Outlook* for 2007 and 2008 (Asian Development Bank 2007, 2008) contains excellent surveys and analyses of this issue. It shows that in many countries the working-age population continued to grow, except in Indonesia; total factor productivity (TFP) rebounded; and financial markets recovered. In addition, saving rates remained high, capacity utilization rates recovered, and there was no sharp decline in public investment. After ruling out these factors as potential explanations of the decline in investment, the *Asian Development Outlook 2007* makes the conjecture that pessimism and uncertainty about future growth may have played an important role.

One possible factor that has not been well examined, but could be considered the "prime suspect" in the decline in investment, is the huge drop and the slow recovery in productivity in the Asian developing economies.[1] But carefully compiled and internationally comparable productivity databases of Asian countries are becoming increasingly available, making such an examination possible. Using the recently developed Asian Productivity Organization (APO) Database (Asian Productivity Organization 2010), this chapter analyzes capital accumulation in Asian developing economies from the viewpoint of productivity.

Figure 4.2 shows how labor productivity changed over time in the major ASEAN countries, Japan, and the Republic of Korea. Labor

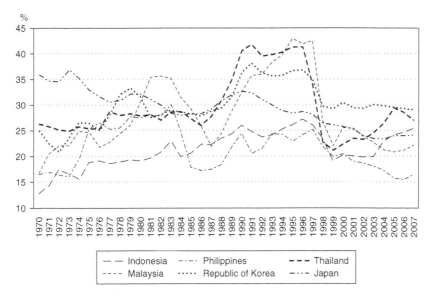

Note: ASEAN = Association of Southeast Asian Nations.

Source: Asian Productivity Organization, APO Productivity Database 2010.

*Figure 4.1   Gross fixed capital formation/GDP (at current prices) in
major ASEAN countries, the Republic of Korea, and Japan*

productivity in Indonesia declined 13 per cent from 1996 to 1999 and took
until 2005 to recover to the pre-crisis level. In Thailand, labor productivity declined 6 per cent from 1996 to 1999 and took until 2003 to recover
to the pre-crisis level. Malaysia and the Philippines experienced milder
drops in labor productivity. In contrast with this, Japan and the Republic
of Korea never experienced a sharp drop in labor productivity from the
early 1980s.

Next, looking at TFP, the decline was even more severe and prolonged
than the drop in labor productivity (see Figure 4.3). In Indonesia, TFP
declined by 19 per cent from 1996 to 1999 and by 2007 had not returned to
the pre-crisis level. In Thailand, TFP declined by 18 per cent from 1996 to
1998 and took until 2006 to recover to the pre-crisis level.

If we exclude the years immediately after the crisis, the TFP growth
trend following the crisis is not substantially lower than that before the
crisis. TFP growth in Indonesia was 2.0 per cent from 1985 to 1996 and 1.7
per cent from 1999 to 2007. In Thailand, TFP growth was 2.7 per cent in
both of these periods. As Figure 4.3 shows, Japan, the Republic of Korea,

Asia rising

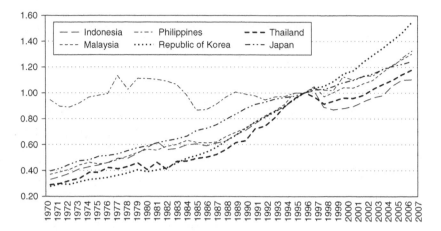

Notes: ASEAN = Association of Southeast Asian Nations; GDP = gross domestic product. Labor productivity for Malaysia is measured as real GDP/total number of workers.

Source: Asian Productivity Organization, APO Database 2010.

Figure 4.2   Labor productivity in major ASEAN countries, the Republic of Korea, and Japan (real gross domestic product/total hours worked 1996=1)

and the Philippines also experienced a TFP drop after 1996, but the drop in TFP in these countries was much milder than that in Indonesia and Thailand.

The sharp drop in TFP and probably several additional factors, such as the decline in output prices caused by weak demand and the increase in imported input prices caused by currency depreciation, reduced the rate of return to capital sharply in Indonesia and Thailand (Figure 4.4).[2] This sharp drop in the rate of return to capital must have contributed to the decline in investment.

This chapter analyzes the drop in the TFP level in crisis-hit Asian countries and its impact on gross fixed capital formation. According to a recent study by the International Monetary Fund (IMF), which examined 88 banking crises and 222 currency crises, a large and prolonged drop in TFP and a sharp decline in investment are not peculiar to the AFC. Many crisis-hit countries around the world experienced similar drops in TFP (International Monetary Fund 2009). It is also interesting to note that the typical impact of a financial crisis on TFP is not a slowdown in the TFP growth trend but rather a sharp drop in TFP. Moreover, in many crisis-hit

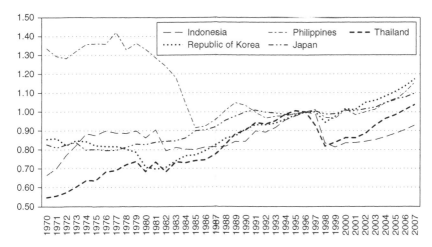

Notes: ASEAN = Association of Southeast Asian Nations. Total factor productivity data
for Malaysia is not available.

Source: Asian Productivity Organization, APO Database 2010.

*Figure 4.3   Total factor productivity level in major ASEAN countries, the
Republic of Korea, and Japan (1996=1)*

countries, TFP growth rates return to their pre-crisis levels several years
after the crisis. These phenomena are very similar to what was seen following the AFC. Therefore, the analysis here will have implications not only
for Asia but also for the rest of the world.

The next section of this chapter presents a standard model of investment and economic growth. A drop in the TFP level will reduce the rate
of return to capital and slow down capital accumulation. But is an 18–19
per cent drop in the TFP level, as observed in Indonesia and Thailand following the AFC, sufficient to explain the huge decline in the gross investment–GDP ratio in these countries? This is the question that the model
developed in next section seeks to address. The analysis suggests that the
impact of a drop in productivity on capital accumulation depends on the
causes of the drop.

This chapter then goes on to explain why TFP dropped so much after
the AFC. Using sector-level labor input and labor productivity data of
Asian and Latin American economies, this issue is analyzed in the chapter's third section, which also reviews preceding studies on productivity
dynamics after financial crises. The final section summarizes the major
results of the chapter.

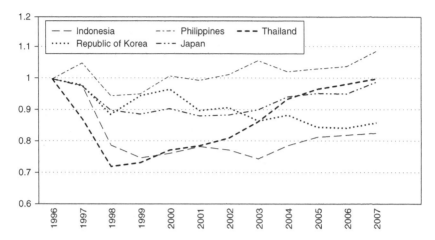

Notes: ASEAN = Association of Southeast Asian Nations. Necessary data for Malaysia
are not available.

Source: Asian Productivity Organization, APO Database 2010.

Figure 4.4   *Changes in the gross rate of return to capital in major ASEAN*
countries, the Republic of Korea, and Japan (gross capital
income/(capital service input × GDP deflator) 1996=1)

THE IMPACT OF A PRODUCTIVITY DROP ON CAPITAL ACCUMULATION: A THEORETICAL EVALUATION

Using a neoclassical growth model, this section analyzes how much of
the decline in capital accumulation after the AFC can be explained by the
drop in productivity.

Open macroeconomics tells us that if the domestic saving rate is low and
there are insufficient international capital inflows, the investment–GDP
ratio will depend on the saving–GDP ratio. Otherwise, the investment–
GDP ratio will depend on the expected future rate of return on capital,
which depends on the capital-deepening process, TFP growth, the growth
rate of the working-age population, and world interest rates. Since saving
rates in the crisis-hit Asian developing countries were high and the countries recorded large current account surpluses, it seems fair to say that
these countries fell into the latter category. In such a situation, domestic
saving is not a binding condition for domestic investment and we cannot
apply ordinary closed-economy growth models.

Therefore, a small open-economy model, in which private firms decide

their investment level, is used here.[3] Assume that international capital
movements are frictionless and all the output is tradable. Under these conditions, we can analyze separately the dynamics of asset accumulation by
households and the dynamics of capital accumulation by firms.

If there is no adjustment cost in capital accumulation, the capital stock
of a small open economy with perfect capital mobility will always be at the
optimal level, at which the rate of return to capital is equal to the world
equilibrium real interest rate. Moreover, when the optimal capital stock
level changes as a result of an unexpected exogenous shock, the actual
capital stock will immediately jump to the new optimal level. In order to
avoid such unrealistic results, I assume that firms incur adjustment costs
when they change their capital stock level.

First, let us specify the production function. A constant returns-to-scale
production function with Harrod-neutral technological change is assumed:

$$Y = F(\Theta N, K)$$

where Y, N, and K denote output, number of workers, and capital stock.
Θ is an index of the productivity level. In per unit labor input terms (labor,
here, includes the Harrod-neutral productivity term),

$$y = f(k)$$

where y and k denote $Y/\Theta N$ and $K/\Theta N$ respectively and $f(k)$ is defined by
$f(k) \equiv F(1, k)$. I assume $f'(k)>0$, $f''(k)<0$, and

$$\lim_{k \to 0} f'(k) = +\infty \text{ and } \lim_{k \to \infty} f'(k) = 0$$

I also assume perfect competition in output, factor input, and financial
markets.

The inter-temporal optimization problem of a representative firm is
expressed by

$$\max_{\{L,i\}} \int_0^\infty \{\Theta L f(k) - wL - \varphi(i)K\} e^{-\rho t} dt$$

subject to the constraints

$$\dot{K} = iK \text{ and } K(0) = K_0,$$

where i and ρ denote the growth rate of capital stock and the world equilibrium real interest rate. $\varphi(i)K$ is a Penrose-Uzawa-type investment cost

function (Uzawa 1969; Hayashi 1982). The following quadratic functional form is assumed:

$$\varphi(i) = (i + \delta) + \frac{a}{2}(i + \delta)^2 \qquad (4.1)$$

A higher value of α means that firms incur larger adjustment costs when they try to change their capital stock level at a high speed. δ denotes the depreciation rate of capital and $(i + \delta)$ denotes the gross investment–total capital ratio.

The necessary conditions of the optimal investment behavior are (Arrow and Kurz 1970; Blanchard and Fischer 1989):

$$f(k) - f'(k)k = w \qquad (4.2)$$

$$\varphi'(i) = q \qquad (4.3)$$

$$\dot{q} = -f'(k) + \varphi(i) - qi + q\rho \qquad (4.4)$$

$$\dot{K} = iK \qquad (4.5)$$

$$K(0) = K_0 \qquad (4.6)$$

where q and w denote the shadow price of capital stock and the real wage rate.

In labor market equilibrium, real wage rates will be set at a level that makes the representative firm's optimal capital–labor ratio (labor, here, includes the technology term), k, equal to the macro-level capital–labor ratio, $K/\Theta N$, which is determined by the economy's factor endowment and technology level. Therefore, we have the following dynamic equation of k:

$$\dot{k} = (i - n - \theta)k \qquad (4.7)$$

where n and θ denote the growth rate of labor, L, and the growth rate of the technology level, Θ. In order to have a meaningful long-run equilibrium, we need to assume that $n+\theta>\rho$; otherwise, the present value of the firm's future cash flow stream does not take a finite value. From equations (4.1), (4.3), and (4.7) we have:

$$\dot{k} = \left\{ \frac{1}{a}(q - 1) - \delta - n - \theta \right\} k \qquad (4.8)$$

From equations (4.1), (4.3), and (4.4), we have the following dynamic equation of q:

$$\dot{q} = -f'(k) - \frac{1}{2a}(q - 1)^2 + (\rho + \delta)q \qquad (4.9)$$

Equations (4.8) and (4.9) simultaneously determine the dynamics of k and q.

Let k^* and q^* denote values of k and q at a steady state. k^* and q^* are uniquely determined by

$$f'(k^*) = -\frac{a}{2}(\delta + n + \theta)^2 + (\rho + \delta)\{1 + a(\delta + n + \theta)\} \qquad (4.10)$$

$$q^* = 1 + a(\delta + n + \theta) \qquad (4.11)$$

From equations (4.10) and (4.11) and the assumption that $n+\theta>\rho$ we can show that a slowdown in productivity growth, θ, will reduce the steady state values of q and k.

Figure 4.5 is the phase diagram of the dynamic system of equations (4.8) and (4.9). We can prove that the unique steady state, point E, is a saddle point (Hirsh and Smale 1974) and the dotted path, which converges to the steady state, is the equilibrium trajectory of the economy.[4]

Usually, developing economies are characterized by a scarcity of capital stock. It is therefore assumed here that their present capital–labor ratio, k, is smaller than the steady state level, k^*. Under such conditions, the shadow price of capital stock, q, which is equal to Tobin's average Q under the assumptions here, is higher than the steady state level, q^*, and firms in this economy actively engage in investment, as equation (4.3) shows. Through this active investment, this economy's capital–labor ratio increases over time. Moreover, this capital accumulation process will gradually reduce the rate of return to capital, $f'(k)$, and the growth rate of the capital–labor ratio.

An examination of what happens when an unexpected drop in the productivity level, Θ, occurs will be helpful. Such a drop will cause an increase of the capital–labor ratio, $k \equiv K/\Theta L$. In Figure 4.5, the economy jumps from point A rightward to, say, point B. This change will reduce the shadow price of capital, q, and slow down capital accumulation. As mentioned earlier, the TPF level declined by about 18 per cent in Indonesia and Thailand after the AFC and did not recover for a long period. Is a TFP drop of this size enough to explain the sharp decline in the investment–GDP ratio, which in the two countries dropped by about 8 percentage points to 15 percentage points?

In order to answer this question, we need to specify the parameter values of our model. A Cobb-Douglas production function is assumed. According to the APO Database 2010, the labor income share in total income (α henceforth) in Indonesia was 0.50 from 1985 to 2007. In Thailand, this value was 0.47 in the same period. The labor income share in the simulation therefore is assumed to be 0.50. According to the same database, the annual growth rate of the total number of employees in Indonesia was 2.1 per cent from 1985 to 2007, while in Thailand it was 1.8 per cent. Thus, labor input growth, n, is assumed to be 2 per cent. Next, again according to the same database, TFP growth in Indonesia was 2.0 per cent from 1985 to 1996 and 1.7 per cent from 1999 to 2007, while TFP growth in Thailand was 2.7 per cent in both periods. Thus, in the simulation it is assumed that annual TFP growth is equal to 2 per cent. Under the assumption of a Cobb-Douglas production function, the annual growth rate of the Harrod-neutral productivity term, θ, is equal to the TFP growth rate times $1/\alpha$. Since it is assumed that the labor income share is 0.50, annual TFP growth of 2 per cent means annual growth of the Harrod-neutral productivity term, Θ, of 4 per cent. That is, θ is assumed to be 0.04. In order to have a meaningful optimization problem, the real interest rate for firms, ρ, needs to be greater than $n + \theta = 0.06$. ρ is therefore assumed to be 0.08. The capital depreciation rate, δ, is assumed to be 0.06. The final assumption required concerns the capital stock–GDP ratio, K/Y, in the steady state. According to the European Union (EU) KLEMS Database 2008, the nominal capital stock–nominal GDP ratio in many developed economies, such as Japan and the United States, is around 3. Since the income share of capital is assumed to be 0.5, we have the following relationship: $f'(k^*)K/Y = 3f'(k^*) = 0.5$. This means that $f'(k^*) = 0.167$.

Under the steady state condition (4.10) and the above assumptions, the value of a becomes 2.81. Moreover, the steady state values of q and the gross investment–capital stock ratio are 1.34 and 0.12, respectively.

Next, an examination of the impact of a productivity drop on the gross investment–capital stock ratio would be helpful. One way to evaluate this impact is to make a linear approximation of the dynamic system around the steady state. But since the system is nonlinear and developing economies' capital–labor ratio, k, seems to be much smaller than the steady state value (that is, these countries are located far to the left of the steady state, E, in Figure 4.5), we evaluate this impact by numerical simulation of our nonlinear dynamic model.

Figure 4.6 shows the equilibrium paths of the capital–labor ratio, k, and the gross investment–GDP ratio over time. In the figure, units are normalized and the steady state value of k is set to 1, that is, $k^*=1$.[5]

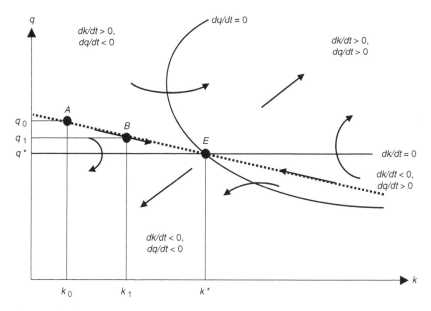

Source: Author.

Figure 4.5   Phase diagram of the investment model

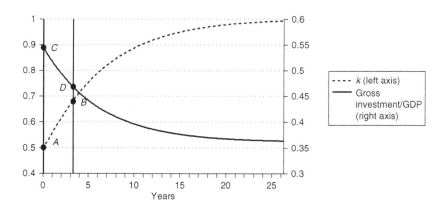

Source: Author.

Figure 4.6   Equilibrium paths of k *and the gross investment–GDP ratio:*
a = 2.81

We assume that when a productivity drop occurs, the capital–labor ratio, k, was 0.5 in year 0. As is well known, there is a huge gap in labor productivity, Y/L, between developing and developed economies. In the model here, this labor productivity gap, $Y/L = 0.333\Theta k0.5$ is explained by two factors: (1) the gap in the capital–labor ratio, $k = K/\Theta L$; and (2) the gap in the productivity level, Θ (and a corresponding parallel gap in capital stock K). Suppose that developed economies are at the steady state. Then, $k = 0.5$ in a developing economy means that the first factor makes this country's labor productivity 29 per cent $((1 - 0.5^{0.5}) \times 100)$ lower than that of the developed economies. Moreover, the remaining gap needs to be explained by the exogenously given Θ (and a corresponding parallel gap in capital stock K). Unfortunately, we cannot assume a very low level of k. As Figure 4.6 shows, if we assume that k is, say, 0.3, we will have an unrealistically high gross investment–GDP ratio.

It is also assumed that TFP drops by 18 per cent. Under the assumptions here, this drop means a 36 per cent decline in the Harrod-neutral productivity term. As already shown in the phase diagram, this drop results in a jump of the state variable, k, by 36 per cent. In Figure 4.6, this change is expressed by a jump of k from point A to point B. This jump reduces the rate of return to capital and the shadow price of capital, q. q will decline from 1.72 to 1.53 and the gross capital–GDP ratio will decline from 54 per cent to 47 per cent, that is, by 7 percentage points. In Figure 4.6, this change is expressed by the decline in the gross investment–GDP ratio from point C to point D. As mentioned, in Indonesia and Thailand, the gross investment–GDP ratio declined about 8 percentage points to 15 percentage points after the AFC. Thus, the decline of the gross investment–GDP ratio in the numerical simulation in Figure 4.6 seems not to be large enough to explain what happened in the two countries.

On the other hand, if we assume a smaller value of α, we obtain a sharp decline in the gross investment–GDP ratio. A smaller α means that capital adjustment costs are low. In this situation, firms increase investment if the rate of return to capital is high. And when the decline in the TFP level reduces the return to capital, firms will cut their investment sharply.

Figure 4.7 shows the equilibrium path in such a situation. Here, it is assumed that $n = 0.02$, $\theta = 0.04$, $\delta = 0.06$, $\rho = 0.09$, $f'(k^*) = 0.1667$, $a = 1.57$, and that the initial value of k is 0.65. Note that under these parameter values, the gross investment–GDP ratio will become unrealistically high if we assume that k is smaller than 0.65. In Figure 4.7, a 36 per cent decline in the Harrod-neutral productivity term will raise k from point A to point B. This change will reduce the gross investment–GDP ratio from point C to point D by 13 percentage points.

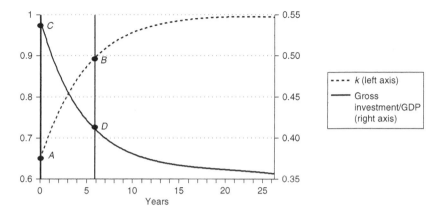

Source: Author.

Figure 4.7   Equilibrium paths of k *and gross investment–GDP ratio:*
         a *= 1.57*

Using the model presented here, we can also analyze what will happen if
the TFP growth rate declines. Assume the same parameter values and initial
conditions as in the simulation in Figure 4.7. Now assume that the TFP
growth rate declines from $\theta = 0.04$ to $\theta = 0.02$ in year 0 and θ stays at that
new level. Also assume that this change was fully unexpected. This time,
there is no assumption of a sudden drop in the TFP level but a downward
bending of the TFP trend. By numerical simulation, it can be shown that
the gross investment–GDP ratio declines 4 percentage points, from 53 per
cent to 49 per cent. Thus, it is possible to explain a drop in the gross investment–GDP ratio by a decline in the TFP growth trend. But it seems difficult
to explain a large drop in the gross investment–GDP ratio by a decline in the
TFP growth trend. As shown in Figure 4.2, Japan, during its "lost decade,"
did not experience a sharp drop in the TFP level. However, Japan's TFP
growth trend declined in the early 1990s, and Japan's gross investment–
GDP ratio gradually declined after that (see Figure 4.1). Thus, the implications of the model regarding the impact of a downward bending of TFP on
the gross investment–GDP ratio seem to be consistent with Japan's experience but not with the experience of Indonesia and Thailand after the AFC.

To sum up the main results of the numerical simulation, when we
assume a relatively low value of the adjustment cost function coefficient,
a, the magnitude of the TFP drop, which we observed in Indonesia and
Thailand just after the AFC, seems to be sufficient to cause the sharp drop
and stagnation of the gross investment–GDP ratio observed afterward in
these countries.

WHAT CAUSED THE PRODUCTIVITY DROP?

The issue in this chapter is an examination of why productivity fell in crisis-hit Asian countries.

A key aspect of the process of economic development is that labor productivity in the primary sector (agriculture, hunting, forestry, and fisheries) is usually much lower than that in other sectors, such as manufacturing and services. Therefore, labor movements from the primary sector to other sectors contribute to labor productivity growth in the economy as a whole (Kuznets 1971; Chenery et al. 1986). Since the manufacturing sector and some service sectors are more capital intensive than the primary sector, this type of structural change is accompanied by capital deepening at the macro level.

Another important aspect of the development process is that the marginal productivity of labor with similar characteristics is also frequently different across sectors (Lewis 1954) and regions. As a result, labor movements from sectors in which the marginal productivity of labor is low, such as agriculture, to other sectors will increase TFP at the macro level (Jorgenson et al. 2007). In the context of the present analysis, this means that if productivity-enhancing structural change and resource allocation came to a halt and were reversed in the wake of the AFC, this may have caused the observed drop in productivity. This issue is addressed later in this chapter.

Another "suspect" factor for the cause of the drop in productivity is micro-level misallocation of resources. If productive firms exit or shrink and less productive firms stay and expand, overall TFP in the economy declines. Unfortunately, there are few studies that examine such productivity dynamics in the crisis-hit ASEAN economies. Therefore, in order to take a first stab, this chapter considers the link between micro-level resource allocation and productivity by reviewing studies on this issue in other countries.

Structural Change and Productivity

The first issue to be examined is whether the productivity drop may have been caused by deterioration in resource allocation across sectors. Industry-level data of labor productivity has been used. As shown in Figure 4.8, with the exception of Malaysia, the percentage of workers in the primary sector is still very high, around 40 per cent, in the major ASEAN countries – Indonesia, the Philippines, and Thailand. Therefore, structural changes in terms of labor allocation across sectors are likely to have a large impact on labor productivity and capital accumulation.

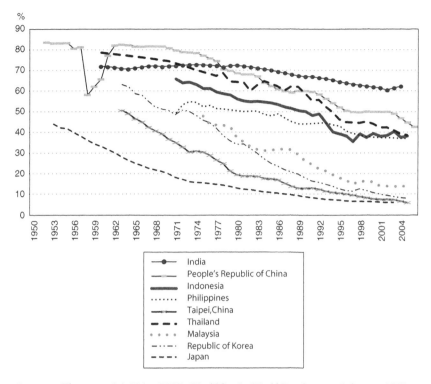

Sources: Timmer and de Vries (2009); World Bank, *World Development Indicators 2007.*

Figure 4.8 *Percentage of workers in agriculture, forestry, and fisheries in Asian countries*

Using a shift–share analysis framework (Chenery et al. 1986; van Ark 1996; Timmer and de Vries 2009), macro-level labor productivity growth can be decomposed as follows:

$$\left(\frac{\sum_i \overset{\wedge}{\overline{P}_i} Y_i}{L} \right) = \left\{ \sum_i \left(\frac{\overset{\wedge}{L_i}}{L} \frac{\overline{P}_i Y_t}{L_i} \right) \right\} = \frac{L}{\sum_i \overline{P}_i Y_i} \sum_i \left\{ \frac{\overline{P}_i Y_t}{L_i} \frac{d}{dt}\left(\frac{L_i}{L} \right) \right\}$$

$$+ \frac{L}{\sum_i \overline{P}_i Y_i} \sum_i \left\{ \frac{L_i}{L} \frac{d}{dt}\left(\frac{\overline{P}_i Y_t}{L_i} \right) \right\} \qquad (4.12)$$

where Li and Yi denote the number of workers and the real value added of sector i. L denotes the economy's total number of workers. $\bar{P}_i$ denotes the value added deflator of sector i in the benchmark year. A circumflex accent over a variable, $\wedge$, denotes the growth rate of that variable.

This equation shows that we can decompose macro-level labor productivity growth (the growth rate of real value added per worker) into two components: the inter-sector labor shift effect (shift effect) and the intra-sector effect.

Given that the discussion in the previous section considers how the optimal level of investment depends on TFP (and not labor productivity), it is important to clarify here how the labor shift and intra-sector effects shown in equation (4.12) are related with TFP. Using a growth accounting framework (Timmer 2000; Jorgenson et al. 2007) and assuming a constant returns-to-scale Cobb-Douglas production function in each sector,

$Yi = Fi(Li,Ki,Ai) = AiLi\alpha iKi1 - \alpha i$, where Ki and Ai denote capital input and the TFP term of sector i, we can further decompose the sum of these two effects, the labor shift effect and the intra-sector effect, in the following way:

$$\left(\frac{\sum_i \hat{\bar{P}_i Y_i}}{L}\right) = \frac{L}{\sum_i \bar{P}_i Y_i}\sum_i\left\{\frac{1}{\alpha_i}\bar{P}_i\frac{\partial F_i}{\partial L_i}\frac{d}{dt}\left(\frac{L_i}{L}\right)\right\}$$

$$+ \frac{\sum_i \bar{P}_i Y_i\hat{A}_i}{\sum_i \bar{P}_i Y_i} + \frac{\sum_i \bar{P}_i Y_i(1 - \alpha_i)\left(\frac{\hat{K}_i}{L_i}\right)}{\sum_i \bar{P}_i Y_i}$$

$$= \frac{L}{\sum_i \bar{P}_i Y_i}\sum_i\left\{\frac{w}{\alpha_i}\frac{d}{dt}\left(\frac{L_i}{L}\right)\right\} + \frac{L}{\sum_i \bar{P}_i Y_i}\sum_i\left\{\frac{1}{\alpha_i}\left(\bar{P}_i\frac{\partial F_i}{\partial L_i} - w\right)\frac{d}{dt}\left(\frac{L_i}{L}\right)\right\}$$

$$+ \frac{\sum_i \bar{P}_i Y_i\hat{A}_i}{\sum_i \bar{P}_i Y_i} + \frac{\sum_i (r_i - \bar{r})K_i\left(\frac{\hat{K}_i}{L_i}\right)}{\sum_i \bar{P}_i Y_i} + \frac{\bar{r}\left(\frac{d}{dt}K - \sum_i\frac{K_i}{L_i}\frac{d}{dt}L_i\right)}{\sum_i \bar{P}_i Y_i} \quad (4.13)$$

where $\bar{r}$ and r_i denote the gross rate of return to capital in the macro economy and the gross rate of return to capital in sector j, respectively.

The right-hand side of the above equations shows that macro-level labor productivity growth can be decomposed into five terms: (1) the effect of the expansion of capital intensive sectors; (2) the labor reallocation effect; (3) TFP growth within each sector; (4) the K/L reallocation effect; and (5) the effect of capital deepening within each sector. Among these five terms, the sum of (2), (3), and (4) is equal to the macro-level TFP growth rate (Timmer 2000). There is a close link between the decomposition shown in equation (4.12) and the decomposition in equation (4.13). The shift effect (the first term on the right-hand side of equation (4.12)) is equal to the sum of (i) the effect of the expansion of capital intensive sectors and (ii) the labor reallocation effect; and the intra-sector effect (the second term on the right-hand side of equation (4.12)) is equal to the sum of (iii) the TFP growth within each sector, (iv) the K/L reallocation effect, and (v) the effect of capital deepening within each sector.

If we had reliable data on sector capital input in developing countries, we could decompose macro-level labor productivity growth into these five components, from (i) to (v), and conduct a detailed analysis of sector resource allocation. For example, we could examine how the resource allocation across sectors affected TFP growth in crisis-hit countries. Unfortunately, it is difficult to obtain such data for Asian developing countries. Therefore, the decomposition results of Timmer and de Vries (2009), which are based on equation (4.12), are used here.

For each country in Asia and Latin America, Timmer and de Vries separate the entire period for which data are available into periods where growth in GDP per worker is accelerating and periods where it is decelerating. They then decompose, for each period, the macro-level growth rate of GDP per worker (labor productivity growth) for each country into the labor shift effect and the intra-sector effect. Table 4.1 shows their results for the Asian countries. In the case of Indonesia and Thailand, we can examine the impact of the AFC by comparing the decomposition results for the growth deceleration from 1996 to 2001 with the results for the pre-crisis growth acceleration period.

In Indonesia, the annual growth rate of labor productivity from 1996 to 2001 was 4.82 percentage points lower than in the period of pre-crisis growth acceleration from 1970 to 1996. Of the 4.82 percentage point decline, 3.36 percentage points are attributable to the shift effect and 1.46 percentage points to the intra-sector effect.

In Thailand, the annual growth rate of labor productivity from 1996 to 2001 was 7.83 percentage points lower than in the period of pre-crisis growth acceleration from 1985 to 1996. Of the 7.83 percentage point

Table 4.1 Sectoral resource allocation and labor productivity growth: Asian countries

Country	Period	Annual productivity growth (%)	Explained by (in percentage points)		Sectoral contribution (intra-industry + shift effect)				
			Total intra-industry effect	Total shift effect	Agriculture	Other industries	Manufac-turing	Market services	Nonmarket services
Hong Kong, China	1975–1993	4.71	3.63	1.08	0.06	0.44	2.08	1.97	0.17
	1993–1998	0.98	-0.53	1.51	-0.04	0.15	0.58	-0.27	0.57
	1998–2005	4.41	3.81	0.6	0	0.15	0.13	3.88	0.24
India	1960–1970	2.93	1.86	1.07	-0.01	0.4	0.65	1.27	0.61
	1970–1979	-0.44	1.29	-1.72	-0.15	0.21	-0.07	0.33	-0.76
	1979–2004	3.65	2.44	1.21	0	0.37	0.62	1.34	1.32
Indonesia	1970–1996	4.08	0.37	3.71	0	0.75	1.48	1.51	0.33
	1996–2001	**-0.74**	**-1.09**	**0.35**	**0**	**-0.03**	**-0.18**	**-0.74**	**0.2**
	2001–2005	3.66	3.65	0.01	-0.02	-0.07	1.7	1.56	0.5
Japan	1960–1990	4.74	4.58	0.16	0.71	0.31	1.53	1.77	0.42
	1990–2003	1.22	1.1	0.12	0.01	-0.15	0.76	0.42	0.18
Republic of Korea	1963–2005	4.45	5.19	-0.74	2.5	0.44	1.77	0.07	-0.32

Malaysia	1975–1997	4.51	4.86	−0.35	1.4	0.97	0.69	1.21
	1997–2005	2.36	2.74	−0.38	0	0.38	1.54	0.47
Philippines	1971–1976	4.62	4.44	0.18	−0.25	1.94	1.18	1.3
	1976–1986	−2.38	−1.79	−0.59	0	−0.59	−0.22	−1.06
	1986–2005	1.35	0.67	0.68	0	0.12	0.31	0.72
Singapore	1970–1996	4.38	3.68	0.7	0.16	0.37	1.02	2.35
	1996–2005	2.05	1.98	0.07	0	−0.21	0.94	1.26
Taipei,China	1963–2005	5.3	5.33	−0.03	1.43	0.32	1.36	1.45
Thailand	1961–1979	4.97	2.27	2.71	0	0.54	1.68	1.82
	1979–1985	1.31	1.05	0.26	0	0.46	0.43	0.26
	1985–1996	6.77	4.17	2.61	0.68	0.79	2.52	2.47
	1996–2001	**−1.06**	**−1.66**	**0.6**	**0.22**	**−0.01**	**0.07**	**−1.4**
	2001–2005	2.96	1.79	1.17	0	0.36	1.88	0.54

Source: Timmer and de Vries (2009).

decline, 2.01 percentage points are due to the shift effect, while 5.83 percentage points are due to the intra-sector effect.

These results suggest that in both countries, a decline in the shift effect played an important role in the slowdown of labor productivity growth after the AFC. Especially in the case of Indonesia, a sharp decline in the shift effect was a major source of the slowdown in labor productivity growth.

Table 4.1 further shows that Malaysia and Singapore also experienced a mild slowdown in labor productivity growth after the AFC. However, the decline in the shift effect was small or negligible: in Malaysia, there was no decline in the shift effect at all; while in Singapore, the decline, although accounting for a quarter of the overall slowdown, was small in absolute terms. The difference between the large decline in the shift effect in Indonesia and Thailand on the one hand and small decline in the shift effect in Malaysia and Singapore on the other hand seems to be caused by the difference in the importance of the primary sector. As Figure 4.8 shows, in Malaysia and Singapore the primary sector already was very small and the shift effect was negligible or negative even in the pre-crisis acceleration period.

It is necessary to review the changes in industrial structure and sector labor productivity in Indonesia and Thailand in more detail.[6] Figure 4.9 shows how labor productivity (real value added per worker) in each sector has changed over time in Indonesia.[7] Labor productivity in the primary sector (agriculture, hunting, forestry, and fisheries) has been less than half of that in almost all the other sectors. Therefore, the shift of labor from the primary sector to other sectors must have a large positive impact on macro-level labor productivity.

Following the AFC, labor productivity declined in most sectors. In the case of manufacturing, as well as transport, storage, and communications, labor productivity recovered within a few years after the AFC. However, in the case of wholesale and retail trade, repair of vehicles and household goods, hotels and restaurants, and construction, labor productivity remained below the pre-crisis level for about 10 years.

Figure 4.10 shows the labor allocation across sectors in Indonesia. The figure indicates that labor shifted from agriculture, hunting, forestry and fisheries to other more productive sectors, such as manufacturing and wholesale and retail trade, repair of vehicles and household goods, and hotels and restaurants, up until 1996. But the shift came to a sudden halt during the AFC and almost no labor shift occurred after that.

How sector labor productivity changed over time in Thailand is shown in Figure 4.11. In manufacturing as well as transport, storage and communications, there was almost no slowdown in labor productivity

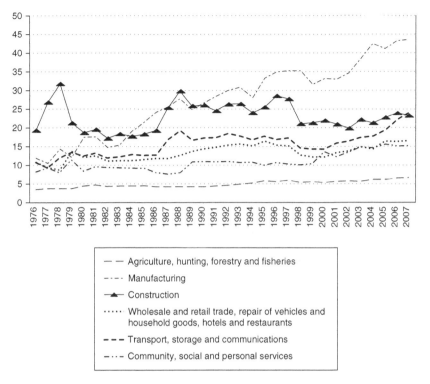

Source: Asian Productivity Organization, APO Database.

*Figure 4.9   Indonesia: labor productivity by sector (value added per
          worker, million rupiah in 2000 prices)*

growth after the AFC, with labor productivity continuing to grow at a
rapid pace. On the other hand, in wholesale and retail trade, repair of
vehicles and household goods, hotels and restaurants, and construction,
labor productivity fell and then stagnated for a long period after the
crisis.

Turning to the shift in labor from agriculture, hunting, forestry and
fisheries to other, more productive sectors in Thailand, Figure 4.12 shows
that this slowed down but continued following the AFC. After the crisis,
the destination of the labor shift changed. The share of the manufacturing
sector, where labor productivity is high, in total labor input stagnated, and
labor moved to less productive service sectors, such as commerce, restaurants, and personal services.

Is the sharp slowdown in the shift effect a phenomenon that is peculiar

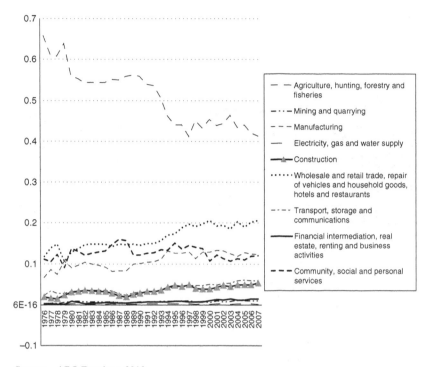

Source: APO Database 2010.

Figure 4.10   Indonesia: labor allocation across sectors

to the AFC or is it something that is common in many crises? To address
this question, it is important to examine what happened after financial
crises in Latin America.

Table 4.2 shows Timmer and de Vries' decomposition results for Latin
American countries. We pick out periods of a deceleration in labor productivity growth that started in the year of a systemic banking crisis.[8]
Information on the timing of banking crises is taken from the database of
Laeven and Valencia (2008). This database covers the universe of systemic
banking crises from 1970 to 2007.[9] Four instances that satisfy the criteria
are identified and the decomposition results for these are highlighted in
bold in Table 4.2.

Let us see for each case how much the shift effect declined after a systemic banking crisis. First, in Argentina following the systemic banking
crisis of 1980, the annual growth rate of labor productivity from 1980
to 1990 was 4.35 percentage points lower than in the period of pre-crisis
growth acceleration from 1950 to 1980. Of the 4.35 percentage point

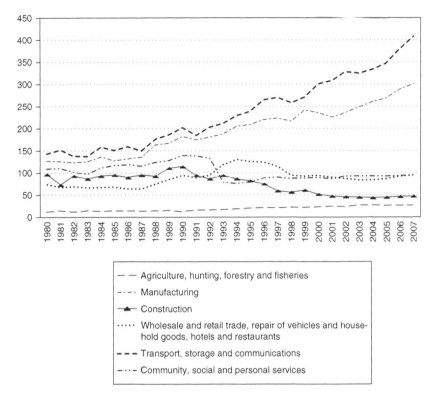

Source: Asian Productivity Organization, APO Database.

Figure 4.11 *Thailand: labor productivity by sector (value added per worker, million baht in 2000 prices)*

decline, 0.32 percentage points are attributable to the shift effect, while 4.02 percentage points were due to the intra-sector effect.

Next, in Chile, following the systemic banking crisis of 1981, the annual growth rate of labor productivity from 1981 to 1985 was 13.20 percentage points lower than in the period of pre-crisis growth acceleration from 1976 to 1981. Of the 13.20 percentage point decline, 1.75 percentage points were due to the shift effect, while 11.46 percentage points were caused by the intra-sector effect.

The third case is Colombia, which experienced a systemic banking crisis in 1998. The annual growth rate of labor productivity from 1997 to 2001 was 7.16 percentage points lower than in the period of pre-crisis growth acceleration from 1993 to 1997, and of this 7.16 percentage point decline,

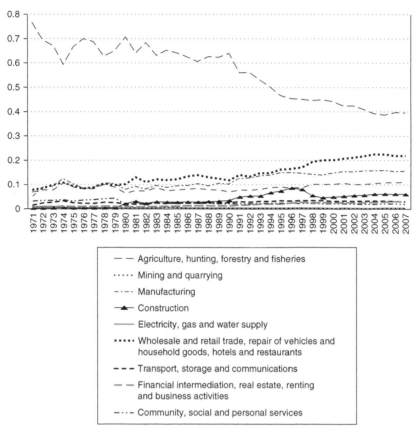

Figure 4.12   Thailand: labor allocation across sectors

1.45 percentage points were attributable to the shift effect, while 5.71 percentage points were due to the intra-sector effect.

Finally, in Mexico, following the systemic banking crisis of 1981, the annual growth rate of labor productivity from 1981 to 1988 was 7.00 percentage points lower than in the period of pre-crisis growth acceleration from 1977 to 1981. Of the 7.00 percentage point decline, 1.85 percentage points were caused by the shift effect, and 5.83 percentage points by the intra-sector effect.

Comparing the results on the AFC with those on crises in Latin America yields two main findings. First, in terms of the magnitude of the decline in labor productivity growth, there is not much difference between the AFC

Table 4.2 Sectoral resource allocation and labor productivity growth: Latin American countries

Country	Period	Annual productivity growth (%)	Explained by (in percentage points):		Sectoral Contribution (intra-industry + shift effect)				
			Total intra-industry effect	Total shift effect	Agriculture	Other industries	Manufacturing	Market services	Nonmarket services
Argentina	1950–1980	1.41	1.08	0.32	0.31	0.12	0.47	0.44	0.06
	1980–1990	**-2.94**	**-2.94**	**0**	**0**	**-0.3**	**-0.49**	**-1.36**	**-0.79**
	1990–1998	5.35	5.58	-0.23	0.47	1.06	1.82	1.86	0.15
	1998–2005	-0.82	-0.47	-0.35	0.24	0.01	0.22	-1.05	-0.23
Bolivia	1950–1954	3.8	1.66	2.15	0.4	0.87	1.26	0.95	0.33
	1954–1959	-1.32	1.15	-2.46	-2.41	0.36	0.37	0.23	0.13
	1959–1969	4.13	1.8	2.33	0.31	1.31	0.85	0.95	0.72
	1969–1982	1.22	-0.64	1.86	0.63	-0.29	0.19	0.44	0.25
	1982–1987	-5.55	-4.61	-0.95	0	-0.2	-0.09	-1.87	-3.39
	1987–2003	0.82	0.9	-0.08	0.61	0.99	-0.37	-0.83	0.42
Brazil	1950–1961	4.77	3.1	1.67	0	0.56	1.71	1.06	1.43
	1961–1966	1.81	-0.07	1.88	0	0.3	0.34	0.82	0.36
	1966–1980	5.43	3.51	1.92	0	1.1	1.56	1.59	1.17
	1980–1992	-1.91	-2.33	0.42	0.19	0.04	-0.84	-0.9	-0.4
	1992–2005	0.79	0.81	-0.02	0.49	0.3	0.39	-0.54	0.15
Chile	1950–1971	2.55	2.27	0.28	0	0.6	1.08	0.6	0.27
	1971–1976	-3.27	-3.35	0.08	0	-0.8	-1.73	-0.9	0.16
	1976–1981	6.75	5.92	0.83	0.53	1.43	2.4	2.5	-0.11
	1981–1985	**-6.45**	**-5.54**	**-0.92**	**-0.66**	**-0.15**	**-0.42**	**-2.81**	**-2.42**
	1985–1997	4.17	3.6	0.57	0.95	1	0.57	1.15	0.49
	1997–2005	0.96	1.44	-0.48	0	0.82	0.77	-0.45	-0.18
Colombia	1950–1987	2.84	1.62	1.22	0	0.34	0.61	1.34	0.54
	1987–1993	-1.13	-2.09	0.96	0	-0.45	-0.36	-0.22	-0.09
	1993–1997	4.04	3.7	0.35	0.56	0.98	0.54	0.75	1.22

Table 4.2 (continued)

Country	Period	Annual productivity growth (%)	Explained by (in percentage points):		Sectoral Contribution (intra-industry + shift effect)				
			Total intra-industry effect	Total shift effect	Agriculture	Other industries	Manufacturing	Market services	Nonmarket services
Colombia	**1997–2001**	**-3.12**	**-2.01**	**-1.1**	**0**	**-0.32**	**0.07**	**-2.57**	**-0.31**
	2001–2005	1.24	1.88	-0.64	0	1.13	0.34	-0.46	0.23
Costa Rica	1950–1958	5.85	4.35	1.5	0	0.44	1.07	2.87	1.47
	1958–2005	1.31	0.07	1.24	0	0.1	0.51	0.72	-0.01
Mexico	1950–1957	5.29	4.28	1.01	0.84	0.21	0.88	2.87	0.49
	1957–1977	2.45	0.96	1.49	0	0.22	0.62	1.21	0.4
	1977–1981	3.69	2.18	1.51	0.43	0.5	0.46	2.07	0.24
	1981–1988	**-3.31**	**-3.65**	**0.34**	**0**	**-0.28**	**-0.62**	**-1.87**	**-0.53**
	1988–2005	1.09	0.06	1.02	0.18	0.04	0.38	0.48	0.01
Peru	1960–1974	3.78	2.63	1.15	0	0.38	0.98	1.68	0.74
	1974–1983	-2.39	-3.44	1.05	0	-0.1	-0.45	-1.29	-0.55
	1983–1987	2.72	1.51	1.22	0	0.37	1.02	0.86	0.47
	1987–1991	-9.77	-10.54	0.77	0	-0.65	-2.04	-4.49	-2.59
	1991–1995	9.62	10.61	-0.99	-1.55	2.09	1.6	6.16	1.33
	1995–1999	-0.63	-1.13	0.5	0	0.67	0.33	-1.38	-0.24
	1999–2005	3.08	2.86	0.21	-0.21	0.7	0.82	1.3	0.47
Venezuela	1950–1957	5.49	4.06	1.43	0	3.48	0.75	1.09	0.17
	1957–1988	-0.82	-0.51	-0.31	0	-0.58	0.17	-0.3	-0.12
	1988–1992	1.54	-0.25	1.79	0.15	1.24	-0.18	0.11	0.22
	1992–2001	-2.24	1.21	-3.45	0	1.59	0.33	-3.91	-0.26
	2001–2005	2.54	4.39	-1.84	-0.63	0.26	1.16	2	-0.25

Source: Timmer and de Vries (2009).

and the Latin American crises. Second, in Asia, the decline in the shift effect played a more important role in the slowdown of labor productivity growth than in Latin America. The contribution of the decline in the shift effect to the total decline in labor productivity growth was 70 per cent in Indonesia and 26 per cent in Thailand, while it was 7 per cent in Argentina, 13 per cent in Chile, 20 per cent in Columbia, and 17 per cent in Mexico.

One probable explanation for this difference between the two regions is that the percentage of workers in agriculture, forestry and fisheries was much higher in Indonesia and Thailand when the AFC occurred than the corresponding values in the Latin American countries when they experienced their crises. In Indonesia and Thailand, the shares were 38 per cent and 45 per cent, respectively, in 1996 (Groningen Growth and Development Centre 10-Sector Database). On the other hand, in Argentina, the share of these workers was only 13 per cent on the eve of its financial crisis in 1979, while in Chile, the share was 21 per cent in 1980, in Colombia it was 24 per cent in 1997, and in Mexico it was 29 per cent in 1980. In the Latin American countries, the economic structure in terms of the three main sectors (primary, secondary, and tertiary) was already more advanced than in Indonesia and Thailand, so that even in the pre-crisis labor productivity acceleration period the role of the shift effect was already relatively small. This means that there was not much room for a further decline in the shift effect in the wake of the various crises.

To summarize, a key factor in the slowdown in labor productivity growth in Indonesia and Thailand following the AFC is a marked slowdown in the shift of labor. Specifically, the labor shift from agriculture to other more productive sectors almost stopped in Indonesia and substantially decelerated in Thailand. Comparing the experience of these two countries with the experiences of Latin American countries that suffered financial crises shows that the magnitude of the slowdown in labor productivity after the AFC was not particularly high. However, the decline in the shift effect played a much more important role in the Asian countries than in Latin America. Turning to the intra-sector effect, in both Indonesia and Thailand, it was mainly service sectors, such as commerce and construction, where the large drop and slow recovery in labor productivity was concentrated, while the manufacturing sector enjoyed rapid labor productivity growth even after the crisis, although the labor share of that sector did not continue to increase.[10]

There is a caveat with regard to the shift effect analysis here. It is true that in economic development, labor tends to shift to sectors in which labor productivity is higher and that are more capital intensive. Moreover, capital accumulation occurs mainly in these productive and capital-intensive sectors. Using theoretical models, it can be shown that if there are obstacles slowing this structural change, TFP will decline and capital accumulation will decelerate. However, as the Rybczynski theorem shows, a reverse causality is also possible. That is, a slowdown in capital accumulation will reduce the expansion of sectors with higher labor productivity and greater capital intensity. In order to judge which direction of causality was more important in the crisis-hit Asian countries, a detailed examination of factor price gaps and factor movements across sectors would be necessary.

Intra-sector Decline in TFP

It is important to examine the intra-sector effect in greater detail. As we have seen, following the AFC, the intra-sector effect also declined substantially, particularly in the case of Thailand. One promising explanation of this intra-sector slowdown of labor productivity growth is that TFP dropped within each sector and capital accumulation within each sector also slowed down because of this drop in TFP.

Such an intra-sector decline in TFP can be caused either by a drop in TFP within firms, the "within effect," or by the misallocation of resources across firms, the "between effect." Unfortunately, there are few studies that examine such productivity dynamics in the crisis-hit ASEAN economies.[11] Therefore, what follows is a brief review of studies on productivity dynamics in crisis-hit Japan, the Republic of Korea, and Latin American countries, which might be useful for future research on the Indonesian and Thai experiences.[12]

Starting with Japan, using long-run unbalanced panel data of plants in Japan's manufacturing sector, which almost covers the universe of establishments (omitting, as it does, only very small plants) from the 1980s to the 2000s, Fukao and Kwon (2006) conducted an analysis of productivity dynamics and found that the slowdown in TFP growth in Japan's manufacturing sector in the 1990s was mainly caused by a decline in TFP growth within each factory and not by a deterioration in resource allocation across factories. Turning to the Republic of Korea, using financial report data of medium and large firms covering almost all sectors, Baek et al. (2009) found that resource allocation across firms improved after the AFC and this change contributed to the acceleration in the Republic of Korea's TFP growth following the crisis.

Next, looking at studies on Latin American countries, Casacuberta and Gandelman (2009), employing data from firms in the manufacturing sector and various services sectors, examined how productivity dynamics in Uruguay changed after the systemic banking crisis of 2002. They did not find a significant increase in resource misallocation after the crisis. Rather, most of the TFP decline was caused by the decline in TFP within firms.

On the other hand, using plant-level data on Argentina's manufacturing sector, Sandleris and Wright (2010) considered productivity dynamics before and after the systemic banking crisis of 2001 and found that more than half of the roughly 10 per cent decline in measured TFP could be explained by the deterioration in the allocation of resources both across and within sectors.

These studies suggest that productivity dynamics after a crisis may differ considerably and it is therefore difficult to distill any stylized facts at the moment. Most likely, the productivity dynamics after a crisis depend on many different factors, such as the kinds of policies taken (Baek et al. 2009) and how the international economic environment has changed.[13]

As already noted, there are few studies that examine such productivity dynamics in the crisis-hit ASEAN economies. However, there is a small number of studies on micro-level productivity dynamics in Indonesia. Using plant-level data for the manufacturing sector, Vial (2008) examined productivity dynamics from 1975 to 1995. She found that positive net entry effects – entry effects plus exit effects – played an important role during this period. That is, relatively productive plants started up, and less productive plants were closed. According to Aswicahyono et al. (2010), the entry rate of manufacturing plants declined sharply immediately after the AFC and continued to decline thereafter. The decline in the entry rate probably had a negative impact on productivity dynamics. On the other hand, Narjoko and Hill (2007) report that foreign-owned firms and firms that were export-oriented prior to the crisis tended to have a higher survival probability during the AFC and recovered well afterward. Since the average TFP level of these firms seems to be higher than the industry average, this selection mechanism must have made a positive contribution to the exit effects.[14]

It is difficult to derive conjectures on the intra-sector decline in TFP in Indonesia from these studies. It will be necessary to wait for studies on productivity dynamics during the AFC to obtain a clear answer to the question why TFP dropped so much. It should also be noted that to answer this question, what is needed first and foremost are micro-data analyses on the service sector, since the large drop and slow recovery in labor productivity in Indonesia and Thailand was mainly concentrated in service sectors such as commerce and construction.

CONCLUSION

After the AFC, crisis-hit Asian countries, particularly Indonesia and Thailand, experienced a sharp decline and a prolonged stagnation in the gross investment–GDP ratio. This chapter considered whether this sharp decline in capital accumulation could be explained by a drop in productivity. It also examined why the productivity drop after the crisis was so large in Indonesia and Thailand. The major results of the chapter are summarized below.

According to the APO Database, Indonesia and Thailand experienced a large drop in labor productivity and TFP after the AFC. In particular, TFP declined 18–19 per cent and took almost 10 years or more to recover to the pre-crisis level. Using a growth model of a small open economy with adjustment costs of investment, the chapter examined how much of the decline in capital accumulation after the AFC can be explained by the drop in productivity. When a relatively low value of the adjustment cost function coefficient is assumed, the magnitude of the TFP drop observed in Indonesia and Thailand seems to be sufficient to cause the sharp drop and stagnation of the gross investment–GDP ratio seen in these countries following the crisis.

Next, the chapter considered why TFP fell so drastically following the crisis. If productivity-enhancing structural change and resource allocation, in particular, and labor movement from the primary sector to more productive modern sectors came to a halt and were reversed in the wake of the AFC, this may have caused the observed drop in productivity. Examining this issue using sector employment and labor productivity data, it was found that the labor shift from less labor productive sectors, such as agriculture, to more labor productive sectors, such as manufacturing, slowed down or stopped after the crisis, particularly in Indonesia.

In addition, the experience of Indonesia and Thailand following the AFC was compared with that of Latin American countries that suffered financial crises. It was found that in terms of the magnitude of the decline in labor productivity growth, there was not much difference between the experiences of the Asian countries and those of the Latin American countries. However, in Asia, the decline in the shift effect played a more important role in the slowdown of labor productivity growth than in Latin America. One probable explanation of this difference between the two regions is that the percentage of workers in agriculture, forestry and fisheries was much higher in Indonesia and Thailand when the AFC occurred than the corresponding values in the Latin American countries when they experienced their crises.

Finally, a brief review was provided of studies that, using micro-data, examined the post-crisis intra-sector decline in TFP. Unfortunately, there are few studies that do so for the crisis-hit ASEAN economies, so the review focused on studies on Japan, the Republic of Korea, and Latin American countries. The review suggested that at this point, it is difficult to derive any stylized facts on intra-sector productivity dynamics following a financial crisis.

Admittedly, we need more data and research to determine why TFP dropped so severely and how much the drop reduced the gross investment–GDP ratio after the AFC. For example, we need empirical studies of productivity dynamics in the service sector to understand the intra-sector TFP decline in Indonesia and Thailand. We also need both a multi-sector growth model and a model with heterogeneous firms to fully understand how the halt in the change in industry structure and productivity dynamics affected the gross investment–GDP ratio. However, the analysis here suggests that the role of productivity in explaining the decline in the gross fixed capital formation–GDP ratio clearly is an issue that deserves further research in order to understand fully how financial crises affect economies in the long run.

NOTES

1. Using a theoretical model of investment with adjustment cost in a small, open economy similar to the theoretical framework of the first half of this chapter, Shioji and Khai (2011) empirically examine factors that contributed to recent changes in investment trends in Asian countries and provide projections of investment trends over the next two decades. However, their study focuses on long-term trends and does not examine the economic impact of the sharp drop in TFP after the AFC on investment. For example, they use the 10-year average TFP growth rate as an explanatory variable for their regression. Another difference between their study and this chapter is that in order to evaluate the quantitative impact of TFP changes on investment, they make a linear approximation of the dynamic system around the steady state, while we evaluate this impact by numerical simulation of a nonlinear dynamic model. Since the system employed in both their study and ours is nonlinear and developing economies' capital–labor ratio seems to be much smaller than the steady state value – that is, these countries are located far from the steady state – it seems preferable to fully take account of the nonlinearity of the dynamic system.
2. Capital stock data for most countries are not available in the APO Database 2010. Therefore, gross capital income/(capital service input × GDP deflator) is used as a proxy for the gross rate of return to capital in Figure 4.4.
3. The model is a modified version of the open economy growth model in Chapter 2 of Blanchard and Fischer (1989).
4. These paths satisfy transversality conditions.
5. This normalization and the assumption $f'(k^*) = 0.167$ imply that the production function is expressed as $Y = 0.333K^{0.5}(\Theta L)^{0.5}$.
6. There is some inconsistency between the database of Timmer and de Vries (2009), the Groningen Growth and Development Centre 10-Sector Database, and the database of the Asian Productivity Organization (APO). The following analysis uses the APO Database because it covers more recent years.
7. Labor productivity in the following three industries: mining and quarrying; electricity, gas and water supply; and financial intermediation, real estate, renting, and business activities, which each account for less than 2 per cent of labor input in the economy, are not shown in Figure 4.9.

8. If the turning point from a pre-crisis acceleration to a post-crisis deceleration coincides with, or is one year before, a banking crisis, the deceleration is regarded as having started in the year of the banking crisis.
9. According to Laeven and Valencia's taxonomy, financial crises consist of systemic banking crises, currency crises, and sovereign debt crises. The financial crises of 1997 in Indonesia and Thailand are classified as systemic banking crises by Laeven and Valencia and the deceleration periods for the two countries, which were examined in Table 4.1, satisfy the criteria of the timing discussed in note 6.
10. Examining Indonesia's manufacturing sector following the AFC, Aswicahyono et al. (2010) find that the sector experienced jobless growth and that it was particularly capital-intensive subsectors that exhibited good export performance. These findings are consistent with the results presented here.
11. A survey of micro-data analyses on Indonesia is provided by Aswicahyono (2008).
12. In this context, another study of interest is that by Ohanian (2001), which examines why TFP declined so much during the Great Depression and finds that a large part of the decline cannot be explained by a deterioration in inter-sectoral resource allocation.
13. For a general discussion of economic policies taken by Indonesia after the AFC, see Hill and Shiraishi (2007).
14. There are many studies on the productivity gap between foreign-owned firms and domestic independent firms in ASEAN countries. On this issue, see Oguchi et al. (2002), Rasiah (2003, 2004), Takii (2004, 2006), Takii and Ramstetter (2005), and Ramstetter (2009).

REFERENCES

van Ark, B. (1996), 'Sectoral growth accounting and structural change in post-war Europe', in Bart van Ark and Nicholas F.R. Craft (eds), *Quantitative Aspects of Post-War European Economic Growth*, CEPR/Cambridge University Press, pp. 84–164.

Arrow, K.J., and M. Kurz (1970), *Public Investment, the Rate of Return, and Optimal Fiscal Policy*, Baltimore: Johns Hopkins Press.

Asian Development Bank (2007), *Asian Development Outlook 2007: Change amid Growth*, Manila: Asian Development Bank.

Asian Development Bank (2008), *Asian Development Outlook 2008: Workers in Asia*, Manila: Asian Development Bank.

Asian Productivity Organization (2010), *APO Productivity Databook 2010*, Tokyo: Keio University Press.

Aswicahyono, H. (2008), 'A survey of micro-data analyses in Indonesia', in J. Corbett and S. Umezaki (eds), 'Deepening East Asian Economic Integration', ERIA Research Project Report 2008, No. 1, Jakarta: Economic Research Institute for ASEAN and East Asia.

Aswicahyono, H., H. Hill, and D. Narjoko (2010), 'Industrialisation after a deep economic crisis: Indonesia', *Journal of Development Studies*, **46**, 1084–1108.

Baek, C., Y.G. Kim, and H.U. Kwon (2009), 'Kinyu Kikigo no Shijo Kyoso to Seisansei Josho: Kankoku Kigyo Data ni Motozuku Jisshobunseki (Market Competition and Productivity after the Asian Financial Crisis: Evidence from Korean Firm Level Data)', Center for Economic Institutions Working Paper Series, No. 2009-12, Institute of Economic Research, Hitotsubashi University.

Blanchard, O.J., and S. Fischer (1989), 'Lectures on Macroeconomics', Cambridge, MA: MIT Press.

Casacuberta, C., and N. Gandelman (2009), 'Productivity, exit and crisis in Uruguayan manufacturing and services sectors', mimeo, Uruguay, Universidad de la República.

Chenery, H., S. Robinson, and M. Syrquin (1986), *Industrialization and Growth: A Comparative Study*, New York: Oxford University Press.

Fukao, K., and H.U. Kwon (2006), 'Why did Japan's TFP growth slow down in the lost decade? An empirical analysis based on firm-level data of manufacturing firms', *Japanese Economic Review*, **57**, 195–228.

Hayashi, F. (1982), 'Tobin's marginal q and average q: a neoclassical interpretation', *Econometrica: Journal of the Econometric Society*, **50**, 213–24.

Hill, H., and T. Shiraishi (2007), 'The Indonesian economy: a decade after the crisis', *Asian Economic Policy Review*, **2**, 127–45.

Hirsch, M.W., and S. Smale (1974), *Differential Equations, Dynamical Systems, and Linear Algebra*, Boston, MA: Academic Press.

International Monetary Fund (IMF) (2009), *World Economic Outlook: Crisis and Recovery*, Washington, DC: IMF.

Jorgenson, D.W. et al. (2007), 'Industry origins of the American productivity resurgence', paper presented at the Conference on Research on Income and Wealth, NBER Summer Institute 2007, accessed at http://www.nber.org/~confer/2007/si2007/PRCR/jorgenson.pdf on 1 October 2007.

Kuznets, S.S. (1971), *Economic Growth of Nations: Total Output and Production Structure*, Cambridge: Harvard University Press.

Laeven, L., and F. Valencia (2008), 'Systemic banking crises: a new database', International Monetary Fund Working Paper Series, No. 08/224, Washington, DC: IMF.

Lewis, A.W. (1954), 'Economic development with unlimited supplies of labour', *The Manchester School*, **22**, 139–91.

Narjoko, D., and H. Hill (2007), 'Winners and losers during a deep economic crisis: firm-level evidence from Indonesian manufacturing', *Asian Economic Journal*, **21**, 343–68.

Oguchi, N. et al. (2002), 'Productivity of foreign and domestic firms in Malaysian manufacturing industry', *Asian Economic Journal*, **16**, 215–28.

Ohanian, L.E. (2001), 'Why did productivity fall so much during the Great Depression', *American Economic Review*, **91**, 34–8.

Ramstetter, E.D. (2009), 'Firm- and plant-level analysis of multinationals in Southeast Asia: the perils of pooling industries and balancing panels', ICSEAD Working Paper Series No. 2009-22, Kitakyushu: International Centre for the Study of East Asian Development.

Rasiah, R. (2003), 'Foreign ownership, technology and electronics exports from Malaysia and Thailand', *Journal of Asian Economics*, **14**, 785–811.

Rasiah, R. (2004), 'Exports and technological capabilities: a study of foreign and local firms in the electronics industry in Malaysia, the Philippines and Thailand', *European Journal of Development Research*, **16**, 587–623.

Sandleris, G., and M.L.J. Wright (2010), 'The costs of financial crises: resource misallocation, productivity and welfare in the 2001 Argentine crisis', mimeo, Universidad Torcuato di Tella.

Shioji, E., and V.T. Khai (2011), 'Physical capital accumulation in Asia-12: past trends and future projections', ADB Economics Working Paper Series No. 240, Asian Development Bank.

Takii, S. (2004), 'Productivity differentials between local and foreign plants in Indonesian manufacturing, 1995', *World Development*, **32**, 1957–69.

Takii, S. (2006), 'Productivity differentials and spillovers in Indonesian manufacturing', in E.D. Ramstetter and F. Sjöholm (eds), *Multinational Corporations in Indonesia and Thailand: Wages, Productivity, and Exports*, Hampshire, UK: Palgrave Macmillan, pp. 85–103.

Takii, S., and E.D. Ramstetter (2005), 'Multinational presence and labour productivity differentials in Indonesian manufacturing, 1975–2001', *Bulletin of Indonesian Economic Studies*, **41**, 221–42.

Timmer, M.P. (2000), *The Dynamics of Asian Manufacturing: A Comparative Perspective in the late Twentieth Century*, Cheltenham, UK and Northampton, MA, USA: Edward Elgar.

Timmer, M.P., and G.J. de Vries (2009), 'Structural change and growth accelerations in Asia and Latin America: a new sectoral data set', *Cliometrica*, **3**, 2, 165–90.

Uzawa, H. (1969), 'Time preference and the Penrose effect in a two-class model of economic growth', *Journal of Political Economy*, **77**, S4, 628–52.

Vial, V. (2008), 'How much does turnover matter? Evidence from Indonesian manufacturing total factor productivity growth 1975–95', *Oxford Development Studies*, **36**, 295–322.

5. Savings and investment

Charles Yuji Horioka and
Akiko Terada-Hagiwara

INTRODUCTION

Developing Asia has been characterized in recent years by high savings rates almost across the board. These high savings rates have provided financing for high levels of domestic investment in the region, but they also have led to large capital outflows or current account surpluses (Park and Shin 2009). Moreover, the stagnation of domestic investment in some of developing Asia since the onset of the Asian financial crisis (AFC) has increased even further the current account surpluses of developing Asia. Given this backdrop, what will happen to savings, investment, and growth in the next two decades?

To answer this question, this chapter presents data on past trends in domestic savings rates in the 12 economies of developing Asia from 1966 to 2007, conducts an econometric analysis of the determinants of domestic savings rates in developing Asia during that period, projects trends in domestic savings rates in developing Asia during the next two decades based on the results of our econometric analysis, and discusses the implications of our findings for investment, growth, and economic policy in developing Asia.

The 12 economies included in our analysis are the People's Republic of China (PRC); Hong Kong, China; India; Indonesia; the Republic of Korea; Malaysia; Pakistan; the Philippines; Singapore; Taipei,China; Thailand; and Viet Nam, which comprise 95 per cent of the gross domestic product (GDP) of developing Asia.

PAST TRENDS IN DOMESTIC SAVINGS RATES IN DEVELOPING ASIA

Past trends in the domestic savings rate in the 12 developing Asian economies in our sample are presented in Table 5.1 and Figure 5.1. They include

Table 5.1 Trends in gross domestic savings rates in developing Asia

	Nominal measure								
	1966–70	1971–75	1976–80	1981–85	1986–90	1991–95	1996–2000	2001–07	Average
PRC	28.9	29.1	33.0	34.8	37.0	41.9	40.7	46.2	37.8
Hong Kong, China	28.2	29.4	33.5	31.6	36.0	32.6	30.4	31.5	31.6
Indonesia	14.3	23.9	30.8	30.1	31.9	32.4	28.1	29.9	27.8
India	15.5	16.7	18.7	19.4	21.9	23.0	22.4	29.0	22.2
Korea, Rep. of	15.2	19.0	27.0	27.8	36.5	36.4	35.6	31.8	28.8
Malaysia	24.3	24.2	31.1	28.1	33.3	37.8	45.8	42.6	33.4
Pakistan	8.9	8.0	7.9	7.2	10.3	16.4	14.9	16.1	11.2
Philippines	21.9	23.6	26.2	21.0	19.0	16.3	17.1	13.8	19.1
Singapore	18.4	26.3	34.9	43.8	41.0	47.3	49.9	46.3	39.8
Thailand	21.2	22.8	22.1	24.3	30.8	35.8	34.3	32.2	27.9
Taipei,China	25.3	30.4	33.0	31.6	33.4	27.2	26.0	26.0	28.7
Viet Nam					3.9	14.6	22.2	29.0	17.4
Average a/	19.8	22.0	25.7	26.6	30.0	33.2	32.9	37.5	

Notes:
PRC = People's Republic of China. Computed as gross domestic savings (current local currency units)/GDP (current local currency units).
a/ weighted by average real GDP of each period.

Data source: World Bank, World Development Indicators.

Real measure

	1966–70	1971–75	1976–80	1981–85	1986–90	1991–95	1996–2000	2001–07	Average
PRC	27.3	28.3	30.1	28.1	27.0	27.7	29.4	35.6	29.2
Hong Kong, China	35.0	34.6	35.7	33.0	33.1	28.2	27.9	33.7	32.6
Indonesia	35.7	39.3	35.2	20.7	26.0	25.8	21.0	19.4	27.9
India	12.2	13.1	14.5	12.0	12.1	12.4	10.9	16.4	13.01
Korea, Rep. of	18.8	21.9	31.8	33.4	39.3	42.2	42.4	43.7	34.2
Malaysia	28.5	31.0	31.5	29.7	37.5	39.0	46.0	42.5	35.7
Pakistan	3.8	3.4	-3.8	-0.8	4.8	5.9	5.2	7.7	3.3
Philippines	10.2	13.2	18.1	18.9	14.2	10.6	9.7	10.8	13.2
Singapore	35.8	40.4	45.4	53.7	51.3	56.2	60.2	56.4	49.9
Thailand	17.9	21.0	21.7	24.8	30.4	35.2	32.8	31.7	26.9
Taipei,China	13.4	18.4	23.1	25.1	25.5	21.7	22.6	26.4	22.0
Viet Nam	-2.4	-2.4	-2.4	-2.4	-1.7	6.9	12.6	16.8	3.1
Average a/	18.8	21.0	23.0	21.2	22.8	24.3	24.8	29.4	

Notes:
PRC = People's Republic of China. Computed as 100−kc−kg, where "kc" is the consumption share of real GDP per capita and "kg" is the government share of real GDP per capita.
a/ weighted by average real GDP of each period.

Data source: Penn World Tables (PWT), version 6.3.

Source: World Bank, World Development Indicators; Penn World tables, version 6.3.

Figure 5.1   Trends in gross domestic savings rates in developing Asia

data on past trends in nominal and real domestic savings rates for each of the 12 developing Asian economies in our sample, as well as for these 12 economies as a whole for each five-year period from 1966 to 2000 and for the most recent period, which includes the years from 2001 to 2007.

Nominal domestic savings rates are computed as the ratio of gross domestic savings in current local currency units to GDP in current local currency units and are taken from the World Development Indicators of the World Bank, while real domestic savings rates are computed by subtracting the consumption and government shares of real GDP from 100 and are taken from the Penn World Tables, version 6.3.

As can be seen from this table and figure, there is enormous variation among the 12 economies in the sample in their domestic savings rates, with the nominal domestic savings rate ranging from 39.8 per cent in Singapore (and also above 30 per cent in the PRC; Hong Kong, China; and Malaysia) to 11.2 per cent in Pakistan (and also below 20 per cent in the Philippines and Viet Nam) from 1966 to 2007. In fact, Viet Nam showed negative real domestic savings rates until it transitioned to a market economy in the 1990s. India, Indonesia, the Republic of Korea, Taipei,China, and Thailand showed intermediate nominal domestic savings rates during this period. Nonetheless, domestic savings rates have been relatively high in developing Asia as a whole relative to the rest of the world from 1966 to 2007.

The real domestic savings rate ranged from 49.9 per cent in Singapore (and also above 30 per cent in Hong Kong, China; the Republic of Korea; and Malaysia) to 3.1 per cent in Viet Nam (and also below 20 per cent in India, Pakistan, and the Philippines) from 1966 to 2007 as a whole. The PRC, Indonesia, Taipei,China, and Thailand show intermediate real domestic savings rates during this period. Thus, the ranking order of the 12 countries is roughly the same regardless of whether we look at nominal or real domestic savings rates, with the biggest difference being that the PRC falls from second to fifth when real domestic savings rates are used.

Turning to trends over time, both the nominal domestic savings rate and the real domestic savings rate have shown upward trends from 1966 to 2007 for the 12 developing Asian economies as a whole, increasing from 19.8 per cent (nominal) and 18.8 per cent (real) in 1966–70 to 37.5 per cent (nominal) and 29.4 per cent (real) in 2001–07.

Moreover, the nominal and real domestic savings rates of most individual economies also showed upward trends during all or most of the period 1966–2007. However, there were some exceptions including declines in recent years of the nominal and real domestic savings rates of the Philippines; the nominal domestic savings rate of Hong Kong, China; Indonesia; the Republic of Korea; and Taipei,China; and the real domestic savings rate of Thailand. In addition, the real domestic savings rate of Indonesia has been declining from 1966 to 2007; and the real domestic savings rates of Hong Kong, China, and of Pakistan declined in the early years of that period before turning upward.

Given that the rank ordering of countries and trends over time are broadly similar regardless of whether we use nominal or real domestic savings rates, given that a real measure is preferable from a theoretical point of view, and given that a number of authors, such as Aghion et al. (2009) and Shioji and Vu (2012), have used a real measure of savings, we decided to use the real domestic savings rate as our dependent variable throughout our regression analysis. Note, however, that we also tried using the nominal domestic savings rate and that the results were qualitatively very similar, with the main difference being that the coefficient of the AGE variable (the ratio of the population aged 65 or older to the population aged 15–64) is higher in absolute magnitude when the nominal domestic savings rate is used than when the real domestic savings rate is used.

ESTIMATION RESULTS CONCERNING THE DETERMINANTS OF DOMESTIC SAVINGS RATES IN DEVELOPING ASIA

In this section, we present our estimation results concerning the determinants of domestic savings rates in the 12 developing Asian economies in our sample from 1966 to 2007. This section and the next section are a condensed version of Horioka and Terada-Hagiwara (2012).

We estimated both a country fixed effects model and a random effects model with robust standard errors, and following past studies, such as Bosworth and Chodorow-Reich (2007) and Park and Shin (2009), we use five-year averages (except for the most recent period, which includes the years from 2001 to 2007) in order to eliminate the impact of cyclical fluctuations. Thus, we have a maximum of eight observations per country and a maximum of 78 total observations. The reduced form estimating equation is given by:

$$SR_{i,t} = \beta_{0,i} + \beta_1*AGE_{i,t} + \beta_2*DEP_{i,t} + \beta_3*LNGDP_{i,t} + \beta_4*LNGDPSQ_{i,t}$$

$$+ \beta_5*CREDIT_{i,t} + \beta_6*CREDITSQ_{i,t} + \beta_7*X_{i,t} + u_{i,t}$$

where $i = 1, 2, 3, \ldots 12$ (1 = PRC, 2 = Hong Kong, China, 3 = Indonesia, 4 = India, 5 = the Republic of Korea, 6 = Malaysia, 7 = Pakistan, 8 = the Philippines, 9 = Singapore, 10 = Thailand, 11 = Taipei,China, and

12 – Viet Nam); and $t = 1, 2, 3, \ldots 8$ ($1 = 1966$ 1970, $2 = 1971$–75, $3 = 1976$–80, $4 = 1981$–85, $5 = 1986$–90, $6 = 1991$–95, $7 = 1996$–2000, and $8 = 2001$–07). $SR_{i,t}$ represents the real domestic savings rate in country i at time t; $AGE_{i,t}$ is the aged dependency ratio (the ratio of the population aged 65 or older to the population aged 15–64); $DEP_{i,t}$ is a youth dependency ratio (the ratio of the population aged 14 or younger to the population aged 15–64); $LNGDP_{i,t}$ is the log of per capita real GDP; $LNGDPSQ_{i,t}$ is the square of $LNGDP_{i,t}$, $CREDIT_{i,t}$ is the ratio of private credit from deposit money banks and other financial institutions to GDP; $CREDITSQ_{i,t}$ is the square of $CREDIT_{i,t}$, and $X_{i,t}$ is a vector of the other explanatory variables included in the estimation model. $\beta_{0,i}$ is a constant plus country fixed effects when a fixed effects model is estimated.

Looking first at the impact of the age structure of the population, since the aged typically finance their living expenses by drawing down their previously accumulated savings, AGE, the aged dependency ratio, should have a negative impact on the domestic savings rate. Similarly, since children typically consume without earning income, DEP, the youth dependency ratio, should also have a negative impact on the domestic savings rate.

We also include $LNGDP$, the log of real per capita GDP; $LNGDPSQ$, the square of the log of real per capita GDP; $CREDIT$, a proxy for the level of financial sector development; and $CREDITSQ$, the square of $CREDIT$, as additional explanatory variables to allow for the possibility of a nonlinear relationship between $LNGDP$ and $CREDIT$ and the domestic savings rate. Finally, in some variants, we also include $CHGNP$, the rate of change of real per capita GDP, and $RINT$, the real interest rate.

The country fixed effects results for the basic specification are as follows (the figures in parentheses are t-statistics):

$$SR_{i,t} = 182.03 + I_i - 0.95*AGE_{i,t} - 0.03*DEP_{i,t} - 43.13*LNGDP_{i,t}$$
$$\phantom{SR_{i,t} = 182.03 + I_i}(5.99) \quad\quad (-2.71) \quad\quad (-0.23) \quad\quad (-8.73)$$

$$+ 2.92*LNGDPSQ_{i,t} + 14.48*CREDIT_{i,t} - 6.46*CREDITSQ_{i,t} + u_{i,t}$$
$$(9.24) \quad\quad\quad (2.94) \quad\quad\quad (-3.99)$$

Number of observations: 78
R-squared: within = 0.76, between = 0.61, and overall = 0.70

where $I_i = \{12.75, -11.82, 2.43, -4.87, 5.32, 7.60, -12.91, -7.23, 11.62, 4.16, -5.97, -2.79\}$ for $i = 1, 2, 3, \ldots 12$. As expected, both AGE and DEP have a negative impact on the domestic savings rate, but only the coefficient of AGE is statistically significant. $LNGDP$ has a nonlinear (convex) impact on the domestic savings rate, with its impact being negative at low-income levels and positive at higher-income levels. Conversely, $CREDIT$

has a nonlinear (concave) impact on the domestic savings rate, with its impact being positive at low levels of *CREDIT* and negative at high levels of *CREDIT*.

As for the impact of the other explanatory variables, the coefficient of *CHGDP* was positive in all cases but was statistically significant only in the random effects model, and the coefficient of *RINT* was not statistically significant in any case. Thus, the results for the variants with *RINT* and *CHGDP* are not shown. (See Horioka and Terada-Hagiwara 2012 for the full set of results.)

The results discussed thus far are based on contemporaneous values for all of the explanatory variables, but the variables relating to *LNGDP*, *CREDIT*, and *CHGDP* are endogenous. Thus, using lagged values for these variables would alleviate the endogeneity problem. Using lagged values for *LNGDP*, *LNGDPSQ*, *CREDIT*, and *CREDITSQ* yields the following country fixed effects results for the basic specification (the figures in parentheses are t-statistics):

$$SR_{i,t} = 102.49 + I_i - 1.34*AGE_{i,t} - 0.02*DEP_{i,t}$$
$$\quad\quad\quad (2.00) \quad\quad\quad (-3.33) \quad\quad\quad (-0.09)$$

$$- 24.63*LNGDP_{i,t}(-1) + 1.96*LNGDPSQ_{i,t}(-1)$$
$$\quad (-2.93) \quad\quad\quad\quad (4.17)$$

$$+ 6.70*CREDIT_{i,t}(-1) - 3.51*CREDITSQ_{i,t}(-1) + u_{i,t}$$
$$\quad (1.08) \quad\quad\quad\quad (-1.65)$$

Number of observations: 78
R-squared: within = 0.60, between = 0.59, overall = 0.66

where I_i = {11.05, −7.56, .07, −5.94, 7.26, 6.41, −14.91, −10.43, 13.22, 4.45, −5.56} for i = 1, 2, 3, ... 12. As can be seen from comparing these estimation results to the estimation results without lags, the results are broadly consistent except that the coefficient of *AGE* is considerably larger in absolute magnitude and the coefficients of all of the other explanatory variables are smaller in absolute magnitude in the case of the estimation results with lags.

In summary, the main determinants of the domestic savings rate in developing Asia from 1966 to 2007 appear to have been the age structure of the population (especially the aged dependency ratio), income levels, and the level of financial sector development, and the impacts of income levels and the level of financial sector development appear to have been nonlinear (convex and concave, respectively).

PROJECTIONS OF DOMESTIC SAVINGS RATES IN DEVELOPING ASIA FOR 2011–30

In this section, we discuss our projections of domestic savings rates in the 12 developing Asian economies in our sample for 2011 to 2030. We show only the projections based on the fixed-effects model because, while the results of standard specification tests such as the Hausman test and the Breusch and Pagan Lagrangian multiplier test suggest the use of random-effects models, a test of the joint significance of the country fixed effects rejected the null hypothesis that the coefficients of all of the country fixed effects are zero. Also, comparing out-of-sample projections based on the fixed-effects and random-effects models suggests that the random-effects model does not perform as well as the fixed-effects model in fitting the domestic savings rate for a number of economies such as the PRC, the Republic of Korea, Singapore, Pakistan, and the Philippines. The projections from the random effects models underestimate the savings rates of the former three economies, while overestimating those of the latter two economies. This is consistently true for every random effects model estimated. For the PRC, omitting the country fixed-effect would yield a far lower savings rate of about 24 per cent of GDP for the 2001–07 period – 10 percentage points lower than the actual rate. A possible explanation for the case of the PRC is omitted factors, such as the increase in the corporate savings rate during this period (International Monetary Fund 2009) and/or the distorted sex ratio of those of marrying age (Wei and Zhang 2009). Another example of an obvious deviation of the fitted savings rate from the actual rate is the Philippines. The fitted savings rate based on the random effects model does not show the decline observed in the actual rate. The rapidly increasing coverage of the Social Security System has been suggested as one of the explanations for why this might be (Terada-Hagiwara 2012).

Our projections for the next two decades, 2011–20 and 2021–30, rely on the United Nations projections of the age structure of the population (the aged and youth dependency ratios, median variant) and the GDP projections of Lee and Hong (2012).

Since projections of financial sector development are not available, we assumed that financial deepening progresses according to the level of per capita income. We projected in which World Bank income group each country would belong in 2011–20 and 2021–30 using Lee and Hong's (2012) GDP projections. We then assigned to each country the 2008 value of the financial sector development variable (private credit–GDP ratio) for the income group to which it is projected to belong in each time period. The exception, however, was that for economies in which

Table 5.2   Future trends in real domestic savings rates in developing Asia

Economy	2001–07 Fitted	2011–20 Projected	2021–30 Projected
PRC	31.8	30.3	31.9
Hong Kong, China	29.8	24.3	20.0
Indonesia	24.1	21.6	20.8
India	14.5	14.9	15.9
Korea, Rep. of	42.0	35.5	37.4
Malaysia	44.7	43.7	42.0
Pakistan	6.7	7.0	10.1
Philippines	14.9	12.9	11.8
Singapore	58.7	47.0	40.4
Thailand	31.3	28.6	23.5
Taipei,China	25.1	20.7	15.7
Viet Nam	16.8	19.2	15.4
Developing Asia	27.4	26.3	27.2

Notes:
PRC = People's Republic of China.
Authors' calculation. Refer to the main text for explanation.

the financial sector has already deepened beyond the average value for the income group to which they are projected to belong (the PRC; Hong Kong, China; Taipei,China; and Viet Nam in 2011–20 and these same countries minus the PRC in 2021–30), the financial sector development variable was assumed to remain at the same value as in the recent past (the average value for 2000–07). The average 2008 values of the financial sector development variable for each income group were 130 per cent for the high-income group, 105 per cent for the upper-middle-income group, and 46 per cent for the lower-middle-income group, as shown in Beck and Demirgüç-Kunt (2008). The PRC; Hong Kong, China; the Republic of Korea; Malaysia; Taipei,China; and Singapore are projected to belong to the high-income group; Thailand to the upper-middle-income group; and India, Indonesia, Pakistan, the Philippines, and Viet Nam to the lower-middle-income group by 2021–30.

Savings rate projections were generated for 2011–20 and 2021–30 using the coefficients in the basic country fixed effects model with lags. Table 5.2 shows future projections of domestic savings rates for the 12 economies in our sample, and as can be seen from this table, domestic savings rates in Hong Kong, China; Indonesia; the Republic of Korea; Malaysia; the Philippines; Singapore; Taipei,China; and Thailand are expected to

Table 5.3   Population aging in developing Asia

Economy	Period during which the population aged 65 and older reaches 14% of the total population
PRC	2020–25
Hong Kong, China	2010–15
Indonesia	2040–45
India	2050–55
Korea, Rep. of	2015–20
Malaysia	2040–45
Pakistan	After 2055
Philippines	2050–55
Singapore	2015–20
Thailand	2020–25
Taipei,China	2015–20
Viet Nam	2030–35
Japan	1990–95

Note: PRC = People's Republic of China.

Data source: United Nations' (UN) projections available at http://esa.un.org/unpp, and the Statistical Yearbook for Taipei,China, available at http://www.cepd.gov.tw/encontent/m1.aspx?sNo=0000063.

decrease (except for a slight upturn in the Republic of Korea in 2021–30); that of Viet Nam is expected to increase in 2011–20, then decrease in 2021–30; that of the PRC is expected to remain roughly flat for the next two decades; and that of India and Pakistan are expected to increase (comparisons are being made to fitted values for the 2001–07 period).

While all the developing Asian economies in our sample are projected to post steady growth, the dramatic differences among these economies in projected future trends in their domestic savings rates are not surprising because there is a 40- to 50-year gap in the timing of population aging in the 12 economies in our sample, as can be seen from Table 5.3. As a result of these dramatic differences in the timing of the demographic transition in the coming decades, the decline in domestic savings rates will not occur simultaneously in the economies of developing Asia but will rather be spread out over close to a half-century, with the decline in domestic savings rates in some economies being offset by the increase in domestic savings rates in other economies until at least 2030.

In particular, economies in which population aging is expected to occur the soonest such as Hong Kong, China; the Republic of Korea; Singapore; Taipei,China; and Thailand are projected to show the earliest declines in domestic savings rates. Economies in which population aging is expected to occur neither early nor late, such as Viet Nam, are projected to show an increase in domestic savings rates early on, followed by a decrease. Economies in which population aging is expected to occur the latest, such as India and Pakistan, are projected to show an increase in domestic savings rates at least until 2030. The primary exception is the PRC, where the domestic savings rate is projected to remain roughly constant for the next two decades because the negative impact of population aging is projected to be roughly offset by the positive impact of higher income levels.

Finally, we calculate the historical and projected domestic savings rates of developing Asia as a whole by weighting the domestic savings rates for each economy by its real GDP (see Table 5.2). According to the fixed effects model, the domestic savings rate in developing Asia as a whole is projected to remain roughly constant for the next two decades – averaging 27.4 per cent in 2001–07 (fitted value), 26.3 per cent in 2011–20, and 27.2 per cent in 2021–30. This is because the domestic savings rate in the largest economy in our sample, the PRC, is projected to remain roughly constant over time and because increases in domestic savings rates in economies projected to show increases in their savings rates will be roughly offset by the projected decreases in domestic savings rates in economies projected to show decreases in their savings rates.

The trajectory of the domestic savings rate in developing Asia as a whole appears to be heavily influenced by trends in the PRC, which will account for more than 50 per cent of regional GDP in the next two decades. Thus, any developments in the PRC that affect its domestic savings rate, such as the worsening of its fiscal balance, increases in expenditures on social services and pensions, and/or changes in the speed of population aging, have important ramifications for developing Asia as a whole.

IMPLICATIONS FOR INVESTMENT AND GROWTH IN DEVELOPING ASIA

This chapter has focused so far on past and future trends in domestic savings rates, but whether domestic savings translate into domestic investment depends on the correlation between domestic savings and domestic investment. In this section, we consider the evidence.

Feldstein and Horioka (1980), using cross-country data for 1960 to 1974 for the member countries of the Organisation for Economic Co-operation and Development (OECD), found that the correlation between domestic savings and domestic investment is very high (in the 0.85–0.95 range), implying that most of any marginal increment to domestic savings will be invested domestically. This result generated considerable surprise, with Obstfeld and Rogoff (2000) calling it one of the six major puzzles in international macroeconomics because it was believed that international capital flows had been liberalized over time and that capital now flowed freely across national borders to where the returns were the highest. By contrast, the result from Feldstein and Horioka (1980) suggests that there are barriers to the international flow of capital and/or that investors prefer to invest their funds in their own countries, so-called "home bias," due to exchange rate risk, risk aversion, differences in legal systems, informational asymmetries, etc.

Since the Feldstein–Horioka (1980) study, there have been literally hundreds of studies that have examined savings–investment correlations using different time periods, different samples of countries, different estimation methods, etc., and these studies are summarized by Apergis and Tsoumas (2009) in a comprehensive literature survey. Apergis and Tsoumas conclude that savings–investment correlations have declined over time but are still high and that savings–investment correlations are lower in developing countries than they are in developed countries but that they are high even in developing countries. Thus, the Feldstein and Horioka (1980) result is surprisingly robust and appears to be alive and well.

Turning next to the applicability of the result found by Feldstein and Horioka (1980) to Asia in particular, Kim et al. (2005) examine the *b* coefficient (coefficient of savings) in Feldstein-Horioka-type investment equations in 11 Asian countries using a panel co-integration framework and fully modified and dynamic ordinary least squares (OLS) estimators and find that this coefficient declined from 0.58 to 0.76 in 1960–79 to 0.39 to 0.42 in 1980–98, indicating increasing capital mobility over time.

In another study, Kim and Park (2010) first replicate the Feldstein and Horioka (1980) methodology for 10 East Asian economies (the PRC; Hong Kong, China; Indonesia; the Republic of Korea; Malaysia; the Philippines; Singapore; Taipei,China; Thailand; and Viet Nam), and for these 10 economies plus Japan, and corroborate the finding of earlier studies that the *b* coefficient has declined over time – from 0.63 in the 1980s to 0.51 in the 1990s and thence to 0.35 in the 2000s (or from 0.63 in 1980–94 to 0.38 or 0.39 in 1993–2007 if a rolling regression with a 15-year window is used).

Kim and Park (2010) then extend the framework of Feldstein and Horioka (1980) in an innovative way to enable them to determine whether investment in East Asia is financed by domestic savings, regional savings, and/or global savings. Whereas Feldstein and Horioka (1980) and most subsequent studies regress domestic investment rates only on domestic savings rates, Kim and Park (2010) include not only domestic savings but also regional (Asian) savings (excluding domestic savings) and global (G7) savings (excluding Asian savings) as additional explanatory variables. The results suggest that Japan has played a key role in financing investment in East Asia, inasmuch as the coefficient of regional savings is significant when Japanese savings are included in regional savings but excluded from global savings, the coefficient of global savings is significant when Japanese savings are included in global savings but excluded from regional savings, and the coefficient of Japanese savings is significant if it is included separately. Moreover, the importance of the role played by Japanese savings has increased over time from the 1980s to the 2000s.

To summarize the findings of the literature related to Feldstein and Horioka (1980), capital markets were relatively closed and Asian investment was financed primarily by domestic savings back in the 1980s, but since then capital markets have opened up and external funds, especially from Japan, have played an increasingly important role in financing investment. However, even now, capital markets have not opened up entirely and investment is still financed largely by domestic savings.

What does this imply for future trends in investment and growth in developing Asia? It implies, first of all, that Asian economies need not rely entirely on domestic savings to finance investment and that they can rely on foreign savings, especially Japanese savings, at least to some extent. However, since Japan's domestic savings rate is projected to plummet in the coming years as the aging of its population continues at a rapid pace (see, for example, Horioka 1989, 1992), developing Asia will not be able to continue relying on Japanese savings to finance investment indefinitely. Fortunately, however, our projection that savings in developing Asia as a whole will remain high during the next two decades implies that, even with a decline in Japan's domestic savings rate, a savings shortage will not constrain investment and growth in developing Asia for at least the next two decades.

Moreover, Shioji and Vu (2012) analyze the determinants of the growth rate of the per capita capital stock in the same 12 economies of developing Asia that we look at, and their estimation results imply that domestic investment rates in developing Asia as a whole will decline during the next two decades but that the decline will be moderate except in the PRC. (This decline in domestic investment rates is due primarily to the "convergence effect," whereby investment rates decline as the per capita capital stock approaches the level of more advanced economies.) This further reduces the probability that savings shortages will constrain investment and growth in developing Asia during the next two decades. It also implies that savings–investment imbalances in developing Asia may increase during the next two decades because domestic savings rates will remain high and domestic investment rates will decline, meaning that global imbalances are not likely to be eliminated any time soon and may, in fact, increase even further.

CONCLUSION

In this chapter, we presented data on past trends in domestic savings rates in the 12 major economies of developing Asia from 1966 to 2007, conducted an econometric analysis of the determinants of domestic savings rates in developing Asia during the same time period, projected trends in domestic savings rates in developing Asia during the next two decades based on the results of our econometric analysis, and discussed the implications of our findings for investment, growth, and economic policy in developing Asia.

To summarize our main findings, we found that domestic savings rates have varied greatly from economy to economy and from year to year in the 12 major economies of developing Asia from 1966 to 2007 but that they have been high and rising in most of these economies during most of the period of analysis (1966–2007). We then analyzed the determinants of domestic savings rates in developing Asia from 1966 to 2007 and found that the main determinants of domestic savings rates during this period were the age structure of the population (especially the aged dependency ratio), the level and growth rate of per capita real incomes, and the level of financial sector development. We also found that the direction of impact of each factor was more or less as expected and that the impacts of income levels and the level of financial sector development were nonlinear (convex and concave, respectively).

We then projected future trends in domestic savings rates in developing Asia over the next two decades based on the results of our econometric analysis and found that future trends in domestic savings rates will vary greatly from economy to economy, with economies experiencing population aging sooner showing declines in their domestic savings rates and economies experiencing population aging later showing further increases in their domestic savings rates, and that the domestic savings rate for developing Asia as a whole is expected to remain roughly constant. We then considered the implications of our findings for future investment and growth in developing Asia and concluded that investment and growth in developing Asia will not be constrained by a savings shortage, despite the heavy reliance on Japanese savings in the past and the projected decline in Japan's domestic savings rate, because domestic savings rates in developing Asia as a whole are projected to remain high during the next two decades and because domestic investment rates in developing Asia as a whole are projected to show a moderate decline over the next two decades (Shioji and Vu 2012).

Looking at the implications of our findings for future trends in the current account surpluses of developing Asia, our projection that the real domestic savings rate in developing Asia as a whole will remain roughly constant at its current high level and that domestic investment rates will decline implies that savings–investment imbalances (current account surpluses) will increase even further during the next two decades, implying that global imbalances may not be eliminated any time soon and may, in fact, increase further. However, the global economic recession has reduced the current account surpluses of developing Asia, at least temporarily, and trends in global imbalances during the next decade will depend on how prolonged the global economic recession turns out to be.

Turning finally to the policy implications of our findings, policies to stimulate consumption and investment and to discourage savings might be warranted in the economies of developing Asia if the amelioration of global imbalances is deemed desirable. And specific measures that might stimulate consumption and discourage savings include further financial sector development and improvements in social safety nets.

REFERENCES

Aghion, P. et al. (2009), 'When does domestic saving matter for economic growth?', mimeo, Harvard University.

Apergis, N., and C. Tsoumas (2009), 'A survey of the Feldstein-Horioka puzzle: what has been done and where we stand', *Research in Economics*, **63**, 64–76.

Asian Development Bank (2009), 'Rebalancing Asia's growth', in *Asian Development Outlook 2009*, Manila: Asian Development Bank.

Beck, T., and A. Demirgüç-Kunt (2009), 'Financial institutions and markets across countries and over time: data and analysis', World Bank Policy Research Working Paper No.4943, May, World Bank, Washington, DC.

Bosworth, B., and G. Chodorow-Reich (2007), 'Saving and demographic change: the global dimension', CRR Working Paper 2007-02, Center for Retirement Research, Boston College, Boston, MA.

Feldstein, M., and C.Y. Horioka (1980), 'Domestic saving and international capital flows', *Economic Journal*, **90**, 314–29.

Horioka, C.Y. (1989), 'Why Is Japan's private saving rate so high?', in R. Sato and T. Negishi (eds), *Developments in Japanese Economics*, Tokyo: Academic Press/ Harcourt Brace Jovanovich, pp. 145–78.

Horioka, C.Y. (1992), 'Future trends in Japan's saving rate and the implications thereof for Japan's external imbalance', *Japan and the World Economy*, **3**, 307–30.

Horioka, C.Y., and A. Terada-Hagiwara (2012), 'The determinants and long-term projections of saving rates in developing Asia', *Japan and the World Economy*, **24**, 128–37.

International Monetary Fund (IMF) (2005), 'Global imbalances: a saving and investment perspective', in International Monetary Fund (ed.), *World Economic Outlook 2005*, Washington, DC: IMF.

International Monetary Fund (2009), 'Corporate savings and rebalancing in Asia', in International Monetary Fund (ed.), *World Economic and Financial Surveys, Regional Economic Outlook, Asia and Pacific 2009*, Washington, DC: IMF.

International Monetary Fund (Various issues), International Financial Statistics, Washington, DC: IMF.

Kim, S.H., and C.Y. Park (2010), 'International capital mobility of East Asian countries: is domestic investment financed by regional or global saving?', mimeo, Seoul National University, Seoul, Republic of Korea.

Kim, H., K.-Y. Oh, and C.-W. Jeong (2005), 'Panel cointegration results on international capital mobility in Asian economies', *Journal of International Money and Finance*, **24**, 71–82.

Lee, J.-W., and K. Hong (2012), 'Economic growth in Asia: determinants and prospects', *Japan and the World Economy*, **24**, 101–13.

Obstfeld, M., and K. Rogoff (2000), 'The six major puzzles in international macroeconomics: is there a common cause?', in *NBER Macroeconomics Annual*, **15**, 340–90.

Park, D., and K. Shin (2009), 'Saving, investment, and current account surplus in developing Asia', ADB Economics Working Paper Series No.158, Asian Development Bank, Manila, Philippines.

Shioji, E., and T.K. Vu (2012), 'Physical capital accumulation in Asia-12: past trends and future projections', *Japan and the World Economy*, **24**, 138–49.

Terada-Hagiwara, A. (2012), 'Have Filipino households become less prudent?', *Journal of Development Studies*, **48**, 673–85.

Wei, C.J., and X. Zhang (2009), 'The competitive saving motive: evidence from rising sex ratios and savings rates in [the People's Republic of] China', NBER Working Paper No.15093, National Bureau of Economic Research, Inc., Cambridge, MA.

World Bank (various issues), *World Development Indicators*, Washington, DC: World Bank.

6. Finance

Shin-ichi Fukuda

INTRODUCTION

Most Asian economies achieved remarkable economic growth during the so-called East Asian Miracle, the period of rapid growth that preceded the Asian financial crisis (AFC). That growth was accompanied by high investment ratios that brought substantial capital accumulation to Asia in the 1980s and the first half of the 1990s. However, the AFC not only caused a temporary slowdown of the growth rates but also the persistent stagnation of capital accumulation. Investments that had plummeted in the late 1990s remained low in the following decade. With the exception of the Philippines, investment ratios had experienced significant upward trends before 1997. However, those ratios dropped sharply after 1998, with the exception of the People's Republic of China (PRC) and Viet Nam, and showed only modest recovery in the 2000s. The modest recovery in investment ratios is in marked contrast with Asian savings rates that remained high both before and after the AFC. This chapter explores how financial development was linked to such investment stagnation in Asia.

The AFC began with the currency crisis in Thailand in July 1997 and quickly spread to other Asian countries. Several economists pointed to the vulnerability of Asian financial systems as largely responsible for the crisis, arguing that those systems had fundamental problems of organization and supervision, with implicit government guarantees creating an inefficient allocation of funds that helped deepen the crisis. Responding to the critics, most Asian countries accelerated the speed of liberalization of their financial systems and institutions after the AFC. The liberalization was based on the idea that "crony capitalism" produced obstacles in transforming high saving rates to high investment rates.

In terms of sources of financing, most Asian emerging economies traditionally relied heavily on either bank lending or internal markets. Bond and stock markets had been less developed in these economies until the 1990s. After the AFC, many Asian emerging economies substantially changed these traditional financial systems. Accompanied by a series of liberalization steps, the role of open markets increased dramatically in these economies after the year 2000. At the same time, the financial sector saw greater profitability and a decline in nonperforming loans in most Asian economies. However, despite the reforms and the improved performance of the financial sector, investment rates remained low after 2000. And the persistent stagnation of capital accumulation continued even though Asian economies enjoyed a substantial recovery. One of the reasons for the stagnant investment climate might have been the "precautionary motives" of Asian economies to insure against the risk of another crisis.[1] The motives may explain temporary investment stagnation immediately after the crisis, but they cannot explain persistent stagnation after that period. It is important to consider why the accelerated liberalization of financial systems failed to increase capital accumulation in Asia.

In light of these perspectives, this chapter first explores how traditional proxies of financial development progressed in Asia after the AFC. Even though most Asian countries liberalized their financial systems and institutions, they could not improve traditional proxies of financial development. Except for the Republic of Korea, the movements of the domestic credit ratios coincided with both the upward trend and the decline of the investment ratios before and after the AFC. Regression results support the view that the failure of traditional financial development might be responsible for the persistent stagnation of capital accumulation after the AFC. Case studies in the Republic of Korea and Thailand provide evidence that loans for the manufacturing sector play an important role in enhancing investment. The results also indicate that in many Asian countries, the traditional policy of promoting bank loans might still be desirable in enhancing investment.

Since Gerschenkron's pioneering study in 1962, an important research topic has involved the study of the most desirable form financial markets should take to promote economic growth. With regard to the effects of financial market liberalization on development, there are conflicting views in the literature.[2] Neoclassical theories propose that liberalization should promote economic growth. In particular, McKinnon (1973) and Shaw (1973) suggest that the development of financial intermediation with few regulations will lead to the increased efficiency of the intertemporal allocation of resources and will provide liquidity to the whole economy. Various models support the view that the development of a financial intermediation system with few regulations will help transform savings in the whole economy to more productive and illiquid assets, as well as promote capital accumulation. Several criticisms of traditional Asian financial systems and financial liberalization were based on these models.

It is probably true that the development of a less-regulated financial market will increase the efficiency of resource allocations when the legal system is sophisticated, the accounting system is transparent, and the disciplines imposed on companies by outside organizations function well. However, neither the legal system nor the accounting system is transparent in most developing countries. In these countries, government needs to intervene in transactions in the financial market and in personal transactions. This is the case in many Asian countries. Although such interventions sometimes have resulted in inefficient allocation due to noneconomic factors such as corruption, policies to promote less regulated financial markets were not necessarily successful in enhancing the economic growth in many Asian countries.

McKinnon insists that it would be better to regulate financial markets if market failures were caused by defective legal and/or accounting systems. Authors such as Stiglitz (1994) and McKinnon and Pill (1996) have proposed some concepts that argue against financial liberalization. In particular, Helleman et al. (2000) provide a theoretical framework to support the case for having less liberalized bank-based financial systems. They suggest that the bank rent created through moderate policy intervention may promote economic growth in developing countries because the banking rent will provide an incentive for private banks to undertake actions to promote development. The view is consistent with the fact that Asia achieved remarkable economic growth under regulated financial systems. The empirical results in this chapter suggest that this might still be true in many of the Asian countries even after the AFC.

Allen and Gale (2000) argue that a country's current development phase and its historical background help determine what financial system is most desirable. For countries that have frontier technology, it is preferable to raise funds through open markets, such as bond and stock markets, rather than through bank lending. However, for countries that import foreign technologies, it is more desirable to use bank lending for reasons of both information-production and risk diversification. For emerging countries that import technologies from developed countries, it is important to monitor how efficiently the introduced techniques and skills are utilized without generating moral hazard. Through repeated monitoring, banks as delegated monitors or personal connections may produce better information than open markets. Even after the AFC, most Asian countries might be in a stage of development that calls for a traditional policy of promoting bank loans.

In the literature, a large number of studies emphasize the positive influence of the development of a country's financial sector on the level and the rate of growth of its per capita income. (See, among others, King and Levine 1993; Levine 1997; and Rajan and Zingales 1998). However,

Levine and Zervos (1998) find that measures of open market development, such as stock market size, are not as robustly correlated with growth and capital accumulation, while bank lending to the private sector has a strong independent effect on growth. The empirical findings in this chapter imply that the proposition of Levine and Zervos is relevant in most of the post-crisis Asian countries.

The next section of this chapter examines how traditional indicators of financial development have contributed to capital accumulation in Asian countries. The chapter then examines the same issue using alternative types of indicators. That discussion is followed by case studies of the Republic of Korea and Thailand. Finally, there is a summary of the chapter's main results and their implications.

THE ROLE OF TRADITIONAL INDICATORS

Traditional Indicators of Financial Development

There are costs and benefits associated with liberalized financial systems. In the following two sections, there is a consideration of how financial development contributed to capital accumulation in Asian countries. While there are active debates on how to measure the degree of financial development, a number of previous empirical studies examined whether financial development promoted economic development. Due to the limited availability of data, earlier studies used crude proxies to measure the degree of financial development. In this section, we focus on three crude but traditional proxies that were widely used in the literature.

The first measure of financial development is the ratio of M2 to gross domestic product (GDP). Money plus quasi money (M2), which is obtained from the International Financial Statistics (IFS) of the International Monetary Fund (IMF) line 35L, comprises the sum of currency outside banks, demand deposits, time savings, and foreign currency deposits of resident sectors. It is a broader notion of financial development in that it covers not only corresponding changes in loans but also changes in securities investments and other assets other than cash and deposits. The second measure of financial development is the ratio of domestic credit to GDP. Domestic credit, which is obtained from line 32 of the IFS, includes credit extended to the private sector, general government, and the nonfinancial public sector, as well as loans to state enterprises. Although it is a narrower notion than M2, it includes credit to the public sectors, which is far from negligible in emerging markets. In order to exclude credit to the public sectors, the literature often used the claims on the private

(a) M2/gross domestic product (GDP)

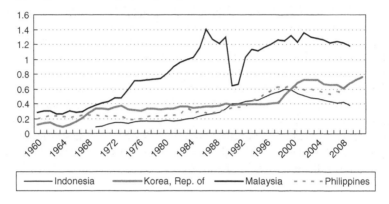

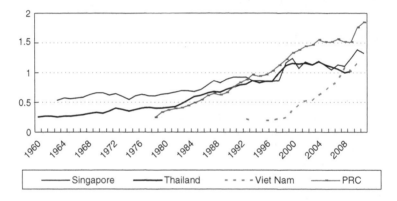

Note: PRC = People's Republic of China.

Sources: International Financial Statistics, International Monetary Fund.

Figure 6.1   Indicators of financial development in Asian countries

sector (IFS line 32D) as the third measure. This includes gross credit from
the financial system to individuals, enterprises, nonfinancial public entities not included under net domestic credit, and financial institutions not
included elsewhere.

   Figure 6.1 shows how these indicators changed in selected Asian countries
(the PRC, Indonesia, the Republic of Korea, Malaysia, the Philippines,
Singapore, Thailand, and Viet Nam) from 1960 to 2010. Except for the
Philippines, the ratio of domestic credit to GDP and the ratio of the claims
on the private sector to GDP showed remarkable upward trends before 1997.

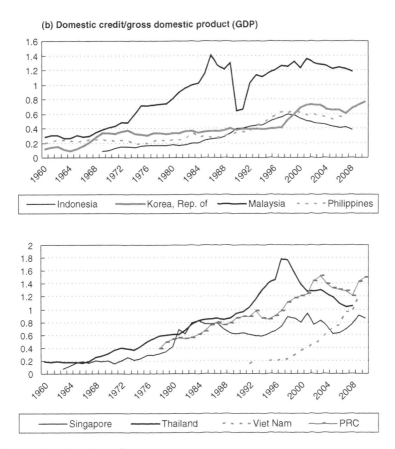

Figure 6.1 (continued)

In particular, the ratios in Indonesia, Malaysia, and Thailand increased dramatically in the 1990s before the AFC. However, except for the PRC, the Republic of Korea and Viet Nam, the ratios dropped sharply in the late 1990s and showed only modest recovery after 2000. This implies that even though most Asian countries accelerated liberalization of their financial systems after the crisis, they could not improve the traditional indicators of financial development as they did before. More interestingly, except for the Republic of Korea, the movements of the domestic credit ratios coincided with both the upward and downward trends of the investment ratios before and after the crisis. This suggests that except for the PRC and Viet Nam, the failure of the traditional financial development might be responsible for the persistent stagnation of capital accumulation after the AFC.

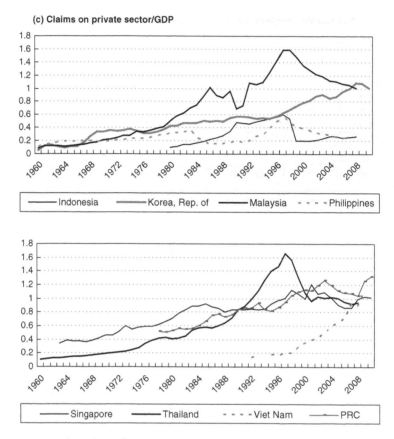

Figure 6.1   (continued)

The essential results still hold even using the ratio of M2 to GDP: in this case, the upward trend before the AFC was more dramatic in Malaysia, Singapore, and Thailand than in Indonesia, the Republic of Korea, and the Philippines. But they moved closely with the upward trend of the investment ratios during the same period. Unlike domestic credit and claims on the private sector, the ratio of M2 to GDP did not show a substantial decline after the AFC. But except for the PRC and Viet Nam, the upward trend ended after the crisis. This also supports the view that the failure of traditional financial development might be responsible for the persistent stagnation of capital accumulation after the AFC.

Regression Results

As described above, even though most Asian countries accelerated liberalization of their financial systems after the AFC, they could not improve the traditional proxies of financial development as they did before. In particular, the failure of traditional financial development might be responsible for the persistent stagnation of capital accumulation after the crisis. This chapter will now explore empirically how traditional proxies of financial development were linked with the investment ratios in selected Asian countries (Indonesia, the Republic of Korea, Malaysia, the Philippines, Singapore, and Thailand). The selected countries are those whose investment ratios had remarkable upward trends before 1997 but stagnated after the AFC. By using the panel data, we estimate the following equation:

$$I_{i,t}/Y_{i,t} = \text{constant} + \Sigma_j \, \alpha_j \, X(j)_{i,t} + \Sigma_k \, \beta_k \, Z(k)_{i,t}, \qquad (6.1)$$

where $I_{i,t}/Y_{i,t}$ = investment ratio in country i in period t, $X(j)_{i,t}$ = a proxy j for financial development in country i in period t, and $Z(k)_{i,t}$ = a macro variable k that may affect the investment ratio in country i in period t.

The annual data of the Asian countries are then pooled and an estimate is derived for the fixed effect models. For each proxy for financial development $X(j)_{i,t}$, we use the ratio of M2 to GDP ($M2/Y$), the ratio of the claims on the private sector to GDP ($Claim/Y$), and the ratio of domestic credit to GDP ($Credit/Y$). The difference between ($Credit/Y$) and ($Claim/Y$) is also used to capture the effect of credits to the non-private sector. For each macro variable $Z(k)_{i,t}$, we assume the accelerator model and use the change of logged GDP ($Log(Y/Y(-1))$) as an independent variable. To control outliers, we include an AFC dummy variable that is equal to 1 for year of 1998 and 0 otherwise. To correct simultaneous bias and serial correlation, we estimate the generalized methods of moment (GMM) by using instruments of one-period lag of all dependent and independent variables except for the dummy variable.

Unless the data are not available, the sample period is from 1962 to 2010. The White cross-section standard errors and covariance was used to calculate t-values. Table 6.1 summarizes the regression results. When only a single proxy for financial development was included, each proxy took a significantly positive coefficient. This suggests that each traditional proxy is a good indicator to link financial development and investment in the Asian countries. When multiple proxies are included, the coefficient of *Claim/GDP* was significantly positive in all of the countries. The coefficient of *Credit/GDP* was significantly positive except for the case that

Table 6.1   Determinants of the investments

	Coefficient	t-statistic	Coefficient	t-statistic	Coefficient	t-statistic
Constant	0.082	2.672	0.115	4.495	0.198	7.067
Claim/Y	0.147	7.579				
Credit/Y			0.120	6.546		
M2/Y					0.074	2.523
Dlog(Y)	0.800	4.131	0.606	3.855	0.181	1.417
dummy(1998)	−0.019	−1.642	−0.016	−1.306	−0.004	−0.38
sample periods	1962–2010		1962–2010		1962–2010	
observations	264		266		266	
Constant	0.136	4.623	0.085	2.785	0.085	2.785
Claim/Y	0.167	2.723	0.232	3.864	0.149	7.704
Credit/Y	0.193	2.663	−0.083	−1.518		
M2/Y	−0.304	−6.845				
(Credit − Claim)/Y					−0.083	−1.518
Dlog(Y)	0.804	4.529	0.793	4.071	0.793	4.071
dummy(1998)	−0.028	−2.998	−0.02	−1.775	−0.02	−1.775
sample periods	1962–2010		1962–2010		1962–2010	
observations	264		266		266	

Notes:
(a)   *Claim/Y* = the ratio of the claims on private sector to gross domestic product (GDP), *Credit/Y* = the ratio of domestic credit to GDP, *M2/Y* = the ratio of M2 to GDP, *(Credit − Claim)/Y* = the difference between *Credit/Y* and *Claim/Y*, *DLog(Y)* = logged difference of GDP, and *dummy(1998)* = year dummy of 1998.
(b)   To avoid simultaneous bias, we use instruments of one-period lag of all dependent and independent variables except for the dummy variable.
(c)   To make the regressions heteroscedasticity and autocorrelation consistent, the White cross-section standard errors and covariance was used to calculate *t*-values.

Source: Estimates by the author.

Claim/GDP was used as an additional independent variable. In contrast, when the other proxy is included for $X(j)_{i,t}$, the coefficient of *M2/GDP* turned negative.

Even when the difference between *Credit/GDP* and *Claim/GDP* was included, the coefficient of *Claim/GDP* was significantly positive. But the difference between *Credit/GDP* and *Claim/GDP* had a negative coefficient. This implies that while increased credits to the private sector enhance investment, increased credits to the non-private sector may discourage investment.

THE ROLE OF ALTERNATIVE INDICATORS

Alternative Indicators of Financial Development

This chapter has already considered how the traditional indicators of financial development were useful in explaining capital accumulation in Asian countries. Due to limited data availability, the traditional indicators have been widely used in the literature. However, they are crude proxies to measure the degree of financial development. Consequently, recent studies tend to use alternative types of indicators to measure the degree of financial development. These include (i) indicators to measure development of stock and bond markets, (ii) indicators to measure performance of the banking sector, and (iii) indicators to measure institutional development.

These indicators tend to face more serious missing data problems in emerging and less-developed economies. Even if available, they are available only in recent years. However, we can obtain various indicators of the first and second types from the data set of Beck and Demirgüç-Kunt (2009) and its updated version and from the database of World Bank's *Global Development Finance*. We can also obtain indicators of the third type in the database of Abiad et al. (2010). Based on these data sets, this section investigates how these alternative types of indicators of financial development were useful in explaining capital accumulation in Asian countries.

In the following analysis, we use "stock market capitalization as a % of GDP" and "private bond market capitalization as a % of GDP" for the first type indicators (Figure 6.2), and "Bank Return On Assets (ROA)" and "nonperforming loan (NPL) ratios (%)" for the second type of indicators (Figure 6.3) for seven East Asian countries (the PRC, Indonesia, the Republic of Korea, Malaysia, the Philippines, Singapore, and Thailand). Although we see short-term fluctuations, Figure 6.2 shows that both of the first type of indicators had upward trends. In particular, most Asian countries experienced remarkable increases in stock market capitalization in the 1990s and accelerated growth rates after 2000. The indicator of private bond market capitalization, in contrast, had heterogeneous growth rates across the Asian countries. The Republic of Korea and Malaysia had higher private bond market capitalization, while Indonesia had small private bond market capitalization even after 2000.

Figure 6.3 shows that most Asian countries experienced substantial improvement in banking sector performance after 2000. Because of the AFC, most Asian banks suffered enormous losses in 1998. Consequently, bank returns on assets in 1998 had large negative values in Indonesia, the Republic of Korea, and Thailand. Except in the Republic of Korea and Singapore, the NPL ratios exceeded 10 per cent in the early 2000s.

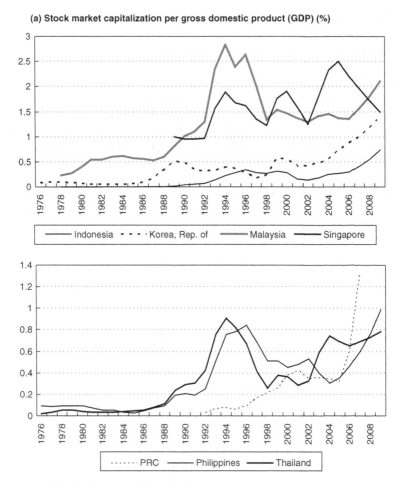

(a) Stock market capitalization per gross domestic product (GDP) (%)

Note: PRC = People's Republic of China.

Source: Data set of Beck and Demirgüç-Kunt (2009) and its updated version.

Figure 6.2   Alternative indicators I: stock and bond markets

However, the NPL ratios declined steadily throughout after 2000 and remained low even during the recent global economic recession (GER). Except in Thailand, bank returns on assets recovered in Asian countries. The improved ratios indicate that most Asian countries succeeded in improving banking sector performance.

Figure 6.4 depicts the third type of indicator to measure institutional development in the financial sector and takes into account different

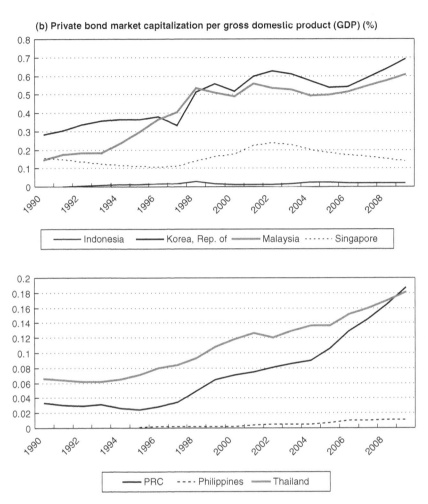

(b) Private bond market capitalization per gross domestic product (GDP) (%)

Figure 6.2   (continued)

dimensions of financial sector policy. Abiad et al. (2010) examined various reforms in the financial sector and constructed an extensive database of the sector. The dimensions they took into account were credit controls, interest rate controls, entry barriers, privatization in the banking sector, capital accounts restrictions, banking supervision, and securities market policy. Scoring the degree of each dimension, they constructed an aggregate index of financial liberalization from 1973 to 2005. The figure depicts the aggregate index for Asian countries. It suggests that the financial sector is most liberalized in Singapore and least liberalized in the PRC

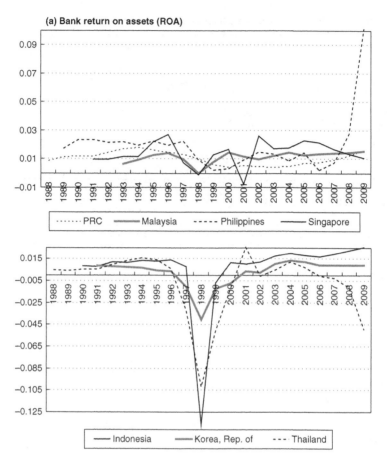

Note: PRC = People's Republic of China.

Source: Data set of Beck and Demirgüç-Kunt (2009) and its updated version.

Figure 6.3   Alternative indicators II: bank performance

and Viet Nam. But most Asian countries experienced substantial financial market reforms in the 1980s and 1990s, and their degree of financial liberalization remained high in the 2000s.

Regression Results

This section has explored alternative types of indicators to measure the degree of financial development and found that many Asian countries

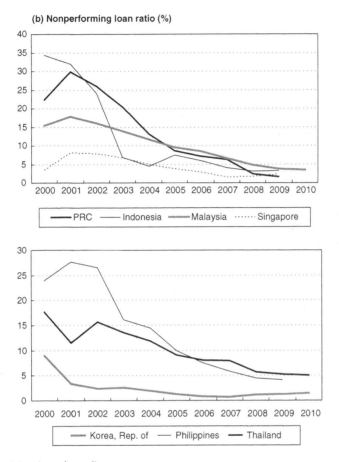

Figure 6.3 (continued)

improved these alternative indicators in the 2000s. The results are in marked contrast with those in the previous section because these countries failed to improve traditional financial development after the AFC. Now, this section examines how alternative types of indicators were linked with the investment ratios in selected Asian countries that had achieved remarkable growth before 1997 but stagnated after the AFC. As in the previous section, we estimate equation (6.1) by using the panel data of Indonesia, the Republic of Korea, Malaysia, the Philippines, Singapore, and Thailand. Because of the limited data availability, the sample period is shorter than that in the previous section.

Except for using alternative proxies for $X(j)_{i,t}$, the explanatory variables

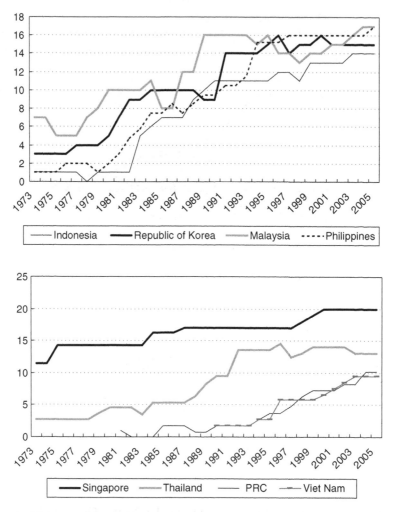

Note: PRC = People's Republic of China.

Source: Database of Abiad et al. (2010).

Figure 6.4   Alternative indicators III: index of financial liberalization

are essentially the same. In the baseline equation, we use the ratio of the claims on the private sector to GDP (*Claim/Y*). We then add one of three alternative types of indicators for $X(j)_{i,t}$. That is, we add either: (i) indicators to measure development of stock and bond markets ("stock market capitalization per GDP (*SMKTCap/Y*)" and "private bond market

Table 6.2   The role of alternative indicators

	Coefficient	t-statistic	Coefficient	t-statistic
Constant	–0.032	–0.435	–0.149	–0.811
Claim/Y	0.204	3.387	0.350	2.808
SMKTCap/Y	–0.04	–1.294	–0.07	–1.085
BMTCap/Y			–0.336	–1.593
Dlog(Y)	1.664	4.122	2.675	2.542
dummy(1998)	–0.011	–0.662	–0.018	–0.306
sample periods	1977–2009		1991–2009	
observations	174		103	
Constant	–0.35	–1.741	0.175	2.946
Claim/Y	0.316	3.459	0.093	3.506
ROA	–4.775	–1.234		
ADT index			–0.013	–0.252
Dlog(Y)	4.003	2.351	0.478	1.675
dummy(1998)	–0.229	–1.276	–0.025	–1.603
sample periods	1989–2009		1974–2005	
observations	107		185	

Notes:
(a)   *SMKTCap/Y* = the ratio of stock market capitalization to GDP, *BMTCap/Y* = the ratio of private bond market capitalization to GDP, *ROA* = bank ROA (return on assets), and *ADT index* = the indicator to measure institutional development in the financial sector. The definitions of the other explanatory variables are the same as those in Table 6.1.
(b)   To avoid simultaneous bias, we use instruments of one-period lag of all dependent and independent variables except for the dummy variable.
(c)   To make the regressions heteroscedasticity and autocorrelation consistent, the White cross-section standard errors & covariance was used to calculate *t*-values.

Source: Estimates by the author.

capitalization per GDP (*BMTCap/Y*)"); (ii) an indicator to measure performance of the banking sector ("Bank ROA (*ROA*)"); or (iii) an index to measure institutional development (the aggregate index of Abiad et al. that was normalized between 0 and 1 [*ADT index*]) to the baseline equation. As in the previous section, we include the AFC dummy variable for year of 1998 (*dummy[1998]*) and estimate GMM by using instruments of a one-period lag of all dependent and independent variables, except for the dummy variable.

Table 6.2 summarizes the regression results of the fixed effect models. Because of the limited data availability, the sample periods become shorter when including the alternative types of indicators. However, the inclusion of the additional indicators and the shortened sample period did not change the essential results in our baseline equation. In particular, the coefficient of *Claim/GDP* was significantly positive. In contrast, all of the additional indicators took a negative coefficient. Among the indicators, the coefficient of "private bond market capitalization/GDP" was marginally significant, but the others were far from statistically significant. This suggests that unlike the traditional indicators, the alternative types might not be good indicators of the link between financial development and investment in the Asian countries.

CASE STUDIES: THAILAND AND THE REPUBLIC OF KOREA

Thailand

The last two sections of this chapter demonstrated that credit to the private sector serve as a good indicator of the link between financial development and investment in Asian countries, although increased credits to the non-private sector are likely to discourage investment. They also showed that indicators might not serve as a link between financial development and investment in Asia. Although the results seem plausible, they were estimated only with the fixed effects that may not capture all of the country-specific features. In general, financial development should be related to how a variety of intermediaries and markets perform the evaluation, monitoring, certification, communication, and distribution functions in each economy. In particular, it is important to clarify why a series of financial liberalization measures did not improve the traditional proxies for financial development in most post-crisis Asian countries. By using a more detailed data set in the Republic of Korea and Thailand, this section strives to answer the question.

In Thailand, securities markets have become as important as loan markets as a source of financing in the 2000s. However, this does not necessarily mean that security markets played as important a role as loan markets in funneling investment into more productive sectors. Figure 6.5 presents the amount of new issuances of securities and their components in Thailand from 1992 to 2010. Unlike the traditional proxies, these proxies have displayed an increase in the 2000s. The total amount of new domestic issues of securities, which was 0.83 trillion baht in 2000, increased to 2.62 trillion baht in 2005 and to 13.93 trillion baht in 2010. Data suggest that the development of securities markets was dramatic in the 2000s, especially in the latter part of the first decade. Looking at the components of new issuances of domestic securities, it appears that public securities, especially

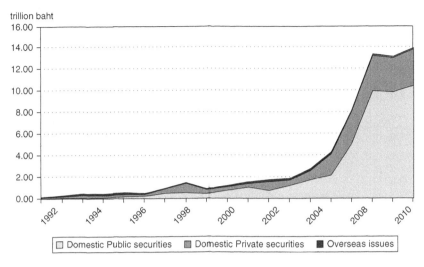

trillion baht

Source: Bank of Thailand.

Figure 6.5   New issuances of securities and their components in Thailand

monetary authority bonds, explain about 75 per cent of new issuances in 2010. But even the amount of new issuances of private securities, which was 0.38 trillion baht in 2000, increased to 3.40 trillion baht in 2010.

Figure 6.6 shows the amount of new issuances of private securities and their components in Thailand from 1992 to 2010. The figure suggests that debt securities and unit trusts are two driving forces increasing the amount of new issuances of private securities. However, when we look into new issuances of private securities by sector, substantial increases occurred mainly because the financial sector increased new issuances of securities in the first decade of the 2000s, particularly in the latter part. Figure 6.7 shows the shares of new domestic private securities issuances classified by type of business in 2005 and 2010, for both debt and equity issues. In the case of new debt issue, the financial intermediation sector had over 50 per cent of shares in both 2005 and 2010. The share of the financial intermediation sector increased from 52 per cent to 68 per cent in the latter part of the first decade of the 2000s. On the other hand, the share of the manufacturing sector declined from 19 per cent in 2005 to 8 per cent in 2010. The results suggest that new issuances of private securities occurred mainly in the financial sector rather than in the manufacturing sector.

In the case of new equity issuances, the dominance of the financial sector was less dramatic. For example, in 2005 the share of the financial intermediation sector was 27 per cent, while the share of the production

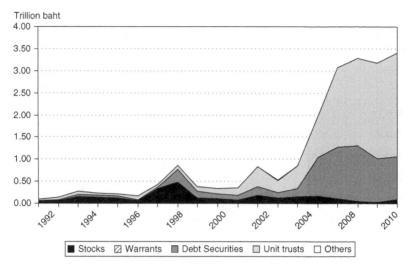

Trillion baht

Source: Bank of Thailand.

*Figure 6.6   New issuances of private securities and their components in
              Thailand*

sector was 49 per cent. This implies that new private equities were issued
more in the manufacturing sector than in the financial sector in 2005.
However, in 2010 the manufacturing sector decreased its share to 20 per
cent and the financial intermediation decreased its share to 7 per cent. In
contrast, the transportation sector increased its share to 19 per cent. More
importantly, the real estate sector increased its share to 49 per cent and
became the largest sector in Thailand in terms of new equities issued in
2010. The results imply that private securities and equity issues did not
contribute to increasing investment in the manufacturing sector. Bank
lending and internal markets continued to play a major role as sources of
finance for the Thai manufacturing sector even in the 2000s.

    If the financial intermediation sector lends money to the manufacturing
sector, the money raised by private securities and/or equities would eventually flow into the manufacturing sector. But this type of intermediation
was rather limited in the 2000s. Figure 6.8 shows changes of all commercial bank credits classified by type of business in Thailand. It shows that
bank credits to manufacturing sector, which was 1.28 billion baht in the
first quarter of 2004, increased to 1.60 billion baht in the third quarter of
2010. Although the increases were significant, they were much smaller
than those of debt securities issued by the financial sector during the same
period. The banking, finance, insurance and leasing sectors, which issued

(a) Private debt

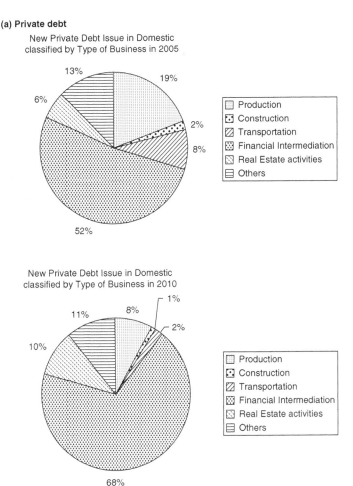

Source: Bank of Thailand.

Figure 6.7 Shares of new domestic private securities issue in Thailand

27 billion baht of debt securities in 2004, issued 989 billion baht of debt securities in 2008, and 552 billion baht in 2010. The amount far exceeded bank credits during the same period. In addition, the figure suggests that even in commercial bank credits, the manufacturing sector is no longer the dominant destination. Financial intermediation and personal consumption became one of the most important destinations of commercial bank credits in 2010. This also coincided with the persistent stagnation of capital accumulation in Thailand after the AFC.

(b) Private equity

New Private Equity Issue in Domestic classified by
Type of Business in 2005

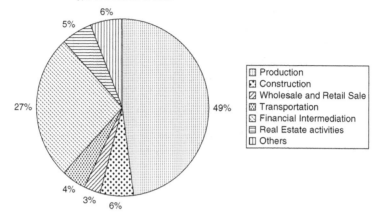

New Private Equity Issue in Domestic classified by
Type of Business in 2010

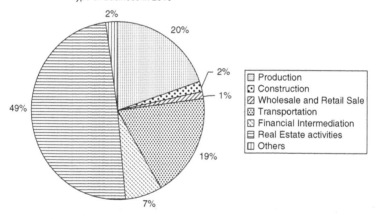

Figure 6.7   (continued)

The Republic of Korea

The Republic of Korea is one of the Asian countries that accelerated liberalization of its financial systems most aggressively after the AFC. But
like most other Asian countries, it also suffered from persistent stagnation of capital accumulation after the crisis. Its investment ratio (gross
fixed capital formation/GDP), which was 0.37 in 1996, dropped sharply
after the crisis and stayed around 0.29 throughout the early 2000s. As in

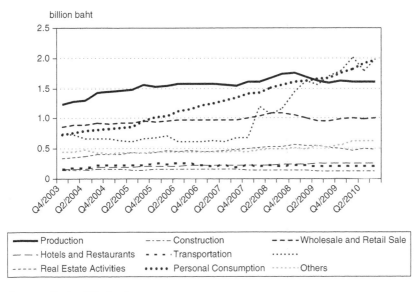

Source: Bank of Thailand.

Figure 6.8 *Commercial bank credits classified by type of business in Thailand*

the other Asian countries, the M2–GDP ratio declined in the Republic of Korea after the crisis. This shows that traditional financial development stagnated in the country after the crisis. But unlike the situation in the other Asian countries, the ratio of domestic credit to GDP and the ratio of the claims on the private sector to GDP increased significantly after the AFC. Unlike in the other Asian countries, some of the traditional proxies in the Republic of Korea continued to show further development after the crisis.

Figure 6.9 shows the number of listings and the volume of transactions in the country's stock markets from 1974 to 2010. In terms of the number of listings, there is a significant upward trend throughout the period. In particular, the number of listed issues and listed corporations had a big jump in the late 1980s and showed only modest increases after that. The volume of transactions, in contrast, showed dramatic changes after the AFC. Even before the crisis, the volume of transactions grew steadily. Total trading volume, which was 0.16 billion shares in 1974, rose to 5.56 billion shares in 1985 and to 11.01 billion shares in 1994. But it was in 1998 and 1999 that the growth rates of total market capitalization, total trading volume, and total trading value, showed dramatic acceleration.

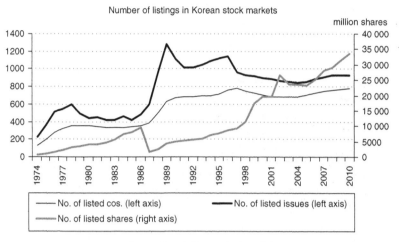

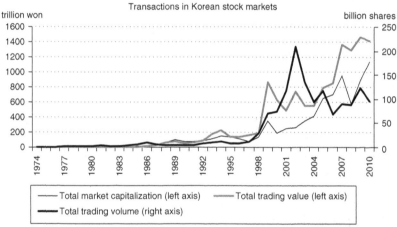

Source: Economic Statistics System (ECOS) in the Republic of Korea.

Figure 6.9   *Number of listings and volume of transactions in Korean stock*
markets

For example, total trading volume, which was 7.79 billion shares in 1996,
rose to 73.79 billion shares in 2000, and to 209.17 billion shares in 2002.
Despite some ups and downs, the dramatic increases continued throughout the early 2000s. The results suggest that there was substantial development in stock markets in the Republic of Korea after the AFC.

However, financial development was not observed in bond markets.
Figure 6.10 shows the number of listings and the volume of transactions

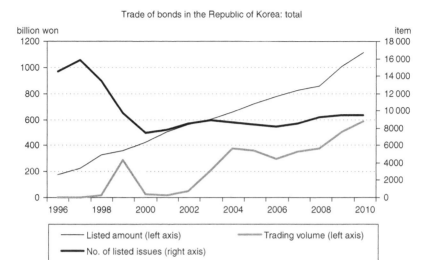

Trade of bonds in the Republic of Korea: total

— Listed amount (left axis) ———— Trading volume (left axis)
—— No. of listed issues (right axis)

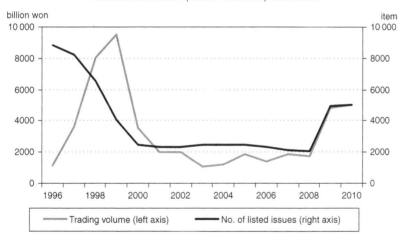

Trade of bonds in the Republic of Korea: corporate bonds

——— Trading volume (left axis) —— No. of listed issues (right axis)

Source: Economic Statistics System (ECOS) in the Republic of Korea.

Figure 6.10   *Number of listings and volume of transactions in Korean bond markets*

in bond markets in the Republic of Korea from 1996 to 2010. Unlike the stock markets, the bond markets show no significant upward trend. The listed amount in total, both public bonds and corporate bonds, showed steady increases throughout the period. But this is rather exceptional.

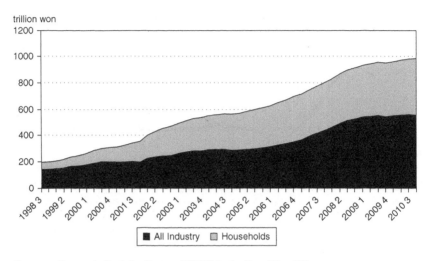

trillion won

Source: Economic Statistics System (ECOS) in the Republic of Korea.

Figure 6.11   The amount of loans and discounts outstanding by Korean banks

Even in total, the number of listed issues dropped sharply during the AFC and remained almost constant throughout the early 2000s. The stagnation was more conspicuous for corporate bonds. Trading volume of corporate bonds, which exceeded 9 trillion won in 1999, dropped below 2 trillion won in 2001, and remained low before a degree of recovery in 2009.

The degree of financial development in credit markets in the Republic of Korea fell somewhere between that of stock markets and bond markets. Figure 6.11 shows the amount of loans and discounts outstanding by commercial and specialized banks from the first quarter of 1998 to the fourth quarter of 2010. The total amount of loans and discounts, which was less than 200 trillion won in 1998, rose steadily throughout the early 2000s and exceeded 9000 trillion won in 2008. However, the increases were largely attributable to increased loans to households. The share of loans to households in total loans and discounts, which was 27 per cent in 1998, exceeded 40 per cent in 2001, and became almost 50 per cent in 2005. The increased loans to households may explain why the increased domestic credits did not enhance the investment ratios in the Republic of Korea after the crisis.

Figure 6.12 shows the changes in the amount of loans and discounts outstanding by industry from the first quarter of 1998 to the fourth quarter of 2010. It shows that bank credits to the manufacturing sector, which were 68 trillion won in 1998, exceeded 200 trillion won in 2010.

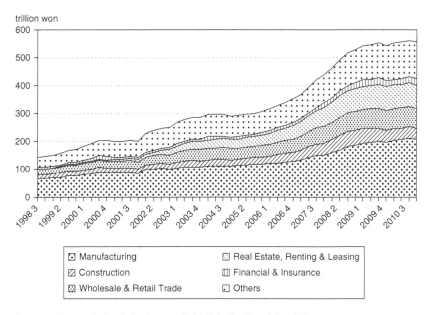

Source: Economic Statistics System (ECOS) in the Republic of Korea.

Figure 6.12   The amount of loans and discounts outstanding by industry

Although the increases were significant, the increased amount was modest compared with dramatic development in stock markets during the same period. Loans to the other industries also increased throughout the early 2000s. Among industries, loans to the real estate, rental and leasing industry, and the wholesale and retail trade industry increased substantially. Loans to the real estate and rental and leasing industry, which were 1.2 trillion won in 1998, exceeded 80 trillion won in 2008. The financial and insurance industry also emerged as borrowers of commercial bank credits in the early 2000s. This may also explain why the increased domestic credits could not enhance capital accumulation in the Republic of Korea after the AFC.

Further Regression Results

Even though there was substantial development in several financial markets, financial development might not have contributed to capital accumulation in the Republic of Korea and Thailand after the AFC. This chapter now suggests further empirical tests to examine which proxies of financial development were linked with the investment ratios in the two countries. By using the seasonally adjusted quarterly time-series data, we estimate equation (6.1) defined earlier in this chapter. Except for the data frequency, we use the same dependent variable $I_{i,t}/Y_{i,t}$ as in the previous sections. We also use the logged difference of GDP ($DLog(Y)$) and the logged GDP ($Log(Y)$) for the macro variables $Z(k)_{i,t}$. We use varieties of new proxies for financial development $X(j)_{i,t}$. For $X(j)_{i,t}$ in the Republic of Korea, we use the ratio of total market capitalization to GDP ($MKTCap/Y$), the ratio of the stock trading volume to GDP ($Svolume/Y$), the ratio of the corporate bond trading volume to GDP ($Bvolume/Y$), the ratio of total loans and discounts to GDP ($Loans(total)/Y$), the ratio of loans for the manufacturing sector to GDP ($Loans(manuf.)/Y$), and the ratio of loans for households to GDP ($Loans(household)/Y$). For $X(j)_{i,t}$ in Thailand, we use the ratio of issued public securities to GDP ($Public/Y$), the ratio of issued long-term debt securities (debt securities whose term to maturity is over a year) to GDP ($LDebt/Y$), the ratio of total loans to GDP ($Loans(total)/GDP$), the ratio of loans for the manufacturing sector to GDP ($Loans(manuf.)/Y$), and the ratio of loans for the non-manufacturing sector to GDP ($Loans(non-manuf.)/Y$).

To avoid simultaneous bias, we took a one-period lag for all explanatory variables except for the $DLog(Y)$ in the Republic of Korea. We took a two-period lag for $DLog(Y)$ in the Republic of Korea because its one-period lag was not significant. The sample period is from Q1 1999 to Q3 2010 for the Republic of Korea and from Q1 2004 to Q2 2010 for Thailand. To make the heteroscedasticity and autocorrelation of the regressions consistent, the Newey-West estimator was used to calculate t-values. Table 6.3 summarizes the regression results. In the case of the Republic of Korea, neither $MKTCap/Y$, $Svolume/Y$, nor $Bvolume/Y$ had a positive coefficient. In particular, the coefficients of $Svolume/Y$ and $Bvolume/Y$ were negative, although their significance level was marginal. This implies that financial development in stock markets or corporate bond markets did not enhance investment in the Republic of Korea. In contrast, the coefficient of loans had significantly positive sign. In particular, the coefficient of loans for the manufacturing sector took large positive values and was statistically significant, while that of housing loans was positive but insignificant. This suggests that loans for the manufacturing sector are a good indicator of the link between financial development and investment in the country.

In the case of Thailand, neither $Stocks/Y$ nor $Public/Y$ had a positive coefficient. This implies that financial development in stock markets or public debt markets did not enhance investment in Thailand. The coefficient of $LDebt/Y$ sometimes took a positive sign but never became significant. Financial development in private debt markets has, if anything, a very weak link with investment. In contrast, the coefficient of loans showed

Table 6.3   Further determinants of the investments

(1) Republic of Korea (Sample: 1999Q2–2010Q3): Dependent variable: *Y/I*					
	Coefficient	t-statistic	Coefficient	t-statistic	Coefficient	t-statistic
---	---	---	---	---	---	---
Constant	0.553	3.937	0.480	5.013	0.490	6.842
MKTCap/Y	−0.001	−0.159	0.000	−0.105		
Svolume/Y	−0.094	−1.655	−0.098	−1.597	−0.097	−1.619
Bvolume/Y	−0.813	−0.936	−1.385	−1.47	−1.412	−1.646
Loans(total)/Y	20.579	2.614				
Loans(manuf.)/Y			70.127	3.306	71.485	3.574
Loans(household)/Y			15.743	1.463	16.469	1.514
Dlog(Y(−2))	0.103	1.950	0.095	1.679	0.095	1.658
Log(Y(−1))	−0.059	−1.919	−0.046	−2.083	−0.048	−2.893
R-squared	0.184		0.222		0.221	

(2) Thailand (Sample: 2004Q1–2010Q2): Dependent variable: *Y/I*					
	Coefficient	t-statistic	Coefficient	t-statistic	Coefficient	t-statistic
---	---	---	---	---	---	---
Constant	0.663	1.611	−0.925	−3.753	−0.41	−1.419
Public/Y	0.000	−0.557	−0.024	−1.562	−0.001	−0.053
LDebt/Y	0.036	0.262	−0.048	−0.225	0.093	0.942
Stocks/Y	−0.405	−2.308	−0.118	−0.842	−0.131	−0.957
Loans(total)/Y	−0.046	−1.798				
Loans(manuf.)/Y			0.310	5.130	0.275	4.785
Loans(non-mf.)/Y					−0.05	−3.118
Dlog(Y(−1))	0.015	0.172	0.253	1.676	0.245	2.330
Log(Y(−1))	−0.032	−0.654	0.127	4.255	0.075	2.387
R-squared	0.527		0.620		0.756	

Notes:
(a) *MKTCap/Y* = the ratio of total market capitalization to GDP, *Svolume/Y* = the ratio of the stock trading volume to GDP, *Bvolume/Y* = the ratio of the corporate bond trading volume to GDP, *Loans(total)/Y* = the ratio of total loans and discounts to GDP, *Loans(manuf.)/Y* = the ratio of loans for manufacturing sector to GDP, *Loans(household)/Y* = the ratio of loans for households to GDP, *Public/Y* = the ratio of issued public securities to GDP, *LDebt/Y* = the ratio of issued long-term debt securities to GDP, *Stocks/Y* = the ratio of issued stocks to GDP, and *Loans(non-mf.)/Y* = the ratio of loans for non-manufacturing sector to GDP.
(b) To avoid simultaneous bias, we took one-period lag for all explanatory variables except for *DLog(Y)* in the Republic of Korea. We took two-period lag for *DLog(Y)* in the Republic of Korea.
(c) To make the regressions heteroscedasticity and autocorrelation consistent, the Newey-West estimator was used to calculate *t*-values.

Source: Estimates by the author.

mixed signs. When total loans and loans for the non-manufacturing sector were used, the coefficient was significantly negative. However, when loans for the manufacturing sector were used, it was significantly positive. This suggests that as in the Republic of Korea, loans for the manufacturing sector are a special indicator of the link between financial development and investment in Thailand.

CONCLUSION

In the globalized world economy, the role of finance is of immense importance. However, since individual countries have different historical backgrounds, it is difficult to categorically judge which system is better than the others. In comparing financial systems, it is extremely important to take into account their historical backgrounds and social and institutional characteristics. This is especially so when exploring the link between financial development and investment in Asia, where legal or accounting systems – or both – may be less mature.

Most emerging Asian economies traditionally have relied heavily on either bank lending or internal markets. After the AFC, there has been criticism that these inherent financial systems might have deepened the seriousness of the crisis. However, despite a series of liberalization measures that strengthened the role of equity markets, investment rates that had plummeted in the late 1990s continued to remain low in the 2000s. Most Asian countries experienced investment stagnation even after further liberalization of financial systems and institutional reforms. At the same time, traditional proxies, such as domestic bank credit, stagnated under the liberalization. This suggests that the failure of traditional financial development might be responsible for the persistent stagnation of capital accumulation after the AFC. Under the traditional Asian financial system, reputation and relationships played an important role in overcoming defective legal and/or accounting systems. Consequently, investment grew remarkably before the crisis, even if several market mechanisms were incomplete. Many Asian countries face essentially the relationship-based environment even after the AFC. In these countries, a traditional policy of promoting bank loans is desirable in enhancing economic growth.

NOTES

1. For example, Aizenman and Lee (2007) compared the relative importance of precautionary and mercantilist motives in accounting for the hoarding of international reserves

by developing countries. Their empirical results suggested that precautionary motives played a more prominent role behind the reserve accumulation by developing countries.
2. For more detailed overviews on finance and economic development, see, among others, Fry (1995).

REFERENCES

Abiad, A., E. Detragiache, and T. Tressel (2010), 'A new database of financial reforms', *IMF Staff Papers*, **57**, 281–302.

Aizenman, J., and J. Lee (2007), 'International reserves: precautionary versus mercantilist views, theory and evidence', *Open Economies Review*, **18**, 191–214.

Allen, F., and D. Gale (2000), *Comparing Financial Systems*, Cambridge, MA: MIT Press.

Beck, T., and A. Demirgüç-Kunt (2009), 'Financial institutions and markets across countries and over time: data and analysis', World Bank Policy Research Working Paper No. 4943.

Fry, M.J. (1995), *Money Interest and Banking in Economic Development, 2nd edition*, Baltimore, MD: Johns Hopkins University Press.

Gerschenkron, A. (1962), *Economic Backwardness in Historical Perspective*, Cambridge, MA: Harvard University Press.

Hellmann, T.F., K.C. Murdock, and J.E. Stiglitz (2000), 'Liberalization, moral hazard in banking, and prudential regulation: are capital requirements enough?', *American Economic Review*, **90**, 147–65.

King, R.G., and R. Levine (1993), 'Finance and growth: Schumpeter might be right', *Quarterly Journal of Economics*, **108** (3), 717–37.

Levine, R. (1997), 'Financial development and economic growth: views and agenda', *Journal of Economic Literature*, **35**, 688–726.

Levine, R., and S. Zervos (1998), 'Stock markets and economic growth', *American Economic Review*, **88**, 537–58.

McKinnon, R.I. (1973), *Money and Capital in Economic Development*, Washington, DC: Brookings Institution.

McKinnon, R.I., and H. Pill (1996), 'Credible liberalizations and international capital flows: the "Overborrowing Syndrome"', in T. Ito and A.O. Krueger (eds), *Financial Deregulation and Integration in East Asia*, Chicago: University of Chicago Press, pp. 7–42.

Rajan, R.G., and L. Zingales (1998), 'Financial dependence and growth', *American Economic Review*, **88**, 559–86.

Shaw, E.S. (1973), *Financial Deepening in Economic Development*, New York: Oxford University Press.

Stiglitz, J. (1994), 'The role of the state in financial markets', in M. Bruno and B. Pleskovic (eds), Proceedings of the World Bank Annual Bank Conference on Development Economics 1993, pp. 19–52.

7. Investment treaties: ASEAN

Diane A. Desierto

INTRODUCTION

Investment treaties significantly interact with macroeconomics, policy, and institutional determinants in attracting, retaining, and sustaining foreign direct investment (FDI). While the precise magnitude of their contribution remains a matter of econometric dispute, the United Nations Conference on Trade and Development (UNCTAD) concluded in 2009 that investment treaties, at the very least:

> appear to have an impact on FDI inflows from developed countries into developing countries. Although most BITs [bilateral investment treaties] do not change the key economic determinants of FDI, they improve several policy and institutional determinants, and thereby increase the likelihood that developing countries engaged in BIT programs will receive more FDI . . . BITs – and other IIAs [international investment agreements] – are important to TNCs [transnational corporations] in terms of investment protection and enhancing stability and predictability of FDI projects. For the majority of surveyed TNCs from all sectors, BIT coverage in host developing countries and transition economies plays a role in making a final decision on where to invest. (UNCTAD 2009, 55)

UNCTAD's 2011 *World Investment Report* indicates that there has been "rapid treaty expansion" worldwide, such that as of 2010, 6092 international investment agreements have been found to account for legal protection for "about two-thirds of global FDI stock" (UNCTAD 2011, 100–102). According to UNCTAD, "countries continue to conclude IIAs, sometimes with novel provisions aimed at rebalancing the rights and obligations between States and investors and ensuring coherence between IIAs and other public policies" (UNCTAD 2011, 100).

The stabilizing effects of investment treaties can be particularly appreciated in the context of Southeast Asia. While there have been few investment arbitration cases in the region, these treaties continue to play a vital role in investment promotion and pre-establishment requirements for potential investors, preservation of host state regulatory flexibility, and the post-establishment protection afforded by legal guarantees (Desierto

2011b).[1] Notwithstanding the debated efficacy of regional investment treaties for determining investment inflows, the regulatory impact of these treaties remains a subject for continued policy scrutiny. This chapter examines the nature of investment treaty regulation following the passage and entry into force of the 2008 Association of Southeast Asian Nations (ASEAN) Charter and its new architecture for regional governance.[2]

Investment treaty regulation in Southeast Asia has changed considerably since the ASEAN member states first initiated internal reforms to address the 1997–98 Asian financial crisis (AFC) (Thompson and Poon 2000). ASEAN's regional responses to the crisis were, in large part, functionally constrained by the nature of ASEAN then as a loose and voluntary economic cooperation association of 10 Southeast Asian states.[3] ASEAN instituted a "surveillance process" to monitor and report on global, regional, and national economic and financial developments, and thereby "detect any sign of recurring vulnerability in the ASEAN financial systems and economies" (Worapot 2002). ASEAN also extended regional capital flow monitoring within the ASEAN Member States and with three key partners: the People's Republic of China (PRC), Japan, and the Republic of Korea (ASEAN+3). In 2000, the ASEAN+3 attempted to establish and implement the Chiang Mai Initiative (CMI), a regional financing arrangement that was supposed to provide a $800 billion facility available to ASEAN countries to meet temporary liquidity shortages or urgent balance-of-payments crises, arranged through a network of currency swap agreements between and among the ASEAN+3 member states.[4] This attempt to devise voluntary collective measures was further challenged by its lack of binding validity, attributable in part to the loose cooperative arrangements of pre-Charter ASEAN.[5]

THE 1987 ASEAN IGA AND ITS 1996 PROTOCOL

Before the AFC, the primary treaty instrument governing international investments in ASEAN was the 1987 "Agreement among the Government of Brunei Darussalam, the Republic of Indonesia, Malaysia, the Republic of the Philippines, the Republic of Singapore, and the Kingdom of Thailand for the Promotion and Protection of Investments," otherwise known as the ASEAN Investment Guarantee Agreement (ASEAN IGA).[6] The ASEAN IGA was to be restrictively applied only to "investments brought into, derived from or directly connected with investments brought into the territory of any Contracting Party by nationals or companies of any other Contracting Party, and which are specifically approved in writing and registered by the host country and upon such conditions as it deems fit for the purposes of [the] Agreement."[7] Apart from standard clauses on expropriation and the duty to compensate for expropriation,[8] the ASEAN IGA obligated its contracting Member States to observe "fair and equitable treatment" and "full protection" of investments as defined in the ASEAN IGA.[9] "Investments" were sweepingly defined in an asset-based manner, contemplating "every kind of asset," such as movable and immovable property, shares of stock, debentures, money claims and contract claims with financial value, intellectual property rights and good will, and business concessions conferred by law or under contract, including natural resource concessions.[10] Investors suffering damages arising from national emergencies were entitled to most-favored nation (MFN) treatment in matters of compensation and restitution.[11] Significantly, the ASEAN IGA provided for an almost unqualified treaty right of investors to the repatriation of their capital and earnings, subject only to the national laws of the ASEAN state from which transfers were to be made:

Article VII: Repatriation of Capital and Earnings
1.   Each Contracting Party shall, *subject to its laws, rules and regulations,* allow without unreasonable delay the free transfer in any freely-usable currency of:
     a)   the capital, net profits, dividends, royalties, technical assistance and technical fees, interests, and other income, accruing from any investments of the nationals or companies of the other Contracting Parties;
     b)   the proceeds from the total or partial liquidation of any investments made by nationals or companies of the other Contracting Parties;
     c)   funds in repayment of loans given by nationals or companies of one Contracting Party to the nationals or companies of another Contracting Party which both Contracting Parties have recognized as investments;
     d)   the earnings of nationals of the other Contracting Parties who are employed and allowed to work in connection with an investment in its territory.
2.   The exchange rate applicable to such transfer shall be the rate of exchange prevailing at the time of remittance.
3.   The Contracting Parties undertake to accord to transfers referred to in paragraph (1) of the Article treatment no less favorable than that accorded to transfer originating from investments made by nationals or companies of any third State.[12]

As a matter of investment law, the above guarantees under the ASEAN IGA arguably offered the highest levels of protection to foreign investors and capital flows.[13] Contracting states bound themselves to ensure "full protection of the investments made," and further committed that they "shall not impair by unjustified or discriminatory measures the management, maintenance, use, enjoyment, extension, disposition, or liquidation of such investments."[14] Due to ASEAN's nature then as a loose economic cooperation association (Desierto 2011a), there was no distinct or specialized institution or intergovernmental body established to administer or monitor compliance with the ASEAN IGA. Disputes concerning the interpretation or application of the ASEAN IGA were to be "settled amicably between the parties" and, failing settlement, were simply to be "submitted to the ASEAN Economic Ministers (AEM)."[15] Investor–State disputes were to be resolved through amicable settlement, conciliation, or arbitration.[16] The ASEAN IGA was amended in a 1996 protocol that obligated Member States to simplify procedures and observe transparency in the investment information and approval process by calling on them to "endeavor to simplify and streamline [their] investment procedures and approval process to facilitate investment flows"; "ensure the provision of up-to-date information on all laws and regulations pertaining to foreign investment in its territory"; and "take appropriate measures to ensure that such information be made as transparent, timely and publicly accessible as possible."[17]

THE 1998 ASEAN INVESTMENT AREA

The AFC ushered in significantly different qualitative reforms to ASEAN investment treaty standards. The 1998 Framework Agreement on the ASEAN Investment Area (AIA Agreement) overhauled the ASEAN IGA's unstructured system of regional investment protection and policies that proved to be largely deferential towards foreign investors' business discretion. The AIA Agreement swung the other way and instead introduced numerous restrictions before qualifying an investment – and an investor – for treaty protection. First, before an investor could invoke the AIA Agreement's protections, the investor had to meet the strict definition of an "ASEAN investor" according to the treaty. The AIA Agreement applied only to a national or juridical person of any ASEAN Member State, who makes "an investment in another Member State, the effective ASEAN equity of which taken cumulatively with all other ASEAN equities fulfills at least the minimum percentage required to meet the national equity requirement and other equity requirements of domestic laws and published national policies, if any, of the host country in respect of that investment."[18] The treaty defines "effective ASEAN equity" somewhat ambiguously as the "ultimate holdings by nationals or juridical persons of ASEAN Member States in that investment," without prescribing the legal test, such as the "control test" to determine the nationality of corporations applicable to determine such "ultimate holdings"(Seidl-Hohenveldern 1999). At best, the AIA Agreement refers to the ASEAN Member State's national rules and procedures for ascertaining such "effective equity."[19] The applicability of the protections of the AIA Agreement thus became de facto a matter of national law instead of being harmonized under treaty law.

Second, the AIA Agreement laid the foundations for an organized regional regulatory administration to facilitate investment cooperation. The 1998 AIA Framework Agreement established the "ASEAN Investment Area" as a distinct market for capital inflows from ASEAN and non-ASEAN sources,[20] intended to coordinate ASEAN's regional investment program, to open all industries for investment to ASEAN investors by 2010 and to all investors by 2020, subject to specified exceptions, and generally extending national treatment to all ASEAN investors by 2010 and to all other investors by 2020, unless otherwise specified in the AIA Agreement.[21] Contrary to the ASEAN IGA, the AIA Agreement expressly provided for the creation of the ASEAN Investment Area Council (AIA Council), composed of the ASEAN Secretary-General and the respective ministers responsible for investment in ASEAN Member States.[22] The AIA Council was tasked with supervision, coordination, and review of the implementation of the AIA Agreement, with the duty to report on these matters regularly to the ASEAN Economic Ministers (AEM).[23] ASEAN Member States were required to periodically submit action plans and investment liberalization programs to the AIA Council.

Third, the AIA Agreement diluted the sweeping investment protection afforded under the standards of the ASEAN IGA, recognizing differences in the levels of economic development of ASEAN Member States as of 1998. States were permitted to submit their respective Temporary Exclusion Lists and Sensitive Lists, which specified the industries or sectors that would not be opened up to investment or for which the ASEAN Member State could not confer national treatment.[24] Even as the AIA Agreement observed MFN treatment for covered investors and investments, the treaty permitted an ASEAN Member State to waive entitlement to MFN treatment and also staggered the time for compliance with MFN treatment for new ASEAN Member States such as Myanmar, Cambodia, the Lao People's Democratic Republic and Viet Nam.[25] Moreover, the AIA Agreement does not contain any reference whatsoever to the ASEAN IGA standards of "fair and equitable treatment," "full protection of investment," or the duty to comply with elements of a lawful expropriation, such as public purpose and compensation.

Finally, the AIA Agreement introduced distinct carve-outs from treaty coverage for areas that appear closely linked to a Member State's regulatory authority over public policy matters. The AIA Agreement provided for a "General Exceptions" clause that appeared remarkably similar to exceptions in trade law, such as Article XX of the General Agreement on Tariffs and Trade.[26] Pursuant to the strict terms of this clause prohibiting arbitrary discrimination or disguised restrictions on investment, Member States could adopt or enforce measures that were "necessary to protect national security and public morals"; "necessary to protect human, animal or plant life or health"; "necessary to secure compliance with laws or regulations which are not inconsistent with the provisions of this Agreement," such as those relating to the "prevention of deceptive and fraudulent practices or to deal with the effects of a default on investment agreement"; and such measures "aimed at ensuring the equitable or effective imposition or collection of direct taxes in respect of investments or investors of Member States."[27] Subject to notification procedures before the AIA Council, ASEAN Member States were also permitted to provisionally and nondiscriminatorily implement any "emergency safeguard measures," if, "as a result of the implementation of the liberalization program under [the AIA Agreement], a Member State suffers or is threatened with any serious injury or threat."[28] Most importantly, unlike the ASEAN IGA, repatriation and transfers of capital and earnings were no longer unfettered. Under the AIA Agreement, Member States could implement "measures to safeguard the balance of payments", described in full below:

Article 15: Measures to Safeguard the Balance of Payments
1. In the event of serious balance of payments and external financial difficulties or threats thereof, a Member State may adopt or maintain restrictions on investments on which it has undertaken specific commitments, including on payments or transfers for transactions related to such commitments. It is recognized that particular pressures on the balance of payments of a Member State in the process of economic development or economic transition may necessitate the use of restrictions to ensure, inter alia, the maintenance of a level of financial reserves adequate for the implementation of its program of economic development or economic transition.
2. Where measures to safeguard balance of payments are taken pursuant to this Article notice of such measures shall be given to the AIA Council within 14 days from the date such measures are taken.
3. The measures referred to in paragraph (1):
    (a) shall not discriminate among Member States;
    (b) shall be consistent with the Articles of Agreement of the International Monetary Fund;
    (c) shall avoid unnecessary damage to the commercial, economic, and financial interests of any other Member State;
    (d) shall not exceed those necessary to deal with the circumstances described in paragraph 1; and
    (e) shall be temporary and be phased out progressively as the situation specified in paragraph 1 improves.
4. The Member States adopting the balance of payments measures shall

commence consultations with the AIA Council and other Member States
within 90 days from the date of notification in order to review the balance
of payment measures adopted by it.
5.   The AIA Council shall determine the rules applicable to the procedures
     under this Article.[29]

As seen from the foregoing description, in terms of treaty design, it
would appear that the AIA Agreement took the opposite direction from
the ASEAN IGA. In the years of liberalization and privatization in the
Southeast Asian region before the 1997–98 AFC, the ASEAN IGA mini-
mally regulated the investment process. Investment protection standards
under the ASEAN IGA were devoid of formal institutional oversight for
treaty compliance. ASEAN Member States assumed heavy legal burdens
to guarantee investment protection, with almost no room for adjusted
or modified compliance with treaty obligations. By contrast, the AIA
Agreement recognized a vast sphere of unregulated discretion for ASEAN
Member States to unilaterally act in key areas of public policy deemed
crucial for sovereign economic interests – placing a high threshold before
investors could qualify for treaty protection through restrictive definitions of covered "investment," diluting standards of investment protection
available to covered investors, and permitting numerous situations where
ASEAN Member States could forego compliance with obligations under
the AIA Agreement. While there was some attempt to harmonize and
monitor treaty compliance through the AIA Investment Council, there
were no means by which ASEAN Member States could challenge another
Member State's unilateral conduct other than on a case-by-case basis in
the AIA Agreement's investor–State dispute settlement mechanism. The
AIA Council's mandate was noncoercive, non-authoritative, and appeared
purely recommendatory. This was consistent with the nature of ASEAN
then as a loose economic cooperation association, wholly dependent on the
mufakat and *mushawarah* consultation and consensus policy of its Member
States, otherwise known as the "ASEAN Way" (Desierto 2008, 2010).

Investment treaty regulation in pre-Charter ASEAN arguably reflects
Southeast Asian policy tensions between liberalization and protectionism before and after the AFC (Desierto 2011b). Investment law scholars
continue to debate the actual impact of investment treaties in attracting
foreign capital, and the actual effectiveness of the ASEAN IGA and the
AIA Agreement in attracting foreign direct investment to ASEAN countries has yet to be determined (Sauvant and Sachs 2009; Sasse 2011). On
the face of it, the scale of total investment flows to ASEAN countries
based on available data from 1995 to 2005 (the period during the operation of the ASEAN IGA and the AIA Agreement, and before the passage
of the ASEAN Charter) demonstrate volatility (Table 7.1).

Table 7.1   Investment flows to ASEAN member countries

Year	Total/aggregated FDI flows to ASEAN ($ million)[a]	Inward intra-ASEAN FDI flows ($ million)[b]
1995	28 231	4 654.42
1996	30 209	4 271.81
1997	34 099	5 235.70
1998	22 406	2 730.75
1999	27 375	1 784.18
2000	23 541	761.92
2001	19 197	2 465.80
2002	15 773	3 667.50
2003	19 664	2 370.68
2004	25 661	2 630.34
2005	38 083	2 220.39

Notes: ASEAN = Association of Southeast Asian Nations. FDI = Foreign Direct Investment.

Sources:
[a] ASEAN Secretariat 2006, Table 2.1.1, at p. 13.
[b] ASEAN Secretariat 2006, p. 229.

From 1995 to 2005, the European Union invested the most in the Southeast Asian region ($79.1 billion), followed by the United States (US) ($48.9 billion), Japan ($34.4 billion), Taipei,China ($8.4 billion), Hong Kong, China ($7.7 billion), the Republic of Korea ($4.2 billion), the PRC ($2 billion), and India ($1.1 billion) (ASEAN Secretariat 2006, 13). The magnitude of the effects of investment treaty regulation (through the ASEAN IGA and AIA Agreement) on the ultimate scale, growth, or decline of foreign direct investment inflows to ASEAN from intra-ASEAN and extra-ASEAN sources from 1995 to 2005 has yet to be determined. Further studies will be required to ascertain the precise effects of the change in investment treaty regulation from the ASEAN IGA to the AIA Agreement in this period.[30]

INVESTMENT IN THE ASEAN CHARTER ERA

Southeast Asian states formalized their regional cooperative commitments into a rules-based system through the 2008 ASEAN Charter (Desierto 2011a; 2008). Under the ASEAN Charter, ASEAN Member States bound themselves as an international legal organization endowed with separate juridical personality.[31] All Member States assumed the primary obligation of "tak[ing] all necessary measures, including the enactment of appropriate domestic legislation, to effectively implement the provisions of this Charter and to comply with all obligations of membership."[32] ASEAN and its Member States became legally bound under the ASEAN Charter to act "in accordance with" organizational principles such as, among others, "adherence to the rule of law, good governance, the principles of democracy and constitutional government"; "respect for fundamental freedoms, the promotion and protection of human rights, and the promotion of social justice"; "upholding the United Nations Charter and international law, including international humanitarian law, subscribed to by ASEAN Member States"; and "adherence to multilateral trade rules and ASEAN's rules-based regimes for effective implementation of economic commitments and progressive reduction toward elimination of all barriers to regional economic integration, in a market-driven economy."[33] The ASEAN Charter also created institutions for regional governance, led by the ASEAN Summit (composed of the heads of state or government of ASEAN Member States), which has the power to issue decisions binding upon all ASEAN Member States.[34] The ASEAN Summit also spearheads a newly integrated "horizontal" bureaucracy drawn from pre-Charter ad hoc bodies embedded in national governments of ASEAN Member States,[35] such as the ASEAN Coordinating Council (composed of the ASEAN foreign ministers), the ASEAN Community Councils (the ASEAN Political-Security Community Council, the ASEAN Economic Community Council, and the ASEAN Socio-Cultural Community Council), ASEAN Sectoral Ministerial Bodies, the ASEAN Secretary-General, and the ASEAN Secretariat (Desierto 2011a) The ASEAN Charter implements ASEAN Vision 2020, which set forth the policy blueprint for the ASEAN Member States' organizational objectives and targets for the year 2020: (1) closer economic integration with the free flow of goods, capital, services, and investments among ASEAN countries; and (2) an increasingly unified ASEAN identity under institutions that promote ASEAN regional political, social, and security interests toward compliance with the international legal order.[36]

The ASEAN Charter also provided for the binding quality of all pre-Charter agreements, protocols, and less formal instruments concluded by the ASEAN Member States during the 40 years that ASEAN functioned as a mere economic cooperation association pursuant to the 1967 ASEAN (Bangkok) Declaration and the 1976 Treaty of Amity and Cooperation (TAC) (Desierto 2011a).[37] Article 52(1) of the ASEAN Charter explicitly provided for the legal continuity of over 300 of these treaty instruments, and conferred binding force, albeit in disputably varying degrees, upon them in the present Charter system.[38] The applicability of the ASEAN IGA and the AIA Agreement remains, unless otherwise stipulated in subsequent treaty arrangements. As will be subsequently shown, the 2009 ASEAN Comprehensive Investment Agreement (ACIA) – the new regional investment treaty that entered into force in April 2012 – has been designed to supersede both the ASEAN IGA and AIA Agreement.[39]

Since the entry into force of the ASEAN Charter on 15 December 2008,[40] ASEAN has pursued regional investment treaty negotiations with key trading partners such as Australia, the PRC, India, New Zealand, and the US, as well as European countries (Fry 2011; ASEAN Investment Report 2009), while simultaneously consolidating intra-ASEAN investment under the ACIA (Zhong 2011; Chia 2010). There has been some delay from the original 2002 target to establish full economic integration within Southeast Asian economies under the auspices of the ASEAN Economic Community (AEC).[41] Instead, the AEC is now scheduled to commence its operational existence by 2015 (ASEAN Economic Community Blueprint; Plummer and Click 2009). The AEC will "transform ASEAN into a region with free movement of goods, services, investment, skilled labor, and freer flow of capital."[42] The AEC's investment objectives are set forth as follows:

A3. Free flow of investment
23. A free and open investment regime is key to enhancing ASEAN's competitiveness in attracting foreign direct investment (FDI) as well as intra-ASEAN investment. Sustained inflows of new investments and reinvestments will promote and ensure dynamic development of ASEAN economies.
26. To enhance regional integration as well as to maintain a competitive investment area, both the Framework Agreement on the AIA and the ASEAN IGA will be reviewed. The objective is to realize a more comprehensive investment agreement which should be forward looking, with improved features, provisions and obligations by considering international best practices that would increase the investor confidence in ASEAN. The ASEAN Comprehensive Investment Agreement (ACIA), which will build on the existing AIA Agreement and ASEAN IGA, will cover the following pillars:

Investment Protection
27. Provide enhanced protection to all investors and their investments to be covered under the comprehensive agreement.
Actions:
i. To strengthen among others the following provisions:
   ● investor–state dispute settlement mechanism;
   ● transfer and repatriation of capital, profits, dividends, etc.;
   ● transparent coverage on the expropriation and compensation;
   ● full protection and security; and
   ● treatment of compensation for losses resulting from strife.

Facilitation and Cooperation

28. A more transparent, consistent and predictable investment rules, regulations, policies and procedures.

Actions:

i.   Harmonize, where possible, investment policies to achieve industrial complementation and economic integration;
ii.   Streamline and simplify procedures for investment applications and approvals;
iii.   Promote dissemination of investment information: rules, regulations, policies and procedures, including through one-stop investment center or investment promotion board;
iv.   Strengthen databases on all forms of investments covering goods and services to facilitate policy formulation;
v.   Strengthen coordination among government ministries and agencies concerned;
vi.   Consultation with ASEAN private sectors to facilitate investment; and
vii.   Identify and work towards areas of complementation ASEAN-wide as well as bilateral economic integration.

Promotion and Awareness

29. Promote ASEAN as an integrated investment area and production network. Since these items are related to capital movements, they should follow the guiding principles of capital movements as stated in section A.4. Freer Flow of Capital, particularly on allowing Greater Capital Mobility . . . .

Liberalization

30. Progressive liberalization of ASEAN Member Countries' investment regime to achieve free and open investment by 2015.

Actions:

i.   Extend nondiscriminatory treatment, including national treatment and most-favored nation treatment, to investors in ASEAN with limited exceptions; minimize and where possible, eliminate such exceptions;
ii.   Reduce and where possible, eliminate restrictions to entry for investments in the Priority Integration Sectors covering goods; and
iii.   Reduce and where possible, eliminate restrictive investment measures and other impediments, including performance requirements.[43]

In line with the foregoing blueprint, ASEAN under its new Charter regime has concluded three regional investment agreements: the intra-ASEAN treaty, designated as the 2009 ASEAN Comprehensive Investment Agreement (ACIA);[44] a regional treaty with the PRC, otherwise known as the 2009 Agreement on Investment of the Framework Agreement on Comprehensive Economic Cooperation between the Association of Southeast Asian Nations and the People's Republic of China (hereafter, "ASEAN–PRC Investment Agreement");[45] and a regional treaty with Australia and New Zealand, which contains a specific chapter on investment, Chapter 11 (Investment) of the 2009 Agreement Establishing the ASEAN–Australia–New Zealand (NZ) Free Trade Agreement (FTA) (hereafter, "ASEAN–Australia–NZ FTA Investment Chapter").[46] All three instruments have entered into force.[47] Before the ACIA's entry into force, its predecessor agreements – the 1998 AIA Agreement and the 1987 ASEAN IGA – had operative legal effect. Following the entry into force of the ACIA, investors may exercise the option, to choose to apply the provisions of the ASEAN IGA or the AIA Agreement in their entirety, within three years from the termination of the latter Agreements.[48]) The ASEAN–PRC Investment Agreement entered into force on 1 January 2010.[49] The ASEAN–Australia–NZ FTA Investment Chapter entered into force on 1 January 2010 for 8 of the 12 countries that signed this agreement (Australia, Brunei Darussalam, Malaysia, Myanmar, New Zealand, the Philippines, Singapore, and Viet Nam), 12 March 2010 for Thailand, 1 January 2011 for the Lao People's Democratic Republic, and finally, 4 January 2011 for Cambodia (Desierto 2011b).[50]

To date, ASEAN is in the process of negotiating similar investment agreements with India (based on commitments under the 2003 India–ASEAN Framework Agreement on Comprehensive Economic Cooperation),[51] and the US (implementing the 2006 United States–ASEAN Trade and Investment Framework Agreement).[52] During the 9th ASEAN–India Summit held in Indonesia on November 2011, Indian Prime Minister Dr. Manmohan Singh expressed confidence that an ASEAN–India Services and Investment Agreement would be concluded by March 2012.[53] At the 18 November 2011 ASEAN Business and Investment Summit in Indonesia, US Secretary of State Hillary Clinton stressed the importance of improving investment rules in the ASEAN region, and ongoing initiatives between ASEAN and the US to strengthen the investment climate within the Southeast Asian region.[54] In anticipation of similar developments in investment treaty regulation with other key trading partners, it is thus significant to examine how investment treaties newly concluded under the ASEAN Charter regime designed investment protection with regard for the host Member State's public policy prerogatives.[55] As will be seen below, none of the three new ASEAN investment agreements favors the excessively liberal terms of the ASEAN IGA or the highly restrictive terms of the AIA Agreement.

INTRA-ASEAN INVESTMENT: THE 2009 ASEAN COMPREHENSIVE INVESTMENT AGREEMENT

The 2011 ASEAN Investment Report indicates that in 2010, intra-ASEAN investment flows "exceeded the $10 billion mark for the first time ($12.1 billion to be exact) since the Asian financial crisis in 1997", and noted that "intra-regional investments (16% of total ASEAN FDI inflows), while rising, are still below their previous peak in 2002 (22.2%) and the pre-crisis level in 1996 (16.4%) . . . By all dimensions, it seems that ASEAN is still not realizing its full potential as an integrated investment area."[56] The report emphasized that in order

> to ensure credibility to foreign investors, it is in ASEAN's best interest to ratify the ASEAN Comprehensive Investment Agreement (ACIA) as soon as possible. The Agreement was signed two years ago but is still yet to be ratified. Recently, the Reservation Lists have been finalized and officials have agreed on the modality for the elimination of those lists over time. But it is crucial that the governments work hard to implement the ACIA as soon as possible to preserve the credibility of the ACIA. In addition, there are also provisions within the ACIA, like the targeted timeline for investment liberalization and provision of preferential treatment, which need to be reexamined to ensure that ACIA leads to optimal investment outcomes for ASEAN."[57]

While intra-ASEAN investment levels admittedly do not comprise the majority of FDI inflows to ASEAN, it should also be noted that intra-ASEAN investment are additional sources of investment urgently needed by ASEAN Member States transitioning from post-socialist regimes into market economies, such as Cambodia, the Lao People's Democratic Republic, Myanmar, and Viet Nam (ASEAN 2006, 243, 245, 247, 250).

In line with the ACIA's key objectives, such as the "progressive liberalization of the investment regimes of Member States" and the "improvement of transparency and predictability of investment rules, regulations, and procedures conducive to increased investment among Member States," it is worth assessing several distinct features of the treaty design of the ACIA.[58] The ACIA is not a replica of standard Model Bilateral Investment Treaties (Model BITs).[59] It applies to "measures adopted or maintained by a Member State relating to investors of any other Member State, and investments, in its territory, of investors of any other Member State,"[60] for sectors not excluded or reserved by ASEAN Member States' respective Reservation Lists, such as manufacturing, agriculture, fishery, forestry, mining and quarrying, among others.[61] Reservation Lists should be submitted to the ASEAN Secretariat, for endorsement of the ASEAN Investment Area Council, and will be integrated as Schedules to the ACIA.[62] ASEAN Member States have 12 months from submission of their respective Reservation Lists within which to modify their commitments therein.[63] The ACIA does not apply to taxation measures, government procurement, supply of services to government, and trade in services.[64]

"Covered investments" under the ACIA refer to those investments in the territory of an ASEAN Member State that are already in existence as of the ACIA's entry into force or to be established afterwards, and which have been "admitted according to [the host Member State's] laws, regulations, and national policies, and where applicable, specifically approved in writing by the competent authority of a Member State."[65] Investments broadly refer to "every kind of asset," such as movable and immovable property and other property rights; shares, bonds, and debentures; intellectual property rights; money claims and financially assessable contract claims; contract rights and business concessions; and particularly, "amounts yielded by investments," such as profits, interest, capital gains, dividends, royalties, and fees.[66] These definitions expand the scope of investments covered beyond those indicated in the ASEAN IGA and the AIA Agreement.

The ACIA obligates ASEAN Member States to observe national treatment with respect to investors and investments of fellow Member States,[67] and MFN treatment consistent with a Member State's treatment of investors of non-ASEAN Member States.[68] Such MFN treatment is said to exclude investor–State dispute settlement procedures that are available in other agreements to which the Member States are parties.[69] Additionally, ASEAN Member States commit to observe "fair and equitable treatment" (requiring a Member State "not to deny justice in any legal or administrative proceedings in accordance with the principle of due process") and "full protection and security" (requiring a Member State "to take such measures as may be reasonably necessary to ensure the protection and security of the covered investments") with respect to fellow Member States' covered investments.[70] Expropriations of covered investments must be for a public purpose, undertaken in a nondiscriminatory manner, with payment of prompt, adequate and effective compensation, and in accordance with due process of law.[71] The benefits of the ACIA may be denied to investors who do not comply with the nationality rules indicated in the treaty, or commit misrepresentations in relation to such nationality rules.[72]

The ACIA contains several provisions that appear to be more extensive than the AIA Agreement's recognition of a host State's policy discretion in crisis situations. While Member States expressly commit to nondiscriminatory treatment with respect to restitution and compensation for investment losses due to armed conflict, civil strife, or state of emergency,[73] Member States are also permitted to prevent or delay all transfers relating to a covered investment, "through the equitable, non-discriminatory, and good faith application of its laws and regulations," related to the following broad areas:

(a) bankruptcy, insolvency, or the protection of the rights of creditors;
(b) issuing, trading, or dealing in securities, futures, options, or derivatives;

(c)   criminal or penal offences and the recovery of the proceeds of crime;
(d)   financial reporting or record keeping of transfers when necessary to assist
      law enforcement or financial regulatory authorities;
(e)   ensuring compliance with orders or judgments in judicial or administra-
      tive proceedings;
(f)   taxation;
(g)   social security, public retirement, or compulsory savings schemes;
(h)   severance entitlements of employees; and
(i)   the requirement to register and satisfy other formalities imposed by the
      Central Bank and other relevant authorities of a Member State.[74]

It is not clear from the text of the ACIA that the above laws and regulations require prospectivity – required to be already in existence at the time
that an ACIA-covered investment is established. Thus, it may be possible
that an ASEAN Member State could, after the admission of an investment,
subsequently enact legislation or adopt regulations on any of the above
subject matter, and thereafter invoke such new legislation and regulations
to prevent or delay a transfer relating to the investment. Furthermore,
Member States are expressly permitted to impose restrictions on capital
transactions, "where, in exceptional circumstances, movements of capital
cause, or threaten to cause, serious economic or financial disturbance in
the Member State concerned."[75] These restrictions must be notified to the
other ASEAN Member States, and shown to be nondiscriminatory, "consistent with the Articles of Agreement of the International Monetary Fund
(IMF)"; "not exceed those necessary to deal with the circumstances";
"temporary and shall be eliminated as soon as conditions no longer justify
their institution or maintenance"; "avoid unnecessary damage to investors
and covered investments, and the commercial, economic, and financial
interests of the other Member States."[76] Subject to similar procedural
conditions, Member States also appear to have broad authority to restrict
capital transfers in the event of serious balance of payments crises and
financial difficulties threatening the level of financial reserves necessary
for a Member State's economic development.[77]

  Beyond the foregoing crisis situations, the ACIA also recognizes that
Member States may adopt or enforce measures under the ACIA's General
Exceptions (Article 17) or Security Exceptions (Article 18) clauses. Such
measures may be necessary to: (1) "protect public morals or to maintain
public order"; (2) "to protect human, animal or plant life or health";
(3) "secure compliance with laws or regulations . . . including those relating to the prevention of deceptive and fraudulent practices to deal with the
effects of a default on a contract, the protection of the privacy of individuals in relation to the processing and dissemination of personal data and
the protection of confidentiality of individual records and accounts, or

safety"; (4) ensure the "equitable or effective imposition or collection of direct taxes in respect of investments or investors of any Member State"; (5) protect "national treasures of artistic, historic, or archaeological value"; or (6) conserve "exhaustible natural resources if such measures are made effective in conjunction with restrictions on domestic production or consumption."[78] The ACIA extends significant latitude to the Member States' own judgment in implementing security measures, declaring that the ACIA may not be construed to "require any Member State to furnish any information, the disclosure of which it considers contrary to its essential security interests"; "prevent any Member State from taking any action which it considers necessary for the protection of its essential security interests"; or to "prevent any Member State from taking any action pursuant to its obligations under the United Nations Charter for the maintenance of international peace and security."[79] Finally, the ACIA explicitly provides for special and differential treatment for the newer ASEAN Member States (Cambodia, the Lao People's Democratic Republic, Myanmar, and Viet Nam), permitting the latter to execute ACIA commitments "in accordance with [each Member State's] individual stage of development.[80]

The AIA Council is the formal implementing authority of the ACIA and is mandated with coordinating the oversight, review, and monitoring of the regional commitments in the ACIA. To assist in these functions, the AIA Council established the ASEAN Coordinating Committee on Investment (CCI), tasked with reporting to the AIA Council, the ASEAN Secretariat, and the AEC's Senior Economic Officials Meeting (SEOM).[81] The ACIA expressly provides for dispute settlement procedures between investors and Member States, such as conciliation, consultations, and arbitration.[82]

ASEAN EXTERNAL INVESTMENT: ASEAN–PRC INVESTMENT AGREEMENT AND THE ASEAN–AUSTRALIA–NZ FTA INVESTMENT CHAPTER

More than a year after the ASEAN–PRC Investment Agreement entered into force in 2010, the PRC's direct investment to ASEAN countries stands at $2.57 billion, while direct investment from ASEAN countries to the PRC reached $6.32 billion. "In 2010, trade volume between [the People's Republic of] China and ASEAN countries reached $292.8 billion, an increase of 37.5% year on year. [The People's Republic of] China has become the biggest trade partner and the first export destination for ASEAN countries. ASEAN countries have also become a major source of investment for [the People's Republic of] China."[83] On the other hand, while ASEAN–New Zealand investments stood at $239 million in 2009 and ASEAN–Australia investments stood at a combined A$70.8 billion in 2006, the annual investment of both Australia and New Zealand into ASEAN reached over $1 billion, a figure expected to increase further with new commercial and business transactions to be expected from the new ASEAN–Australia–New Zealand free trade area involving a combined total population of 600 million and total estimated gross domestic product (GDP) of $2.7 trillion.[84] While the European Union (EU), the US, and Japan remain the top capital exporters to ASEAN, the 2011 ASEAN Investment Report notes that "nontraditional suppliers of capital into the region have increased their share of FDI investments in ASEAN. Australia, [the People's Republic of] China and [the Republic of] Korea easily stand out – with combined investments of $8.2 billion in 2010 (10.9% share) from an average of $3.2 billion (6.3% share) over the last 10 years."[85]

Unlike the ASEAN–Australia–NZ FTA Investment Chapter, the ASEAN–PRC Investment Agreement contains more provisions that distinctly recognize the host Member State's broad policy discretion as a basis to adjust its compliance with a treaty obligation. "Investments" refer to "every kind of asset *invested by the investors of a Party in accordance with the relevant laws, regulations, and policies* of another Party," with "policies" ambiguously defined only as those "affecting investment that are endorsed and announced by the Government of a Party."[86] This requirement of compliance with domestic laws and "policies" would make it difficult to qualify a transaction or subject matter as an "investment" protected by the treaty. Similar to the ACIA, the ASEAN–PRC Investment Agreement does not apply to taxation measures; procurement laws, regulations and policies; grants or subsidies; the supply of services to government agencies; and trade in services.[87] The Agreement also enables treaty parties to deny the benefits of the treaty to investors not complying with the prescribed nationality rules to qualify for treaty coverage.[88]

The ASEAN–PRC Investment Agreement also adopts investment protection standards of national treatment and MFN treatment,[89] but carves out certain "non-conforming measures" enumerated by the treaty parties from these standards of protection.[90] The ASEAN–PRC Investment Agreement provisions on fair and equitable treatment of investment, full protection and security of investment, and expropriation, are virtually identical with those indicated in the ACIA.[91] The ASEAN–PRC Investment Agreement likewise contains provisions similar to those in the ACIA on compensation for losses in times of strife, war, or state of emergency;[92] permitted prevention or delay of all transfers upon the application of laws and regulations relating to certain subject matter (identical to the enumeration in the ACIA);[93] measures to safeguard the balance of payments;[94] general exceptions and security exceptions clauses.[95]

Oversight, supervision, coordination, and review of the implementation of the ASEAN–PRC Investment Agreement are to be undertaken by a permanent body created in the treaty, or such entity succeeding the ASEAN Economic Minsters–PRC Minister of Commerce (AEM–MOFCOM).[96] Disputes between ASEAN (or an ASEAN Member State) and the PRC arising from the agreement will be governed by the 2004 Agreement on Dispute Settlement Mechanism of the Framework Agreement on Comprehensive Economic Cooperation between ASEAN and the PRC.[97] Disputes between a treaty party (or a host Member State) and an investor may be submitted for consultations or negotiations, and failing the latter, may be submitted, at the choice of the investor to either local or domestic court adjudication; arbitration at the International Centre for Settlement of Investment Disputes (ICSID); ad hoc arbitration under the United Nations Commission on International Trade Law (UNCITRAL) rules; or arbitration before any other arbitral institution, with the consent of both the investor and the host Member State.[98]

The ASEAN–Australia–NZ FTA Investment Chapter bears some similarities to the ACIA and the ASEAN–PRC Investment Agreement, but also some critical differences that empower the treaty parties with more discretion to determine compliance with treaty obligations. The Investment Chapter does not apply to government procurement, subsidies or grants, and supply of services to government agencies.[99] It also has a broad, asset-based definition of investment, but deliberately excludes from the sample asset enumeration all orders or judgments entered in judicial or administrative actions.[100] The benefits of the Chapter may be denied to investors that are juridical persons who do not have "substantive business operations in the territory" of the host Member State; who, in the particular case of Thailand, do not comply with its definitions of ownership and control by a juridical person; and in the Philippines, those who breach anti-dummy or nationalization laws.[101] Moreover, the Investment Chapter does not provide for MFN treatment of investment, restricting the applicable standards of investment protection to national treatment,[102] and customary international law standards of fair and equitable treatment (defined as requiring a Member State "not to deny justice in any legal or administrative proceedings") and full protection and security (defined as requiring a Member State "to take such measures as may be reasonably necessary to ensure the protection and security of the covered investment").[103] The Investment Chapter contains provisions similar to the ACIA and the ASEAN–PRC Investment Agreement on permissible prevention or delay of transfers relating to investments through the application of laws in given subject-matter areas;[104] expropriations;[105] reservation lists;[106] and special differential treatment for the newer ASEAN Member

States (Cambodia, the Lao People's Democratic Republic, Myanmar, and Viet Nam).[107] In contrast, the Chapter applies both national treatment and MFN treatment for cases of losses suffered by investments owing to armed conflict, civil strife, or state of emergency.[108]

The Investment Chapter contains some distinct innovations, such as an institutional mechanism or "contact point" to facilitate treaty parties' compliance with transparency obligations relating to "all relevant measures of general application" and "international agreements affecting investors or investment activities."[109] Parties may withhold information in emergency situations, or in situations when the disclosure would "impede law enforcement" or operate "contrary to the public interest," "or which would prejudice the legitimate commercial interests of particular juridical persons."[110] The Chapter also enables a treaty party to seek administrative review of a fellow treaty party's compliance with its transparency obligations.[111] The Chapter designates a Committee on Investment for the oversight, monitoring, and review of the implementation of obligations under the Chapter.[112] Perhaps the most unique feature of the Investment Chapter lies with its dispute settlement procedures. Apart from providing for consultation, conciliation, and arbitration as possible options for investor–State disputes,[113] the Chapter permits parties to issue a "joint decision" that declares "their interpretation of a provision of this Agreement," which would be binding and controlling upon any arbitral tribunal constituted under the Chapter.[114] Clearly, this provision on "joint decisions" could very well authorize the treaty parties to de facto resolve investor–State disputes beyond the conventional forms of dispute settlement provided for in the Chapter. It is a treaty innovation that has yet to be tested through actual application.

CONCLUSION

Investment treaty regulation under the new ASEAN Charter regime affirms the cautious, gradual, and differentiated strategies of ASEAN toward full economic integration by 2015. Unlike the minimal regulation and full liberalization policies seen in the ASEAN IGA, and the increased regulation and restrictive terms of the AIA Agreement, the new regional investment treaties of ASEAN appear to balance between the demands for consistent and stable investment rules with the regulatory latitude that Southeast Asian states need to retain in order to advance their respective development agendas. Under the new Charter regime, ASEAN has taken more direct and participatory institutional roles in the monitoring, coordination, oversight, and review of the implementation of regional investment agreements, but at the same time it has also permitted treaty parties to exercise discretion in more policy areas that conceivably affect returns on investment. Left unaddressed, this tension of interests and institutional roles could undermine ASEAN's investment competitiveness.

The challenges to regional and developmental investment regulation are not new. In 2008, the UN Conference on Trade and Development (UNCTAD) issued its survey of the qualitative protections and standards commonly prevalent in the international investment agreements (IIAs) concluded by Asia-Pacific Economic Cooperation (APEC) countries (UNCTAD 2008):

> A recent trend in a small but growing number of APEC IIAs [is] to include significant revisions to the wording of various substantive treaty obligations. Prominent amongst these are more detailed treaty language on the meaning of fair and equitable treatment . . . [and] significant innovations to the inves-tor–State dispute resolution process. The main purpose of these innovations is to increase transparency, to promote judicial economy, and to foster sound and consistent results. At the same time, all these changes increase the complexity of the IIA dispute settlement system.
>
> In an overall increasingly complex IIA system, three changes relating to the content of APEC IIAs are evident . . . First is the challenge of promoting policy coherence. Coherence requires that a country's IIAs are consistent with domestic economic and development policy, and with other IIAs signed by that country . . . Second, there is a challenge relating to how best to reflect in IIAs a balancing of investors' interests with the public interest. Long-term sustainabil-ity of the system requires maintaining this balance . . . Third, there is the chal-lenge of how to incorporate development issues most relevant to developing countries into IIAs. This is made more difficult by the fact that the development interests of different countries cannot be uniformly addressed in all IIAs . . . flexibility in the approach to certain core elements of APEC IIAs is required, for example, in the way investment is defined, the use of positive lists to identify sectors to which commitments apply, the use of limited and temporary deroga-tions from an investor's right to freely transfer investment-related capital, and in the use of performance requirements provisions. By definition this introduces a tension with the challenge of coherence outlined. (UNCTAD 2008, 95–6)

The above recommendations are particularly apropos to investment treaty regulation under the new ASEAN Charter regime. Barely three years from the entry into force of the ASEAN Charter, ASEAN continues to build institutions to realize its Vision 2020, this time under a legally binding international mandate from all 10 Southeast Asian nations. The success of ASEAN's projected economic integration by 2015 depends upon the same policy coherence, regulatory balancing, and reliable institutional monitor-ing and oversight urged by UNCTAD. These factors are just as critical for the prospects for increased regional investment in Southeast Asia, particu-larly at a time when regional and global financial crises afflict the world's more developed regions, such as Europe and the US. Having already experienced the volatility of capital flows and their grossly destabilizing effects on national economies during the 1997–98 AFC, ASEAN's cautious path in investment treaty regulation under the new Charter regime should, perhaps, be seen as a prudent long-term regional policy.

NOTES

1. There have been two reported investor–State arbitrations involving regional investment agreements in Southeast Asia: the ad hoc arbitration in *Yaung Chi Oo Trading Pte Ltd v. Myanmar,* 42 ILM 540 (2003), where the tribunal declared it did not have jurisdiction; and the ICSID request for application in *Cemex Asia Holdings Ltd v. Indonesia,* ICSID Case No. ARB/04/3, 23 February 2007, which did not reach final adjudication by the tribunal due to the settlement reached by the parties. See also Sornarajah and Arumugam 2007, 163–8.
2. Full text of the ASEAN Charter available at http://www.aseansec.org/publications/ASEAN-Charter.pdf (last accessed 15 November 2011).
3. For a comparison of pre-Charter ASEAN cooperation and the present structure of legal arrangements in the Charter-based ASEAN, see Desierto (2011a).
4. The bilateral swap arrangements under the CMI have been regarded as "more symbolic than truly effective". See Sussangkarn (2010), Chey (2009), and Kawai (2010).
5. For a description of national, bilateral, and regional efforts taken by ASEAN member states during the 1997–98 Asian financial crisis, see Soesastro (1998). On the proposal for stronger regional institutions to prevent and manage financial crises, see Kuroda and Kawai (2005). See also Koh (2009) and Chesterman (2008).
6. Agreement among the Government of Brunei Darussalam, Indonesia, Malaysia, the Philippines, Singapore, and Thailand for the Promotion and Protection of Investments, Manila, 15 December 1987 (hereafter, ASEAN IGA). Full text of the ASEAN IGA available at http://www.asean.org/6464.htm (last accessed 15 November 2011).
7. ASEAN IGA, Art. II(1).
8. ASEAN IGA, Arts. VI(I) and VI(2).
9. ASEAN IGA, Art. III(2). See ASEAN IGA Art. IV(1) ad IV(2).
10. ASEAN IGA, Art. I(3).
11. ASEAN IGA, Art. IV(3): "Investor of any Contracting Party who within the territory of another Contracting Party suffers damages in relation to their investment activities – in connection with their investments, owing to the outbreak of hostilities or a state of national emergency, shall be accorded treatment no less favorable than that accorded to investors of any third country, as regards restitution, compensation, or other valuable consideration. Payments made under this provision shall be effectively realizable and freely transferable subject to Article VII."
12. ASEAN IGA, Article VII. Italics added.
13. On the evolution of standards of treatment in international investment law from customary minimum treatment protecting aliens to modern treaty standards, see McLachlan et al. (2008).
14. ASEAN IGA, Art. IV (1).
15. ASEAN IGA, Art. IX(1) and IX(2).
16. ASEAN IGA, Art. X.
17. Protocol to Amend the Agreement among the Government of Brunei Darussalam, the Republic of Indonesia, Malaysia, the Republic of the Philippines, the Republic of Singapore, and the Kingdom of Thailand for the Promotion and Protection of

Investments, Jakarta, 12 September 1996, Arts. 2 and 3. Full text available at http://www.asean.org/12813.htm (last accessed 15 November 2011).

18. Framework Agreement on the ASEAN Investment Area, Makati, Philippines, 7 October 1998 (hereafter, "AIA"), Article 1.

19. AIA, Art. 1 para. 4: "For purposes of this Agreement . . . 'effective ASEAN equity' in respect of an investment in an ASEAN Member State means ultimate holdings by nationals or juridical persons of ASEAN Member States in that investment. Where the shareholding/equity structure of an ASEAN investor makes it difficult to establish the ultimate holding structure, the rules and procedures for determining effective equity used by the Member State in which the ASEAN investor is investing may be applied. If necessary, the Co-ordinating Committee on Investment shall prepare guidelines for this purpose."

20. ASEAN AIA, Art. 3.

21. ASEAN AIA, Art. 4.

22. ASEAN AIA, Art. 16(1).

23. ASEAN AIA, Art. 16 (3) to 16(5).

24. ASEAN AIA, Art. 7.

25. ASEAN AIA, Arts. 9(1) and 9(2).

26. ASEAN AIA Art. 13 (General Exceptions), and GATT Art. XX (General Exceptions).

27. ASEAN AIA, Art. 13.

28. ASEAN AIA, Art. 14.

29. ASEAN AIA, Art. 15.

30. On the importance of political institutions within ASEAN Member States to cope with the Asian financial crisis, see McIntyre (2001).

31. ASEAN Charter, Article 3 ("ASEAN, as an intergovernmental organization, is hereby conferred legal personality"). Full text of the ASEAN Charter available at http://www.asean.org/archive/publications/ASEAN-Charter.pdf (last accessed 15 November 2011).

32. ASEAN Charter, Article 5(2).

33. ASEAN Charter, Article 2(2), specifically Articles 2(2)(h), 2(2)(i), 2(2)(j), 2(2)(n).

34. ASEAN Charter, Article 7.

35. ASEAN Charter, Articles 8, 9, 10, and 11.

36. Full text of ASEAN Vision 2020 at http://www.aseansec.org/1814.htm (last accessed 15 November 2011).

37. ASEAN Declaration, Bangkok, 8 August 1967, available at http://www.asean.org/1212.htm (last accessed 15 November 2011); Treaty of Amity and Cooperation in Southeast Asia, Indonesia, 24 February 1976, available at http://www.asean.org/1217.htm (last accessed 15 November 2011).

38. ASEAN Charter, Article 52(1): "All treaties, conventions, agreements, concords, declarations, protocols, and other ASEAN instruments which have been in effect before the entry into force of this Charter shall continue to be valid." On the disputed effects of such legal continuity, see among others Chan (2010) and Wu (2010).

39. 2009 ASEAN Comprehensive Investment Agreement, Art. 47 (Transitional Arrangements Relating to the ASEAN IGA and the AIA Agreement):

    "1. Upon entry into force of this Agreement, the ASEAN IGA and the AIA Agreement shall be terminated.

    2. Notwithstanding the termination of the AIA Agreement, the Temporary Exclusion List and the Sensitive List to the AIA Agreement shall apply to the liberalization provisions of the ACIA mutatis mutandis, until such time that the Reservation List of the ACIA comes into force.

    3. With respect to investments falling within the ambit of this Agreement as well as under the ASEAN IGA, or within the ambit of this Agreement and the AIA Agreement, investors of these investments may choose to apply the provisions, but only in its entirety, of either this Agreement or the ASEAN IGA or the AIA Agreement, as the case may be, for a period of 3 years after the date of termination of the ASEAN IGA and the AIA Agreement."

40. For basic information and background on the ASEAN Charter, see http://www. aseansec.org/21861.htm (last accessed 15 November 2011).

41. The ASEAN Free Trade Area was supposed to have been fully implemented by 2002, and full phase out of exclusions from investment into the manufacturing sector by 2003. See Manupipatpong (1999).

42. For the overview of AEC, see http://www.aseansec.org/18757.htm (last visited 15 June 2011).

43. ASEAN Economic Community Blueprint, at pp. 12–14, available at http://www. aseansec.org/5187-10.pdf (last visited 15 June 2011).

44. 2009 ASEAN Comprehensive Investment Agreement, Art. 48(1), at http://www. aseansec.org/documents/FINAL-SIGNED-ACIA.pdf (last visited 15 June 2011) [hereafter, "ACIA"].

45. Agreement on Investment of the Framework Agreement on Comprehensive Economic Cooperation between the Association of Southeast Asian Nations and the People's Republic of China, 2009, available at http://www.aseansec.org/22974.pdf (last accessed 15 November 2011) [hereafter, "ASEAN–PRC Investment Agreement"].

46. Agreement Establishing the ASEAN–Australia–New Zealand FTA, Chapter 11 (Investment), 2009, available at http://www.dfat.gov.au/fta/aanzfta/chapters/aanzfta_chapter11.PDF (last visited 15 November 2011) [hereafter, "ASEAN–Australia–NZ FTA Investment Chapter"].

47. The ACIA entered into force on 6 April 2012. See http://www.pia.gov.ph/news/index.php?article=1781333691163.

48. ACIA Arts. 47(1) to 47(3).

49. Agreement on Investment of the Framework Agreement on Comprehensive Economic Cooperation between the Association of Southeast Asian Nations and the People's Republic of China, 2009, available at http://www.aseansec.org/22974.pdf (last accessed 15 November 2011) [hereafter, "ASEAN–PRC Investment Agreement"].

50. Agreement Establishing the ASEAN–Australia–New Zealand FTA, Chapter 11 (Investment), 2009, available at http://www.dfat.gov.au/fta/aanzfta/chapters/aanzfta_chapter11.PDF (last accessed 15 November 2011) [hereafter, "ASEAN–Australia–NZ FTA Investment Chapter"].

51. "India pushes for services and investment agreement with ASEAN", The Economic Times, 13 August 2011, available at http://articles.economictimes.indiatimes.com/2011-08-13/news/29884263_1_asean-countries-trade-in-goods-agreement-services-and-investment (last accessed 15 November 2011). See Joint Statement of the 2nd United States – ASEAN Leaders Meeting (2010).

52. Framework Agreement on Comprehensive Economic Cooperation Between the Republic of India and the Association of Southeast Asian Nations, Indonesia, 8 October 2003, available at http://www.asean.org/15278.htm (last accessed 15 November 2011).

53. Statement by the Prime Minister at the 9th ASEAN–India Summit, Press Information Bureau, Government of India, available at http://pib.nic.in/newsite/erelease.aspx?relid577320 (last accessed 15 November 2011).

54. Remarks by U.S. Secretary of State Hillary Clinton at the ASEAN Business and Investment Summit, 18 November 2011, available at http://www.state.gov/secretary/rm/2011/11/177349.htm (last accessed 20 November 2011).

55. For a more detailed discussion of applicable investment law, see Desierto (2011b).

56. ASEAN Secretariat, ASEAN Investment Report 2011: Sustaining FDI Flows in a Post-Crisis World, November 2011, p. V (Executive Summary).

57. Ibid., at p. 25.

58. ACIA Art. 1(a) and 1(c).

59. See Canada's 2004 Model BIT (Agreement for the Promotion and Protection of Investments) at http://italaw.com/documents/Canadian2004-FIPA-model-en.pdf (last accessed 15 November 2011); the United States' 2004 Model BIT at http://italaw.com/documents/USmodelbitnov04.pdf (last accessed 15 November 2011); Germany's 2008

Model BIT at http://italaw.com/investmenttreaties.htm (last accessed 15 November 2011).

60. ACIA Art. 3(3).
61. ACIA Art. 3(1).
62. ACIA Art. 9.
63. ACIA Art. 10.
64. ACIA Art. 3(4).
65. ACIA Art. 4(a).
66. ACIA Art. 4(c).
67. ACIA Art. 6.
68. ACIA Art. 5.
69. ACIA Art. 6, footnote 4(a) of the treaty text.
70. ACIA Art. 11.
71. ACIA Art. 14.
72. ACIA Art. 19.
73. ACIA Art. 12.
74. ACIA Art. 13(3).
75. ACIA Art. 13(4)(c).
76. ACIA Art. 13(5).
77. ACIA Art. 16.
78. ACIA Art. 17(1).
79. ACIA Art. 18.
80. ACIA Art. 23(c).
81. ACIA Art. 42.
82. ACIA Arts. 28–41. See note 65.
83. "[The People's Republic of] China's direct investment to ASEAN countries reaches $2.57 b", Xinhua News, 2 March 2011, available at http://www.chinadaily.com.cn/business/2011-03/02/content_12104984.htm (last visited 15 August 2011).
84. See Overview of ASEAN–New Zealand Relations, at http://www.asean.org/5826.htm (last visited 15 August 2011); Australia Trade and Investment with ASEAN, at http://www.dfat.gov.au/facts/asean.html (last visited 15 August 2011); Gemma Daley and Shammim Adam, "ASEAN, Australia, New Zealand sign free-trade deal", Bloomberg, 27 February 2009, at http://www.bloomberg.com/apps/news?pid5newsarchive&sid5aul8rxM98Jg4 (last visited 15 August 2011).
85. 2011 ASEAN Investment Report, at p. 7.
86. ASEAN–PRC Investment Agreement, Art. 1(d) and footnote 1 of the treaty.
87. ASEAN–PRC Investment Agreement, Art. 3(4).
88. ASEAN–PRC Investment Agreement, Art. 15.
89. ASEAN–PRC Investment Agreement, Arts. 4–5.
90. ASEAN–PRC Investment Agreement, Art. 6.
91. ASEAN–PRC Investment Agreement, Arts. 7–8.
92. ASEAN–PRC Investment Agreement, Art. 9.
93. ASEAN–PRC Investment Agreement, Art. 10(3).
94. ASEAN–PRC Investment Agreement, Art.11
95. ASEAN–PRC Investment Agreement, Arts. 16–17.
96. ASEAN–PRC Investment Agreement, Art. 22.
97. ASEAN–PRC Investment Agreement, Art. 13. See Agreement on Dispute Settlement Mechanism of the Framework Agreement on Comprehensive Economic Co-operation between the Association of Southeast Asian Nations and the People's Republic of China, Vientiane, Laos, 29 November 2004, available at http://www.asean.org/16635.htm (last accessed 15 November 2011).
98. ASEAN–PRC Investment Agreement, Art. 14(4).
99. ASEAN–Australia–NZ FTA Investment Chapter, Art. 1(2).
100. ASEAN–Australia–NZ FTA Investment Chapter, Art. 2(c) and footnote 2 of the treaty text.

101.   ASEAN–Australia–NZ FTA Investment Chapter, Art. 11.
102.   ASEAN–Australia–NZ FTA Investment Chapter, Art. 4.
103.   ASEAN–Australia–NZ FTA Investment Chapter, Art. 6.
104.   ASEAN–Australia–NZ FTA Investment Chapter, Art. 8(3).
105.   ASEAN–Australia–NZ FTA Investment Chapter, Art. 9.
106.   ASEAN–Australia–NZ FTA Investment Chapter, Art. 12.
107.   ASEAN–Australia–NZ FTA Investment Chapter, Art. 15.
108.   ASEAN–Australia–NZ FTA Investment Chapter, Art. 7.
109.   ASEAN–Australia–NZ FTA Investment Chapter, Art. 13(1), 13(5).
110.   ASEAN–Australia–NZ FTA Investment Chapter, Art. 13(1), 13(8).
111.   ASEAN–Australia–NZ FTA Investment Chapter, Art. 13(9) to 13(12).
112.   ASEAN–Australia–NZ FTA Investment Chapter, Art. 17.
113.   ASEAN–Australia–NZ FTA Investment Chapter, Articles 18–28.
114.   ASEAN–Australia–NZ FTA Investment Chapter, Art. 27(3).

BIBLIOGRAPHY

ASEAN Economic Community Blueprint. Available at http://www.aseansec. org/5187-10.pdf (accessed 15 June 2011).

ASEAN Investment Report (2009). Available at http://www.aseansec.org/docu-ments/AIR2009.pdf.

ASEAN Secretariat (2006), *Statistics of Foreign Direct Investment to ASEAN*, Eighth Edition. Available at http://www.asean.org/5187-1.pdf (accessed 15 November 2011).

Chan, W.T. (2010), 'ASEAN legal personality under its new charter: its nature, meaning, and implications: status of the work and issues involved', in S. Tiwari (ed.), *ASEAN: Life after the Charter*, Singapore: Institute of Southeast Asian Studies.

Chesterman, S. (2008), 'Does ASEAN exist? The Association of Southeast Asian Nations as an international legal person', *Singapore Yearbook of International Law, Vol. 12*, pp. 199–211.

Chey, H.K. (2009), 'The changing political dynamics of East Asian financial coop-eration: the Chiang Mai initiative', *Asian Survey*, **49** (3) (May/June), 450–67.

Chia, S.Y. (2010), 'Accelerating ASEAN trade and investment cooperation and integration: progress and challenges', in Philippe Gugler (ed.), *Competitiveness of the ASEAN Countries: Corporate and Regulatory Drivers*, Cheltenham UK and Northampton, MA, USA: Edward Elgar.

Desierto, D.A. (2008), 'Postcolonial international law discourses on regional developments in South and Southeast Asia', *International Journal of Legal Information*, **36** (3), Winter, 387–421.

Desierto, D.A. (2010), 'International law: regional developments in South and Southeast Asia', *Max Planck Encyclopedia of Public International Law (MPEPIL)*, Heidelberg and Oxford University Press.

Desierto, D.A. (2011a), 'ASEAN's constitutionalization of international law: challenges to evolution under the new ASEAN charter', *Columbia Journal of Transnational Law*, **49** (2), 268–330.

Desierto, D.A. (2011b), 'For greater certainty: balancing economic integration with investment protection in the new ASEAN investment agreements', in G. Born and M. Maniruzzaman (eds), *Transnational Dispute Management*, **5**

(Special Issue on International Business Dispute Resolution in Asia). http://www.transnational.dispute.management.com/article.asp?key=1768.

Egger, P., and M. Pfaffermayr (2009), 'The impact of bilateral investment treaties on foreign direct investment', in K.P. Sauvant and L.E. Sachs (eds), *The Effect of Treaties on Foreign Direct Investment: Bilateral Investment Treaties, Double Taxation Treaties, and Investment Flows*, Oxford University Press.

Fry, J.D. (2011), 'ASEAN: regional trends in economic integration, export competitiveness, and inbound investment for selected industries', United Nations Conference on Trade and Development.

Hallward-Driemeier, M. (2009), 'Do bilateral investment treaties attract FDI? Only a bit . . . and they could bite', in K.P. Sauvant and L.E. Sachs (eds), *The Effect of Treaties on Foreign Direct Investment: Bilateral Investment Treaties, Double Taxation Treaties, and Investment Flows*, Oxford: Oxford University Press.

Joint Statement of the 2nd United States–ASEAN Leaders Meeting, 24 September 2010. Available at http://www.whitehouse.gov/the-press-office/2010/09/24/joint-statement-2nd-us-asean-leaders-meeting (accessed 15 November 2011).

Kawai, M. (2010), 'From the Chiang Mai initiative to an Asian monetary fund', at http://aric.adb.org/grs/papers/Kawai%205.pdf (accessed 15 November 2011).

Koh, T.B. (ed.) (2009), *The Making of the Asean Charter*, Singapore: World Scientific.

Kuroda, H., and M. Kawai (2005), 'Strengthening regional financial cooperation in East Asia', in G. De Brouwer and Y. Wang, *Financial Governance in East Asia: Policy Dialogue, Surveillance and Cooperation*, London: Routledge.

Manupipatpong, W. (1999), 'ASEAN economic integration', (26 August). http://www.asean.org/2830.htm (accessed 15 June 2011).

McIntyre, A. (2001), 'Institutions and investors: the politics of the economic crisis in Southeast Asia', *International Organization*, **55** (1), Winter, 81–122.

McLachlan, C., L. Shore, and M. Weiniger (2008), *International Investment Arbitration: Substantive Principles*, Oxford: Oxford University Press.

Neumayer, E., and L. Spess (2009), 'Do bilateral investment treaties increase foreign direct investment to developing countries?', in K.P. Sauvant and L.E. Sachs (eds), *The Effect of Treaties on Foreign Direct Investment: Bilateral Investment Treaties, Double Taxation Treaties, and Investment Flows*, Oxford: Oxford University Press.

Plummer, M.G., and R.W. Click (2009), 'The ASEAN economic community and the European experience', in K. Hamada, B. Reszat, and U. Volz (eds), *Towards Monetary and Financial Integration in East Asia*, Cheltenham, UK and Northampton, MA, USA: Edward Elgar.

Rose-Ackerman, S. (2009), 'The global BITs regime and the domestic environment for investment', in K.P. Sauvant and L.E. Sachs (eds), *The Effect of Treaties on Foreign Direct Investment: Bilateral Investment Treaties, Double Taxation Treaties, and Investment Flows*, Oxford: Oxford University Press.

Salacuse, J.W., and N.P. Sullivan (2009), 'Do BITs really work: an evaluation of bilateral investment treaties and their grand bargain', in K.P. Sauvant and L.E. Sachs (eds), *The Effect of Treaties on Foreign Direct Investment: Bilateral Investment Treaties, Double Taxation Treaties, and Investment Flows*, Oxford: Oxford University Press.

Sasse, J.P. (2011), *An Economic Analysis of Bilateral Investment Treaties*, Springer Gabler.

Sauvant, Karl P., and Lisa E. Sachs (eds), *The Effects of Treaties on Foreign Direct Investment: Bilateral Investment Treaties, Double Taxation Treaties and Investment Flows*, Oxford University Press.
Seidl-Hohenveldern, I. (1999), *International Economic Law*, Kluwer Law International, p. 55.
Soesastro, H. (1998), 'ASEAN during the crisis', *ASEAN Economic Bulletin*, 3 (Southeast Asia's Economic Crisis: Origins, Lessons, and the Way Forward) (December).
Sornarajah, M., and R. Arumugam (2007), 'An overview of foreign direct investment jurisprudence, in Denis Hew (ed.), *Brick By Brick: The Building of an ASEAN Economic Community*, Institute of Southeast Asian Studies, pp. 144–74.
Sussangkarn, C. (2010), 'The Chiang Mai initiative multilateralization: origin, development and outlook', Asian Development Bank Insititue Working Paper Series No. 230 (July). http://www.adbi.org/files/2010.07.13.wp230.chiang.mai. initiative.multilateralisation.pdf (accessed 29 November 2011).
Thompson, E.R., and P.H. Poon (2000), 'ASEAN after the financial crisis: links between foreign direct investment and regulatory change', *ASEAN Economic Bulletin*, 17 (1) April.
UNCTAD (United Nations Conference on Trade and Development) (2008), 'Identifying core elements in investment agreements in the APEC region', UNCTAD Series on International Investment Policies for Development.
UNCTAD (2009), 'The role of international investment agreements in attracting foreign direct investment to developing countries', UNCTAD Series on International Investment Policies for Development.
UNCTAD (2011), 'World Investment Report 2011: Non-Equity Modes of International Production and Development'.
Worapot, M. (2002), 'The ASEAN surveillance process and the East Asian monetary fund', *ASEAN Economic Bulletin*, 19 (1) April.
Wu, C.H. (2010), 'The ASEAN economic community under the ASEAN charter: its external economic relations and dispute settlement mechanisms', in C. Hermann and J.P. Terhechte (eds), *European Yearbook of International Economic Law*, *Volume 1*, Heidelberg, Dordrecht, London, New York: Springer.
Zhong, Z. (2011), 'The ASEAN comprehensive investment agreement: realizing a regional community', *Asian Journal of Comparative Law*, 1, 1–39.

PART III

Country Studies

8. Malaysia

Tham Siew Yean

INTRODUCTION

As a small and open economy rich in natural resources, Malaysia has grown rapidly since independence in 1957, as shown by the growth in gross national per capita income from $380 in 1970 to $6,760 in 2009. This growth was achieved along with a reduction in both poverty and income inequality, as well as improvements in the quality of life. Malaysia also aspires to be a developed country by 2020, based on the Vision 2020 goals that were launched by the former Prime Minister Mahathir bin Mohamad in 1991. In 2010, Prime Minister Datuk Seri Najib Tun Razak, after a review of economic performance, announced the need to accelerate growth over the next 10 years in an effort to achieve a high-income economy with a per capita income of $17,000.

Setting this target poses a great challenge to Malaysia as growth has almost halved since the 1997 Asian financial crisis (AFC). Externally, Malaysia is also facing increasing competitive pressures, especially from other developing countries that have sizeable domestic consumer markets such as the People's Republic of China (PRC), India, and Viet Nam. Internally, the country is at a crossroads politically, economically and socially. Other challenges include faltering private investment and outflows of human and financial capital. Furthermore, the manufacturing sector, despite being the engine of growth for more than five decades, has failed to nurture deep linkages domestically, while new engines of growth have yet to be cultivated.

In view of these aspirations and challenges, the first objective of this chapter is to review Malaysia's growth performance since independence, especially the macroeconomic performance and savings-investment gap after the AFC. The second objective is to analyze the pattern and constraints on long-term private investment in the country. This will provide the basis for policy recommendations for sustaining future growth and investment. The conclusion summarizes the main findings of this chapter.

MALAYSIA'S ECONOMIC PERFORMANCE

Malaysia's overall development strategy first needs to be outlined as
it exerts a strong influence on the country's development policies. The
New Economic Policy (NEP), which was launched in 1971 in response
to domestic interethnic riots in May 1969, sought to reduce poverty and
redistribute income in favor of the *bumiputeras*.[1] However, the government also recognized that growth is a fundamental condition for both
objectives of the NEP and hence there is ". . . a continuing obsession on
growth and distribution" (Zainal 2009). It is important to bear in mind
this twin obsession as it helps explain the policy choices of the country.
For example, pro-growth strategies include accelerating industrialization
as the manufacturing sector was identified as an engine of growth due to
the volatility in commodity prices and its adverse effects on the terms of
trade. Concurrently, NEP redistribution policies placed a cap on foreign
equity ownership, as well as other restrictions.[2] This set the pattern in
policy formulation whereby the road to development has been and continues to be a constant search for balance between the twin needs of the
country: growth and redistribution.

Despite its rich natural resources and supporting research infrastructure in this sector, Malaysia embarked on industrialization by focusing
and developing the non-resource-based sector as a new engine of growth
after independence. Import substitution, export promotion strategies,
and foreign direct investment (FDI) were used to develop the country's
manufacturing sector. Early import substitution policies after independence were withdrawn by the end of the 1960s due to a limited domestic
market and the need to create employment. As a result, export promotion
started early in Malaysia relative to other developing countries, thereby
providing "early mover" advantages for the development of the manufacturing sector from 1970 to 1980. But import substitution strategies
were reinstated with the implementation of the heavy industries program
in 1980, inspired by Korean and Japanese models of industrial development. These, however, had twin objectives of deepening industrialization
through the development of linkages and, at the same time, fostering the
development of *bumiputera* entrepreneurship. Heavy industries, such as
the national automobile project, were born out of government and foreign
partnerships, instead of the private partnerships in the first phase of export
orientation. Subsequently, twin deficits – fiscal and external – led to the
reinstatement of export- and FDI-promotion strategies in 1985, alongside
the government-led heavy industry program. Export- and FDI-promotion
policies continue to be utilized for developing the manufacturing sector.
Since 2005, there has been an increasing emphasis on the services sector

Table 8.1   Key economic indicators by percentage (1970–2010)

	1970–84	1985–86	1987–97	1998	1999–2008	2009	2010
Real GDP growth[a]	7.9	0.1	8.9	−7.4	5.5	−1.7	7.2
Inflation	5.9	0.5	3.2	5.4	2.4	0.6	1.7
Unemployment rate	5.8	6.6	4.1	3.1	3.4	3.7	3.2
Current account (% of GNI)	−3.0	−1.2	−3.0	13.2	13.0	17.5	12.2

Notes:
GDP = gross domestic product.
a.   Based on different base years.

Source: Sukhdave (2011a).

as a new source of growth. Nevertheless, the same export- and FDI-promotion strategies used for the development of the manufacturing sector have applied for the development of the services sector, without resolving the underlying problems that are hindering industrial deepening.

Overall, Malaysia registered higher average growth rates before the AFC, compared to the post-crisis period (see Table 8.1). There were economic crises in 1985, 1998, and 2009 with negative growth rates. Nonetheless, the economy recovered the following year on each of these occasions. The highest inflation rates occurred between 1970 and 1984. Inflation averaged 5.9 per cent during that period, due largely to the relatively high inflation rate in 1973 and 1974, respectively 9.8 per cent and 17.0 per cent. This, in turn, can be attributed to imported inflation when the ringgit appreciated with the shift to a floating exchange rate regime, as well as a rapid growth in government expenditure due to the discovery of oil and a boom in commodity prices (Thillainathan 2011, 44). But inflation ceased to be a problem by the mid-1980s due to tight monetary policy. Subsequently, inflation has been well controlled, except during the AFC, when the ringgit depreciated by almost 50 per cent against the dollar from July 1997 to January 1998. Similarly, while unemployment was relatively high from 1970 to 1984, the unemployment rate fell rapidly during the period of rapid industrialization and high growth from 1987 to 1997. In fact, by the early 1990s, Malaysia had achieved full employment and had to resort to the use of migrant workers. Unemployment increased slightly in 2009 as a result of the global economic recession (GER), but it has decreased with economic recovery in 2010. The current account was in deficit before the AFC, while it had a surplus post-crisis.

The main contributors to growth by expenditure items differed over time (see Table 8.2). Before the first economic crisis in 1985 and 1986,

Table 8.2   Contribution to gross domestic product (GDP) growth by percentage (1970–2009)

	1970–84	1985–86	1987–97	1998	1999–2008	2009
Consumption	3.78	−2.71	4.13	−4.80	3.48	0.35
Government expenditure	1.22	0.03	0.73	−0.93	1.06	0.43
Investment	2.80	−4.88	4.79	−18.01	0.98	−3.13
Exports	3.91	3.41	11.27	−18.88	7.85	−12.27
Imports	4.47	−4.39	12.09	−4.36	7.66	−12.91
Net exports	−0.56	7.80	−0.81	19.38	0.19	0.63
GDP growth	7.2	0.2	8.8	−4.4	5.7	−1.7

Note: Based on a common base year, 2000.

Source: Computed based on data from the World Bank, http://databank.worldbank.org/ddp/home.do.

Table 8.3   Contributions to growth, by inputs and total factor productivity (1971–2010) by percentage

	1971–90	1991–2000	1991–95	1996–2000	2001–05	2006–10
GDP growth	6.7	7.0	9.5	4.8	4.2	4.2
Labor	2.4	1.7	2.3	1.5	1.5	1.3
Capital	3.4	3.5	4.7	2.2	1.7	1.4
TFP	0.9	1.8	2.5	1.1	1.3	1.5

Source: Mahadevan (2007) and Malaysia (2010).

consumption had been the main contributor. For the subsequent period of high growth before the AFC, investment had been the main driver, although consumption was also important. After the crisis, however, the contribution of consumption has been significantly higher than investment. Moreover, although export contribution is also large, it has been accompanied by an equal, if not larger, import contribution so that the net contribution of trade is negative, except for the crisis years when the drop in imports is larger than that of exports.

Despite differences in approaches and estimates obtained for total factor productivity (TFP) growth for the country, there appears to be a consensus that the Malaysian economy is very much driven by input growth, especially capital input (see Table 8.3). Estimations from the Economic Planning Unit (EPU) lend further support to that conclusion, although its estimates also show that TFP growth has increased over time.[3] The relative contributions of capital and labor to growth have fallen over time when the period before the AFC (1991–95) is compared to the post-crisis period.

STRUCTURAL TRANSFORMATION

Over the last five decades, Malaysia has shifted from a primarily commodity-producing economy to an industrialized economy (see Figure 8.1). At the time of independence, Malaysia was a key producer of tin and rubber. By 1970, agriculture's share of gross domestic product (GDP) had fallen and was almost the same as the share of nongovernment services (29 per cent and 31 per cent, respectively) due to increasing industrialization. However,

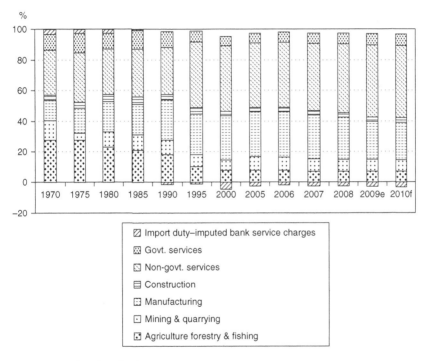

Note: e = estimation; f = forecast.

Sources: Government of Malaysia (various years), *Economic Report,* Kuala Lumpur: Ministry of Finance.

Figure 8.1   Sector shifts in gross domestic product 1970–2010 (%)

manufacturing's share was only 14 per cent in 1970 despite the pursuit of import substitution after independence.

Subsequently, the shift into export-oriented manufacturing activities in 1969 and the opening of Free Trade Zones in 1970, as well as a concerted effort to attract FDI into the country, changed the pace of industrialization. The share of manufacturing in Malaysia's GDP grew steadily to a peak of 32 per cent in 2000. Its share of total employment also grew gradually from 9 per cent in 1970 to 28 per cent in 2000. This sector also registered the highest average annual growth rate from 1970 to 2000. But growth has declined after the AFC due in part to increasingly adverse external circumstances, such as the dot.com crisis in 2001, the emergence of the GER in 2008, and the escalating competitive pressures from the rise of the PRC and Viet Nam. While the share of manufacturing in GDP has declined since 2000, its employment share has been maintained at around 29 per cent due to the use of migrant labor.

The share of nongovernment services has also grown from 21 per cent in 1970 to 38 per cent in 2000. After 2000, this sector recorded higher average annual growth rates than manufacturing and its share in GDP and employment continued to grow to 50 per cent and 42 per cent, respectively, in 2009.

Within manufacturing, non-resource-based manufacturing has a larger share than resource-based manufacturing. Production continues to be highly concentrated in electrical and electronics production, which is dominated mainly by multinational production. The manufacture of transport equipment, sheltered from competition by both tariff and non-tariff barriers, is the next largest non-resource-based manufacturing subsector.

Recent Macroeconomic Performance: 1996–2010

The Central Bank of Malaysia aims to promote monetary stability with the primary objective of maintaining price stability, while giving due regard to the developments in the economy (Sukhdave 2011b; Hannoun 2007). Interest rate targeting by means of the Overnight Policy Rate has been used since 1996 to achieve price stability. Figure 8.2 shows that inflation continues to be well managed after the AFC, with an average inflation rate of 2.2 per cent from 1999 to 2010. The use of monetary policy to manage price stability is also supported by the use of non-inflationary sources of financing for financing government expenditure (Thillainathan 2011). The Employee Provident Fund (EPF) is a national pension fund with mandatory contributions from both employers and employees. The law further requires 70 per cent of EPF's funds to be invested in Malaysian Government Securities. Thus, the EPF provides a captive market for

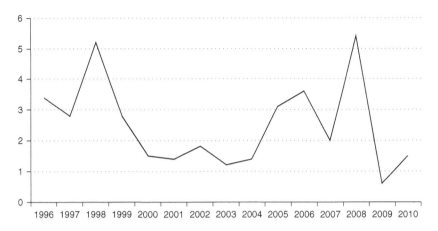

Note: CPI = Consumer Price Index.

Source: Ministry of Finance, various years (figures for 2010 are estimates).

Figure 8.2   Inflation rate in Malaysia 1996–2010 (CPI based) (%)

government borrowing. In addition, the use of price controls and subsidies, especially fuel subsidies, has also helped to maintain relatively low inflation.

In the 15 years since the onset of the AFC, Malaysia moved from a managed float that was implemented from 1993 to 1998 to a pegged exchange rate. The latter was implemented from 1998 to 2005. The peg was further defended by a new regime of comprehensive capital controls when it was imposed in 1998. The purpose of these controls was to restrict outflows, in contrast to its earlier use in 1993–94 to restrain capital inflows. International trading of the ringgit was restricted, unlike its unrestricted tradability before the AFC. Thus, all travelers taking more than RM10000 outside the country need to make a declaration to the Central Bank. All payments and borrowing by residents to non-residents, or vice versa, have to be in foreign currency rather than in ringgit. The imposition of capital controls, a fixed exchange rate and the non-internationalization of the ringgit allowed the Central Bank to lower interest rates and shift to an expansionary monetary policy in order to stimulate economic recovery.

These exchange rate control measures were gradually removed over time, even though the economy recovered the following year. The exit levy on portfolio foreign investments was abolished in 2001. Other liberalization measures were implemented, as guided by the Financial Master Plan and the Capital Market Plan, which were launched in 2001. In particular,

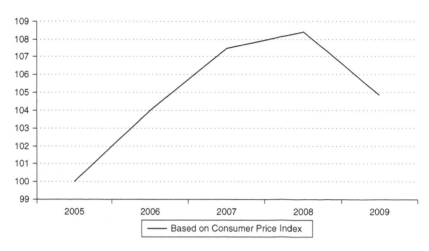

Source: International Financial Statistics.

Figure 8.3   The real effective exchange rate (2005–09)

the deregulation of capital outflows by residents in response to the surges in capital inflows in 2006 and 2007 contributed to the large jump in outflows of direct investment from Malaysia after 2006.

In 2005, the peg was removed and a managed float was reinstated. However, the non-internationalization of the ringgit is still maintained. The real effective exchange rate appreciated from 2005 to 2008 (see Figure 8.3). In fact, the ringgit appreciated against the dollar by as much as 14 per cent from 2005 to 2007. The huge outflows in 2008, as well as declining demand for exports in the wake of the GER resulted in the depreciation of the ringgit in 2009.

Although the Central Bank has emphasized that the exchange rate is determined by economic fundamentals and market conditions, it has occasionally intervened in the foreign exchange market to moderate large fluctuations. The aim of these interventions is minimize disruptions to trade and investment, reduce misalignments, and to facilitate orderly adjustments – but not to influence the underlying trend (Ooi 2006, 2008).

The use of a fixed exchange rate in 1998 led to a heavier burden on fiscal policy to achieve the domestic objectives for reviving the economy. Consequently, an expansionary fiscal policy was used (see Table 8.4). The budget deficit grew from 1.8 per cent of GDP in 1998 to a peak of 6.6 per cent in 2000, before it was reduced progressively to 3.2 per cent by 2007. In 2008–09, the deficit grew again due to the use of fiscal stimulus to overcome the negative impact of the GER on the domestic economy. The two

Table 8.4   Selected indicators of fiscal policy

Year	Total government expenditure (% of GDP)[a]	Gross development expenditure (% of total expenditure)[a]	Budget deficit (% of GDP)[b]	Total public debt (% of GDP)[a]	Foreign debt/ total public debt (%)[a]
1996	23.1	25.0	0.7	35.3	11.7
1997	21.4	26.1	2.4	31.9	14.4
1998	22.1	28.9	−1.8	36.4	14.5
1999	23.0	32.6	−3.2	37.3	16.4
2000	23.7	33.1	−6.6	35.2	15.0
2001	28.1	35.6	−5.5	41.3	16.7
2002	27.3	34.4	−5.8	43.0	22.0
2003	27.4	34.3	−5.3	45.1	19.8
2004	25.3	24.0	−4.1	45.7	16.0
2005	24.6	23.8	−3.6	43.8	13.1
2006	25.0	25.0	−3.3	42.2	10.3
2007	25.5	24.8	−3.2	41.5	7.3
2008	26.5	21.8	−4.8	41.4	6.6
2009	30.4	24.0	−7.0	53.3	3.8
2010	26.9	26.2	−5.6	50.7	4.4

Notes: GDP = gross domestic product.

Sources: [a] Economic Planning Unit (Malaysia), published time series economic statistics (figures for 2009–10 form source 1), http://www.epu.gov.my/ accessed 20 April 2011; [b] Malaysia Ministry of Finance, various years (figures for 2010 are estimates).

stimulus packages used for this purpose amounted to RM7 billion (or 1.04 per cent of GDP) and RM60 billion (or 9 per cent of GDP). The budget deficit increased steeply to 7 per cent in 2009, before it was brought down to 5.6 per cent in 2010. Total public debt has also grown from 36 per cent of GDP in 1998 to a peak of 53 per cent in 2009, before it was brought down to 51 per cent in 2010. Much of the public debt is financed domestically, as shown by the relatively low foreign debt to GDP, and that is due to a relatively high rate of domestic savings.

Three emerging patterns in the fiscal deficit indicate an urgent need for fiscal reforms (Narayanan 2012). The first pattern is the decreasing share of gross development expenditure in total expenditure, which fell from a peak of 36 per cent in 2001 to 22 per cent in 2008, before increasing to 26 per cent in 2010 (see Table 8.4). This implies a converse increase in operating expenditure, the bulk of which is spent on the emoluments of the civil servants. However, the amount spent on subsidies for both consumption

Table 8.5   Banking sector: solvency, profitability, and asset quality

	2000 (%)	2009 (%)
Solvency position		
Risk-weighted capital ratio	12.0	14.0
Core-capital ratio	11.0	12.5
Profitability		
Return on assets	1.75	2.0
Return on equity	19.5	20.0
Asset quality		
Net nonperforming loans (NPL) ratio[a]	9.7	4.7

Source: UNDP 2009; [a] Central Bank Annual Reports.

and production has grown from 7.4 per cent of operating expenditure to 27 per cent in 2009, before decreasing to 21 per cent in 2010. In particular, the fuel subsidy is unsustainable (Thillainathan 2008). The second pattern is the increasing dependence on petroleum-based taxes as a source of tax revenue. In 2004, petroleum-related taxes contributed about 27 per cent of all tax revenue. That increased to 32 per cent in 2008. The third pattern is a compromise in fiscal prudence due to institutionalized leakages, a lack of transparency in the government procurement system, and the huge amount of debt owed by states, ministries, local councils and other government entities to the federal government. This is estimated at RM12.06 billion in 2005.

On the other hand, the banking system has emerged stronger after the AFC due to the broad-based financial sector reforms and capacity-building measures that were undertaken as a result of the crisis (see Table 8.5). All three indicators show that the banking sector was more resilient at the time of the GER. Moreover, Malaysia, as well as other Southeast Asian countries, had little exposure to the collateral debt obligations that triggered the subprime mortgage crisis in the United States (Athukorala 2012).

The impact of the GER, therefore, differed from the impact of the AFC as the source of instability in the GER was external in origin, specifically the subprime crisis in the United States. The AFC had domestic sources of instability, namely the domestic credit boom and the bubble in the share market.[4] In the case of the GER, the improved resilience of the banking sector and swift policy responses in terms of expansionary monetary and fiscal policies contributed to the economic recovery in 2010.

The impact of the GER on Malaysia was mainly transmitted through its

Table 8.6   Merchandise exports, Malaysia, 2008–09 (%)

Sector	Composition of exports			Annual change in exports			Share in export contraction/ expansion	
	2008	2009	2010[a]	2008	2009	2010[a]	2009	2010[a]
Primary products	23.5	20.4	22.3	36.0	−27.6	26.9	−38.9	35.2
Minerals	13.2	10.7	11.4	41.4	−32.2	23.4	−25.6	16.0
Crude oil	6.6	4.6	4.8	33.0	−42.0	21.3	−16.6	6.3
Liquefied natural gas	6.1	5.6	6.0	51.2	−23.4	22.1	−8.7	8.0
Agriculture	10.3	9.7	10.9	29.7	−21.6	30.8	−13.3	19.1
Palm oil	6.9	6.6	7.1	43.5	−20.9	25.4	−8.7	10.7
Rubber	1.2	0.8	1.4	10.6	−45.0	106.5	−3.3	5.5
Manufactures	74.1	77.8	76.1	3.8	−12.5	13.0	−55.7	65.1
Electronics	29.5	32.4	30.4	−8.3	−8.6	9.9	−15.3	17.8
Electrical machinery & appliances	12.3	12.3	12.0	9.9	−16.6	13.3	−12.3	10.4
Others	2.4	1.8	1.6	−1.7	−37.2	−2.4	−5.4	−0.3
Total	100.0	100.0	100.0	9.8	−16.6	15.6	−100.0	100.0
RM billion	663	553	639					

Source: Athukorala 2012; [a] Central Bank Annual Report 2010; preliminary figures.

trade links due to the adverse impact of the GER on its main trading partners. As shown in Table 8.6, exports contracted by 16.6 per cent in 2009. The contraction in the share of exports of primary products exceeded their share in total exports due to the sharp fall in the world prices for crude oil, palm oil, and rubber (Athukorala 2012). The contraction in manufacturing exports was 12.5 per cent, but its share in the total contraction of exports amounted to 56 per cent. Subsequently, the sharp rebound in exports in 2010 also helped to contribute to the rapid recovery in 2010, when economic growth shot up to 7.2 per cent.

The surplus in Malaysia's current account balance has resulted in growing international reserves since the current account surplus exceeded the deficit in the financial account, except in 2000 and 2008 (see Table 8.7). Since 2004, there have been episodes of large inflows and outflows of portfolio investments in response to changes in the domestic and global markets. In particular, the collapse of the Lehman Brothers Holdings Inc. in the fourth quarter of 2008 led to large outflows of portfolio investments and other short-term capital in that year.

Table 8.7 Current account, capital flows and reserves RM million (1999–2010)

	1999	2000	2001	2002	2003	2004	2005	2006	2007	2008	2009	2010
Current account	47895	32252	27687	30494	50625	57302	78367	96029	102190	129513	112139	90511
% of GNP	17	10	9	9	14	13	16	17	16	18	18	12
Financial account	-25152	-23848	-14791	-11941	-12146	19347	-36991	-43488	-38954	-118501	-80208	-21918
Outward direct investment (from Malaysia)	-5405	-7699	-1014	-7238	-5204	-7833	-11647	-22086	-38892	-50192	-27948	-42632
Inward (FDI) investments	14802	14393	2105	12173	9398	17572	15396	22230	29545	24134	5040	27649
Portfolio (shorter-term) investments	-4392	-9395	-2466	-6506	4168	32994	-14116	12786	18548	-82171	-1689	44942
Other investments	-30157	-21147	-13416	-10370	-20508	-23386	-26624	-56112	-47991	-8066	-58064	-51122
Foreign reserves Expressed in US dollars (million)	30854	29879	30843	34577	44856	66235	70193	82451	101338	91530	96688	106518
Ringgit equivalent (RM million)	117244	113541	117203	131394	170453	251690	265240	290399	335695	317445	331277	328649

Note: RM = Malaysian Ringgit. Current account balance is stated as % of Gross National Income (GNI) from 2006 onward.

Source: Central Bank Malaysia, Annual Report, various years.

The reserves are used to ensure that the domestic economy is shielded in the event of the large repatriation of capital, given the very open nature of Malaysia's economy. When the ringgit was pegged from 1998 to 2005, the reserves were adjusted to absorb changes in the current and financial accounts. However, with the removal of the peg, the ringgit was not allowed to float freely and instead the reserves were used to support the ringgit. For example, the Central Bank intervened from August 2008 to June 2009 to support the ringgit in response to the massive outflow of portfolio funds in 2008, resulting in a RM18 billion decrease in international reserves (International Monetary Fund 2010).

Foreign exchange regulations restricting the free inflow and outflow of foreign funds have been progressively liberalized since the AFC (Khor 2009; International Monetary Fund 2010). In 2001, repatriation of the principal sum and profits by non-resident portfolio investors was freely allowed. Other measures facilitated foreigners in borrowing in foreign or local currencies, purchasing property, and in operating in foreign or local currencies. Residents may now use their own funds to invest in foreign currency assets, to borrow in foreign currency the equivalent of RM100 million, without permission, and to open foreign currency accounts in Malaysian banks or abroad.[5] These measures therefore expanded the savings and investment choices for Malaysians. Malaysians can now invest in unit trusts and other investment vehicles that have their investments abroad, while Malaysian companies can also invest in projects abroad.

Hence, in terms of managing the trilemma of having to choose among exchange rate stability, free capital mobility, and monetary policy independence, Malaysia has chosen an intermediate solution of a managed float that is maintained through a combination of reserve accumulation, as well as liberalizing outflows (Hannoun 2007).

Savings–Investment

The negative savings–investment gap (by 6.6 per cent of GDP) in the period before the AFC turned positive after the crisis (see Figure 8.4). The average savings–investment gap was 12.6 per cent of GDP from 1999 to 2007. This fell to 9.4 per cent from 2008 to 2010. Gross domestic savings as a percentage of GDP fell from 49 per cent in 1998 to 42 per cent in 2001, but remained at around 42 per cent of GDP until 2008. Savings continue to remain high due primarily to the demographic bonus and a lack of social safety nets in the country.

In contrast, Gross Fixed Capital Formation as a percentage of GDP grew rapidly from 16 per cent in 1970 to a peak of 39 per cent in 1983. Subsequently, there was a marked drop in this measure after the AFC.

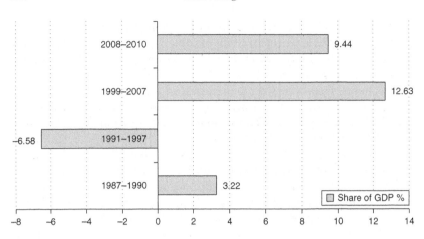

Note: ª 2010; preliminary figures.

Source: GDP from Money and Banking in Malaysia 35th Anniversary Edition (1987–1992); Annual Report Central Bank Malaysia from 1993–2011 for the years 1993–2010; Gross Fixed Capital Formation and Saving from *The Central Bank and The Financial System in Malaysia,* BNM 40th Anniversary Edition (1987–1995); Annual Report Central Bank Malaysia from 2000–2010 for the years 1996–2010)

Figure 8.4   Average annual savings–investment balance, 1987–2010ª

The average annual share was 35.3 per cent from 1986 to 1997, but it averaged at 21 per cent annually from 1999 to 2010. The share of public investment was generally lower than the share of private investment, until 1981 when the big push for the heavy industry projects was implemented with the government as an investor and partner in the production of heavy industries such as the national automobile project (see Figure 8.5). Its share again exceeded the share of private investment from 1999 to 2003 and again from 2008 to 2009 due to the AFC. The average annual share of public investment to GDP was 11.8 per cent from 1986 to 1997, and this was almost the same from 1999 to 2010 (11.0 per cent). In contrast, the share of private investment to GDP averaged 23.6 per cent for 1986–97 and 9.6 per cent for 1999–2010. Likewise, the share of FDI to GDP fell from an average of 5.0 per cent in 1986–97 to 3.2 per cent in 1999–2010.

LONG-TERM GROWTH CHALLENGE: REVIVING PRIVATE INVESTMENT IN MALAYSIA

A consumption-driven growth strategy for a small country such as Malaysia needs to have high per capita income in order for its

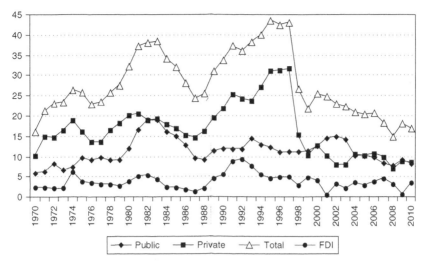

Note: Current price, 2010; preliminary figures.

Source: Money and Banking in Malaysia 35th Anniversary Edition (1970–1992) and Annual Report Central Bank Malaysia from 1993–2011 for the years 1993–2010.
http://www.epu.gov.my/nationalaccounts (accessed on 6 June 2010).
http://www.epu.gov.my/balanceofpayments (accessed on 6 June 2010).

*Figure 8.5   Public, private and foreign investment to GDP (1970–2010)
(share of GDP %)*

purchasing power to increase. However, Malaysia has been a middle-income economy for more than three decades, so the growth in its purchasing power is limited. Investment in high-value-added production, therefore, plays a critical role in terms of contributing to future growth. However, as shown in Table 8.2, the contribution of investment to growth in the last decade or so has been subdued. Sustaining future growth needs a strategy for enhancing investment in the country. In view of this, the pattern of private long-term investment is examined in the following sections.

Foreign Direct Investment

After the AFC, foreign direct investment (FDI) grew at an average of 3 per cent of GDP annually, with a peak in 2007 (Figure 8.5). Two pronounced dips can be observed from 2000 to 2009. The first was due to the dot. com crisis in 2001, and the other can be attributed to the GER in 2009. Table 8.8 shows a shift in inward FDI from the manufacturing sector to

Table 8.8   Cumulative net foreign direct investment flows by sector
(1990–2009)

Sector	1990–99 (% of total)	2000–09 (% of total)
Manufacturing	63	41
Oil and gas	17	17
Services	15	37
Others	5	5

Source: Central Bank Malaysia, Annual Report 2009.

the service sector, despite the fact that 100 per cent foreign ownership is allowed in the former as opposed to the latter.

The increase in the share of FDI services is due largely to the liberalization in financial services to promote the development of Islamic finance. The Central Bank estimated that FDI in the financial sector, including Islamic finance, amounted to RM41.6 billion from 1999 to 2009, after the liberalization of the sector (Central Bank Malaysia 2009). This is in line with the government's plan to build Malaysia as a global hub for Islamic finance. In particular, the relaxation of foreign equity restrictions in financial services has been mapped out in the Financial Master Plan in 2001. For example, foreign equity limits for investment banks, insurance companies and Islamic insurers were raised from 30 per cent to 49 per cent in 2005, and later to 70 per cent in 2009 (World Trade Organization 2009, 60). An increasing number of banking licenses with 100 per cent foreign-owner equity were given for Islamic banks. This also explains why there was a net inflow in the financial sector from 1999 to 2009. On 22 April 2009, foreign equity restrictions on 27 service subsectors were removed. This was followed a week later with the relaxation of foreign equity ownership in financial services.

The sterling performance of FDI in the period before the AFC can be attributed to a match between the internal conditions in the country or "pull factors" and "push factors" in terms of the external surge in outward labor-intensive FDI at that time (Tham 2004). However, after the AFC, while Malaysia sought to attract high-quality FDI to facilitate the shift up the value chain, its domestic structural problems in terms of human capital did not provide a suitable environment to host these investments. Concurrently, competition for FDI had intensified.

Domestic Investment

There are no published data on total domestic private investment in the country, which also includes investment by the government-linked

Table 8.9 Growth in value of fixed assets and capital–labor ratio (1986–2007)

Year	Growth in value of fixed assets (%)	Capital–labor ratio
1986	–	0.05
1987	7.7	0.04
1988	7.5	0.04
1989	10.0	0.04
1990	30.3	0.04
1991	30.0	0.05
1992	22.8	0.05
1993	19.6	0.06
1994	19.8	0.07
1995	22.2	0.07
1996	14.3	0.08
1997	13.3	0.09
1999	–	0.11
2000	14.0	0.10
2001	–2.4	0.11
2002	10.6	0.12
2003	3.7	0.12
2004	0.7	0.12
2005	3.3	0.11
2006	1.3	0.11
2007	–5.5	0.10

Source: Department of Statistics, Time Series Data Malaysia.

companies (GLCs). Two indicators that suggest that domestic investment in manufacturing may be subdued in the wake of the AFC are the growth in fixed assets and the rate of capacity utilization in the manufacturing sector.

Within manufacturing, the value of fixed assets grew significantly from 1986 to 1996, with the capital-labor ratio also increasing steadily (see Table 8.9). However after the AFC, the growth in the value of fixed assets slowed down and was affected by the dot.com crisis in 2001. The capital-labor ratio as shown in Table 8.9 indicates that this ratio stagnated at around 0.11 to 0.12 from 2000 to 2006, before falling to 0.10 in 2007.

It is possible that in the post-crisis environment, investment in the man-ufacturing sector has been affected by the undervalued ringgit due to the import-dependent nature of this sector. Although this has helped exports to be competitive, it has also affected imports. Hence, instead of increas-ing investment, Malaysia has increasingly depended on migrant labor to

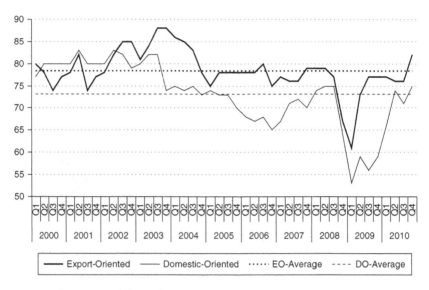

Source: Quarterly Bulletin, Bank Negara Malaysia, 2000–10.

*Figure 8.6   Capacity utilization rates in the manufacturing sector
              (2000–10)*

maintain its competitiveness in terms of costs. The use of migrant labor
also provided flexibility as these workers can be laid off during downturns
in the business cycle. This flexibility is seen in the relatively low rates of
unemployment during the AFC, as well as the recent GER.

Following the AFC, the capacity utilization rate in manufacturing has
averaged around 78 per cent for export-oriented manufacturing and 73 per
cent for domestic-oriented manufacturing (see Figure 8.6). The presence
of excess capacity is due to overinvestment before the crisis, as well as a
subdued demand for manufactured goods after the crisis.

However, cumulative net direct investment abroad (DIA) amounted
to RM32 billion in 1995–99 and further escalated to RM182 billion from
2000 to 2009 (Central Bank Malaysia 2009). In 2007, outward flows
exceeded inward flows for the first time since independence, with the new
trend continuing to 2010.

Is private manufacturing investment moving outward? While the data
support a progressive shift of manufacturing investment out of the country,
Table 8.10 shows that the bulk of direct investment abroad is in the service
sector, with the share increasing from 49 per cent to 70 per cent over
the two subperiods shown. In particular, while earlier investments were
reported to be undertaken mainly by Petronas and government-linked

Table 8.10 *Cumulative net direct investment abroad flows by sectors
(1995–2009)*

Sector	1995–99 (% of total)	2000–09 (% of total)
Services	49	70
Manufacturing	7	8
Oil and gas	7	10
Construction	4	2
Agriculture	5	7
Others	28	3

Source: Central Bank Malaysia, Annual Report 2009.

plantation companies, investment in the subsequent period was reported to be undertaken by GLCs in services such as financial services, telecommunications, utilities and private companies.[6] It should be noted that GLCs dominate the service sector due to their incumbent positions as government monopolies in key service sectors such as utilities, air transport, and electricity before these entities were privatized.

Anecdotal evidence and data from annual reports reveal that GLCs that have investments abroad include Telekom Malaysia Berhad (TMB) and banks such as CIMB and Maybank. These banks are expanding rapidly in order to create a regional presence. TMB, on the other hand, has an internationalization strategy that focuses primarily on emerging markets in Asia and the Pacific that have low penetration rates and high potential for growth under relatively stable governments. This is driven by the highly competitive non-fixed-line telephone sectors and saturated markets at home (Tham 2007). Tenaga Nasional Berhad, the national electricity company, reported in its 2009 annual report that it has investment holding companies in India, Mauritius, and Pakistan. It also operates a power plant and generates electricity in Pakistan. It would appear that these GLCs are market-seeking investors, as they need growth beyond Malaysia's limited domestic market.

The peculiar nature of services, chiefly their proximity burden, also renders investments abroad a necessary mode of delivery in many of these services. Malaysia has increasing export revenues in medical tourism and private higher education, leading to some of these providers venturing overseas. For example, KPJ Healthcare Limited has health care facilities in Bangladesh, Indonesia, and Saudi Arabia, and eight private higher education institutions in the country have branch campuses overseas, mainly in developing countries such as Bangladesh, the PRC, India, Indonesia and several countries in Africa.

Constraints to Long-term Private Investment

Inward FDI and domestic investments are faltering due to four main reasons: institutional quality, human capital, competitiveness of the manufacturing sector, and regulatory barriers in the service sector.

Institutional quality

Although the ease of doing business has improved in Malaysia, corruption is perceived to have worsened steadily from 1996 to 2010 based on Transparency International's Corruption Perceptions Index (Table 8.11). Similarly, the control of corruption also shows some deterioration from 2004 to 2009. While this is a deterrent to investment, Malaysia's ranking on corruption is ahead of the PRC and selected member countries of the Association of Southeast Asian Nations (ASEAN), with the exception of Singapore (Table 8.12; Hill 2012). It would appear that the PRC's poor ranking on corruption has not deterred investors from entering the country as there are compensating factors such as high economic growth, a large domestic market, and the availability of labor. By contrast, the domestic market in Malaysia is relatively small, while human capital is highly constrained due to inflows of unskilled labor and outflows of skilled labor.

Human capital

While Malaysia's productivity is ahead of most of her ASEAN neighbors, except Singapore, the growth in its labor productivity has fallen over time. From 1990 to 1995, the growth in labor productivity in Malaysia exceeded the ASEAN average. From 2000 to 2005 it was the same as ASEAN, while it fell below the ASEAN average from 2005 to 2010 (Table 8.13). The slower growth in labor productivity can be attributed to outflows of skilled labor, thereby aggravating the shortage of skilled labor in the country, while inflows are mainly unskilled.

Shortage of skilled labor   The lack of skilled labor further compounded labor problems in the country and this may explain why some approved investments in the manufacturing sector were not realized. Although the ringgit has been appreciating since the removal of the peg in 2005, investment is still muted, while the share of migrant workers continues to increase. Survey evidence from the World Bank (2009) indicates that skill shortages are perceived to be the top constraint by 40 per cent of firms. These skill shortages, coupled with an unresolved graduate unemployment problem, show that both education and human capital in the country have problems meeting the demand for skills.

Table 8.11 *Indicators of governance and regulation (1996–2011)*

Malaysia governance and regulation	2011	2010	2009	2008	2007	2006	2005	2004	2003	2002	2001	2000	1999	1998	1997	1996
Ease of doing business (rank)[a]	21/183	23/183	21/183	25/181	25/175	25/175	..	..	..	..	..	..	..	..	..	..
Economic freedom[a]	66	65	65	64	64	62	62	60	61	60	60	66	69	68	67	70
Corruption perceptions index (rank)[b]	..	56/178	56/180	47/180	43/180	44/163	39/159	39/146	37/133	34/102	36/91	36/90	33/99	29/85	32/52	26/54
World governance indicators[a]																
Voice and accountability	..	..	32	31	32	31	45	42	38	38	..	40	..	44	..	38
Political stability, absence of violence	..	..	47	51	53	55	61	58	58	59	..	52	..	45	..	58
Governance effectiveness	..	..	80	83	85	84	83	84	81	79	..	79	..	69	..	..
Regulatory quality	..	..	60	63	67	66	66	67	71	66	..	65	..	69	..	..
Rule of law	..	..	65	64	66	66	66	65	63	63	..	61	..	64	..	75
Control of corruption	..	..	58	62	68	67	65	70	67	67	..	66	..	72	..	..

Source: [a] World Bank http://databank.worldbank.org/ddp/home.do (accessed 20 April 2011); [b] Transparency International Secretariat, various years.

233

Table 8.12   *Indicators of governance and regulation in selected countries*
                  (2009)

Governance and regulation	Malaysia	Singapore	Thailand	PRC	Indonesia	Philippines
Ease of doing business (rank)	21/183	1/183	12/183	86/183	129/183	141/183
Economic freedom[a]	65	87.1	63	53.2	53.4	56.8
Corruption perceptions index (rank)[a]	56/180	3/180	84/180	79/180	114/180	142/180
World governance indicators						
Voice and accountability	32	34	35	5	48	45
Political stability, absence of violence	47	90	15	30	24	11
Governance effectiveness	80	100	60	58	47	50
Regulatory quality	60	100	62	46	43	52
Rule of law	65	92	51	45	34	35
Control of corruption	58	99	51	36	28	27

Note: PRC = People's Republic of China.

Source: World Bank http://databank.worldbank.org/ddp/home.do (accessed 20 April 2011); [a] Transparency International Secretariat, 2009.

Outflows of skilled labor from the country, especially to Singapore, have further aggravated the shortage of skills in the country. Although there are few data on outflows of labor, estimates provided by the National Economic Advisory Council (NEAC) of Malaysia indicate there are roughly 350 000 Malaysians working abroad, with over half of them having tertiary education (Fong 2010). The estimates further showed that the number of Malaysian migrants with tertiary education residing in

*Table 8.13   Cross-country comparisons of labor productivity growth
(% average annual growth rate at constant prices per worker),
1990–2010*

	1990–95	1995–2000	2000–05	2005–10
Malaysia	6.4	0.9	3.1	3.5
Singapore	5.2	1.9	3.7	2.6
Thailand	8.3	0.1	2.6	3.6
Viet Nam	5.6	4.1	4.8	6.1
Indonesia	6.5	−1.5	3.8	2.7
Philippines	−0.4	2.4	1.1	5.0
ASEAN	5.4	0.5	3.1	3.9

Source: Asian Productivity Organization, 2010.

member countries of the Organisation for Economic Co-operation and Development (OECD) has increased from 72 649 in 1990 to 102 321 in 2000, or an increase of 41 per cent over 10 years. The World Bank (2011) found that the main factors motivating Malaysians to move overseas include differences in earnings potential, career prospects, quality of education, and quality of life. More importantly, discontent with Malaysia's inclusiveness policies is a key factor for outward migration, especially among the non-*bumiputeras*, who make up the bulk of the diaspora, particularly in Singapore.

Increasing use of migrant workers   The share of migrant workers increased from a mere 1.0 per cent in 1980 to 14.1 per cent in 1996, on the eve of the AFC (see Table 8.14). This fell back slightly, increased again to 14.1 per cent in 2000 and has increased steadily to 28 per cent by 2007, before dropping slightly to 27 per cent in 2008. These workers are generally low-skill production workers making up for the lack of domestic workers in these occupational groupings, thus leading to increasing excess demand (Tham and Liew 2004, 2010). Tham and Liew (2004, 2010) found that these workers have a negative impact on labor productivity as they substitute for capital and slow down automation.

Decreasing competitiveness in manufacturing
The relative competitiveness of the manufacturing sector, based on the United Nations Industrial Development Organization's (UNIDO) Competitive Industrial Performance index (CIP), indicates increasing competitiveness from 1990 to 2000. However, competitiveness has deteriorated steadily from 2000 to 2005 (see Table 8.15). In contrast, Singapore

Table 8.14 Migrant workers as percentage of total workers in Malaysian manufacturing (1981–2008)

Year	Migrant workers (%)
1981	1.0
1985	1.6
1990	2.0
1995	10.2
1996	14.1
1997	13.9
1998	13.6
1999	13.2
2000	14.1
2001	15.3
2002	16.2
2003	18.2
2004	20.5
2005	22.1
2006	23.8
2007	28.4
2008	26.9

Source: 1981–99 is extracted from Henderson and Phillips 2007; 2000–08 is extracted from unpublished data from Department of Statistics (DOS).

Table 8.15 Ranking of economies by CIP Index, 1990, 2000, 2005

Country	1990	2000	2005
Indonesia	54	38*/38	42
Malaysia	23	15*/13	16
Philippines	43	25*/30	30
Singapore	1	1*/1	1
Thailand	32	23*/26	25
PRC	26	24*/31	26

Notes:
For the year 2000, rankings have been revised from UNIDO's 2004 report (asterisked) to its 2009 report.
CIP = Competitive Industrial Performance.
PRC = People's Republic of China.

Source: Tham (2008), United Nations Industrial Development Organization (2009).

has maintained its competitive position throughout that period, while the PRC and Thailand have improved in their respective rankings.

Entry barriers in services

Despite the recent liberalization of foreign equity ownership, especially in financial services, foreign ownership is still relatively small, as shown in Table 8.16.

Based on Tham and Loke (2012), apart from equity restrictions on foreign ownership, there are also various other barriers that affect both domestic and foreign service providers as summarized in Table 8.17.

Another barrier is preferential government procurement procedures, but these are also a form of protection. Locally owned businesses are generally favored in government procurement, with international tenders being invited only when the service is not available locally (World Trade Organization 2009, 24). Malaysia is not a party to the World Trade Organization Agreement on Government Procurement. Given the size of the government sector, government procurement can constitute a substantial discriminatory practice, as for example in the use of the national airlines for the official travel of civil servants.

There are also natural barriers and policy barriers to entry. The former prevail in natural monopolies such as water, air transport, energy, telecommunications, and water as these subsectors involve huge investments that serve as entry barriers. For example, the amount of capital required for the development of fixed telephone lines has deterred new entrants, despite the provision of five additional licenses that were issued in line with the National Telecommunication Policy to encourage competition.

The service sector is also governed by a licensing system whereby service providers are required to apply for a license before they can provide a service in most subsectors.[7] Approval for licenses is granted by the minister in charge of the subsector. For instance, the license for operating a higher education institution is awarded by the Ministry of Higher Education. The criteria used for awarding the licenses are not necessarily disclosed publicly. To illustrate, as stated in the Private Higher Education Act 1996, private higher education institutions have to be invited to apply, but the conditions for invitation are not stated. Similarly, the establishment of hospitals is subject to an economic needs test, but the criteria for the test are not explicitly stated.

Apart from licensing requirements, the service sector is also governed by a complex web of regulations at the local, state and federal levels. But there is no systematic and comprehensive assessment of the impact of these regulations on the economy (Lee 2012). The closest attempt to assess the impact is the World Bank's annual *Ease of Doing Business* survey, which

Table 8.16   Ownership of selected services subsectors in Malaysia

Year	Services subsector	No. of establish-ments	Ownership Foreign No. (%)	Malaysian No. (%)	Joint
2006	Highway operations	21	0 (0)	21 (100)	0
2006	Storage and warehousing	42	0 (0)	42 (100)	0
2006	Car parks	202	0 (0)	202 (100)	0
2006	Cargo handling/ stevedoring	299	9 (3)	290 (97)	0
2006	Health	6040	5 (0.08)	6035 (99)	0
2007	Selected healthcare	225	0 (0)	225 (100)	0
2007	Private hospitals	194	0 (0)	194 (100)	0
2006	Computer	1137	79 (7)	1054 (93)	4
2006	Inland water transport	320	0 (0)	320 (100)	0
2007	Specialist medical clinics	623	0 (0)	623 (100)	0
2007	Maternity homes	36	0 (0)	36 (100)	0
2007	General medical clinics	3821	0 (0)	3821 (100)	0
2007	Dental	966	0 (0)	966 (100)	0
2006	Post and courier	157	6 (4)	151 (96)	0
2006	Road haulage	1938	7 (0.3)	1931 (99.7)	0
2006	Shipping/forwarding agencies and freight forwarding	1019	36 (4)	979 (96)	4
2006	Telecommunications	170	9 (5)	161 (95)	0
2006	Travel agencies and tour operators	1135	0 (0)	1135 (100)	0
2007	Veterinary	175	0 (0)	175 (100)	0
2007	Accommodation	2144	28 (1)	2116 (99)	0
2006	Public bus transport	390	0 (0)	390 (100)	0
2007	Colleges and universities	245	0 (0)	245 (100)	0
2007	Private education	6318	15 (0.2)	6303 (99.2)	
2006	Sea transport	395	4 (1)	391 (99)	
2009	Commercial banks	23	14 (61)	9 (39)	0
2009	Islamic banks	17	11 (65)	6 (35)	0
2009	International Islamic banks	4	4 (100)	0 (0)	0
2009	Investment banks	15	0 (0)	15 (100)	0
2009	Life and general insurance	7	3 (43)	4 (57)	0
2009	Life insurance only	9	3 (33)	6 (67)	0
2009	General insurance only	24	9 (38)	15 (63)	0
2009	Takaful (Islamic insurance)	8	0 (0)	8 (100)	0
2009	International takaful	1	1 (100)	0 (0)	0

Source: Department of Statistics and Central Bank Malaysia.

Table 8.17   Overview of market access barriers in selected services

Subsector	Principal barriers
Banking	Foreign banks operate under a grandfathering provision and no new banking licenses have been granted to foreign banks, except for Islamic banks. Foreign banks must normally operate as locally controlled subsidiaries. Foreign equity restriction (aggregate maximum permitted per institution) is 30% for commercial banks, and 70% for investment/merchant banks.
Insurance	Local incorporation is required, except for professional reinsurers. Foreign shareholding of 70% is permitted for conventional insurance companies. A higher limit is considered on a case-by-case basis. Islamic insurers are also allowed 70% foreign equity ownership. 100% foreign equity ownership is allowed for international Islamic insurers and also for Islamic reinsurers.
Telecommunications	Malaysia guarantees market access and national treatment for basic telecom services only through acquisition of up to 30% of the shares of existing licensed public telecommunications operators and limits market-access commitments to facilities-based providers. Value-added suppliers are similarly limited to 30% of foreign equity; investments exceeding the 30% limits are sometimes allowed. Retail prices for fixed-line services are regulated by the government.
Legal services	Lawyers must be Malaysian citizens or permanent residents, pass a Malay language exam (unless exempted), and admitted to the Malaysian Bar. Foreign lawyers may provide legal advisory services in foreign law and offshore legal corporations of Malaysia through GATS Modes 1 and 2. However, foreign law firms may not establish operations in Malaysia except in the Federal Territory of Labuan to provide limited legal services to offshore corporations established in Labuan. The Attorney General has the power to issue a Special Admission Certificate.
Accounting	Foreign firms can provide accounting and taxation services only through affiliates. Aggregate foreign shares in affiliates are restricted to 30%. Accountants must be registered with the Malaysian Institute of Accountants (MIA) before they can apply for a license, which allows them to provide auditing and taxation services.

Table 8.17   (continued)

Subsector	Principal barriers
	Registration with the MIA requires proof of citizenship or permanent residency. Foreign accountants need to have an address in Malaysia, as well as recognized qualifications.
Architecture	Foreign architects cannot be licensed in Malaysia but can be involved in Malaysian firms. Only licensed architects may submit architectural plans. Foreign architect firms can operate only as joint ventures in specific projects with approval of the Board of Architects. Foreign architects may hold up to 30% shares in a multidisciplinary consultancy firm providing architectural, engineering and/or surveying services in Malaysia.
Engineering	Foreign engineers can work on specific projects under the license of the Board of Engineers and must be sponsored by the Malaysian company undertaking the project. The Malaysian company must demonstrate that they are unable to find a Malaysian engineer. Foreign engineering companies may collaborate with a Malaysian company, but the latter is expected to design the project and is required to submit the plans. Up to 30% foreign equity is allowed in a company providing multidisciplinary practices.
Health	For private hospital services, commercial presence of a foreign investor must be through a joint venture and foreign equity participation is limited to 30%.

Source: World Trade Organization (2005, 2009).

seeks to measure the impact of regulations on the ease of doing business in various countries. Malaysia's ranking has fluctuated from 25 in 2006 to 23 in 2010 (Table 8.11), out of a total of approximately 180 countries that participate in the survey. However, Malaysia's worst ranking is found in the section on "Dealing with Licenses" in earlier reports, and in "Dealing with Construction Permits" in the 2010 report. This concurs with the findings of World Bank surveys in 2002 and 2003 that also showed that regulatory burdens are a constraint to doing business in Malaysia (World Bank 2005). The poor ranking and bureaucratic impediments have led to the establishment in 2007 of a special task force to facilitate business called

PEMUDAH, a committee of high-level government and private sector leaders tasked with making recommendations to reduce bureaucratic impediments.

CONCLUSION

Although Malaysia has achieved quite a good record of growth since independence in 1957, economic growth has faltered after the AFC. While overall macroeconomic stability has been maintained, fiscal management has worsened. The huge current account surplus due to the commodity price boom is reflected in the positive savings–investment gap in the country since the crisis. As the current account surplus is greater than the deficit in the financial account, Malaysia's international reserves have increased. Although savings have continued to be high, investment behavior after the crisis is different, as private investment as a percentage of GDP has fallen quite significantly. FDI as a percentage of GDP has fallen, while direct investment abroad has grown with outflows exceeding inflows since 2007.

While direct investment abroad has increased, declining labor productivity growth and the lack of core research and development capabilities and competences in the country imply that Malaysia will face deindustrialization without new domestic investment to revitalize its manufacturing sector. Sustaining long-term growth will therefore require Malaysia to increase domestic and foreign investment in the country. This is particularly important in view of the increasing fiscal constraints and dire need for fiscal reform, including curtailing the burgeoning growth in government operational expenditures and dependency on depleting resources as a key contributor to government revenues.

Numerous government initiatives have been launched since 2009 in response to the need for change. The Malaysian Anti-Corruption Commission Act was enacted, followed by the establishment of the Malaysian Anti-Corruption Commission in 2009. Subsequently, the Government Transformation Plan, the Economic Transformation Plan, the New Economic Model (NEM) and the Tenth Malaysia Plan were launched in 2010, with the common agenda of government and economic reforms to facilitate the shift to a high-income economy. In particular, the issue of inclusiveness is one of the three goals of the NEM.[8] The NEM's approach toward inclusion represents a shift from ethnic-based targets to one based on socioeconomic status, with assistance targeted at the bottom 40 per cent of households (National Economic Advisory Council 2010a). However, the use of affirmative action programs based on the NEP is not abolished. Rather, market-friendly affirmative action programs are suggested that "will focus on building capacity and capability rather than the imposition of conditions to meet specific quotas or targets" (National Economic Advisory Council 2010a). This is reiterated in the Tenth Malaysia Plan as well as the concluding part of the NEM (National Economic Advisory Council 2010b). Moreover, the Tenth Malaysia Plan also continues to emphasize the need for increased participation of the *bumiputera* community in the economy, as in all the previous national plans. It appears that the use of affirmative action will therefore be continued, albeit in a different form.

This does not augur well for attracting and retaining talent in the country, given the recent findings of the World Bank (2011). The brain drain is particularly damaging as outflows of skilled labor reduce the already narrow base of such labor in the country. Therefore, the availability of skilled labor, or talent, remains an issue, as domestic and foreign investment will continue to move to where talent can be found to work together with capital. This is particularly important for Malaysia due to a slowdown in the rate of growth in labor productivity. While the Talent Corporation Malaysia is working toward wooing back Malaysian talent from abroad, a fundamental shift in policy focus is needed. Inclusive policies based on merit and need are critical for creating, retaining and sustaining talent management in the country. While the World Bank (2011) has made many useful suggestions toward a deeper engagement with the diaspora, it does not seem likely that those who left due to the discontent with Malaysia's inclusiveness policies can be reengaged without this fundamental shift.

Second, in terms of sector focus, there is a shift from manufacturing to services. Only the electrical and electronics sector is chosen as one of the 12 national key economic areas in the ETP, while nine others are service oriented. This shift is premature, given the importance of manufacturing in exports while services are still protected and predominantly oriented toward the domestic market. The use of a segmented approach in the development of the service sector is similar to the segmented approach that was used earlier for the development of manufacturing. In the latter's case, the development of manufacturing was not leveraged on the earlier development of the agricultural sector by a more focused development of resource-based manufacturing. Instead, manufacturing development focused on the development of non-resource-based manufacturing. Similarly, the current focus on the development of services is not linked to the development of manufacturing in that the service sector is viewed as a new source of growth rather than as an integrated segment in the value creation of goods. This segmented approach, as epitomized by targeting selected sectors for development, uses essentially an old industrial policy format while a shift to a high-value-added process requires an integrated approach toward manufacturing and services development. Such an integrated approach is also fundamentally different from the project-based approach (or entry-point projects) taken by the ETP.

Finally, deepening the development of services requires reform of their entry barriers, especially domestic regulations that are still the main barriers in the development of this sector (Dee 2004). This in turn requires political will since GLCs dominate the services sector, and deregulating the sector and increasing competition can be a threat to incumbents.

In conclusion, reviving private investment in Malaysia requires a shift toward more inclusive policies based on merit and need, an integrated approach toward the development of manufacturing and services to enhance the competitiveness of the manufacturing sector, and reforms in the services sector.

NOTES

1. This refers to Malays and indigenous groups of the country.
2. This was limited at 30 per cent during the NEP period, although its implementation has been flexible and discretionary to a large extent.
3. Estimations by EPU are based on the Cobb-Douglas production function.
4. See Thillainathan 2011 and Athukorala 2012 for further details on the causes and impact of the AFC in Malaysia.
5. Prior to the AFC, there were strict rules on residents borrowing in foreign currency.
6. GLCs are defined as companies that have a primary commercial objective and in which the government has a direct controlling stake. It should be noted that GLCs are considered as private companies and their investments are listed as private investment.
7. There were some exceptions, as in the case of services that did not fall under the jurisdiction of any of the ministries, such as computer service firms. But these subsectors have subsequently been placed under the Ministry of Domestic Trade and Consumer Affairs.
8. The other two are high income and sustainability.

REFERENCES

Asian Productivity Organization (APO) (2010), *APO Productivity Databank*, Tokyo: APO.

Athukorala, P. (2012), 'The Malaysian economy during three crises', in H. Hill, S.Y. Tham, and H.M. Ragayah (eds), *Graduating from the Middle: Malaysia's Development Challenges*, London: Routledge.

Central Bank Malaysia (various years), Annual Report, Kuala Lumpur: Central Bank.

Dee, P. (2004), 'Measuring the cost of regulatory restrictions on services trade in Malaysia', background report to a study on Improving the Investment Climate

by Reducing the Regulatory Burden in Malaysia, Washington, DC: World
Bank for the Economic Planning Unit of Malaysia.

Fong, C.O. (2010), 'Tracing the brain drain trend', *The Star*, Sunday 16 May,
Kuala Lumpur, Malaysia.

Hannoun, H. (2007), 'Policy responses to the challenges posed by capital inflows in
Asia', Speech delivered by the Deputy General Manager of the BIS, at the 42nd
SEACEN Governors' Conference in Bangkok, 28 July.

Henderson, J., and R. Phillips (2007), 'Unintended consequences: social policy,
state institutions and the "stalling" of the Malaysian industrialization project',
Economy and Society, **36**, 78–102. doi:10.1080/03085140601089853

Hill, H. (2012), 'Malaysian economic development: looking backward and
forward', in H. Hill, S.Y. Tham and H.M. Ragayah (eds), *Graduating from the
Middle: Malaysia's Development Challenges*, London: Routledge.

International Monetary Fund (IMF) (2010), Staff Report for the 2010 Article IV
Consultation.

Khor, M. (2009), 'Financial policy and management of capital flows: the case of
Malaysia', Third World Network (TWN) Global Economy Series 16, Penang:
TWN.

Lee, C. (2012), 'Microeconomic reform in Malaysia', in H. Hill, S.Y. Tham and
H.M. Ragayah (eds), *Graduating from the Middle: Malaysia's Development
Challenges*, London: Routledge.

Mahadevan, R. (2007), *Sustainable Growth and Economic Development: A Case
Study of Malaysia*, Cheltenham, UK and Northampton, MA, USA: Edward
Elgar.

Malaysian Government (2010), *Tenth Malaysia Plan: 2011–2015*, Putrajaya:
Economic Planning Unit, Prime Minister's Department.

National Economic Advisory Council (2010a), 'The new economic model for
Malaysia', Putrajaya. www.neac.gov.my (accessed 22 August 2010).

National Economic Advisory Council (2010b), 'The new economic model for
Malaysia: concluding part', Putrajaya. www.neac.gov.my (accessed 22 April
2010).

Narayanan, S. (2012), 'Public sector resource management', in H. Hill, S.Y. Tham
and H.M. Ragayah (eds), *Graduating from the Middle: Malaysia's Development
Challenges*, London: Routledge.

Ooi, S.K. (2006), 'The monetary transmission mechanism in Malaysia: current
development and issues', BIS papers no. 35.

Ooi, S.K. (2008), 'Capital flows and financial assets in emerging markets: determinants, consequences and challenges for central banks: the Malaysian experience', BIS Papers no. 44.

Sukhdave, S. (2011a), 'A brief overview of the Malaysian economy', www.fstep.org.
my/. . ./Overview%20Week%20Notes/Dr%20Sukhdave_Monetary%20Framew
ork_Dr%20Sukhdave_120411_Slide%201_BNM.pd (accessed 18 April 2011).

Sukhdave, S. (2011b), 'Monetary policy framework in Malaysia', www.fstep.org.
my/. . ./Monetary%20Framework_Dr%20Sukhdave_120411_Slide%202_BNM.
pdf (accessed 25 April 2011).

Tham, S.Y. (2004), 'Malaysia', in D.H. Brooks and H. Hill (eds), *Managing FDI in a
Globalizing Economy: Asian Experiences*, Houndmills, UK: Palgrave Macmillan.

Tham, S.Y. (2007), 'Outward foreign direct investment from Malaysia: an explora-
tory study', *Southeast Asian Affairs*, **26**, 45–72.

Tham, S.Y. (2008), 'The economic rise of China and its implications on the industrial development in Malaysia', Chapter 9 in Liao Shaolian (ed.), *Malaysia and Sino-Malaysian Relations in a Changing World*, Xiamen: Xiamen University Press.

Tham, S.Y., and Liew Chei Siang (2004), 'Foreign labor in Malaysian manufacturing: enhancing Malaysian competitiveness?', A.R. Embong (ed.), *Globalization, Culture and Inequalities: In Honour of the Late Ishak Shari,* Bangi: Penerbit Universiti Kebangsaan Malaysia.

Tham, S.Y., and C.S. Liew (2010), 'The impact of foreign labor on labor productivity in Malaysian manufacturing, 2000–2006', World Bank, Final Report (submitted).

Tham, S.Y., and W.H. Loke (2012), 'Services liberalization: the need for complementary policies', in H. Hill, S.Y. Tham and H.M. Ragayah (eds), *Graduating from the Middle: Malaysia's Development Challenges*, London: Routledge.

Thillainathan, R. (2008), 'A critical review of price control and subsidies in Malaysia', Presented at the LSE Alumni's Forum on the Rise and Fall of Subsidies, 26 May, Kuala Lumpur.

Thillainathan, R. (2011), 'Macroeconomic stabilization', in *Malaysia: Policies and Issues in Economic Development*, Kuala Lumpur: Institute of Strategic and International Studies.

United Nations Development Program (UNDP) (2009), 'The global financial crisis and the Malaysian economy: impact and response', a Joint Report by the Institute of Strategic and International Studies (ISIS) and the Faculty of Economics and Administration (UNDP Malaysia).

United Nations Industrial Development Organization (UNIDO) (2009), *Industrial Development Report 2009*, Vienna: UNIDO.

World Bank (2005), *Malaysia: Firm Competitiveness, Investment Climate and Growth*, Washington, DC: World Bank.

World Bank (2009), 'Malaysia: productivity and investment climate assessment update', Washington, DC: World Bank.

World Bank (2011), 'Malaysia Economic Monitor: Brain Drain', April, Washington, DC: World Bank.

World Trade Organization (2005), 'Trade policy review: report by the secretariat – Malaysia', WT/TPR/S/156, Geneva: WTO.

World Trade Organization (2009), 'Trade policy review: report by the secretariat – Malaysia', WT/TPR/S/225, Geneva: WTO.

Zainal, A.Y. (2009), 'The Malaysian economic model; a case of heterodoxy', in A.R. Nungsari and S.A. Suryani (eds), *Readings on Development: Malaysia 2057: Uncommon Voices, Common Aspirations*, Kuala Lumpur: Khazanah Nasional.

9. Indonesia

Ari Kuncoro

INTRODUCTION

Before the Asian financial crisis (AFC), Indonesia and other East Asian economies had been the model of successful economic development. Investment is believed to have been one of the key elements of this success. But high investment growth and the availability of savings are not sufficient explanations for the rapid and sustained growth of these economies and the subsequent reduction of poverty. While investment and savings contribute to high growth, it is achieved largely by getting the basics right (Basri and Hill 2011). Another key to success is often thought to be economic liberalization that brings both competition and external trade, which also are essential to rapid economic growth and stability (Kuncoro and Resosudarmo 2006).

The AFC, however, raises many questions about the success of East Asian economies. And while there is some disagreement about the role of competitiveness and trade in fostering growth, the high growth rates prior to the AFC often mask many country-specific characteristics that spur growth. It is also clear that more information, particularly from the perspective of microeconomic agents who make investment decisions, needs to be examined to determine what measures boost the quality and quantity of investment, thus fostering growth. In Indonesia, economic growth has improved to around 6 per cent annually, but it may not be sufficient to absorb the unemployed and new entrants in the labor market. Indonesian economic growth was impacted by the global economic recession (GER) in 2008–09 and the slow and uncertain recovery that followed. High energy prices also slowed down the Indonesia recovery. The government has pursued a more expansionary policy to boost growth, but in the end sustained growth must come from the private sector in the form of investment and exports.

On the financial side, this chapter looks at the system that finances investment. The domestic financial architecture can amplify or dampen the impacts of a recession on developing Asian countries. The collapse of the Indonesian banking system has deeply traumatized the mind-set of both Bank Indonesia (BI), which is the country's central bank, and bankers. Various protective measures and risk-free financial assets such as Bank Indonesia Certificates (SBIs) have been created to provide banks with almost risk-free income. As a result, banks have become overly cautious or reluctant to provide loans, particularly for corporate or productive investment.

The traditional neoclassical model of investment implicitly assumes the existence of a perfect capital market. In this setting, the optimal capital stock is determined by the interaction between the demand schedule for capital and the supply schedule, where expected marginal profitability of capital equals the interest rate. As a consequence, financial factors are not determinants of actual capital stock.

But the reality, especially in developing countries, is very different. Financial factors often become formidable hurdles that hamper firms in financing their productive investments, and thus eventually will be detrimental to economic growth. In this respect, modern theories of investment account for the assumption of a perfect capital market by recognizing the existence of information asymmetries and incentive problems. Financial intermediaries' information on profitable investment opportunities often differs from the information available to firms that have to make investment decisions, which ultimately leads to financial discrimination against less-favored types of firms. Thus, financial factors become an important determinant of actual capital cost – and ultimately economic growth. Financial constraints can bind firms by creating less than optimal circumstances for the formation of capital stock. So from the microeconomic perspective, this chapter looks at both sides: investment decisions and their sources of finance.

The availability of savings at a sufficient level is a necessary condition for economic growth. What also matters is how efficiently financial intermediaries channel savings to users. The dominance of commercial banks in financial systems is a common factor in East Asian countries. Bond markets are often very thin. Equity markets – though quite well developed in recent years – limit themselves to accumulating funds for large firms in the formal sector. Banks are inherently conservative and pro-cyclical. The AFC and banking regulations have prompted banks to look for easy profits. With the availability of risk-free assets like government bonds (*surat utang negara* or SUN) and SBIs, this comes at the expense of extending credit to the real sector. To examine bank-lending behavior with respect to productive investments, this chapter looks at bank portfolios.

Firms operate optimally if their environments are supportive. It is generally agreed that the primary function of government includes maintaining law and order, providing basic infrastructure, and regulating firms and transactions to address information asymmetries, externalities, and market power. But there also are other government policies and behaviors that play critical roles affecting the costs, risks, and barriers to competition that firms face. They include approaches to regulation and taxation, the functioning of markets for finance and labor, and the broad aspect of governance, including corruption. Firms assess investment opportunities and related government policies and behavior as a package, not in a partial fashion. The investment decisions of firms reflect their expectations about the future, not just current conditions. That makes it essential for government to foster credibility and stability.

Government must mediate and seek a balance between two potentially conflicting goals. Firms are primary creators of wealth, thus a good investment climate must be responsive to their needs. But a sound investment climate should serve a society as a whole – not only firms – and the preferences of the two may diverge. Creating a sound investment climate requires governments to "fine-tune" between firms and society. It also requires governments to restrain rent-seeking, establish credibility, foster public trust and legitimacy, and ensure policy responses that reflect a good institutional fit.

ECONOMIC PERFORMANCE

Table 9.1 summarizes the performance of the Indonesian economy over three decades, beginning in 1984. The drop in oil prices in the 1980s brought a strong impetus for the first round of economic reforms. It was acknowledged that export revenues from oil and primary commodities were unreliable, and there was a sense of urgency to develop and to diversify non-oil sectors in the economy, particularly manufacturing and agriculture. The economic reforms covered four broad categories of measures relating to: exchange rate management; monetary and financial policies; fiscal policy; and trade policy and other regulatory reforms. The primary objective of stimulating non-oil exports was achieved relatively quickly. Growth in gross domestic product (GDP) bounced back from the average of 4.8 per cent in 1984–86 to 6.4 per cent in 1987–93 (Table 9.1). Meanwhile in the same period investment growth soared from as low as 1.9 per cent to 10.3 per cent annually. Exports also were rejuvenated, growing from 4.2 per cent to 10.8 per cent annually.

The second wave of deregulation measures commenced in 1994, with an emphasis on boosting investment. This time there were no looming crises of the magnitude seen in the 1960s and 1980s. The economy continued to

Table 9.1   Average annual growth (%)

Expenditure components	1984–86	1987–93	1994–96	2000–04	2004–09
Private consumption	1.6	5.0	10.6	3.6	4.6
Government consumption	5.6	5.2	2.2	8.3	8.5
Investment	1.9	10.3	14.1	8.8	8.8
Exports	4.2	10.8	8.6	9.3	8.1
Imports	2.9	7.2	16.2	12.0	9.7
GDP	4.8	6.4	7.9	4.6	5.5

Note: GDP = gross domestic product.

Source: CEIC Asia Database.

perform well (see Table 9.1), but the government continued to press on with a bold economic deregulation, mainly related to investment and trade policies, including the abolition of the limitation on foreign ownership, a reduction of trade barriers in the form of tariff cuts, and the opening up of 10 previously closed sectors to foreign investment.[1]

From the expenditure side, the immediate impact of the deregulation was to improve investment growth from an average of 10 per cent in 1986–93 to 14.1 per cent in 1994–96 (Table 9.1). Export performance, however, did not follow suit. The growth of exports in the post-1994 deregulation period was 8.6 per cent, below what was achieved in 1987–93. The rather disappointing export performance was more than compensated for by the high growth of investments that enabled the economy to grow by 7.9 per cent from 1994 to 1996, well above the preceding period.

The period following the AFC saw the subdued investment growth of 8.8 per cent annually that led to the low GDP growth in Indonesia since the crisis (Table 9.1). It appears that the growth in exports could not compensate fully for the sluggishness of investment, which again gives weight to the importance of investment in the growth dynamic. To reach more definitive conclusions, we will be looking at a longer time horizon when analyzing the growth dynamic.

THE GROWTH DYNAMIC

Expenditure Side

Indonesian GDP growth and its expenditure components are depicted in Figure 9.1. We consider GDP components that are truly autonomous in

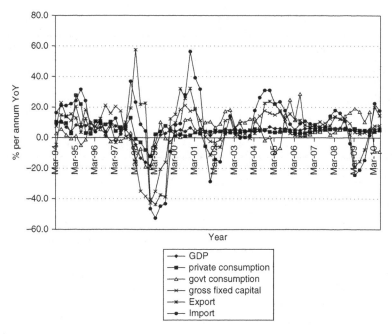

Note: GDP = gross domestic product.

Source: CEIC Asia Dabatase.

Figure 9.1   GDP growth 1994–2010: expenditure side

the sense that they are dynamic enough to affect GDP but relatively independent from the GDP movement over time. These factors may explain
the subdued economic growth in Indonesia after the AFC. It becomes
apparent that private consumption may not fit into this category. The
movement of private consumption is virtually indistinguishable from that
of GDP, thus they are interrelated or endogenous in nature. It is true that
in developed economies a portion of private consumption, especially big-
ticket items or consumer durables such as cars and electronic appliances,
may have their own dynamic traits since their purchase involves large sums
of money, thus the decision to purchase may sometimes mimic investment.

Investment and import growth, on the other hand, oscillate around the
time path of GDP growth, with large swings. They are both sources of
dynamism for GDP. To a lesser extent government consumption is also
autonomous from GDP (Figure 9.1). The path tends to be countercyclical, with GDP growth that indicates the role of government as a stabilizer.
This countercyclical pattern has been more pronounced after the AFC.

Table 9.2   Share of expenditure components of GDP (%)

Year	Private consumption	Government consumption	Investment	Exports	Imports
1983	61	11	25	26	26
1993	58	9	26	27	24
1995	62	8	28	26	28
1997	62	7	28	28	28
2000	62	7	20	41	30
2003	68	8	20	30	23
2006	63	9	24	34	26
2009	59	10	31	24	21

Note: GDP = gross domestic product.

Source: CEIC Asia Database.

The Indonesian government budget took an expansionary stance at the time of the GER in 2008–09, with considerable success. It smoothed out GDP growth so that it could be maintained at a reasonable annual pace of around 4–5 per cent, lower than the previous 6 per cent rate. Certainly this has something to do with different budget principles applied during those times – a balanced budget in the pre-crisis regime and a more flexible budget in the post-crisis era.

Another consideration that should not be overlooked when examining the growth dynamic is the respective share of each factor within GDP (Table 9.2). Government consumption may play an important role in smoothing business cycles, but after considering leakage and import content, its impact is limited by its share of GDP. The share of government consumption within GDP has only once exceeded 10 per cent, which limits its impact to conduct countercyclical policy.

The share of private consumption in GDP is about 60 per cent, but Figure 9.1 suggests that it does not have its own dynamism – it depends very much on GDP. The share of non-food items in private consumption is about 50 per cent, but we do not know the share of non-durables. Whatever the number, it would be insignificant in terms of producing large periodic swings in private consumption. The share of imports in GDP is also substantial, reaching 30 per cent in 2000 (Table 9.2). But it is tied closely to export movement due to the relatively high import content in Indonesian manufactured exports, which are dominant in the total figure. This leaves investment and exports as the possible main sources of the GDP growth dynamic.

In Figure 9.2 we plot GDP, investment and export growth, along with the share of exports in GDP. The intention is to examine the impact of export dynamism on GDP growth more closely.[2] Three years prior to the AFC, high investment growth – along with about a 30 per cent share in GDP – had succeeded in producing economic growth averaging 8 per cent annually. Besides the growth level, the impact of investment on GDP is reflected in its oscillation pattern.

The period of high growth ended with the AFC. The sharp turnaround of investment growth had caused a severe contraction in the economy. The recovery of investment in late 2000 helped the economy achieve a modest recovery, with average growth of 4.6 per cent annually from 2000 to 2004 (Table 9.1). But the recovery stalled after the latter half of 2001 and only resumed in the second half of 2002. Negative investment growth appears to be behind the slowdown of the recovery. In this period, investment posted negative growth of −1.2 per cent to −3.2 per cent annually. To make matters worse, the share of investment also dropped sharply, to about 20 per cent of GDP from about 30 per cent (see Figure 9.2).

The reason behind the slowdown can be tracked to the worsening investment climate due to the chaotic days of the administration of President Abdurrahman Wahid, his eventual impeachment, and the accession of Vice-President Megawati Sukarnoputri to the presidency. This political development had a big impact on market confidence (Siregar 2001). The launching of a decentralization law in 2001 also created huge uncertainty for the business sector (Deuster 2002). The most visible impact immediately after the decentralization law went into effect was the race among districts to create new local regulations. At the local government level a number of new local regulations concerning taxes, levies, and various types of permits were created to be artificially complementary and as a way to extract indirect revenues in the form of bribes, as well as direct revenues (Kuncoro and Resosudarmo 2006).

The Megawati administration brought short-lived optimism into the business sector. The investment growth recovered briefly in the second half of 2002. Subsequently, the controversy surrounding a new labor law caused this renewed optimism to wane in a very short time. Overregulation in the labor market as a consequence of the introduction the new labor law acted as a disincentive for new investments, both domestic and from abroad (Alisjahbana and Manning 2002). Unresolved disputes between the business sector and labor revolved around controversial articles of the new law dealing with severance pay, minimum wages, layoffs in the modern sector, conditions governing the right to strike, and rent-seeking on the part of Ministry of Labor officials. So once again, investment growth dipped into negative numbers or very low growth throughout 2003.

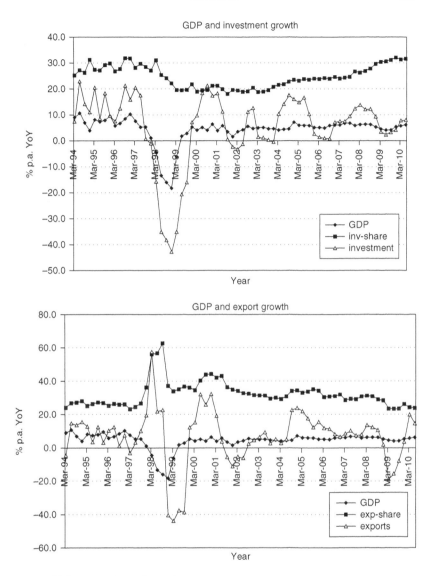

Note: GDP = gross domestic product.

Source: CEIC Asia Database.

Figure 9.2   Impact of export dynamism on GDP growth

Things began to improve in 2004 in the aftermath of the presidential election. But in the end, the cycle of surging new optimism and eventual disappointment reappeared. GDP growth slowed from 6.7 per cent in Q4 2004 to 5.3 per cent in Q3 2005 (Figure 9.2). Looking at the record of economic growth before and after Q4 2004, it appears that the election of President Susilo Bambang Yudhoyono in September renewed some optimism for economic actors that led to a surge of investment and GDP growth in that particular quarter. But the perceived lack of a concrete action plan to turn around the economy saw that optimism gradually turn to apathy (Kuncoro and Resosudarmo 2006). It came as no surprise when the apparent lack of government direction in pursuing an economic reform agenda increased uncertainty and eventually lowered economic expectations, creating little enthusiasm for risky investments. Increased uncertainty led many entrepreneurs to adopt a wait-and-see attitude.

There was not a massive drop in investment, as occurred at the height of the AFC in 1998, but rather a gradual loss of momentum (Kuncoro and Resosudarmo 2006). The slowdown of investment could be traced to Q4 2004 to Q3 2005. The growth rate of investment in Q4 2004 was 17.6 per cent and in Q3 2005 it was 16.1 per cent (Figure 9.2). The investment growth rate in Q1 2005 was well below these numbers at only 14.9 per cent. The downward trend of investment growth continued well into 2006. The first three quarters of 2006 recorded very low growth, below 2 per cent, before improving to 7.2 per cent in the last quarter of 2006. As a result the economy reverted back to the previous path, with annual growth ranging from 4.9 per cent to 5.1 per cent.

It is worth noting that the Yudhoyono administration's performance on investment is by no means poorer than that of the previous administration. On the contrary, on average it was better since it has never posted negative investment growth in any quarter. Also, in the Q4 2006, the investment growth rate is well above the GDP growth rate and far above consumption growth. But to make the economy grow faster and increase employment, higher investment growth is needed.

Some attribute the dismal performance of the Yudhoyono government to "finding the right person for the right job" and the delay in the appointment of top-tier officials, who would eventually be responsible to implement the government economic agenda (McLeod 2005). The government tried many things to restore investor confidence, including a Cabinet reshuffle. The December 2005 reshuffle rejuvenated public optimism. Investment moved back to a higher gear, with investment growth ranging from 7.2 per cent to 9.6 per cent in 2006 and from 12 per cent to 13 per cent in 2007. The economy was back to a 6 per cent growth rate before the GER struck at the end of 2008.

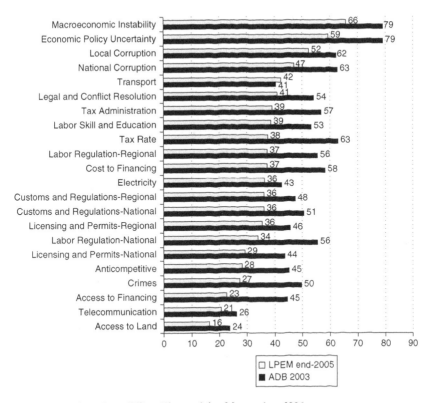

Source: Lembaga Penyelidikan Ekonomi dan Masyarakat, 2006.

Figure 9.3   Monitoring the investment climate in Indonesia

The urgency of the Cabinet shake-up can be traced in Figure 9.3, which shows a survey on manufacturing firms conducted in mid-2005 by *Lembaga Penyelidikan Ekonomi dan Masyarakat* (LPEM). It asked respondents to rank the severity of 22 constraints on business.

Overall, according to the perception of firms, the investment climate improved between 2003 and 2005, suggesting the difference between the Megawati and the Yudhoyono administrations. The perception indicators for 2003 were obtained from the *Country Governance Assessment Report, Republic of Indonesia* (Asian Development Bank 2004). At first glance it appears that except for transportation, all constraints have become less severe. Interestingly, from 2003 to 2005 the ranking of constraints has changed very little. The biggest impediments are still macroeconomic instability, policy uncertainty, and corruption – all macro indicators. This result provides a glimpse of the mind-set of investors. It may suggest that no matter how good the picture when considering more microeconomic indicators, new investment may not be forthcoming if the macroeconomic situation is bad or uncertainty about government policies is higher than usual, due to either policy inconsistencies or a lack of credibility.

Macroeconomic instability, policy uncertainty, and corruption are bigger problems than the regulatory environment. But that does not necessarily mean that microeconomic problems are not important. On the contrary, simplifying procedures and regulations reduces opportunities for corruption. Thus, regulatory reform can address one of the biggest investment constraints.

In 2009, investment once again was subdued, growing at 2.4 per cent to 4.2 per cent before improving to around 8 per cent in the first half of 2010 (see Figure 9.2). At the same time, economic growth was slow – below 5 per cent before recovering to a 6.2 per cent annual rate in the second quarter of 2010. The government attempted to offset the impact by increasing the speed of budget disbursements. This is apparent from the jump in government consumption growth from 5.3 per cent in Q1 2008 to above 14 per cent in Q2 2008. In Q1 2010 the figure dropped dramatically into negative territory, with −8.8 per cent annual rate in Q1 2010 and −9 per cent rate in Q2 2010. There was an intention to speed up budget disbursements even more in the second half of 2010, but the capacity of government agencies to absorb disbursements in a relatively short time was limited.

Exports

The impact of 2008–09 GER was very modest. Exports bore the brunt of the shock, with huge negative growth numbers for three consecutive months in 2009. Only in the last quarter in 2009 did it move back to a low positive growth rate (Figure 9.2). This decline, however, was largely offset by a decline in imports, which posted even larger negative growth numbers in the same period. The continuing decline in exports and investment made the growth of consumption, particularly private consumption which accounts for about 60 per cent of GDP, a very important determinant for national economic growth. However, the growth in private consumption only modestly increased – from 6.0 per cent in Q1 2009 to 4.0 per cent in Q4 2009 – which was just enough to make GDP grow from 4.1 per cent to 4.5 per cent during that period.

Components of Investment

In the above analysis, this chapter has shown the role of investment in Indonesia during the boom and bust. But an important question remains:

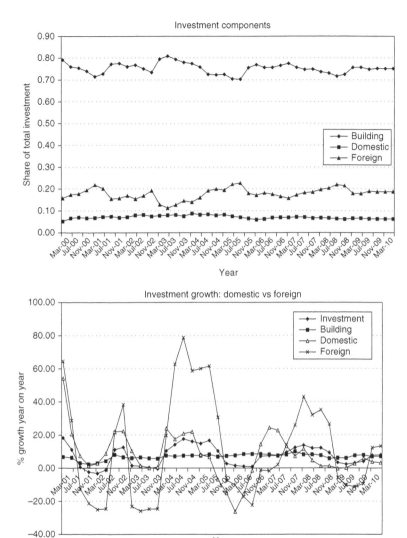

Source: CEIC Asia Database.

Figure 9.4   Components of investment: domestic versus foreign

what factors are behind the cyclicality of investment? Figures 9.4 and 9.5 graph the different components of investment.

Indonesia's slowdown in investment can be tracked to growth stagna-tion in the building sector because of its commanding share – around

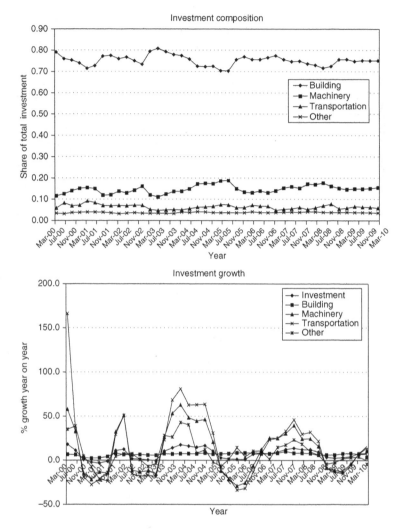

Source: CEIC Asia Database.

*Figure 9.5   Components of investment: building, machinery and
            transportation*

75 per cent or so of total investment. The building sector captures residential and other construction investments, including infrastructure.[3] The movement over time tends to be flat, showing very little dynamism. This is a far cry from before the AFC when its growth was fueled by domestic credit and capital inflows.[4]

The investment dynamic is determined by other types of investment by domestic and foreign parties. Both domestic and foreign categories consist of machinery, transportation, and other investments. Foreign investment is very important for the economy since its share is about 20 per cent of the country's total capital expenditures (Figure 9.4). Not only is its share significant, but foreign investment is also the largest contributor to investment dynamism, with its large upward and downward swings that reflect volatile business expectations since the AFC.

The most consistent period of foreign investment growth was from early March 2004 until the early part of 2006. Again in early 2007, foreign investment was trending up with expectations of growth well into 2010. But then the GER struck in 2008. The pattern of domestic investment is more or less similar to foreign investment, only more subdued and less volatile, possibly reflecting a wait-and-see attitude of domestic entrepreneurs concerned about moving too aggressively ahead of the cycle.

Figure 9.5 shows the investment series broken down into machinery, transportation, and other categories, regardless of ownership. Machinery forms around 15 per cent of the total investment. With building in a steady-state mode, machinery is clearly the most important factor behind the investment dynamic, with transportation playing a minor role.

Earlier, this chapter made the case for the importance of boosting the quality of investment. Due to its sheer size, the building sector is obviously one candidate for investment growth. But the building sector has been sluggish. We need to look at factors that affect investment decisions on building if we are to understand why building remains sluggish in the aftermath of the AFC. One important factor is interest rates, which will be discussed later in this chapter. Another factor is overinvestment before the AFC. This could be attributed to rapid growth in non-tradable sectors such as utilities, construction, communications, and finance. So there is a possibility that subdued investment growth since the AFC, particularly in areas related to building and construction, is just a process by which investment is returning to its more sustainable long-run growth path.

Machinery could be the other candidate for investment growth. With its effect on current investment and future output, its impact on GDP growth may be comparable to that of the building sector. Efforts to revive investment growth in machinery could be more complicated since it involves factors beyond the cost of funds. As indicated in Figure 9.3, the government must sustain business expectations by implementing consistent economic policies, combating corruption, controlling the cost of doing business at the national and local levels, and maintaining infrastructure and transportation.

Asia rising

Table 9.3   Sector average annual growth and share of GDP 1983–2009 (%)

	1983–93		1994–96		2000–03		2004–09	
	Annual growth	GDP share	Annual growth	GDP share	Annual growth	GDP share	Annual growth	GDP share
Agriculture	3.6	20.6	2.7	17.1	3.2	15.2	3.5	14.0
Mining	2.2	16.9	6.2	8.7	1.4	9.8	1.5	10.6
Manufacturing[a]	11.9	13.4	13.0	21.7	5.9	24.5	5.0	22.8
Utilities	12.6	0.6	14.0	1.2	7.4	0.8	8.6	0.9
Construction	7.7	5.7	13.7	7.6	5.5	6.0	7.7	7.9
Trade	7.5	15.4	7.9	16.6	4.9	16.4	6.5	14.8
Transportation	7.0	4.8	6.8	5.7	7.2	3.6	5.5	3.8
Communication	10.7	0.6	18.9	1.1	14.5	1.7	25.6	2.7
Finance	8.8	6.7	9.3	8.7	6.2	8.4	6.8	7.9
Services	5.2	11.1	3.1	8.9	3.4	9.6	5.9	10.1
GDP	6.1	100.0	7.9	100.0	4.5	100.0	5.6	100.0

Note: a.   Excluding oil and gas.

Source: CEIC Asia Database.

Production Side

The Indonesia economy has undergone a structural transformation over the past three decades, going from an economy dominated by agriculture to one dominated by manufacturing, signifying a metamorphosis to a more modern economy. Agriculture's share of GDP dropped from around 20 per cent in the 1980s to about 15 per cent in 2000, while manufacturing has increased its share from around 13.4 per cent in the 1980s to about 24 per cent in 2000 (see Table 9.3).[5] The structural transformation has changed the growth dynamic. Now anything that hinders growth in manufacturing will translate into diminished GDP growth, despite the fact that other sectors may provide some offsetting influences. The slow growth of manufacturing provides some explanation for the modest growth of GDP in the aftermath of the AFC (Table 9.3).[6]

Various deregulation measures announced in 1994–95 changed many aspects of existing economic incentives, including consumption and investment activities, and an orientation toward exports versus the domestic market (Kuncoro and Resosudarmo 2006). From 1994 to 1996, the impact of the deregulation measures was immediately seen. GDP grew at an annual average of about 8 per cent (Table 9.3).

Looking more deeply, however, after the initial burst of growth in manufacturing, economic growth took place primarily in non-tradable

Table 9.4   GDP growth by sector (1993 prices; % per annum year on year)

	March 1994	December 1994	March 1995	December 1995	March 1996	December 1996
GDP	9.0	3.9	8.1	9.5	5.7	10.3
Agriculture	−2.5	−2.0	5.0	4.3	1.4	5.1
Mining	3.4	5.7	8.3	6.5	6.4	6.0
Manufacturing	23.4	4.8	11.4	17.8	8.6	14.8
Utilities	11.1	13.8	16.6	13.3	14.1	14.2
Construction	12.5	9.3	22.1	7.9	4.9	12.9
Trade	8.3	5.6	9.5	8.1	7.5	10.9
Transportation	5.5	8.2	8.0	3.7	6.6	6.8
Communication	24.1	15.3	17.7	19.0	21.6	19.5
Finance	21.5	0.5	0.0	0.9	19.2	15.9
Services	4.1	2.2	2.4	3.3	3.0	3.9

Note: GDP = gross domestic product.

Source: CEIC Asia Database.

sectors, such as utilities, construction, communications, and finance, that mainly served domestic demand and hence contributed very little to foreign exchange generation (Table 9.4). For example construction grew at a 22.1 per cent annual rate in Q1 1995 compared to an 11.4 per cent rate for manufacturing. The growth of other supposedly more productive non-tradable sectors, such as transportation, was a little slower. For example, transportation rose at an annual rate of 8.0 per cent in Q1 1995 and fell thereafter.[7]

In the aftermath of the AFC, manufacturing has gone from the primary driver of the economy to a significant source of drag on GDP growth simply because of its sizeable share of the economy (see Table 9.3). Along with transportation, manufacturing was the only sector that recorded growth below GDP in 2004–09. Amid the sluggishness of the other sectors, the communications sector, boosted by booming cellular phone services, appears to have its own life. The growth was extraordinarily high at around 26 per cent annually from 2004 to 2009.

To examine the growth dynamic more closely, we must look at GDP growth after the 1997–98 AFC. Figure 9.6 summarizes the growth dynamic from the output side since 2000. Due to its relatively high share of GDP, the manufacturing growth path for the most part resembles GDP. After starting with a modest recovery in Q1 2001, it began to lose steam in Q1 2005.

The peak was reached in Q4 2004 with an 8.7 per cent annual growth

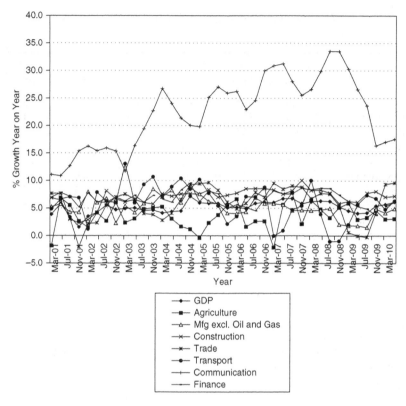

Note: Mfg = manufacturing.

Source: CEIC Asia Database.

Figure 9.6   Sectoral GDP growth: 2001–10

rate; thereafter growth declined gradually. The GER only made matters worse. From Q4 2008 to Q3 2009, manufacturing growth fell below 2 per cent. This caused GDP growth to drop to around 4.5 per cent. Other sectors provided little help since the slowdown occurred uniformly across sectors.

Looking at Figure 9.6, transportation, communications, and construction show some sign of countercyclicality, relative to GDP, but their share is still too small to have any meaningful impact. Also their cycles are not completely independent from GDP, so they are not truly autonomous factors. The high growth of communications can be explained by the increasing demand for cellular phone services. Some of the demand is based on necessity, especially in rural areas where the fixed-line phone service is not reliable. The demand, especially in urban areas, is often due

Table 9.5 *Non-oil manufacturing average growth (% per annum year on year)*

ISIC	2001	2002	2003	2004	2005	2006	2007	2008	2009
Food	1.1	0.2	2.7	1.4	2.7	7.2	5.1	2.3	11.3
Textile	3.4	3.2	6.2	4.1	1.3	1.2	−3.7	−3.6	0.5
Wood	0.5	0.6	1.2	−2.1	−0.9	−0.7	−1.7	3.5	−1.5
Paper	−4.8	5.3	8.4	7.6	2.4	2.1	5.8	−1.5	6.3
Chemicals	0.5	4.7	10.7	9.0	8.8	4.5	5.7	4.5	1.5
Non-metal	19.1	6.6	7.1	9.5	3.8	0.5	3.4	−1.5	−0.6
Basic-iron	−1.0	−1.3	−8.0	−2.6	−3.7	4.7	1.7	−2.1	−4.5
Machinery	17.2	18.1	8.9	17.7	12.4	7.5	9.7	9.8	−2.9
Others	12.6	−11.1	17.7	12.8	2.6	3.6	−2.8	−1.0	3.1
All	4.9	5.7	6.0	7.5	5.9	5.3	5.2	4.0	2.5

Share (fraction)

ISIC	2001	2002	2003	2004	2005	2006	2007	2008	2009
Food	0.33	0.31	0.30	0.28	0.27	0.28	0.28	0.27	0.30
Textile	0.14	0.13	0.13	0.13	0.12	0.12	0.11	0.10	0.10
Wood	0.06	0.06	0.05	0.05	0.05	0.04	0.04	0.04	0.04
Paper	0.05	0.05	0.06	0.06	0.05	0.05	0.05	0.05	0.05
Chemicals	0.12	0.12	0.13	0.13	0.13	0.13	0.13	0.13	0.13
Non-metal	0.03	0.03	0.04	0.04	0.04	0.03	0.03	0.03	0.03
Basic-iron	0.03	0.02	0.02	0.02	0.02	0.02	0.02	0.02	0.01
Machinery	0.23	0.26	0.27	0.29	0.31	0.32	0.33	0.35	0.33
Others	0.01	0.01	0.01	0.01	0.01	0.01	0.01	0.01	0.01

Source: CEIC Asia Database.

to its status as a new symbol of affluence. It is very uncommon now for someone not to have a cellular phone.

Basri and Hill (2011) found that the persistent slowdown of manufacturing is rather puzzling because after the AFC, manufacturing has enjoyed currency depreciation and there had been no constraint on domestic demand, except for a brief time in 2008 when GER occurred. The slow growth of manufacturing might be attributed to the same factors that made investments grow slowly – the deterioration of the business climate, policy uncertainty, and labor market rigidity. Competition from cheap, low-end manufactured products from the People's Republic of China (PRC) might also be a factor. The appreciation of the exchange rate due to capital inflows makes things more precarious for manufacturing. There is also another argument that puts the blame on the reluctance of the banking sector to provide loans to the real sector.

Table 9.5 provides useful information regarding the manufacturing dynamic. In terms of value-added creation, machinery and food rank as the top two categories. But within a relatively short time after the AFC, the position of food as a value-added generator was slowly being replaced by machinery. In 2009 the share of machinery within non-oil manufacturing was 33 per cent, while food commanded about 30 per cent of the total value added. These two categories, along with chemicals and textiles, constitute about 60 per cent or more of non-oil manufacturing value-added creation, so any dismal performances in that sector can be traced back to these categories. Other sectors are either too small or too static – or both – to have a significant impact on manufacturing growth.

From its peak in 2004, manufacturing showed successive declining growth, which accelerated during the 2008 GER (Table 9.5). Overall growth immediately dropped from 5.2 per cent in 2007 to 4.0 per cent in 2008 and 2.5 per cent in 2009. In 2008, the two mainstays of manufacturing – machinery and food – were able to withstand the shock, with 9.8 per cent and 2.3 per cent growth, respectively, while other categories, except for wood and chemicals, posted negative growth. In the following year, machinery succumbed with a negative growth of −2.9 per cent, while food did very well with exceptional growth of 11.3 per cent. The final tally, however, still resulted in a low, albeit positive, growth rate of 2.5 per cent for non-oil manufacturing. Due to the sheer size of its contribution, it was difficult to compensate for the loss in machinery.

Aftermath of the Global Economic Recession

Table 9.6 includes data from Q1 2009 to Q2 2010 that show how the economy – from the output side – navigated through the GER.

On the output side, the highest growth rate was recorded by the communications sector. The second-highest growth rate was achieved by the utility sector (electricity, gas, and water supply), of which electricity was the main contributor. The growth of agriculture was positive, which provided some reprieve to the economy. After posting very low growth, the recovery of manufacturing began in Q4 2009 with growth of 4.5–5.0 per cent. Construction and trade performed reasonably well, providing a further boost to the recovery. Meanwhile the financial sector appeared to be pro-cyclical, just following the movement of GDP. In the end, despite the sluggishness of the manufacturing sector, the recovery went well, so much so that in Q2 2010 the economy was able to achieve the psychological threshold of a 6 per cent annual growth rate.

Table 9.6   GDP growth by sector (2000 prices; % per annum year on year)

	March 2009	June 2009	September 2009	December 2009	March 2010	June 2010
GDP	4.5	4.1	4.2	5.4	5.7	6.2
Agriculture	5.9	2.9	3.3	4.6	3.0	3.1
Mining	2.6	3.4	6.2	5.2	3.1	3.8
Manufacturing excl. oil and gas	1.9	1.8	1.5	4.9	4.1	4.9
Utilities	11.2	15.3	14.5	14.0	8.2	4.8
Construction	6.2	6.1	7.7	8.0	7.1	7.2
Trade	0.6	0.0	−0.2	4.2	9.4	9.6
Transportation	2.0	5.7	7.4	6.7	4.8	6.3
Communication	30.3	26.6	23.7	16.3	17.0	17.5
Finance	6.3	5.3	4.9	3.8	5.3	6.1
Services	6.7	7.2	6.0	5.7	4.6	5.3

Note: GDP = gross domestic product.

Source: CEIC Asia Database.

SOURCE OF FINANCE

Figure 9.7 shows the growth of the financial sector and the banking subsector. Before the AFC, the financial sector for the most part behaved more erratically than GDP. The pattern of growth, however, resembles that of GDP, which is the pro-cyclical nature of the sector. The financial sector is dominated by the banking subsector, which explains why the financial sector and the banking series move together very closely. After the AFC, the financial sector path was less oscillatory but more pro-cyclical than before. It is interesting to note that the non-bank financial sector tends to outperform GDP after 2000. One explanation is that most of the excess liquidity was invested in financial assets rather than in the real sector.

Many economic commentators in Indonesia question why the banking sector – as the biggest recipient of taxpayer money in the form of recapitalization – failed to give something back to the economy, a reference to bank reluctance to extend loans to the real sector. The gap between total deposits and the amount of outstanding loans to the economy continues to persist after the AFC. There is no sign that the gap will diminish in the foreseeable future.

There are many explanations for this. First, banks are now excessively

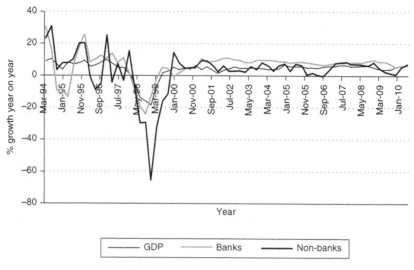

Source: CEIC Asia Database.

Figure 9.7   Growth of banking and non-bank sector

averse to risk. With the availability of risk-free assets such as Bank Indonesia Certificates (SBIs) and government bonds (SUN), there is less pressure for banks to extend loans to borrowers. These financial instruments, which provide some protection for banks, were created by the government authorities, who are still traumatized by the massive bank failures in 1998 and do not want to see that happen again. The social cost of this policy is excess liquidity in the economy, which otherwise could be used to produce more growth and employment (Figures 9.8 and 9.9).

Besides the prevalence of excess liquidity, there is also a shift of bank portfolios from sectors and activities that used to be the primary drivers of economic growth – manufacturing from the output side and investment from the expenditure side – toward other sectors with lesser weight or multiplier effects on the economy. Table 9.7 shows that the share of credit allocated to manufacturing declined from its peak of 39.7 per cent in 2000 to merely 17 per cent in 2009. On the expenditure side, the share of credit allocated to investment fell from 28.4 per cent in 1993 to 20.8 per cent in 2009. So the engines of economic growth have experienced greater borrowing constraints that in fact may be growth impediments.

Banks have gradually increased their loan portfolios and reduced their risk-free assets (SBIs and SUN) as seen in Figure 9.9, but the new pattern of credit allocation still favors sectors and activities other than

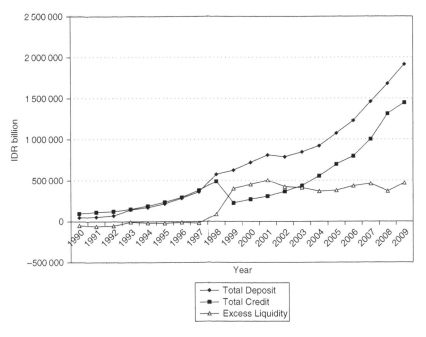

Source: Calculated from CEIC Asia Database.

Figure 9.8   Excess liquidity: 1990–2009

manufacturing and investment (Table 9.7). As mentioned earlier, banks may be more cautious in lending to manufacturing and investment projects, but the change may also be attributed to firms that after the AFC are less inclined to borrow, preferring to rely on cash accumulation (retained earnings) or other sources of borrowing.

Some suspect that the reluctance of firms to borrow can be attributed to high domestic interest rates. The gap between lending rates for all types of loans and deposit rates is around 5 per cent, which indicates the high fixed costs and inefficiency of banks (Figure 9.10). But this does not explain why in the period before the AFC, investment growth was high.

Figure 9.11 shows that there is no relationship between the trend of interest rates and growth of all types of credit. Despite a downward trend, the interest rate on a six-month deposit was virtually flat after the AFC. Growth in consumer credit picked up quickly after the AFC but then steadily declined, reflecting competition among credit providers as well as excess liquidity.

In terms of the speed of the recovery, credit for working capital ranks

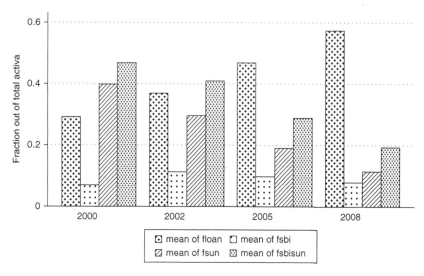

Note: FLOAN = foreign loan; FSBI = Surat Berharga Bank Indonesia (Bank of Indonesia Certificate); FSBISUn = sum of FSBI and FSUN; FSUN = Surat Utang Negara (government bonds).

Source: Calculated from Bank of Indonesia balance sheet.

Figure 9.9   Bank placement in SBI and SUN

Table 9.7   Credit allocation to selected sectors and by usage to investment (%)

Year	Sectors							Usage to invest-ment
	Agricul-ture.	Mining	Manu-facturing	Trade	Utilities	Constr-uction	Trans-port	
1993	8.0	0.5	34.2	25.2	0.4	7.4	–	28.4
1997	6.9	1.4	29.5	21.8	1.1	7.9	1.1	24.0
2000	7.3	2.5	39.7	16.4	1.7	2.5	3.6	24.3
2005	5.4	1.1	24.3	19.4	0.8	3.8	1.8	21.7
2009	5.3	2.9	17.0	20.9	1.7	4.4	5.0	20.8

Source: Financial and Economic Statistics, Bank of Indonesia.

second after credit for consumption. The trend of consumption credit, however, is quite erratic, with a sharp decline in 2003 owing to macro-economic uncertainty in the administrations of President Abdurrahman Wahid and President Megawati Sukarnoputri in 2001 to 2004. The trend

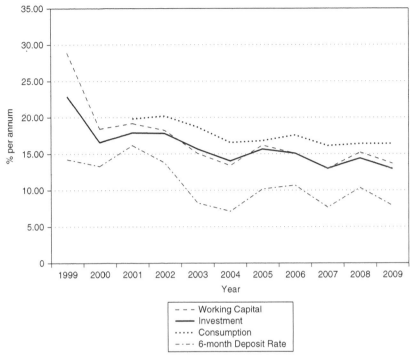

Source: Calculated from CEIC Asian Database.

Figure 9.10 Interest margin

only recovered late in 2004, with the election of President Susilo Bambang Yudhoyono. Ranking third, after consumption credit and credit for working capital, is credit for property. The property market reached its peak in 2003 but then declined steadily before falling sharply at the time of the GER.

Of the four types of credit listed in Figure 9.11, credit for investment ranks the lowest. After huge negative growth in 1999, growth of investment credit remained flat until 2003. A slight improvement occurred in 2004, followed by another loss of steam. Growth picked up again in 2006, but by 2009 the GER drove it below a 20 per cent annual rate.

Figure 9.12 supports this observation for investment credit. Since 1999 the rate of investment lending has been virtually flat, but investment credit growth has exhibited its own pattern. After being long dormant, growth was poised to gain momentum in 2008 when the GER occurred. The recovery of investment credit in 2006 took place without lowering

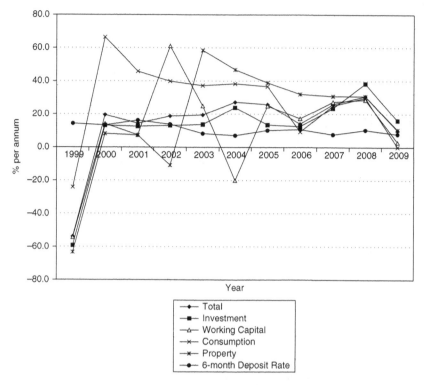

Source: Calculated from CEIC Asian Database.

Figure 9.11   Credit growth and interest rate

investment-lending rates, thus investment credit and the lending rate are
driven more by demand than supply. Investment is a forward-looking
activity, anticipating future opportunities rather than waiting for lending
rates to come down.[8]

Figure 9.13 suggests that this does not necessarily mean that there
are no credit or external borrowing constraints. The graph of investment credit growth and investment growth, which are from different
sources but resemble one another, are able to match at almost every
turning point, very much like shifting up the graph by a constant factor.
This implies that investment credit is determined by demand. There is
also a possibility that most of the funding might come from elsewhere,
including retained earnings. Domestic bank credit and non-bank foreign
borrowing might provide only residual financing. The recovery of investment growth in 2006 also suggests that credit for investment is driven by

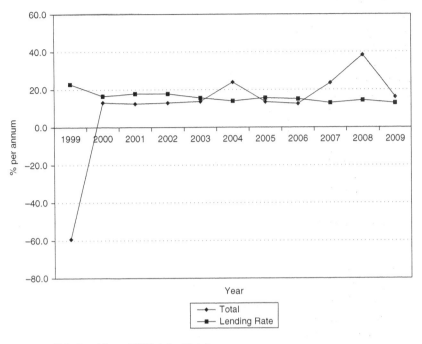

Source: Calculated from CEIC Asian Database.

Figure 9.12   Investment credit and lending rate

demand as it is almost perfectly matched by the corresponding rise in
the growth of domestic credit. Again this shows that interest rates may
matter little.

The issue becomes more complicated when Bank Indonesia (BI),
which has to maintain the competitiveness of the domestic currency, the
rupiah, has to sterilize the impact of capital inflows on currency appreciation. That requires BI to buy foreign exchange in the market, which will
increase domestic liquidity. In order to rein in inflation, BI has to use its
SBI bonds to absorb excess liquidity. This is an expensive operation since
BI has to offer attractive rates, which will eventually be used as a benchmark for other banks if they are to compete with the high-yielding government bonds. So coupled with bank inefficiency and excessive aversion
to risk on the part of commercial banks, this creates a situation in which
it is difficult for lending rates to fall significantly. Excess liquidity in the
economy – at an interest rate higher than it should be under a situation
where demand meets supply – allows firms to face a near perfectly elastic
supply of credit (Figure 9.14).[9]

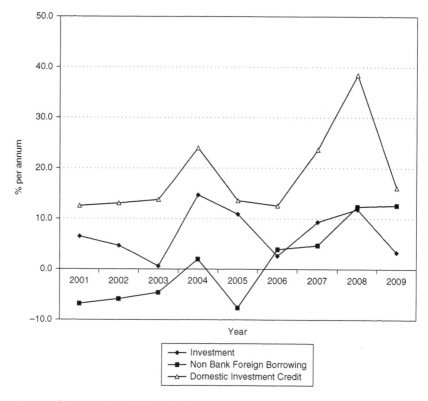

Source: Calculated from CEIC Asian Database.

Figure 9.13   Financing investment

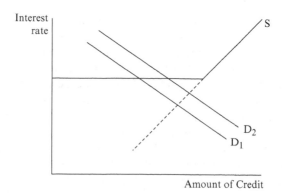

Figure 9.14   Interest rates and credit: a theoretical framework

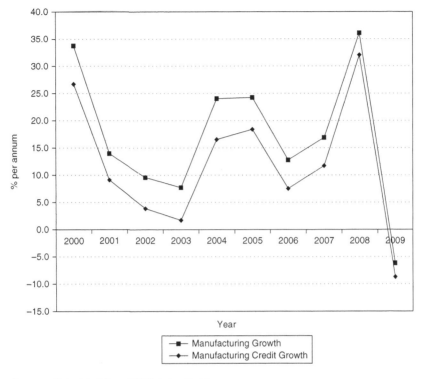

Source: Calculated from CEIC Asian Database.

Figure 9.15 Financing manufacturing growth

This does not mean that loans are not readily available given the present state of excess liquidity; the only problem is that the loans are expensive. Therefore, firms have to rely on other sources of funding, including internal sources. With the limited ability of firms to borrow externally from banks as well as other sources, their ability to share risks with external parties is also limited. Sources of investment funding from friends, relatives, family, and informal connections should not be counted as external financing since firms may not want their long-term relationships with their personal networks to go awry if there is a downturn in their investment projects.

This would make firms even more cautious when it comes to investment decisions. The data show that business confidence is still fragile. The recovery of investment growth in 2000 and again in 2003 failed to gain momentum because of deteriorating business confidence (Figure 9.12).

Bringing down interest rates on credit may be one important ingredient in reviving investment. Bank Indonesia has tried to lower rates mainly through moral suasion, but to no avail. The latest draconian measure is to use required reserves, which essentially punish banks that fail to extend enough credit to the private sector. It remains to be seen how this measure will work. Investment is a forward-looking activity that weighs future prospects, uncertainty, and costs. If investment credit remains a source of residual financing due to its high borrowing cost, reviving investment will depend solely on the future prospect for the economy – which is uncertain – and less on financial costs.

MICROECONOMIC PERSPECTIVE

This chapter has asserted that the reasons behind subdued investment growth are complex. They range from high borrowing costs; slowing demand; some deterioration in the business climate, especially uncertainty in economic policymaking; local corruption; transportation and infrastructure; and change in the attitude of entrepreneurs toward risks and thus investment – all of which have contributed to a slowdown of investment and ultimately to lower economic growth since the AFC.

Given what happens at the macro-aggregate level, a micro-level examination of how entrepreneurs invest and how they finance that investment must consider the impact of high borrowing costs, the limited access to external financing, and the risk appetite of entrepreneurs themselves. Fazzari et al. (1988) and Hubbard (1998) provided the theoretical and empirical framework underpinning the relationship between the cost and access of borrowing on one hand and investment on the other. In this setting, a firm is considered as financially constrained if the cost or availability of external funds prevents it from exercising the level of the optimum investment I_{it}^* (Bhaduri 2005). The actual investment can differ from the optimum level if the available internal funds from cash flows (CF) are less than they should be. In the other case, the level of CF is binding below the level of the optimum investment I_{it}^*. Formally, the investment decision is expressed as

$$I_{it} = Min(I_{it}^*, CF_{it}) \qquad (9.1)$$

This method has been applied widely in studying the impact of external financial constraints on the investment behavior of firms. See for example Athey and Laumas (1994), Bhaduri (2005), and Harris et al. (1994) for Indonesian manufacturing firms.[10]

The interpretation of the empirical model implied by equation (9.1) is not straightforward, so instead of pursuing an econometric analysis we rely on a simpler method to examine firm investment behavior at the micro

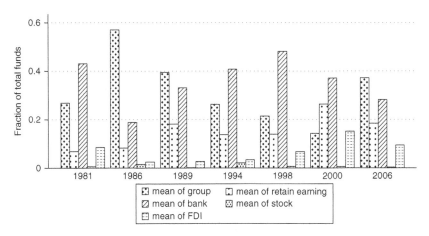

Source: Calculated from manufacturing survey of medium and large establishments.

Figure 9.16   Sources of finance for investment

level. To examine the idea that investment behavior is influenced by high borrowing costs since the AFC, we look at the establishment-level data sets. The survey of medium and large manufacturing firms from *Badan Pusat Statistik* (BPS) has recorded various sources of finance for investment. To gain insight we compare the situation before and after the AFC. The result is presented in Figure 9.16. In this figure the "group" category captures the method of financing investment from a firm's own money, family and relatives, and from its own business group. The method of using retained earnings from a firm's operations is captured by the category "retained earnings." External financing is represented by "bank," which covers both domestic and foreign banks. Foreign direct investment (FDI) records all financing from partners or the parent company abroad. Finally "stock" is financing through selling stock in the capital market.

In 1981, just two years before banking deregulation, interest rates on credit were low. This was manifested by firms' high leverage (high fraction in the "bank" category). External financing from banks became the main mode for financing investment. The pivotal change came in 1983 when the banking system was deregulated. The shift was immediately apparent. External financing through banks was no longer dominant as credit now became more expensive. Financing from groups became the most popular method of financing. Higher interest rates, however, were accompanied by easier access to funds.

As the government continued with deregulation in trade- and investment-related matters, businesses boomed. Easier access to bank financing enabled the private sector to use the opportunity to expand businesses, albeit at higher interest rates (Harris et al. 1994). In addition, external financing came with a distinct advantage – a firm could now share its risks with creditors (Asanuma and Kikutani 1992). This explains why entrepreneurs went ahead with risky investment projects, despite the fact that interest rates were higher compared to the pre-deregulation period. Gradually, external financing from banks regained its importance (Figure 9.16). As a result, investments grew faster after 1986 (Table 9.1).

The AFC changed the composition of investment financing sources. External financing by banks since 1998 has become less important. The composition of retained earnings almost doubled in 2000, though the share of bank financing was still higher. The situation changed completely when the "group" category, whose funds may come from its own money and from the same business group, became the most important source of financing. So, similar to the aggregate level (Figure 9.13), at the micro level this may indicate an aversion to bank financing on the part of manufacturing firms due to the traumatic experience of the AFC. The role of financing from partners or parent companies abroad (direct foreign investment) after the AFC is also interesting. In 2000 it provided partial compensation for the decline of bank financing, but by 2006 it was replaced by financing from the "group" category.

The new financing strategy changes the way business risks are absorbed. Previously, they were more balanced between internal (a company's retained earnings and the group) and external parties (banks). But now most risks cannot be shifted to others. It may explain why entrepreneurs are more averse to risk when it comes to making new investments.

How the decline in external financing impacts investment behavior presents an interesting question. To find an answer we must look at the investment–output ratio at the firm level. From the previous narrative (Figure 9.2), it is clear that at the aggregate level the investment–GDP ratio falls when investment growth slows down. When we repeat this analysis at the firm level, the change in the investment–output ratio also explains the nature of its growth, in terms of growing faster or slower. We refrain from using the value of investment of firms directly since we do not have a credible deflator.

Before we examine the impact of external constraints on a firm's investment behavior, we must look at a microeconomic factor that may also be important in investment sluggishness, and that is excess capacity. In Figure 9.17, we compare investment to output and capacity utilization. It appears that there is a relationship between the investment–output ratio and capacity utilization. Over time, the investment–output ratio shows a slight downward trend, while capacity utilization points to slight increase

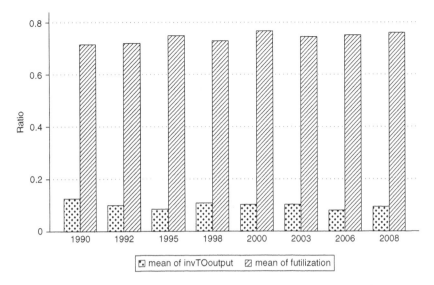

Note: invTOoutput = ratio of investment to output; futilization = capacity utilization ratio.

Source: Calculated from manufacturing survey of medium and large establishments.

Figure 9.17   Investment to output ratio and capacity utilization

over time. It is interesting to note that the utilization ratio did not exceed 80 per cent before and after the AFC. There was some indication that manufacturing firms were reluctant to invest because of the prevalence of excess capacity. The decline in the propensity to invest had some effect on reducing excess capacity, but not much. The overall pattern, however, is too noisy to conclude that excess capacity is the sole cause of the slow-down since investment still grew quite rapidly before the AFC, despite the fact that excess capacity was just over 20 per cent.

In Figure 9.18 we examine the relationship between the investment–output ratio and access to external borrowing. Each variable is regressed to its respective trend, and the resulting regression lines are compared. The trends for both variables unambiguously exhibit a downward trend. The less frequently firms rely on external financing, the lower is the input–output ratio.

We perform a similar exercise between the input–output ratio and retained earnings (Figure 9.19), as well as for the "group" (Figure 9.20). The result indicates that the more a firm uses retained earnings to finance investment, the lower the input–output ratio.[11] Financing from

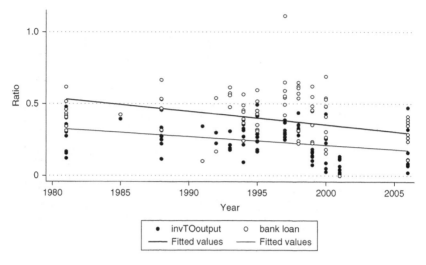

Note: invTOoutput = ratio of investment to output.

Source: Calculated from manufacturing survey of medium and large establishments.

Figure 9.18   Investment to output ratio and bank loans

the "group" category appears to be a substitute for bank loans, at least temporarily. So it resembles quasi-external financing, where the risks are spread out among different companies in the same group. The slope of the "group" time trend is also negative, though flatter than bank loans which means investment is less sensitive to funding from the "group" category. The negative slope of the investment ratio suggests that the propensity to invest declines as financing from these sources dry up. Both results confirm Fazzari et al. (1988), who said that if investment is more sensitive to cash flows or retained earnings, then a firm is externally constrained because the cost of borrowing is too high or simply because external financing is unavailable or inaccessible. Thus, Figure 9.18 and Figures 9.19 and 9.20 are two sides of the same coin.

So we may find bidirectional causality between investment and economic growth after the AFC. Although the cost of borrowing is still important, investors may now be more cautious. Instead of preempting the business cycle, they are waiting for good economic news before committing themselves to invest. Therefore, efforts to boost growth after the AFC appear more complicated, since "trigger factors" are required, rather than just lower borrowing costs.

The surge of investment growth after the election of President Susilo

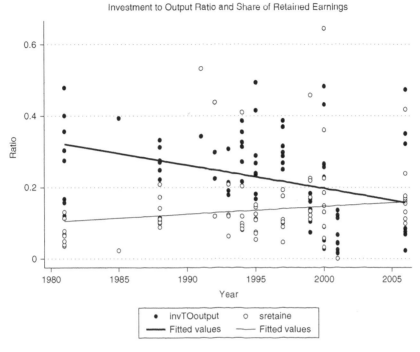

Note: invTOoutput = ratio of investment to output; sretaine = share of retained earnings.

Source: Calculated from manufacturing survey of medium and large establishments.

Figure 9.19 Investment sources of income – retained earnings

Bambang Yudhoyono in September 2004 and the loss of momentum thereafter can be explained by this behavior. Investment growth becomes more erratic when alternating between a sudden short burst of growth and a longer period of stagnation or decline. This behavior may not continue indefinitely if the external situation improves or the marginal cost of not doing anything is negative. The most recent surge of investment growth might have signified a longer trend of recovery had the GER not occurred in 2008.

Earlier we touched on the idea of the quality of investment. Using the marginal-product analogy, from Figure 9.4 and Figure 9.5 we suggested that building and machinery – both domestic and foreign – for different reasons could potentially contribute more to GDP growth compared to other types of investment. So these types of investments may qualify for our definition of "high-quality investment." To mimic this exercise, we look at the composition of investments at the firm level (Figures 9.21 and 9.22).

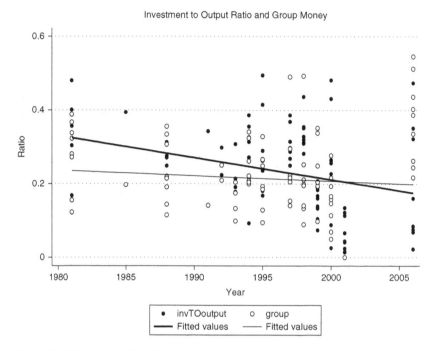

Note: invTOoutput = ratio of investment to output.

Source: Calculated from manufacturing survey of medium and large establishments.

Figure 9.20   Investment sources of income – own group money

The decline of machinery investment is more pronounced for domestic firms. It has been partially compensated by building investment (Figure 9.21). FDI firms have also experienced the same problem, although it is much less severe than their domestic counterparts (Figure 9.22). So in addition to a decline in the propensity to invest – as less productive types of investment such as land acquisition are carried out – the driving force for investment has become more diluted, producing slower economic growth.

CONCLUSION

In this chapter, we attempted to identify factors behind the subdued investment climate that has been observed in Indonesia since the AFC. From the growth analysis, we have shown that investment explained much

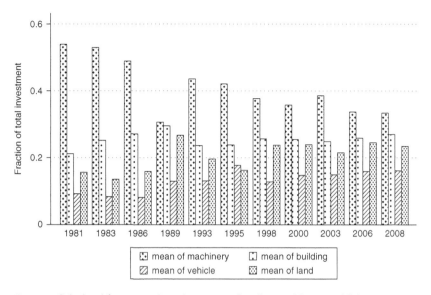

Source: Calculated from manufacturing survey of medium and large establishments.

Figure 9.21   *Components of investment in Indonesian manufacturing –*
                 domestic firms

of the past growth in Indonesia. Thus, reviving investment growth is the key to maintaining sustained growth. We employed a neoclassical model as a framework where investment is basically an interaction between demand and the supply schedule of capital.

As for sources of finance, firms increasingly use more internal sources to finance investment. This situation is driven primarily by high lending rates beyond the market-clearing level. The open-market operation policy intended to keep the exchange rate from appreciating amid capital inflows requires Bank Indonesia to absorb the excess liquidity in order to keep inflation low by issuing the SBI certificates with attractive rates. This makes it difficult for lending rates to go down. The situation becomes more complicated when inefficiency of the banking system, as well as the presence of the government bonds, is taken into account. The presence of all of these high-return, risk-free assets makes banks more reluctant to extend loans to the real sector.

As a consequence, external financing, such as bank and overseas loans, are only a last resort after the use of internal sources, such as retained earnings and contributions from the business group and family, are exhausted. But using internal sources also implies that firms will likely be

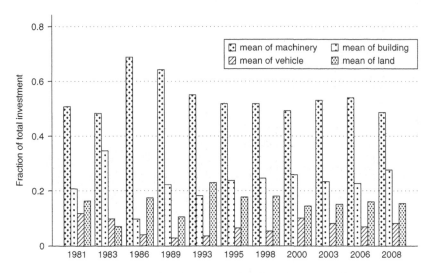

Source: Calculated from manufacturing survey of medium and large establishments.

Figure 9.22   *Components of investment in Indonesian manufacturing –*
                FDI firms

more reluctant to carry out risky investment projects since this method of
financing limits their ability to shift risks to the third parties.

This explains why investment credit is determined more by demand
rather than serving as the driver of investment. Investment is a forward-
looking activity, which should react favorably to good news – especially
in terms of macroeconomic stability, consistent government policy, and
good governance. The volatile growth of investment suggests that it is difficult to sustain positive expectations in the private sector, where attitudes
have become more conservative. Macroeconomic stability, economic
policy consistency, and vigorous implementation of announced economic
plans are the keys to building private-sector confidence.

Resolving this problem is difficult and requires a coordinated effort
from the government and Bank Indonesia. Paramount is the issue of
private sector "crowding-out." To lessen the crowding-out effect, government must reduce its budget deficit and seek more balanced financing
between bond issuance and funding from multilateral donor agencies.
Those agencies may have lower costs of funds, but their role has been
reduced since the AFC as a result of nationalist issues that emerged after
the AFC, particularly in response to the unpopular oversight by the IMF.

In the meantime, Bank Indonesia should seek a less expensive method
to contain the impact of capital inflows into the domestic economy. To

control excess liquidity from the open-market operation in the foreign exchange market, Bank Indonesia could use a more direct method, for example a required reserve ratio instead of SBI certificates. Along with increasing the efficiency of the banking system, the ultimate goal should be to reduce interest rate protection from risk-free SBI certificates and government bonds in an effort to induce more competition among banks to extend loans to the economy.

NOTES

1. The divestment rule, which had been a major deterrent to foreign investors, was abolished. Under the new rule, foreign investors were allowed to form either a joint venture with 95 per cent majority equity ownership without any further divestment obligation or to have full ownership (100 per cent stake) of a business entity in Indonesia with the provision that within 10 years some unspecified divestment would take place in favor of Indonesian partners. In addition, firms 100 per cent owned by foreigners were also allowed to invest in all areas in Indonesia (Azis and Pangestu 1994). Deregulation also eliminated minimum investment requirements, which previously were set at $1 million. In May 1989, this was lowered to $250 000 for certain sectors, such as the distribution of the joint-venture products.

2. Another potential relationship to explore is between export and GDP growth, but the relationship appears to be bidirectional, though the dynamic of GDP growth appears to have a relationship with the oscillation of export growth around the path of GDP (Figure 9.2). Only in the case of investment does the Granger causality suggest that the causality runs from investment growth to GDP growth and not the other away round. So in the strictest sense investment is the closest to being "autonomous."

3. Unfortunately we do not have a separate category for domestic and foreign building investment.

4. Included in this other component is public infrastructure, which is dominated by government capital expenditure, which tends to move countercyclically. Before 2000 there are no data on investment components. Thus, before the AFC the growth of the building sector can only be inferred from the construction sector (Table 9.3).

5. The importance of manufacturing is even more pronounced considering that in 1971 the agriculture sector was 34 per cent of GDP, while manufacturing was only 8 per cent.

6. While in the previous case the relationship between investment and economic growth is more straightforward, there is no evidence that the causality runs one way from manufacturing growth to GDP growth.

7. To complicate the matter, most capital inflows were also used to finance expansion in these sectors. This bred the seed of the 1998 crisis.

8. Certainly one can resort to a formal causality test to determine the direction of relationship but this is beyond the scope of this chapter.

9. To illustrate this point we replicate this exercise by plotting manufacturing growth against manufacturing credit growth. Both come from different data sources (Figure 9.15). The two lines on the graph again resemble each other.

10. The general function of the empirical counterpart of (9.1) is given by

$$\left(\frac{I}{K}\right)_{it} = G\left[\left(\frac{I}{K}\right)_{it-1}, \left(\frac{\Delta S}{K}\right)_{it-1}, \left(\frac{CF}{K}\right)_{it-1}, \left(\frac{D}{K}\right)_{it-1}, e_{it}\right]$$

In the above equation I is gross investment in machinery, K is capital stock, D is bank loans and S is sales. In addition, we also control for firm characteristics, such as being exporters and foreign direct investment (FDI) firms. The lagged value of the changes in sales (*S*) captures the future prospect of profits. Value added instead of output is used as a proxy for sales, since otherwise we have to control for intermediate inputs and raw materials. For cash flow (*CF*) we use the firm's retained earnings and the private contribution from its own cash and relatives.

11. In this situation, the slope differential between the two time-trend regressions represents the degree of tightness of the constraint.

REFERENCES

Asian Development Bank (2004), *Country Governance Assessment Report, Republic of Indonesia*, Manila. Accessed at www.adb.org/Documents/Reports/CGA/ino. asp.

Alisjahbana, A.S., and C. Manning (2002), 'Survey of recent developments', *Bulletin of Indonesian Economic Studies*, **38**, 277–305. doi:10.1080/00074910215539.

Asanuma, B., and T. Kikutani (1992), 'Risk absorption in Japanese sub-contracting: a micro-econometric study of the automobile industry', *Journal of the Japanese and International Economies*, **6**, 1–29. doi:10.1016/0889-1583(92)90016-W.

Athey, M.J., and P.S. Laumas (1994), 'Internal fund and corporate investment in India', *Journal of Development Economics*, **45**, 287–303. doi:10.1016/0304-3878(94)90034-5.

Azis, I.J., and M. Pangestu (1994), 'Survey of recent developments', *Bulletin of Indonesian Economic Studies*, **30**, 3–47.

Basri, M.C., and H. Hill (2011), 'Indonesian growth dynamics', *Asian Economic Policy Review*, **6**, 90–107. doi:10.1111/j.1748-3131.2011.01184.x.

Bhaduri, S.N (2005), 'Investment, financial constraint and financial liberalization: some stylized facts from a developing economy, India', *Journal of Asian Economics*, **16**, 704–18. doi:10.1016/j.asieco.2005.06.001.

Deuster, P.R. (2002), 'Survey of recent developments', *Bulletin of Indonesian Economic Studies*, **38**, 5–37. doi:10.1080/000749102753620257.

Fazzari, S.M., R.G Hubbard, and B.C. Petersen (1988), 'Financing constraints and corporate investment', *Brookings Papers on Economic Activity*, pp. 141–208. doi:10.2307/2534426.

Harris J.R., F. Schiantarelli, and M.G. Siregar (1994), 'The effects of financial liberalization on the capital structure of and investment decision of Indonesian manufacturing establishments', *World Bank Economic Review*, **8**, 17–47. doi:10.1093/wber/8.1.17.

Hubbard, G. (1998), 'Capital market imperfection and investment', *Journal of Economic Literature*, **36**, 193–225.

Kuncoro, A., and B. Resosudarmo (2006), 'Understanding Indonesian economic reforms: 1983–2000', in J.M. Fanelli and G.M. McMahon, *Understanding Market Reforms*. Melbourne: Palgrave Macmillan.

Lembaga Penyelidikan Ekonomi dan Masyarakat – Faculty of Economics, University of Indonesia (2006), 'Monitoring investment climate in Indonesia: a survey of 2005', Jakarta.

McLeod, R.H. (2005), 'Survey of recent developments', *Bulletin of Indonesian Economic Studies*, **41**, 133–57. doi:10.1080/00074910500117271.

Siregar, R. (2001), 'Survey of recent developments', *Bulletin of Indonesian Economic Studies*, **37**, 277–303. doi:10.1080/00074910152669127.

10. India

Rajendra R. Vaidya

Achieving a high rate of growth of gross domestic product (GDP) and sustaining it over a prolonged period has been the chief aim of successive Indian governments over the last two decades. Maintaining moderate to low inflation has also been addressed by the government, but with much less frequency and vigor. In India, recent periods of high growth have been coupled with high inflation. The government has been quick to take credit for high growth rates, but is reluctant to accept blame for high inflation – citing supply shocks, which it says are outside its control. But high inflation is sure to have a moderating influence on growth in the near future, leading to concerns about the economy's ability to sustain high GDP growth rates.

Economists know that a rather complicated relationship exists between trade, investment, and growth and that the specifics of this relationship are likely to be unique for each country. This has made it difficult to arrive at universal agreement on policy choices for realizing sustainable growth. The recent global economic recession (GER) and the slowdown in the growth of world trade have somewhat muted confidence about the continued success of outward-oriented growth policies. Moreover, there seems to be uncertainty regarding the elements of a more inward-looking growth strategy. In such an uncertain environment, policy makers remain convinced that investment plays a key role in growth strategy, irrespective of whether or not it is an inward- or outward-looking strategy. The academic literature seems far less convinced in this regard, as empirically it is not yet clear whether growth drives investment or vice versa. There seems to be a general consensus that public investment, especially in infrastructure, is critical for growth in underdeveloped countries.

Government policies on investment in India largely have focused on investment by the private corporate sector, and a number of recently published papers have examined the Indian corporate sector. That research has focused on the financial constraints facing firms (Athey and Laumas 1994; Ganesh-Kumar et al. 2001), and it concluded that Indian firms face severe finance constraints. By contrast, relatively little attention has been paid to investment by both the public and household sectors. There is very little a government can do to influence investment in the short term given that major reforms, such as industrial reforms and trade and financial liberalization, have already taken place. Attempts at keeping the cost of capital low through low interest rates seem to be running the risk of increasing inflation. Most of the other policy suggestions, such as improving the legal framework (bankruptcy laws and contract enforcement) and improving the efficiency of the financial sector by reducing finance constraints for firms, are likely to be effective only in the medium and long term. In addition, the large budget deficits in recent years have raised fears that private investment will be crowded out.

Recent advances in the real business cycle theory suggest that policies aimed at facilitating household capital accumulation should be a key element of domestic demand-led growth strategy. There are three reasons. First, capital stock held by households globally is larger than capital stock held by the private corporate sector. Second, household investments, which predominantly consist of investments in residences, lead the business cycle. Third, increases in household capital stock are likely to have a direct impact on labor productivity – and thus on growth.

In addition, recent empirical evidence has shown that macroeconomic stabilization policies have been pro-cyclical rather than countercyclical in underdeveloped countries, including India. This raises the possibility that macroeconomic policies could be destabilizing, thus pushing the economy to lower growth and investment levels. Thus, there is a real possibility that policies aimed at macroeconomic stabilization and at achieving higher GDP growth rates could be working at cross purposes. The incidence of high GDP growth rates accompanied by high inflation in recent years seems to be indicative of this possibility.

This chapter discusses India's growth performance and attempts to identify policy options necessary to sustain high growth in the near future in light of the issues discussed above. It attempts to focus on issues that have not received appropriate attention in academic literature and policy discourse in India. The first section of this chapter provides a brief outline of economic reforms in India and is followed by a section outlining empirical observations about India's economic performance over the period 1981 to 2009. The next section provides a short summary of the views of several economists with respect to this performance. The chapter then provides a brief discussion of the empirical literature on the nexus between investment and growth. It also includes a short discussion of India's policy on residential investments. That is followed by a discussion of issues pertaining to the pro-cyclical nature of macroeconomic stabilization policies, and a conclusion.

POLICY REGIMES

Indian policy regimes have had three distinct phases. The first phase was the era of planning from 1951 to 1984 when the state had strict control over resource allocation. The industrial sector was dominated by public sector enterprises during those years. The second phase (1984–91) was a period of partial deregulation. The state retained a major role in resource allocation, even as private agents were given greater freedom in investment decisions. The third phase (1991–2009) saw far-reaching reforms of industry, finance, and trade. After 1991, resource allocation was primarily market driven.

Phase 1: 1951–84

In this first policy phase self-reliance was introduced as an explicit policy objective. Exports were not seen as an engine of growth, and planners regarded import substitution as the prime means of achieving self-reliance. During this period, India had highly restrictive trade and industrial policies. Imports were discouraged through extraordinarily high tariffs. Even exports were not actively encouraged. Until 1975 the Indian rupee was pegged to the British pound sterling. Over a substantial part of this period, the pound sterling fell in relation to other currencies, and so in consequence did the rupee. In September 1975, the peg was altered to a basket of currencies with undisclosed weights.

Various five-year plans set out industry-specific capacity targets accompanied by a financial plan that attempted to ensure those targets were met. The principal instrument of industrial policy was an elaborate industrial licensing framework under the Industries Development and Regulation Act of 1951. With respect to financial sector policy, this was a period of increasing financial repression. In 1969, 14 of the largest commercial banks were nationalized, followed by 6 more in 1980. Moreover, commercial banks were increasingly pressured to lend to what was considered the priority sector, which includes agriculture, small-scale industry, retail trade, transport operators, professionals, and craftsmen. Bank-lending rates were regulated through an elaborate arrangement that tied interest rates to loan amounts. Deposit rates also were tightly regulated.

In 1947 the Industrial Disputes Act was enacted. It was amended in 1976, with a requirement that firms employing 300 or more workers obtain government permission for layoffs, retrenchments, and closures. A further amendment in 1982, which took effect in 1984, expanded its ambit by reducing the threshold to 100 workers. It has been argued that this law made it more or less impossible for large firms to retrench workers. Over this period an extensive command-and-control system was set up, which constrained every aspect of firm behavior and made public sector enterprises the most important players in the economy.

Phase 2: 1985–91

In 1985, piecemeal reforms were initiated in trade and industrial policy. Several initiatives were taken to limit the role of licensing, expand the role large business houses played in contributing to growth, encourage modernization, and allow existing firms in certain industries to operate more economically. Most of these measures favored existing firms and made no attempt to reduce entry barriers. The shift from quantitative import controls to a protective system based on tariffs, which was initiated in the mid-1970s, was considerably quickened after 1985. Gradual reforms of the money market were initiated, although there were no changes in policies relating to the provision of credit to firms. In the mid-1980s, there was a renewed emphasis on export promotion. In this period, there was a steady devaluation of the rupee. Effectively, India operated with an "active" crawling peg from 1986 to 1990, producing a sharp devaluation of the rupee. This was seen to be consistent with new efforts to promote exports.

One of the most significant reform measures in this period was the reform of the call money market and the market for government securities. By the late 1980s there was significant deregulation and a development of the short-term segment of financial markets, with little progress in the deregulation of credit and capital markets.

Phase 3: 1991–2009

In mid-1991, India experienced a severe balance-of-payments crisis, with foreign exchange reserves falling so low that they covered less than two weeks of imports. The immediate cause of the crisis was the increase in world oil prices and the drop in remittances of migrant workers, following the Iraqi invasion of Kuwait in August 1990. It has been argued that the roots of the crisis in India lay in the increasing deficits at all levels of the government and in particular the central government deficit. The crisis helped convince political parties that a market-friendly development model was more likely to succeed. In 1991, a systematic attempt was made to dismantle the command-and-control regime that had been set up to achieve a more socialistic society.[1]

The crisis provided an enabling environment for some initial bold steps that included de-licensing of domestic production and investment, extensive decontrol of foreign trade, an opening to foreign direct investment

(FDI), and improvements in the tax system. As a part of the structural adjustment program, there was a significant cut in tariff rates. Cutting tariff reductions continued steadily over the years. Industrial licensing was abolished, except for a select list of environmentally sensitive industries. There was a distinct change in the mindset of policy makers with regard to FDI, which was suddenly seen as an important source of capital, technology, and managerial skills. In 1991 the government launched its first major push for FDI, and over subsequent years India gradually opened its markets to FDI. But these liberalization efforts did not lead to FDI inflows that were comparable to some neighboring countries, notably the People's Republic of China (PRC).

Since 1992, foreign institutional investors, such as pension funds, mutual funds, investment trusts, and asset management companies have been allowed unrestricted entry, in both primary and secondary markets for corporate securities. As a result, foreign investment inflows – both direct and portfolio – into India have risen substantially. In July 1991, as a part of the stabilization package, the rupee was devalued 18 per cent against the United States dollar. From 1991 to 1993, India moved gradually to full current account convertibility of the exchange rate. In the initial years after 1993, there were strict controls over the capital account, especially on capital outflows. Over the years these capital controls have systematically been reduced in small steps. Although some capital controls remain in place, the capital account is largely open.

In the financial sector the two most important changes were the deregulation of interest rates and freeing price restrictions on new share issues in stock markets. In order to improve the health of the banking system – and of the nationalized banks in particular – the Reserve Bank of India (RBI) introduced a risk-asset ratio system for banks as a measure of capital adequacy. All banks were instructed to achieve a capital adequacy ratio of 8 per cent by March 1994. Since March 2007, banks in India have adopted the "Basel II" norms. The banking sector became more competitive, as a significant number of new private sector banks and foreign banks entered the market, and healthier, with nonperforming assets significantly reduced. In addition, a regulatory mechanism was in place to prevent banks from excessive risk taking.

In 1992, the Securities and Exchange Board of India (SEBI) Act was approved. SEBI was established as the regulatory authority overseeing new issues of shares by companies. In addition, SEBI was given the legal powers to regulate and reform capital markets. The most important fallout of the establishment of SEBI was to free up the pricing and the issuance of new guidelines for new share issues. Companies are now free to approach the capital market after clearance is obtained from SEBI.

According to SEBI guidelines, most categories of new issues – except for new companies – were allowed complete freedom in pricing.

From 1991 to 2009 India dismantled the command-and-control regime of the 1950s and substantially reformed both the financial and real sectors to become a far more open, market-friendly economy. Since 1991, no attempt has been made to amend or repeal the Industrial Disputes Act of 1947. But it has been argued that labor market reforms have never been seriously contemplated in India, and there has been much debate about how inaction on labor reform has impacted economic performance.

PERFORMANCE OF THE INDIAN ECONOMY: 1980–2009

Growth and Inflation

Figure 10.1 presents data pertaining to the growth rate of real GDP and the inflation rate measured on the basis of the wholesale price index. From 1980 to 1991, high growth rates were achieved only in fiscal years 1980–81,[2] 1983–84, and 1988–89. For the rest of the period, the growth rates were rather sluggish. In the wake of India's structural adjustment program, the growth rate dipped sharply in 1991–92, after which it recovered to levels above 5 per cent. In 1997–98 the growth rate dipped to 4.3 per cent due to the AFC. After 2002–03 the growth rate had good momentum. From 2005 to 2008 growth exceeded 9 per cent. In 2008–09, the growth rate dipped to

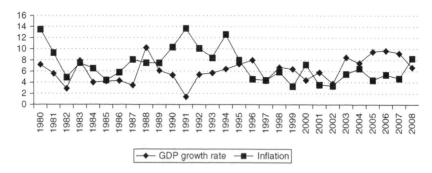

Note: GDP = gross domestic product.

Source: *Handbook of Statistics on the Indian Economy*, Reserve Bank of India, Mumbai.

Figure 10.1 GDP growth rate and inflation (%)

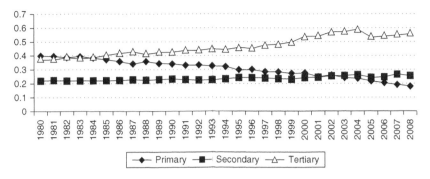

Note: GDP = gross domestic product.

Source: *Handbook of Statistics on the Indian Economy*, Reserve Bank of India, Mumbai.

Figure 10.2   Shares of primary, secondary and tertiary Sectors in GDP (by ratio)

6.7 per cent due to the aftermath of the GER. Data on inflation indicate that it was very rarely under control from 1980 to 2009.

The Structure of the Economy

Figure 10.2 presents the shares of GDP of the primary sector (agriculture, and mining and quarrying), the secondary sector (manufacturing, electricity, and gas and water supply), and the tertiary or service sector (trade, hotels and restaurants, transport, storage, communications, finance, insurance, real estate, business services, and community and social services). The share of the primary sector has declined from about 40 per cent in 1980–81 to 18 per cent in 2008–09. The share of the secondary sector in general has remained in the 20 per cent range throughout the period. In 2008–09 its share stood at 25 per cent. The share of the services sector has increased from 38 per cent in 1980–81 to 56 per cent 2008–09. It has been argued that this large increase in the share of the services sector has been an important and distinctive feature of Indian growth.

The External Sector

Figure 10.3 presents the ratio of exports and imports to GDP, the ratio of the current account deficit to GDP, the import cover of reserves, and the ratio of foreign investment to GDP. The ratio of export and imports to GDP has risen dramatically from 1980 to 2009. It was a meager 15 per cent

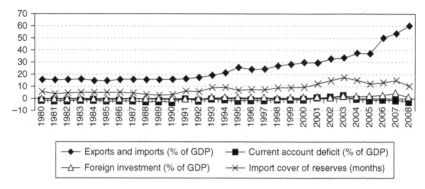

Exports and imports (% of GDP)   Current account deficit (% of GDP)
Foreign investment (% of GDP)   Import cover of reserves (months)

Note: GDP = gross domestic product.

Source: *Handbook of Statistics on the Indian Economy*, Reserve Bank of India, Mumbai.

Figure 10.3   Trade and balance of payments (by ratio)

in 1980–81 but by 2008–09 it had risen to 59 per cent. The current account deficit to GDP ratio has almost always been negative, the exception being the fiscal years 2001–02, 2002–03, 2003–04. From 1985 to 91, there were high current account deficits, with the largest deficit in 1990–91 at −3 per cent of GDP. In 2009 this ratio had fallen to −2.4 per cent, and it is being viewed as an added threat to the economy. The import cover of foreign exchange reserves has steadily improved after touching an all time low of 1.9 months in 1989–90, as a prelude to the 1990–91 economic crisis. From 2001 to 2008 there were extremely high reserves capable of financing more than a year of imports. The ratio of foreign investment to GDP rose from zero to a small positive number for the first time in 1986–87. The fiscal years 2006–07 and 2007–08 saw a substantial hike in this ratio. In fact, it reached a high of 5 per cent in 2007–08. It fell in 2008–09 due to the GER. Overall, India has not been able to attract foreign investment in large amounts compared to its GDP.

Government Finances

Figure 10.4 presents four sets of data. The first is the ratio of the gross fiscal deficit to GDP, with the gross fiscal deficit being the excess of total expenditure including loans net of recoveries over revenue receipts, external grants, and non-debt capital receipts for the central and state governments. The second is total receipts of central and state governments as a ratio of GDP, the third is central government transfers to states as a ratio of the aggregate receipts of the central government, and the fourth is the

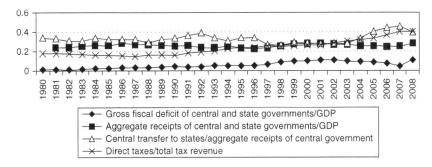

Note: GDP = gross domestic product.

Source: *Handbook Economy of Statistics on the Indian Economy,* Bank of India, Mumbai.

Figure 10.4 Government finances and taxes (by ratio)

ratio of direct taxes to total tax receipts of central and state governments. Fiscal prudence has rarely been a characteristic of governments in India. The ratio of the gross fiscal deficit to GDP rose dramatically after 1988–89 and this was in fact one of the reasons for the 1991 crisis. The fiscal year 2008–09 saw a substantial rise in the gross fiscal deficit–GDP ratio to 0.11 as a result of the large increases in government spending in response to the GER. The ratio of aggregate receipts to GDP has not changed much over the years and has ranged between 0.24 and 0.28. The ratio of central transfers to states as a ratio of the receipts of the central government rose from 0.34 in the early 1980s to over 0.4 since 2005–06. The importance of direct taxes in total tax revenue also has increased substantially from about 18 per cent in the early 1980s to 40 per cent in 2008–09.

Money and Credit

Figure 10.5 presents the ratio of GDP to money supply (velocity of money) and the ratio of bank credit to GDP. Over the years, the velocity of money has declined. This is not unexpected and is mainly driven by the improvements in payment mechanisms. The ratio of bank credit to GDP stagnated between 17 per cent and 26 per cent from fiscal year 1980–81 to fiscal year 2001–02. Subsequently this ratio has seen significant increases and in 2008–09 it stood at 50 per cent. A significant part of the increase in bank credit has been attributed to large increases in loans to households, especially home loans.

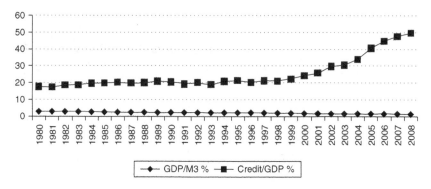

Note: GDP = gross domestic product.

Source: *Handbook of Statistics on the Indian Economy*, Reserve Bank of India, Mumbai.

Figure 10.5   Money and credit (%)

Savings and Investment Rates

Figure 10.6 presents the ratios of investment represented by gross fixed capital formation (GFCF) and gross domestic savings to GDP. Both these ratios were about 18 per cent in 1980–81 and have slowly and consistently risen to about 33 per cent in 2008–09. From 2004 to 2009, there were investment rates in excess of 32 per cent of GDP. These have also been the years when the highest growth rates were recorded. These recent years bring out clearly the empirical link between investment and growth. There is no doubt that the real sector and financial sector reforms have resulted in higher savings and investment rates.

An important aspect of aggregate savings is its distribution between households, the private sector, and the public sector. Figure 10.7 presents this distribution. As would be expected, the household sector's share is the largest. It has varied between a low of 62 per cent in 2007–08 and a high of 91 per cent in 2001–02. The share of the private corporate sector was 8.7 per cent in 1980–81, and has risen to a high of 26 per cent in 2008–09. This reflects the increasing importance of internal sources of funds to finance investments. The share of the public sector has consistently declined from a high of 28 per cent in 1981–82 to a figure consistently below 10 per cent between 1996–97 and 2005–06. In fact in the period between 1998–99 and 2002–03, the share of the public sector in aggregate savings was negative (indicating "dis-savings" of the government). This share rose to 13.9 per cent in 2007–08, but again fell to 4.4 per cent in 2008–09. This was due to large increases in government expenditures in response to the GER.

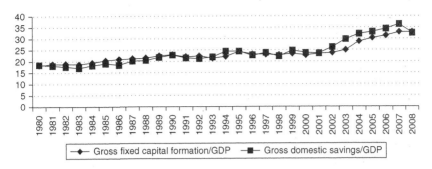

Note: GDP = gross domestic product.

Source: National Accounts Statistics, Central Statistical Organization, Ministry of Statistics and Programme Implementation, Government of India, New Delhi.

Figure 10.6   *Gross fixed capital formation and gross domestic savings (% of GDP)*

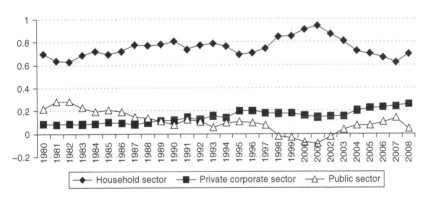

Source: National Accounts Statistics Central Statistical Organization, Ministry of Statistics and Programme Implementation, Government of India New Delhi.

Figure 10.7   *Sector-wise domestic savings (by ratio)*

Overall, the low and generally falling share of the public sector in aggregate savings reflects the general erosion of fiscal discipline.

The distribution of investment (GFCF) among the public sector, private corporate sector, and household sector (Figure 10.8) shows some interesting patterns. The share of the public sector has fallen from 44.5 per cent in 1980–81 to 25.7 per cent in 2008–09. It touched a high of 53.4 per cent in 1986–87 and a low of 22.8 per cent in 2004–05. This decline is due to

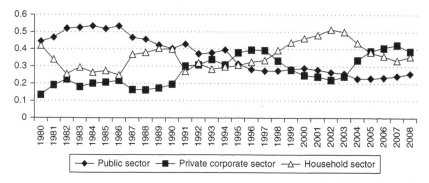

Source: National Accounts Statistics, Central Statistical Organization, Ministry of
Statistics and Programme Implementation, Government of India, New Delhi.

*Figure 10.8   Gross fixed capital formation by type of institutions and
               assets (by ratio)*

withdrawal of the government from many activities after the onset of
reforms in 1990–91 and the inability of the government to boost public
investment, especially in infrastructure. The share of the private corporate
sector has risen consistently from 13.5 per cent in 1980–81 to 38.7 per
cent in 2008–09. The shares are significantly larger in years when investment booms took place (1995–96 to 1998–99 and 2004–05 to 2007–08).
In terms of investment, the private corporate sector has now become the
most important source of investment. The share of the household sector
has always been high and has fluctuated between a high of 51.4 per cent
in 2002–03 and a low of 25.5 per cent in 1982–83. Figure 10.9 presents the
shares of construction and machinery of the household sector in investment. A distinct pattern emerges for the household sector, which includes
unincorporated enterprises owned by households. The share of construction has risen from 56.5 per cent in 1980–81 to 74.7 per cent in 2008–09.
This shows the rising importance of investment in residential housing for
households in recent years and the fact that bank lending to the household
sector, especially for home loans, grew rather rapidly.

  Investment in infrastructure is of critical importance to the growth
process. We designate, as is the general practice, two infrastructure
sectors: the first is electricity, gas, and water supply, and the second
is transport, storage, and communications. Figure 10.10 presents the
share of these two sectors – both private and public – in total investment (GFCF). The share of investment in the transport, storage, and
communications sector rose substantially in the years 1999–2000 to
2003–04. These were years when substantial investments took place in

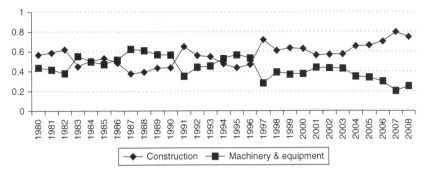

Source: National Accounts Statistics, Central Statistical Organization, Ministry of Statistics and Programme Implementation, Government of India, New Delhi.

Figure 10.9 Composition of household sector's gross fixed capital formation (by ratio)

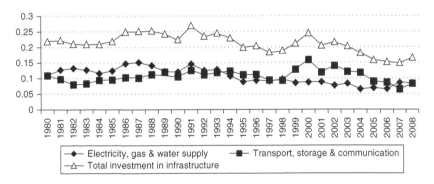

Note: GFCF = gross fixed capital formation.

Source: National Accounts Statistics, Central Statistical Organization, Ministry of Statistics and Programme Implementation, Government of India, New Delhi.

Figure 10.10 Share of GFCF in infrastructure sectors (public and private) (by ratio)

the telecommunications and roads. In recent years this share has dropped from a high of 14 per cent in 2002–03 to 8.3 per cent in 2008–09, suggesting a fall in investment in this sector. A countrywide chronic shortage of electricity has plagued the economy. The share of electricity, gas, and water supply was about 11–14 per cent between 1980–81 and 1993–94. This fell to 8.4 per cent in 2008–09. This indicates underinvestment in this sector. The share of investment in these sectors has ranged from a

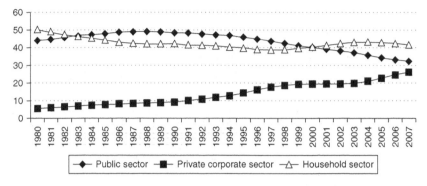

Source: National Accounts Statistics, Central Statistical Organization, Ministry of
Statistics and Programme Implementation, Government of India, New Delhi.

*Figure 10.11   Distribution of real net fixed capital stock across public
                 private corporate and household sectors (%)*

high of 25.2 per cent in 1987–88 to a low of 15.3 per cent in 2006–07, with
substantial fluctuation over the years. Particularly worrying is the fall of
this share in recent years (2005–06 to 2008–09), in which both investment
rates and growth rates have been high. This slowing down of investment
in infrastructure sectors has called into question the sustainability of the
high growth rates of recent years.

All investment activity ultimately increases the capital stock available
in the economy. Figure 10.11 presents the distribution of the real net
fixed capital stock among the public sector, private corporate sector,
and the household sector. From 1981 to 2008 total real capital stock was
augmented almost by 428 per cent. In 1981 the private corporate sector
accounted for only 5.6 per cent of the capital stock. Households accounted
for the largest share (50.3 per cent), followed by the public sector (44.0 per
cent). By 1990 the share of the public sector and private corporate sector
had risen to 49 per cent and 9 per cent, respectively. The share of the
household sector fell to 42 per cent. In 2008 the public sector accounted for
only 32.3 per cent, while the private corporate sector accounted for 26.2
per cent and the household sector's contribution was 41.6 per cent. Clearly
after reforms the importance of the government in capital formation has
significantly decreased while the importance of the private corporate
sector has seen a major increase. The household sector has seen a small
decline in its share. Households own the largest share of capital stock. This
simple fact has been overlooked by policy makers.

SOME RECENT INTERPRETATIONS OF INDIA'S GROWTH PERFORMANCE

Various economists have analyzed the growth of the Indian economy over the last 10 years or so. We now present a short review of what various economists have had to say about economic growth in India.

The relatively high growth rates experienced in the mid-1980s need an explanation that goes beyond the half-hearted reforms initiated in this period. Srinivasan and Tendulkar (2003) argue that the growth was the consequence primarily of fiscal expansionism – documented earlier in this chapter – and thus cannot be sustained. Rodrik and Subramanian (2004) disagree with this interpretation, arguing that the moderate increase in growth in the mid- and late 1980s was in fact accompanied by productivity increases that could not have been triggered by fiscal expansionism. According to their productivity calculations, productivity surprisingly declined after 1991. They attribute the increase in growth rates to an attitudinal shift in policy in the mid-1980s in favor of private business. These policies helped to increase the profitability of established firms. They describe the 1991 reforms as pro-market rather than pro-business. These pro-market policies involved the removal of impediments to better functioning markets, but this did not have a discernable impact either on productivity or growth. They thus locate the first real policy push to higher growth and productivity to the economic reforms undertaken in the mid-1980s rather than to the 1991 reforms.

It has been well documented that India's overall productivity growth after 1991 has been rather slow, especially when compared to the PRC. Why did this occur? Bosworth and Collins (2008) compare the economic performance of India and the PRC from 1978 to 2004. The PRC has consistently outperformed India over this period in almost every aspect of economic performance, including productivity. The authors argue that this was due to the PRC's willingness to rapidly lower its trade barriers and attract vast amounts of FDI. These policies led to a significant increase in the size and diversity of the industrial sector. In contrast, India's growth, the authors argue, has been led by rapid growth of the services sector and not by low-wage manufacturing. Comparing the growth of total factor productivity (TFP), the authors find that it grew much faster for the services sector in India compared to the PRC, while the PRC's TFP growth in manufacturing surpassed India's by a wide margin over this period. Inadequate infrastructure and the structure of exports, such as the excessive reliance on the export of services, are identified are the key constraints for India.

As India is a large country, regional disparities in growth there are

of particular relevance. Ahluwalia (2000) argues that interstate disparities in the growth rate of state domestic product (SDP) and per capita
SDP had increased sharply after the 1991 reforms. Aghion et al. (2003)
analyze the impact of globalization to understand how it influences
various industries and regions in India, using data from 1980 to 1997.
They found that the 1991 reforms had strong "inequalizing" effects
across both industries and regions. Those industries that were close to
their productivity frontiers experienced faster growth in productivity
and profits. These gains were larger for industries located in states that
had put in place more flexible labor market institutions. In the light of
these findings, they argue that initial conditions matter. Those industries
and regions that were already in an advantageous position benefited
more from reforms. The fact that regional disparities have increased
sharply after reforms is now widely recognized, but the appropriate
policy response to this phenomenon has as yet not been worked out. On
the basis of their empirical results, the authors make a strong plea for
labor market liberalization as a means of enhancing growth. Earlier in
this chapter, we noted that there has been almost no movement on labor
market reform throughout this period.

We also noted earlier that in recent years the services sector in India
has made rapid strides and has emerged as the largest contributor to
GDP. Would the services sector be able to provide adequate employment
in the future given the fact that low-wage manufacturing has not shown
adequate growth and by all counts is unlikely to experience robust growth
in the future? Kochhar et al. (2006) point out that 13 million people are
expected to enter the Indian workforce each year over the next 40 years.
The need to generate gainful employment for such a large prospective
workforce is a key challenge for the country. They argue that past experience suggests that India's manufacturing sector has been incapable of
absorbing the labor released from the agricultural sector. While it is true
that the services sector has made rapid progress, the sector's ability to
absorb labor is under some doubt because of the fact that employment
in this sector requires higher skill levels. In the early 1980s the industrial
sector, due to past policies, was specialized in those industries that were
more skill and capital intensive. Industries that were labor intensive and
less capital intensive formed a very small part of the industrial sector.
Such a specialization in an economy that has abundant labor and scarce
capital looks to be a little out of place. After the 1991 reforms, the growth
of skill-intensive industries has continued and disparities among states
with respect to various indicators of development have increased. In
faster-growing states, a sharp decline in the share of manufacturing in
state domestic product and a rapid increase in the share of the services

sector has been recorded. The poor states remain predominantly agricultural economies. The largest additions to the labor force are expected to
originate in these less-developed states. It is precisely in these states that it
would be difficult to acquire the requisite skills to gain employment in the
skill-intensive industrial and services sectors. The authors suggest that the
way out of this conundrum would be to stimulate those resources in short
supply, namely skilled labor. One way to do this would be to "de-license"
higher education and allow FDI in this sector.

The growth of the services sector has led to a heated discussion in India.
Opinions on the quality and sustainability of growth in the services sector
are varied. Panagariya (2008) doubts the scope of productivity improvement in this sector. The possible lack of spillovers is cited as a reason why
this sector cannot lead the growth process. This sector requires a skilled
workforce and is unlikely to be able to absorb the unskilled workforce
released from agriculture.

From a macroeconomic perspective the nature of the trade-off between
growth and inflation is likely to be the most important factor that could
influence future growth, given the fact that episodes of high growth have
generally been accompanied by high inflation. Singh and Kalirajan (2003)
studied the growth–inflation trade-off in the Indian context from 1971 to
1998. They attempted to estimate empirically an inflation threshold for
the Indian economy. They did this because of a widespread belief that
inflation above a particular threshold hurts growth, and if inflation can
be maintained below that threshold, negative influences on growth would
be absent. They found that any increase in inflation from the previous
year has a significant negative impact on growth. Consequently, they
recommended a policy stance that puts continuous downward pressure on
inflation. Their model indicates that if India succeeds in bringing down its
inflation rates to match its major trading partners – essentially the developed world – this would increase its per capita growth by 2 percentage
points. In light of the data presented earlier in this chapter, the importance
of this conclusion is obvious in terms of the nexus between growth and
inflation in India.

The literature cited above emphasizes that inflationary pressure,
regional disparities, infrastructure issues, the industrial sector's inability
to absorb surplus labor from agriculture, and the lack of robust productivity growth in industry are major constraints to the growth process. The
literature has not focused on the investment–growth nexus and the role of
macroeconomic stabilization policies. We deal with each of these issues in
the following sections.

THE INVESTMENT–GROWTH NEXUS

Aggregate investment increases the capital stock available to the economy and thus determines future potential output. Aggregate investment is the most volatile part of GDP. A large part of this volatility arises because investment depends on expectations of private agents about future growth. Increased uncertainty about future growth, which may arise because of both domestic and external factors, can potentially be decreased by sound macroeconomic management but can never be completely eliminated. Volatility of private investment must thus be accepted as a fact of life. To the extent that public investment and household investment have an autonomous component (i.e., a component that does not depend on future prospects of the economy) both would have a role to play in reducing the volatility of aggregate investment. Research on aggregate investment and its components (private, public, and household) and their relationship with growth has not provided any generally accepted and robust results. We provide below a short summary of some recent papers in this regard.

Determining which components of private investment have the strongest influence on growth is a question with obvious policy relevance. De Long and Summers (1991), in an oft-quoted paper, examine the influence of different components of investment on economic growth using panel data on countries from the *Penn World Tables* for 1960 to 1985. They find that the machinery and equipment of producers have a very strong association with productivity growth in the cross section of nations. They also argue that equipment investment causes productivity growth, rather than the other way around. In the Indian context, this conclusion has been verified using data from 1954 to 1996 by Athukorala and Sen (2002).

Blomstrom et al. (1996), and more recently Orazio et al. (2000), challenge the view of De Long and Summers. They argue that per capita GDP growth in a period is more closely related to subsequent capital formation than to current or past capital formation. Thus they conclude that there is no clear evidence that fixed investment is the key to economic growth. The general assumption that investment causes growth does not seem to be validated by data.

Clearly in a cross-country context there is some controversy about whether investment determines growth. In any case, the policy implications of this literature seem unclear. It is obvious that governments should attempt to put in place policies that make it easy for firms to augment capital stock. The problem is that firms would first need to expect high growth in the future to have an incentive to invest. Moreover, it is when the economy grows fast that firms build up savings (internal sources of funds) needed to fund investments in a financial environment that imposes binding financial constraints on firms. It is unclear which particular policy measures would be successful in such a scenario. Governments are forced to do their best in given circumstances, and then wait and watch. The success of a proactive government policy aimed at increasing investments of the private corporate sector depends on the growth performance of the economy as a whole. Given the fact that investment in India has been very volatile, government policies to boost investment have at best seen sporadic success.

We have noted earlier in this chapter that a substantial share of capital stock is owned by households and that a major part of this is accounted for by residential investment. Let us now turn to a discussion of some recent literature regarding investment by households and its relationship with growth.

Greenwood and Hercowitz (1991) are among the earliest to incorporate the home production model in a real business cycle context. They argue that by and large the business cycle literature is silent on capital stock held by households and its role in the growth process. They point out that there are two striking facts about capital accumulation in the household sector. The first is the fact that the stock of household capital (defined as the combined stock of consumer durables and residential capital) is higher than the stock of business non-residential capital, indicating that household capital accumulation is quantitatively important. Secondly, investment in household capital is highly pro-cyclical. It moves together and even leads movements in business investments.

Implicitly, the earlier literature assumes that household and business capital are perfect substitutes, and thus the composition of total capital investment between businesses and households is indeterminate and possibly of no consequence. Their modeling strategy involves a Beckerian view of household production (see Gronau 1997 for a review of the contribution of these models). There are two production functions: one for market activities and another for non-market activities. In market activities, labor interacts with market capital (equipment and structures) to produce market goods and services. In home activities, labor interacts with household capital (consumer durables and residences) to produce home goods and services. The model allows for dissimilarity between home and market production: capital goods can be produced in the market sector only.

Suppose a positive technological innovation is introduced into the economy. In response, the optimal level of household and business capital increases. Given that capital goods are produced in the business sector only, the induced scarcity of market goods reduces the shadow price of home goods in terms of market goods. A shift of resources to the business sector in terms of both time and capital ensues. Hence, this mechanism implies a tendency for business capital to be built first and only then will household capital be built. The model thus implies negative co-movement between the two investments. This is contrary to what the data actually show. Thus, the model fails to rationalize the lead of household investment over business investment. The main point that the authors make is that considerations of capital accumulation and technological change are important for activities of households as well as firms. This aspect of capital accumulation has largely been ignored in the literature.

Fisher (2007) attempts to reconcile real business cycle theories and the empirical generalizations with respect to household and business investment, as noted in Greenwood and Hercowitz (1991). It is assumed that household capital directly affects labor productivity. Household capital is considered a complimentary input to market production. Household capital contributes to the production of both home and market goods, and business capital produces only market goods. Thus there is a strong incentive to build household capital before business capital. If household capital is a complimentary input in market production, then output per worker should be increasing in the quantity of household capital per worker. Empirical estimates indicate that workers with the same education and working with the same business are more productive in states with more rooms per household. Thus, Fisher provides, perhaps for the first time, both theoretical and empirical reasons why household capital and thus household investment would have a role to play in the growth process.

In the Indian context, the above arguments are likely to have quite a bit of relevance. India has an enormous amount of underinvestment in housing. A technical group set up by India's Planning Commission estimated that the housing shortage at the end of the 10th Five-Year Plan (2007) was 24.7 million units for 64.7 million households. They also found that 99 per cent of this shortage could be located in economically weaker sections and low-income groups. The working group on urban housing for the 11th Five-Year Plan (2007–12) estimated that meeting housing requirements by 2012 would require Rupees 3.61 trillion, which is about 1.3 per cent to 1.5 per cent of GDP per year, over this five-year period. These are daunting numbers and a major policy push would be needed if there were hope of achieving these targets.

Sivam and Karuppannan (2002) have argued that despite the obvious importance of housing, this sector has not received a very high priority in public policy. Although the government on various occasions has introduced a variety of housing programs and policies, especially for low-income groups, these schemes have had a marginal impact in relation to the overall housing requirements. In 1985 the government launched *Indira*

Awas Yojana, a scheme to directly provide homes to families below the poverty line. From the inception of the scheme until 2009 only 21.3 million houses were constructed. Clearly, too little has been done.

Until 1988 there was no cohesive housing policy. The policy only attempted to offer indirect support – mainly through tax concessions and subsidies, and augmentation of land and credit available to the housing sector – to increase housing stock. In 1988, the first National Housing Policy was announced, which for the first time recognized shelter as a basic human need. In the same year the government set up the National Housing Bank to promote and regulate housing finance. A new draft of the housing policy was introduced in 1990, which emphasized the importance of the housing sector on the employment front. The details of the actual policy changed very little, with the government still adopting only indirect methods to incentivize increases in housing stock. The 1994 housing policy had the explicit aim of providing affordable housing for all sections of society. The government committed itself to make appropriate investments in the required infrastructure, such as roads, water supply, and sewage, which would provide an enabling environment, while not taking on the responsibility of building houses directly. After the mid-1990s the banking sector made a major attempt to induce middle- and higher-income groups to take advantage of tax concessions available for home loans to invest in housing. These efforts were effective as indicated by increases in the share of construction in gross capital formation in the household sector after 1997–98.

The National Urban Housing and Habitat Policy was announced in 2007. Its main instrument to achieve affordable housing for all was through various types of public–private partnerships. The role of the government again was envisaged as a facilitator, creating an enabling environment by provision of basic infrastructure and a legal and regulatory framework. As housing is a basic need, the government has a large role to play in its provision to poorer segments of society. Policies aimed at substantial increases in investment in residential buildings, especially for poorer sections of society, should be high on the government's priority list. The possibility of the large-scale provision of cheap housing to economically weaker segments of society across the country needs to be considered. Investment in housing has the potential to increase labor productivity, which is another reason why public policy must urgently address this issue. Moreover, public investments differ from private investments in that they can be undertaken by the government quite independently of the current or future growth prospects of the economy. If the government were able to develop fiscally sustainable public investment programs, especially to build cheap houses for poor households and for other infrastructure, this would go a long way to reduce the volatility of aggregate investment.

MACROECONOMIC POLICIES

The literature recognizes that macroeconomic policies intended to be countercyclical may in fact turn out to be pro-cyclical, and thus further complicate the problems they sought to solve. The finding that fiscal policy is pro-cyclical is incompatible with the general expectation that these policies should be countercyclical. If these policies were pro-cyclical they would have a negative impact on growth because of their destabilizing nature. Gavin and Perotti (1997) were possibly the first to empirically establish that fiscal policy in Latin America was, in fact, pro-cyclical while those of the G-7 countries were countercyclical. The reason they identified such an outcome is the fact that Latin American countries had major difficulties in accessing international credit markets in bad times. In the face of an adverse shock to the economy, these countries lost access to international credit. When faced with a fall in output these countries were forced to prepay loans, which required fiscal contractions. From a policy perspective, the problem that needed to be fixed was located in international credit markets.

Talvi and Vegh (2000) studied the fiscal policies of a group of 56 countries (India was not a part of the sample) from 1970 to 1994. They report that the fiscal policies of developing nations were far more pro-cyclical than the rest of the sample. They find that only the G-7 countries had countercyclical fiscal policies. They offer an alternative explanation for pro-cyclicality focusing more on the domestic political economy. Developing countries have tax bases that fluctuate much more compared with developed countries. In such a scenario, there would be a need to have large budget surpluses in good times and large deficits in bad times if fiscal policy is to be stabilizing. However, running large surpluses in good times is likely to be an extremely difficult thing to do politically. This would be particularly true for countries organized as federations, which typically involve revenue transfers from the central government to subnational governments. In good times when revenues are high, subnational governments lobby for higher allocations to fund their expenditures thus making it extremely difficult for central governments to maintain large surpluses. Central governments may have an incentive to lower tax rates in good times and increase their own spending in order to neutralize pressures emanating from subnational governments for higher allocations. This would lead to a pro-cyclical fiscal policy. India is a federation, and as pointed out earlier in this chapter, central government transfers to the states are rather large. If these transfers are pro-cyclical then there is a good chance that fiscal policy could be pro-cyclical in India.

Kaminsky et al. (2004) using data on 104 countries (including India) from 1960 to 2003 confirm the finding that fiscal policies in developing countries are pro-cyclical. Woo (2009) studied the cyclical behavior of fiscal policy for a sample of 96 countries (including India) from 1963 to 2003. Woo reports that underdeveloped countries in general have pro-cyclical fiscal policies. The author built a theoretical model to provide an explanation for this pro-cyclicality. The model identifies social polarization of preferences, as measured by inequality of income and education across the population, as the reason why fiscal policy is pro-cyclical. In a situation where there is a high degree of social polarization, policy makers, who represent different socioeconomic groups and thus push different agendas, would find it extremely difficult to arrive at an agreement on the most preferred policy. When the going is good, such as during an economic upswing with rising revenues, each of their diverse agendas and their implied policy actions might seem to be feasible. When coupled with weak institutional constraints, this could lead to pro-cyclical fiscal policy. At an empirical level, a positive correlation is found between social polarization (measured by income inequality, as in the Gini coefficient) and education distribution (dispersion of educational attainment) on the one hand and the extent of pro-cyclicality of fiscal policy after controlling for real per capita GDP, government size, openness and political uncertainty on the other. Another significant empirical finding reported by Woo is the negative relation between pro-cyclicality of fiscal policy and growth.

On the policy front, Woo argued that in the interest of long-term growth there is an urgent need to introduce checks and balances in fiscal decision making to limit the possibility of pro-cyclical fiscal responses to business cycles. It is also suggested that more direct policies to reduce social polarization would facilitate more responsible fiscal decisions. There is considerable evidence that indicates that India is heavily polarized socially. In fact, there seems to be general consensus that India's income distribution has worsened in the post-reform period (see Acharyya 2006 for an excellent discussion).

Given the fact that India is a federation and is rather heavily polarized socially, one would be tempted to believe that fiscal policy in India would be pro-cyclical. We now turn to an evaluation of whether fiscal and monetary policies in India have in fact been pro-cyclical. We use data from 1971 to 2009. In the empirical exercise that follows, we adopt the methodology suggested by Kaminsky et al. (2004, 17). They define a procyclical fiscal policy as one that "involves higher (lower) government spending and lower (higher) tax rates in good (bad) times. [They] call such a policy procyclical because it tends to reinforce the business cycle (i.e, fiscal policy is expansionary in good times and contractionary in bad times)."

They argue that two sets of variables potentially could be used to check for the cyclical behavior of fiscal policy, namely tax rates and government expenditures. The problem is that no systematic data on tax rates are available and thus the only variable that is used is government expenditures. On the monetary policy front they suggest the use of the rate of growth of central bank domestic credit, among other measures. To distinguish between good and bad times they use the Hodrick–Prescott filter and the Baxter–King filter. Using these filters on data on real GDP, various aspects of real government expenditures, and the rate of growth of real central bank domestic credit, they decompose these series into their trend and cyclical components. If the correlations between the cyclical components of real GDP and cyclical components of the variables used to measure policy stance are positive, they argue that one can unambiguously say that the policy is pro-cyclical.

We use real GDP, six different measures of government spending (central government expenditure, central government expenditure minus interest payments, expenditure of central and state governments, expenditure of central and state governments minus interest payments, central government transfers to state governments, and wages and salaries of the central government) and the rate of growth of central bank credit to the domestic sector. We use both the Hodrick–Prescott filter and the Baxter–King filter to decompose these series into their trend and cyclical components. The correlations between the cyclical component of real GDP and the cyclical components of the other variables are presented in Table 10.1. All the correlations with respect to government expenditures are positive, rather large, and significant. Fiscal policy is thus clearly pro-cyclical in India. It is interesting to note that central government transfers to states are also highly pro-cyclical, thus it is likely that the federal structure of the country is actually driving the result. The indicator we use for monetary policy turns out to have a rather low and insignificant correlation coefficient, and thus monetary policy can be said to be acyclical or neutral.

The studies quoted earlier use cross-country panel data sets. The policy implications of each of the papers discussed above are, therefore, unlikely to be directly relevant to a particular country. When considering a particular country, one needs to take note of the institutional and social realities surrounding it. Generally speaking, all the papers point toward the need to design fiscal arrangements that make it possible to run surpluses in good times. India desperately needs to develop fiscal

Table 10.1   Correlation of cyclical components of GDP with cyclical components of variables indicating fiscal and monetary policy stance

Variables	HP Filter	BK Filter
Central govt. expenditure	0.3994[b]	0.4045[b]
Central govt. expenditure (minus interest)	0.3600[b]	0.3718[b]
Central + state govt. expenditure	0.3895[b]	0.4264[b]
Central + state govt. expenditure (minus interest)	0.3815[b]	0.4294[b]
Transfer to states	0.3751[b]	0.3437[c]
Wages and salaries	0.3692[b]	0.4636[a]
Monetary policy indicator	–0.1348	–0.2192

Notes:
GDP = gross domestic product.
a.   significant at 1%,
b.   significant at 5%,
c.   significant at 10%.

Source: Author's estimates based on data from the *Handbook of Statistics on the Indian Economy*, Reserve Bank of India, Mumbai.

rules that force the government to save in good times. Thus, there is a need to find ways to conduct fiscal policies in countercyclical or at least neutral ways.

Our finding that fiscal transfers to states form a substantial part of central government revenues and that these transfers themselves are pro-cyclical suggest that there is a need to develop institutional mechanisms that would make transfers to subnational governments independent of the business cycle. Of course, this is more easily said than done. The Constitution of India has clearly set out a system of a transfer of funds from the central government to states. This system has evolved over a number of years and any major changes to this system would be extremely difficult politically to achieve in the short or medium term. The fact that social polarization in India is high and rising could be another reason for the pro-cyclicality of fiscal policy. A direct and effective policy to reduce polarization might be feasible, at least in the medium term, although the exact nature of such a policy is obviously an open question. An increased direct government provision of housing to weaker segments of society, which we have discussed earlier in this chapter, would contribute to decreasing social polarization. If successful, this could possibly go a long way toward reducing the pro-cyclicality of fiscal policy and provide an enabling environment for reaching a sustainable growth path.

CONCLUSION

As a consequence of far-reaching economic reforms undertaken after 1991, India has been transformed into an economy that is open to the rest of the world through trade and capital flows and whose resource allocation is market driven. The reform process has forced the government to give up most of the direct levers it possessed to influence resource allocation. Over the years both the savings rate and the investment rate have risen. Exports and imports have grown dramatically. The financial sector (banks and stock markets) is well regulated. The rise in government revenues has been consistently outpaced by expenditures, leading to chronic fiscal deficits. A striking feature of the economy is the rapid strides that the service sector has taken. It is now the largest segment of the Indian economy.

India has recently seen some years of robust growth, but inflation has never really been tamed. There have been periods when investments by the private corporate sector have boomed, but it needs to be recognized that the ability of the government to influence private corporate investment is rather limited and ultimately depends on expectations of future growth rates. Public and household investments have not received the kind of policy attention they deserve. We have demonstrated that fiscal policy is highly pro-cyclical and this inevitably influences growth negatively. It is under these circumstances that policy makers have to design an inward-looking growth strategy that would be capable of putting India on a higher growth path.

Our analysis suggests a three-fold approach. First, macroeconomic policies that keep inflation low are a necessary prerequisite to enhance growth. This of course is easier said than done in light of the persistent fiscal deficits and the pro-cyclical stance of India's fiscal policies. Given the fact that India is a federation, running surpluses in good times is difficult because of pressures from states for larger shares of central government revenues. Thus, there is a need for a mechanism that keeps transfers to subnational governments independent of the business cycles. Social polarization could also be contributing to the pro-cyclicality of fiscal policies. Clearly, more direct efforts at reducing social polarization are needed.

Second, public investment needs to be substantially increased. This again looks to be a monumental task given high fiscal deficits. There is a silver lining in that government revenues have been buoyant in recent years. Major expenditure reforms to curtail current expenditures and expand capital expenditures are needed to achieve higher public investment. Third, the government needs to work out a detailed housing policy for rural and semi-urban areas. This would provide a major impetus to household investment, decrease social polarization, and increase labor productivity. Given the fact that private corporate investment inevitably goes through booms and busts, there is a need for policies to promote the stability and the consistent growth of public and household sector investment. This may make aggregate investment itself relatively less volatile. Low inflation, anti-cyclical or neutral fiscal policies, and less volatile aggregate investments would make it possible for India to reach higher and more sustainable levels of growth.

NOTES

1. See Bhagwati and Srinivasan (1993) for an excellent discussion of the rationale and nature of reforms initiated in 1991.
2. This and other subsequent two-date ranges refer to India's fiscal year, which runs from 1 April of the earlier year to 31 March of the latter year. Thus 1980–1981 refers to the fiscal year that ran from 1 April 1980 until 31 March 1981.

REFERENCES

Acharyya, R. (2006), 'Trade liberalization, poverty and income inequality in India', Asian Development Bank, India Resident Mission Policy Brief No. 10.

Aghion, P., et al. (2003), 'Unequal effects from liberalization: theory and evidence from India', Mimeo, Harvard University and University College London.

Ahluwalia, M.S. (2000), 'Economic performance of states in post reforms period', *Economic and Political Weekly*, **35**, 1637–48.

Athey, M.J., and P.S. Laumas (1994), 'Internal funds and corporate investment in India', *Journal of Development Economics*, **45**, 287–303. doi:10.1016/0304-3878(94)90034-5.

Athukorala, P., and K. Sen (2002), *Saving, Investment and Growth in India*, New Delhi: Oxford University Press.

Bhagwati, J., and T.N. Srinivasan (1993), 'India's economic reforms', Government of India, Ministry of Finance, New Delhi.

Blomstrom, M., R.E. Lipsey, and M. Zejan (1996), 'Is fixed investment the key to economic growth?', *Quarterly Journal of Economics*, **111**, 269–76. doi:10.2307/2946665.

Bosworth, B., and S.M. Collins (2008), 'Accounting for growth: comparing [the People's Republic of] China and India', *Journal of Economic Perspectives*, **22**, 45–66. doi:10.1257/jep.22.1.45.

De Long, J.B., and L.H. Summers (1991), 'Equipment investment and economic growth', *Quarterly Journal of Economics*, **106**, 455–502.

Fisher, J.D.M. (2007), 'Why does household investment lead business investment over the business cycle', *Journal of Political Economy*, **115**, 141–68. doi:10.1086/511994.

Ganesh-Kumar, A., K. Sen, and R.R. Vaidya (2001), 'Outward orientation, investment and finance constraints: a study of Indian firms', *Journal of Development Studies*, **37**, 133–49. doi:10.1080/00220380412331322071.

Gavin, M., and R. Perotti (1997), 'Fiscal policy in Latin America', *NBER Macroeconomics Annual*, Cambridge: MIT Press, pp. 11–61.

Greenwood, J., and Z. Hercowitz (1991), 'The allocation of capital and time over the business cycle', *Journal of Political Economy*, **99**, 1188–214. doi:10.1086/261797.

Gronau, R. (1997), 'The theory of home production: the past ten years', *Journal of Labour Economics*, **15** (2), 197–205.

Kaminsky, G.M., C.M. Reinhart, and C.A. Vegh (2004), 'When it rains, it pours: pro-cyclical capital flows and macroeconomic policies', *NBER Macroeconomics Annual*, **19**, 11–53.

Kochhar, K., et al. (2006), 'India's pattern of development: what happened, what follows?', *Journal of Monetary Economics*, **53**, 981–1019. doi:10.1016/j.jmoneco.2006.05.007.

Orazio, P.A., P. Lucio, and A.E. Scorcu (2000), 'Saving, growth and investment: a macroeconomic analysis using a panel of countries', *Review of Economics and Statistics*, **82** (2), 182–211.

Panagariya, A. (2008), *India: The Emerging Giant*, New York: Oxford University Press.

Rodrik, D., and A. Subramanian (2004), 'From Hindu growth to productivity surge: the mystery of Indian growth transition', International Monetary Fund Working Paper No. WP/04/77.

Singh, K., and K. Kalirajan, (2003), 'The inflation growth nexus in India: an empirical analysis', *Journal of Policy Modeling*, **25**, 377–96. doi:10.1016/S0161-8938(03)00011-5.

Srinivasan, T.N., and S.R. Tendulkar (2003), *Reintegrating India with the World Economy*, Washington, DC: Institute for International Economics.

Sivam, A., and S. Karuppannan (2002), 'Role of state and market in housing delivery for low income groups in India', *Journal of Housing and the Built Environment*, **17**, 69–88. doi:10.1023/A:1014831817503.

Talvi, E., and C.A. Vegh (2000), 'Tax base variability and pro-cyclical fiscal policy', NBER Working Paper No. 7499.

Woo, J. (2009), 'Why do more polarized countries run more procyclical fiscal policy?', *Review of Economics and Statistics*, **91**, 850–70. doi:10.1162/rest.91.4.850.

11. People's Republic of China

Siow Yue Chia

INTRODUCTION

The economy of the People's Republic of China (PRC) is the most remarkable economic growth and transformation story of the recent decades. It has transformed from a centrally planned economy to a transitional mixed economy and from a poor agrarian economy into an industrial powerhouse and economic superpower. The growth and transformation originated with the economic reforms that began in 1978 and have propelled the roles of exports and foreign direct investment.

Following the onset of the global economic recession (GER) in 2008 the world has had two perspectives of the PRC. The positive perspective views the PRC as an engine of growth that is crucial to recovery of the Asian and global economies. The negative perspective blames the PRC for the problems associated with global imbalances and puts the country under intense pressure to address its trade and current account surpluses and to appreciate its undervalued currency.

This chapter analyzes the PRC's economic growth and transformation from the period prior to the recent GER to the policy responses and performance in the wake of the crisis. The chapter then examines the issue of structural imbalances and the challenge of rebalancing. Finally, it examines the PRC's growth prospects and the features of the 12th Five-Year Development Plan (2011–15), and ends with a conclusion.

THE PRC'S ECONOMIC GROWTH AND TRANSFORMATION

Pre-Crisis Growth and Structural Transformation

The PRC has been experiencing spectacular economic growth performance of nearly 10 per cent a year on average since its economic reforms and its open-door policy were launched in 1978. However, it is still a developing

Table 11.1 Gross domestic product indicators

	1990	1995	2000	2001	2002
GDP at PPP (current international dollars), millions			2 985 366	3 306 472	3 665 958
GDP per capita at PPP (current international dollars)			2355	2591	2854
GNI per capita (current US$)	330	530	930	1000	1100
Growth rates of real GDP (%)	3.8	10.9	8.4	8.3	9.1
Growth rates of real GDP per capita (%)	2.3	9.7	7.6	7.5	8.4

Notes: PPP = Purchasing Power Parity. GNI = Gross National Income. GDP = Gross Domestic Product.

Source: Asian Development Bank. Key Indicators for Asia and the Pacific (2011).

country with nominal per capita gross national income (GNI) of $4,260 and purchasing power parity (PPP) gross domestic product (GDP) per capita at $7,554 in 2010 (Table 11.1). The number of people living in absolute poverty declined from 250 million in 1978 to just over 20 million by 2008.

The PRC's 1978–79 reforms led to agricultural reforms and the adoption of an open-door policy, which initially focused on Special Economic Zones (SEZs) in an experiment with the free-market system. Price controls were gradually lifted for all products, and tax holidays and low-interest credit were introduced to promote foreign investment for industries and export production. Domestic and foreign investments grew rapidly and exports surged. Following the Asian financial crisis (AFC) of 1997–98, the government adopted enterprise and financial reforms. The number of state-owned enterprises (SOEs) declined from above 300 000 to less than 100 000 through privatization and re-grouping, and millions of redundant workers were laid off. Four asset-management companies were established to deal with bad loans, and a radical transformation of banks brought in foreign strategic investors and public listings. Meanwhile, the government improved tax collection through campaigns to crack down on tax evasion. With the PRC's accession to the World Trade Organization (WTO) in December 2001, establishing a free-market system became an official policy goal and the PRC undertook further reforms to conform to WTO rules and obligations. As a result, most export subsidies were abolished, import tariffs were brought down from 35 per cent to 12 per cent, and many domestic market distortions were abolished. The Chinese

2003	2004	2005	2006	2007	2008	2009	2010
4 119 472	4 664 101	5 364 252	6 242 144	7 372 801	8 257 241	9 091 142	10 120 628
3188	3588	4102	4749	5580	6218	6811	7554
1270	1500	1760	2050	2490	3050	3650	4260
10.0	10.1	11.3	12.7	14.2	9.6	9.2	10.3
9.3	9.5	10.6	12.1	13.6	9.0	8.7	9.9

economy entered a period of extraordinary growth, with real GDP growth averaging 11 per cent from 2003 to 2008.

When economic reforms were launched in 1978, the PRC was primarily an agrarian economy. After that, economic development shifted towards heavy capital-intensive industry and later to labor-intensive industry more in tune with the country's comparative advantage. Even in 1990, 79.6 per cent of the PRC's population lived in rural areas, and primary products comprised 27.1 per cent of GDP; by 2009 these shares declined to 27.3 per cent and 11.3 per cent, respectively. Likewise, the PRC's export composition has been transformed so that almost all of its exports are now manufactured goods and the PRC has become the "factory of the world." In the process the PRC has rapidly built up its foreign reserves, which, at nearly $2.9 trillion in 2010, are the largest in the world.

The PRC's rapid economic growth is driven by exports and investments, eventually giving rise to unsustainable current account surpluses. From 2002 to 2007, annual export growth averaged 29 per cent and investment growth averaged 24 per cent. Both the export–GDP ratio and investment–GDP ratio are very high (see Table 11.2).

Export-led Growth

Export-led growth began with the 1978 open-door policy. By 2006, the total goods trade–GDP ratio had peaked at 65 per cent and the export (goods and services)–GDP ratio had peaked at 39 per cent, declining in subsequent

*Table 11.2   Consumption, saving, investment, trade, current account
             balance*

	1990	1995	2000	2001	2002	2003
Private consumption expenditure (% of GDP)	50.6	46.7	46.2	44.9	43.7	41.8
Government consumption expenditure (% of GDP)	14.1	13.8	15.8	16.1	15.9	15.2
Gross domestic savings (% of GDP)	35.2	39.6	38.0	39.0	40.4	43.0
Gross domestic capital formation (% of GDP)	36.1	41.9	35.1	36.3	37.9	41.2
Merchandise exports ($ million)	62091	148780	249203	266100	325600	438228
Growth rates of merchandise exports (%)	18.2	23.0	27.8	6.8	2.4	34.6
Merchandise imports ($ million)	53345	132084	225094	243550	295170	412760
Growth rates of merchandise imports (%)	(9.8)	14.2	35.8	8.2	21.2	39.8
Trade in goods (% of GDP)	29.6	38.6	39.6	38.5	42.7	51.9
Exports of goods & services (% of GDP)	14.7	20.2	23.3	22.6	25.1	29.6
Imports of goods & services (% of GDP)	12.0	18.6	20.9	20.5	22.8	27.6
Trade in goods balance (% of GDP)	2.3	2.5	2.9	2.6	3.0	2.7
Trade in services balance (% of GDP)	0.4	−0.8	−0.5	−0.4	−0.5	−0.5
Current account balance (% of GDP)	3.1	0.2	1.7	1.3	2.4	2.8

Note: GDP = Gross Domestic Product.

Source: ADB, Key Indicators for Asia and the Pacific 2011.

2004	2005	2006	2007	2008	2009	2010
40.8	39.3	38. 0	36.0	35.2	35.6	33.5
14.0	14.3	14.1	13.5	13.3	13.4	13.5
45.2	46.4	47.9	50.5	51.5	51.0	53.0
43.3	42.1	43.0	41.7	44.0	48.3	48.2
593 326	761 953	968 969	1 217 780	1 430 690	1 201 610	1 577 900
35.4	28.4	27.2	25.7	17.5	(16.0)	31.3
561 229	659 953	791 461	955 950	1 132 560	1 005 920	1 394 800
36.0	17.6	19.9	20.8	18.5	(11.2)	38.7
59.8	63.0	64.9	62.2	56.7	44.3	50.6
34.0	37.1	39.1	38.4	35.0	26.7	29.8
31.4	31.6	31.4	29.6	27.3	22.3	25.9
3.1	5.9	8.0	9.0	8.0	5.0	4.3
−0.5	−0.4	−0.3	−0.2	−0.3	−0.6	−0.4
3.6	5.9	8.6	10.1	9.1	5.2	5.2

years. Smaller economies such as the Asian newly industrialized countries (NIEs) and the member countries of the Association of Southeast Asian Nations (ASEAN) have much higher export–GDP ratios. But the PRC's export–GDP ratio is way above those of the European Union, India, the United States (US), and other large economies. Export and import ratios increased further with WTO accession. Foreign direct investment (FDI) accounted for over 50 per cent of the PRC's exports of manufactured goods in recent years. The PRC's exports rely heavily on the processing trade, and it has become a major regional center for processing and assembling components into finished consumer goods, as well as the final link in the Asian supply chain. By the end of the 1990s, processing trade accounted for 60 per cent of the PRC's total trade. The exports of manufactured goods to North America and Western Europe contributed to growing trade surpluses.

The export-led growth model has been highly successful in Asia, from Japan to the Asian NIEs and ASEAN and now the PRC. It enables exploitation of comparative advantage and depends on increasing trade liberalization, production networks and the FDI–trade nexus. The export-led model also leads to the accumulation of unsustainably large current account surpluses in some countries and to structural imbalances. And when it involves large economies such as the PRC, it also has serious international repercussions. Also, in some countries, the GER of 2008–09 led to the collapse of export demand from the US and Europe, and exposed the PRC's export vulnerability.

Investment has long been the single most important factor contributing to the PRC's economic growth, with the investment growth rate rising persistently since 2001. An enabling factor is the PRC's high savings ratio, which reached over 50 per cent of GDP from 2007 to 2010. The PRC's restrictions on outward investment until recent years meant that the high savings were used for domestic investments. With the fast growth of corporate income and government revenue, enterprises have reinvested most of their profits and the government has spent a large proportion of its revenue on capital formation, so that the PRC is an investment-driven economy. The gross domestic capital formation (GDCF) share of GDP rose to over 40 per cent from 2003 to 2008 and to over 48 per cent from 2009 to 2010. Despite the GER, the PRC's GDP is growing at 7–8 per cent, investment/GDP in the range 40–45 per cent, with investment in construction growing at an even faster pace.

GLOBAL FINANCIAL CRISIS AND THE PRC'S POLICY RESPONSE: FISCAL STIMULUS PACKAGE AND MONETARY EXPANSION

The GER in 2008 did not badly affect the PRC's finances due to its sound economic fundamentals of a current account surplus, strong public sector finances, sound financial sector, and capital controls that limit capital flow instabilities. The financial system had abundant liquidity and the People's Bank of China (PBC), which is the central bank of the PRC, had abundant foreign reserves. Instead, the Chinese economy was adversely affected by the collapse of its major export markets. Exports declined by 2.2 per cent in November 2008 and fell by 16 per cent in 2009. Real GDP growth, after achieving a sizzling 14.2 per cent rate in 2007, dropped to 9 per cent in Q3 2008 and further to 6.8 per cent in Q4 2008, resulting in 9.6 per cent for the year before declining further to 9.2 per cent in 2009. Investment growth fell due to inventory adjustments, a drop in export-related investment, and in investments in real estate. Unemployment became a serious issue by February 2009, with approximately 20 million migrant workers out of 130 million such workers having lost their jobs. An estimated 1.5 million out of 5.6 million college graduates could not find jobs by the end of 2009. The total urban unemployment rate reached 9.4 per cent by the end of 2008.

The government's response to the crisis was swift and decisive. In November 2008 the central government announced a RMB4 trillion fiscal stimulus package for 2009–10, amounting to 14 per cent of GDP. Unlike the situation in many other countries, the PRC's stimulus package was heavily weighted toward spending on investments, with infrastructure – especially airports, railways, and roads – accounting for 38 per cent. The Sichuan earthquake reconstruction accounted for another 26 per cent, with low-cost housing another 10 per cent, rural livelihood and infrastructure a further 10 per cent, and other categories representing 16 per cent. Investments in infrastructure would provide employment and offset the job losses of migrant workers from the collapse of export demand. In addition to the central government, provincial and local governments launched their own complementary stimulus packages, amounting to RMB1.8 trillion, with the bulk financed by commercial loans. The stimulus package financing was 30.6 per cent by local governments, 29.5 per cent by the central government in the form of direct grants and interest rate subsidies, and 39.8 per cent by bank lending. In addition to the fiscal stimulus, the PBC adopted a highly expansionary monetary policy. In the first half of 2009, bank credit increased by RMB7.3 trillion, compared with the annual increase of RMB3.18 trillion in 2006 and RMB3.63 trillion in 2007. M2 grew at a record rate relative to GDP, so that the interbank money market was flooded with liquidity. With the healthy state of the banking institutions, onward lending by banks to local governments and enterprises did not pose a problem.

The fiscal stimulus package ended at the end of 2010. It played a pivotal role in stabilizing and reviving the Chinese economy. The GDP growth rate rebounded from 6.1 per cent in Q1 2009 to 7.8 per cent in Q2 2009 and 10.3 per cent for 2010. Exports rebounded strongly since early 2009 and grew by 31.3 per cent for 2010. To ensure economic and financial stability after the stimulus package, policy attention shifted to mitigating the risks of a property bubble and the strains on local government finances. Government began to adopt tough measures to adjust the economy, as government-led investment decelerated.

Inflationary pressures have been rising. The PRC's consumer price index (CPI) reached 6.1 per cent by September 2011, with soaring food and property prices. To combat inflation and property speculation, the PBC raised the bank reserve requirement ratio and bank deposit interest rates several times in 2010 and 2011. The government also ordered a range of measures to ensure supplies of key goods and offer financial help to the needy, and vowed to impose price caps if necessary. It also tried to ease consumer price inflation with measures such as agricultural subsidies, reducing transportation fees, and releasing grain reserves. It took measures to dampen soaring property prices, and committed to boost the housing supply. The government and enterprises also launched a round of hikes in the minimum wage after a spate of labor disputes and employee suicides highlighted growing discontent among the country's millions of low-paid workers, as inflationary pressures, particularly food and housing prices, seriously eroded their purchasing power. The media reported that several Chinese provinces and cities raised the minimum wage by as much as one-third. Beijing raised the minimum wage by 20 per cent in July 2010 and by another 20 per cent in January 2011.

The stimulus package and expansionary monetary policies have succeeded in arresting a fall in economic growth, but Yu Yongding (2009) argued that there are negative impacts on growth in the longer term. First, the investment rate has increased to over 50 per cent as a result of the investment-centered stimulus package, worsening the PRC's overcapacity in the future. Second, with such a high investment rate and a GDP growth rate of 8 per cent, the incremental capital output ratio (ICOR) has exceeded 6 as compared with 4.1 from 1991 to 2003, and this drop in investment efficiency will impact negatively on the PRC's long-term growth. Infrastructure investment is long term, but without accompanying investment in manufacturing capacity it means investment in infrastructure will not bring returns. Also waste in infrastructure construction lowers efficiency and possibly increases nonperforming loans. Third, provincial and local governments were encouraged to raise money to launch their own complementary stimulus packages, and the many grandiose investment projects could lead to suboptimal resource allocation and increase the central government's contingent liabilities. Fourth, the PRC's loose monetary policy resulted in the too rapid growth of credit and money supply, possibly leading to rising nonperforming-loans, worsening economic structure, and creating stock market and real estate asset bubbles.

The PRC was one of the first countries to recover from the GER. As its recovery accelerated, the PRC became increasingly viewed as an engine of growth to spur global recovery.

STRUCTURAL IMBALANCES AND REBALANCING

The GER exacerbated the structural imbalances in the Chinese economy that had been evident for some years. In particular, going forward, the PRC will not be able to rely on the export-led model of economic development because of its unsustainable current account imbalances. The next phase of the PRC's economic development will have to depend much more on domestic demand.

Relationships among Consumption, Savings, Investment, and the Current Account Balance

For an open economy, $Y = C + I + G + X - M$; $Y - (C+G) = I + CA = S$; $CA = S - I$. The root cause of the PRC's large and persistent current account (CA) surplus is the high degree of dependence on external demand as an engine of growth. Another interpretation of the CA surplus is an excess of savings over investment. A country can reduce its CA surplus by reducing savings – that is, increasing private and public consumption – or raising the level of investment. A CA surplus can also be offset by lending funds abroad, making investments abroad, or by the PBC increasing its holdings of foreign reserves. If a CA surplus country were also a net recipient of FDI, as with the PRC, balance would have to be achieved through even greater foreign lending, or through more rapid acquisition of foreign reserves by its PBC. Although high savings rates have served Asia in the past, the key question highlighted by the financial crisis is whether the region now suffers from oversaving. For the PRC, given the country's high savings rate relative to its level of income and low consumption levels and low living standards, the welfare costs of oversaving could be high.

Consumption

Empirical evidence shows countries usually experience a U-shaped trajectory in consumption: as per capita income rises, the household share of the consumption–GDP ratio declines while the share of the investment–GDP ratio rises, but eventually the consumption–GDP share will rise and the investment–GDP share will fall.

The PRC's private consumption declined from 46.2 per cent of GDP in 2000 to 33.5 per cent in 2010, lowest among the world's major economies. There is concern over the PRC's low and declining consumption–GDP ratio, with international pressure on the PRC to focus more on domestic demand rather than exports as a growth driver. The decline reflects the falling share of household consumption and corresponding rise in household savings. The PRC's private consumption has been declining, alongside the widening income gap between rural and urban areas and between eastern coastal and western interior regions. The greatest consumption growth potential can be found in stronger demand for consumer durables from the rapidly rising middle class, stronger demand from rural areas and from the fast-growing western interior, stronger demand for services, and reduction in the savings rate, with strong political commitment to develop and expand coverage of a social security system. As the PRC reaches the Lewis turning point, an accelerated increase in real wages will lead to a rising wage share of income. This in turn is likely to lead to an increase in the consumption share and a corresponding reduction in the national savings rate.

Savings

The *Asian Development Outlook (2009)* noted that the national savings rates on average are high in Asia, with the PRC leading the pack. The PRC's savings rate has been rising sharply in recent years, reaching over 50 per cent after 2006. This is high by the PRC's own historical experience, as well as model predictions and international standards. All the sectors – household, corporate, government – have high savings rates.

The household sector used to be the main source of national savings, but its share has been declining in recent years. This reflects the declining share of households in overall national income, as the household savings rate relative to household disposable income has continued to rise. Explanations of the rising household savings rate include: life cycle hypothesis; precautionary motives due to the absence of a social safety net; and minimal health, education, unemployment compensation and pension coverage. Pension reform in 1997 reduced pension benefits, increased contributions and introduced pre-funded individual pension accounts, and contributed to the higher savings rate.

Corporate savings increased markedly in recent years to account for over half of the national savings by 2006. From 1995 to 2005, the PRC's corporate restructuring resulted in large-scale labor retrenchments at SOEs and the enterprise-based social safety net shrank rapidly. SOEs no longer provide housing for their employees and in exchange have increased contributions to housing provident funds. Such corporate restructuring lifted corporate savings. Government policies contributed to high corporate savings through massive state subsidies for land and energy to SOEs, administrative monopolies, and low-dividend payouts, and repressed the financial system that provides capital at low real interest rates to favored firms, thus increasing corporate profitability. The distorted financial system forces private firms to save through retained earnings to fund growth due to credit scarcity. Although interest rates were partially liberalized in 2004, when the ceiling on interbank lending rates was lifted, there are still limits on the floor of interbank lending rates and a ceiling on deposit rates, distorting investment decisions. If interest rates were liberalized, it would reduce financing costs for firms and reduce the savings incentive.

There is plenty of room for increased government spending on social security. As a share of GDP it was 13 per cent in 2008 and approached 20 per cent in 2009 only because of the massive fiscal stimulus package. This is lower than the Organisation for Economic Co-operation and Development (OECD) average and lower than most developing economies.

Structural shifts contributed to higher savings, with a rising profit share in national income, accelerated capital accumulation and faster economic growth, leading to a higher savings rate. The PRC has experienced rapid structural changes, as its agriculture–GDP ratio fell from 30 per cent to 10 per cent from 1980 to 2008. Large-scale, rural-to-urban labor migration and urbanization shrunk the agricultural share of total employment from 70 per cent to 40 per cent, while the urban share rose from 20 per cent to 45 per cent. Additionally, the PRC's demographic transition has been very compressed with the one-child policy, resulting in a low child-dependency ratio and a high working population ratio, which surged to 74 per cent, and thus a high household savings rate. All these factors will eventually result in the PRC's savings rate easing off from current highs.

The PRC's high savings rate has important implications for its internal balance and external balance. First, a high savings rate has financed strong economic growth, with low inflation and manageable exposures to adverse external shocks. Second, a rising savings rate implies a falling consumption rate and hence an investment-intensive internal demand structure. A rising savings rate interacted with a high investment rate from 1998 to 2008 and the investment–GDP ratio surged from 37 per cent to 45 per cent. Policies that can shift household savings toward consumption and channel corporate savings into productive investment will help to reduce the existing savings–investment gap.

Investment

Even before the GER, authorities in the PRC were concerned over the heavy dependence of aggregate demand on investment expenditures. The investment ratio increased further as a result of the investment-biased stimulus package. Provincial and local governments competed to invest in infrastructure and housing projects. Traditionally, investment growth was particularly strong in the tradable sectors, so sectors with higher export ratios on average saw more rapid growth in fixed asset investment (FAI).[1] In 2007 the PRC's urban FAI was concentrated in manufacturing (30.2 per cent), real estate (24.3 per cent), public facilities and hydraulic (7.8 per cent), and utilities (7.7 per cent). When the GER erupted, the pattern changed. First, investment in export-oriented manufacturing slowed with the global slump and emergence of spare capacity, and secondly, the stimulus package boosted investment in infrastructure. The rising share of investment in GDP increases the risk of excess capacity and low returns.

The PRC needs to pay more attention to the quality of its domestic investment rather than to the overall investment ratio. This would entail a shift away from low-wage, low-productivity, labor-intensive production to higher value-added production; from eastern coastal to western interior regions; and from urban to rural areas. It also would entail a shift from physical infrastructure to social infrastructure investments in education, health care, and housing; from polluting production to environment-friendly green technology products and processes; and from SOE investments to market-determined private enterprise investments.

Current Account Surplus

The PRC's growing current account surplus is a relatively recent phenomenon, jumping from 2.8 per cent of GDP in 2003 to 10.1 per cent by 2007. The current account surplus fell 35 per cent in 2009 to $284.1 billion as US and European demand for Chinese exports slumped, but the surplus rebounded by 25 per cent in 2010 to $306.2 billion.

The PRC's current account surplus is the subject of fierce international debate. It has given rise to growing trade tensions and threat of protectionism by major trading partners, as well as growing external pressure to let the RMB appreciate in value. The Chinese government has made various efforts to limit export growth by lowering export tax rebates, further liberalizing import barriers, and increasing exchange rate flexibility. But the PRC has thus far resisted pressure for a substantial one-off RMB appreciation. It argues that the current account surplus is driven by structural factors and that the exchange rate has little role to play in influencing the savings–investment balance. It has also made it a priority to "rebalance" growth in the PRC by stimulating private consumption.

Chinese economists have also been uneasy about the rapidly growing trade and current account surpluses. For example, Yu (2008) argued that these surpluses are neither desirable nor sustainable for the PRC. First, running a persistent current account surplus means that the PRC as a poor country is exporting capital to finance the consumption and investment of rich countries, such as the US and those in Europe. Many of the PRC's export products are produced at the expense of the PRC's environment, and the rapid increase of the PRC's exports and current account surplus has led to a deteriorating terms of trade for the PRC. Second, overdependence on the processing trade based on cheap labor runs the risk of the PRC being locked into the lower rung of the international division of labor and renders its economy highly vulnerable to external shocks. Third, trade frictions are worsening and the threat of protectionism against the PRC is rising as a result of the growing current account surplus. Fourth, accumulation of foreign reserves is making the Chinese economy vulnerable to any US adjustment, as a falling US dollar would mean tremendous losses in the PRC's foreign reserves.

RMB undervaluation argument

Whether the RMB is undervalued is a matter of heated debate, with critics arguing that the RMB undervaluation is evident from the huge bilateral trade surpluses that the PRC had with the US and the EU (see Table 11.3). US economists at the Peterson Institute (Bergsten, Cline, Williamson) and Paul Krugman have argued that the RMB is undervalued, as has the US Congress and the International Monetary Fund (IMF).

Plasschaert (2011) argues that it is incorrect to attribute the PRC's large export surplus to the US and its large foreign reserves to an undervalued RMB. The record growth of the PRC's exports to the US is largely due to joint ventures and affiliates of multinational corporations (MNCs) in the PRC. Exports often contain a high percentage of imported components, with only moderate Chinese value added. Further, the PRC's large foreign exchange reserves are not due primarily to its export surplus but also to the large net inward FDI and "hot money" inflows, the latter notwithstanding the non-convertibility of capital flows.

Table 11.3   *Bilateral trade between the People's Republic of China, the*
United States, and the European Union (US$ billion)

Year	PRC exports to US	PRC imports from US	PRC–US balance	PRC exports to EU	PRC imports from EU	PRC–EU balance
2007	322	63	259	233	72	161
2008	338	70	268	248	79	169
2009	296	69	227	215	82	133

Note: PRC = People's Republic of China.

Source: Plasschaert (2011).

Bergsten (2010) argues that the PRC's currency remains substantially undervalued, largely due to the PRC's massive intervention in the foreign exchange market, which is a major cause of its large and growing trade and current account surplus. The PRC had appreciated the RMB by 21 per cent against the US dollar during from June 2005 to December 2008 but discontinued the policy in the wake of the US financial crisis. Bergsten argues that a similar appreciation should be pursued over the next two years. The safe haven effect boosted the US dollar, and thus pushed up RMB, and when the US dollar peaked in March 2009, the real effective exchange rate (REER) of RMB was 25.8 per cent above its June 2005 level. This strong increase in the RMB contributed to the reduction of the PRC's current account surplus from a peak of 11 per cent of GDP in 2007 to less than 6 per cent by 2009. On 19 June 2010, the PRC signaled a return to a more flexible and more market-based exchange rate regime. The Peterson Institute (Borst 2011) in an update found that the RMB had appreciated 6.8 per cent. However, it argues that if the PRC is to rebalance its economy, the RMB will need to appreciate relative to all the PRC's major trade partners (trade-weighted REER) and not just the US. It found that while the RMB may be appreciating bilaterally against the US dollar, it is actually depreciating globally.

Some critics argue that RMB revaluation would be ineffective in correcting the current account imbalances and that the PRC needs to stimulate domestic demand, while the US needs to reduce its budget deficit by reducing consumption.

Huang's factor market distortions argument
Huang (2010) argues that the PRC's current account surplus reflects not only its export-led growth model and exchange rate distortions, but also

hot money inflows, savings–investment gap, the processing trade that transfers trade surpluses of other East Asian countries to the PRC, and above all, the PRC's factor-market distortions arising from asymmetric liberalization of goods and factors. He argues that while exchange rate policy is important, an exclusive focus on exchange rate policy is not likely to be productive for dealing with the problem, although keeping the exchange rate fixed to the dollar will give rise to asset bubbles and inflation. Still, liberalizing factor markets should be placed at the top of the PRC's policy agenda. While the PRC's products market has been largely liberalized, factor markets have not. Prices of almost all factors, including capital, energy, environment, labor and land, remain highly distorted. The resultant lower production costs, increased corporate profits and returns on investment, and the improved international competitiveness of Chinese goods contributed to the PRC's extraordinary economic growth. Factor-market distortions depressed consumption and contributed to emergent structural problems. The PRC needs to accelerate factor-market liberalization in order to complete the transition to a market economy and ensure a more sustainable growth path.

Labor market distortions   A key factor in the PRC's success in labor-intensive manufacturing exports is its abundant and cheap labor supply. Labor costs are suppressed by labor-market segmentation and the underdeveloped social welfare system. Notwithstanding the millions of migrant workers in the PRC's eastern coastal region, the household registration system (HRS) restricts population and labor mobility as it requires government approval for migration. The HRS also discriminates against migrant workers, who normally receive only half the wages of their urban counterparts, and are excluded from social welfare benefits received by residents, such as compulsory education, medical insurance, pensions, and unemployment support. Huang estimates that if urban employers made social welfare contributions for their migrant workers, their payrolls, including contributions to pensions, medical insurance, work injury insurance, maternity benefits, and housing entitlements, could rise by 30–40 per cent.

Capital and financial market distortions   Domestically, the financial system remains repressed, with state interventions on interest rates and on credit allocation. Although the PRC's financial system has undergone a major transformation, with the growth of commercial banks, entry of foreign banks, and establishment of stock exchanges in Shenzhen and Shanghai, most large banks are still majority-owned by the state. Financial intermediation remains overly dependent on large state banks, and SOEs account for a dominant share of funds raised from the market. The financial repressions likely reduced capital efficiency and reduced access of small and medium-sized enterprises (SMEs) to funding. While the government has liberalized and actively promoted inflows of FDI since the late 1970s, it adopted a much more cautious approach toward commercial bank borrowing and portfolio investment flows; only in recent years has the government adopted a qualified foreign institutional investor (QFII) system to experiment with inflows of portfolio capital. Controls on capital outflows were partially liberalized more recently and include liberalization of outward direct investment by Chinese enterprises, allowing residents to convert \$50000 a year for current account items, as well as the introduction of the QFII system. Liberalization in the capital account could potentially lead to more capital outflows and push up domestic costs of capital. Additionally, exchange rate policy also contributes to cost distortions. In 1994 the PBC unified the official and swap market exchange rates at 8.7 RMB to the dollar, substantially devaluing the official rate. In July 2005, the PBC appreciated the currency by 2.1 per cent and adopted a managed float with reference to a basket of currencies. The RMB showed slow but steady appreciation against the US dollar, reaching 6.84 RMB by the end of 2008 and around 6.4 RMB in mid-2011. Most economists believe that the RMB is undervalued, although they may disagree on the extent of undervaluation.

Land cost   Urban land is owned by the state, while rural land is owned by collectives. There is no market mechanism for determining land prices for industrial use, and prices are often set by government departments, with underpricing to investors a common phenomenon. Regional and local governments in an effort to attract investment and promote growth often offer land use rights to investors at discounted or even zero cost. This led the Ministry of Land Resources to issue a directive in 2006 on minimum prices for industrial land.

Energy cost   The state regulates prices of key energy products such as oil, gas, and electricity. In 1998, the government announced a formula linking domestic prices of oil to the weighted average of prices in New York, Rotterdam, and Singapore. In 2000, oil prices were raised seven times to bring them closer to international levels. However, when international prices moved sharply upward, the government became reluctant to follow up for fear of disrupting economic growth. Hence, oil price distortions are highly volatile.

Environmental cost   Although the PRC has environmental laws and regulations, they have not been strictly enforced. Pollution of air, water, and land has not only adversely affected productivity and quality of life but also generated serious health consequences. Since producers do not always fully compensate for their damage to the environment, this reduces short-term production costs at the expense of long-term development. One estimate of the costs of environmental damage amounted to about 3 per cent of GDP in 2004.

Preferential taxes for foreign enterprises In an effort to attract FDI, income tax rates for foreign-invested firms were set at only 15 per cent, while domestic enterprises had to pay 33 per cent. In 2008, the government unified these tax rates at 25 per cent. However, foreign-invested firms are often exempt from corporate income tax during the first three years of operation and pay only half of the tax in the following two years. Likewise, export tax rebates are offered to promote export growth, with the rates frequently adjusted, with the average rebate rate rising from 8.3 per cent in 1997 to 15 per cent in 2000, and falling back to 12.1 per cent in 2004. Resource tax rates averaging 1.2 per cent are also significantly lower than international levels.

The various cost distortions contribute to imbalances such as overinvestment, underconsumption, and a strong export orientation. Also, the very rapid expansion of capital stock without accompanying technological progress could drag down economic efficiency and economic growth. Huang argues that the PRC needs to focus on reforms to complete the liberalization of factor markets. First, labor market liberalization should entail removing the HRS system and developing the social welfare system. Narrowing the rural–urban income gap should come as a result of reducing the number of farmers, not just building rural infrastructure or raising agricultural prices. Liberalizing the labor market would stimulate consumption. Second, financial market liberalization would necessitate market-based interest rates and exchange rates. Free capital flows are important for economic efficiency. Residents need to be able to diversify their assets and should also be able to borrow from overseas. Third, collective ownership in the rural areas is ambiguous, creates room for corruption, and hinders modernization of the rural economy. In addition, more clearly defined land ownership is needed. In the urban areas, the government should at least stay out of direct negotiation of land prices or private property development. Fourth, energy prices should be determined by the market, while fiscal subsidies can be used to support specific target groups. Fifth, the government's role in environmental protection should be strengthened significantly, particularly in enforcing existing environmental regulations.

THE PRC'S REBALANCING CHALLENGES

Before the onset of the GER in 2008, growing economic and social imbalances in the PRC had already become problematic.

Rebalancing Domestic Demand–Export Demand

Exports grew at more than 20 per cent annually from 2002 to 2007 and their share of GDP rose from 25.1 per cent in 2002 to 38.4 per cent in 2007. The continued rapid growth of exports caused significant structural adjustments and political resistance in the US and Europe. The PRC is dependent on imported raw materials to support its robust growth, and this import demand has contributed to sharp increases in international commodity prices in recent years.

Pressure for a shift toward domestic demand grew with the slowdown in exports in the wake of GER as merchandise export growth slowed to 17.5 per cent in 2008 and fell to 16.0 per cent in 2009. Rebalancing would mean the PRC needs faster growth of domestic demand and slower growth of export demand. Unlike much smaller economies, the PRC has considerable potential to achieve a sustained growth of domestic demand. Its dynamic and enormous domestic market enables economies of scale and scope, while its varied resource endowment and technological capabilities would reduce import dependence. Going forward, domestic demand should grow with the current trend of rising wages, a rapidly growing middle class demanding consumer durables and services, improvement of the social security system, and faster development of the western interior and rural regions of the PRC.

The external imbalance can be tackled on both the export and import sides. Increasing the PRC's imports would help to rebalance its external trade and help major trading partners that have bilateral trade deficits with the PRC. The PRC could increase imports of consumer goods and technology goods, as only a very small proportion of its imports are consumer goods, and these are still subject to relatively high tariffs and value-added or sales taxes, as well as cumbersome customs procedures. Technology goods are usually big-ticket items that can shift bilateral trade balances, but a major stumbling block lies in the severe restrictions on such exports to the PRC from the US and European countries on national security grounds.

Achieving fast and sustained growth of domestic demand will also depend in large part on the PRC's exchange rate policy. Chinese Premier Wen Jiabao told European leaders in October 2010 (Channel News Asia, 10 October 2010) that the 20–40 per cent appreciation demanded by critics would destroy Chinese firms, as many exporters had profit margins of just 2–3 per cent, and would lead to widespread unemployment and trigger social upheaval. He pledged to gradually allow more flexibility in the RMB exchange rate while maintaining its basic stability. Analysts agree that a sudden sharp RMB revaluation would trigger mass factory closures and job losses in the PRC, and would be harmful not only to the PRC's export-driven economy but also to a global economy struggling to recover from the financial crisis.

Rebalancing Domestic Consumption Demand–Investment Demand

Achieving sustainable growth of domestic demand needs consumption–investment balancing by raising the share of consumption and lowering the share of investment. This growing imbalance has raised serious questions about the sustainability of growth. From 2000 to 2007 the PRC's household consumption–GDP ratio declined from 46.2 per cent to 36 per cent while its investment–GDP ratio rose from 35.1 per cent to 41.7 per cent. Expanding investment is relatively less problematic in a system where SOEs are fed with substantial amounts of public funds that they can promptly channel into expansion. In contrast, raising private consumption requires raising household purchasing power and changing saving habits.

Reasons for the PRC's low consumption ratio have been discussed earlier. There is significant room to expand both household and public sector consumption. Growth in consumption is limited by the declining share of household income to national disposable income, which fell from 66 per cent in 1997 to 58 per cent in 2007, while that of the corporate sector rose from 17 per cent to 22 per cent and that of the government sector from 17 per cent to 20 per cent. Household savings rose faster than incomes, prompted by concerns with saving for housing, education, and health care. For a significant increase in consumption, there is a need to address the precautionary motive for household saving and strengthen the social safety net and provision of public goods, such as education, health care, and affordable housing.[2] Specific policies that transfer more corporate savings to households and that dilute the precautionary motive for saving among households will strengthen domestic demand. To transfer corporate savings, firms should be encouraged to pay dividends to stockholders and use the tax system to distribute profits to households. The advent of credit cards would also spur consumption among middle-class and wealthy households and individuals.[3] There is also much potential for greater public consumption in view of the government's strong fiscal situation and low public debt. With the new emphasis on greater social inclusiveness, the government has set up several social development programs, such as a minimum living wage guarantee and basic health insurance for eligible urban and rural households whose annual incomes are below the minimum living wage level.

Investment growth is still critical for industrial upgrading, provisions of public goods, and provisions for environmental protection and the development of green economy sectors. A shift from the current energy-consuming and environmentally damaging economic growth would require more reliance on skills, technology and innovation, with large investments in education and training, and research-and-development spending on green technology.

Rebalancing Inward and Outward Direct Investment

Although the PRC has been a net capital exporter for more than 15 years, it consistently ran an investment account deficit. Due to underdevelopment of financial markets, excess savings in the economy are not readily translated into financial capital for enterprises and foreign exchange for imports. Essentially, the PRC's domestic savings have often to be intermediated by foreign capital markets for domestic investment. As a result, there are large inward FDI and foreign reserves. Despite returns required on inward FDI being much higher than yields of US Treasury bills, the PRC is dependent on inward FDI for enterprise, technology, management, and market networks. The PRC's fiscal system and institutional arrangements also give local governments great incentive to attract inward FDI. About 65 per cent of inward FDI takes the form of contractual or equity joint ventures with Chinese companies, although 100 per cent foreign-owned enterprises are now the fastest-growing sector. The majority of inward FDI is "greenfield" investment. However, in order to give new impetus to the reform of SOEs and state-owned banks, mergers and acquisitions of Chinese firms by foreign investors are also encouraged.

In 1986 the investment environment for inward FDI was further improved with the "Twenty-two Regulations" that included lower fees for labor and rent, tax rebates for exporters, the conversion by foreign companies of RMB into foreign exchange and the repatriation of profits, joint venture contracts that extended beyond the original 50-year limit, and the creation of a legal basis for wholly foreign-owned enterprises. In 1992, following on Deng Xiaoping's tour of the southern region of the PRC, the reform and opening-up process intensified and FDI inflows surged until the outbreak of AFC in 1997. Following the PRC's entry into the WTO in December 2001, the policy focus shifted from providing preferential treatment to fulfilling WTO liberalization commitments, which include relaxing local content and export requirements and restrictions on foreign ownership; dismantling the requirement for the self-balancing of foreign currency; lowering barriers to sensitive sectors such as telecoms, banking, insurance and professional services; and participation in the agreements on trade-related investment measures (TRIMS) and trade-related aspects of intellectual property rights (TRIPS). The central government also has had to constrain excessive competition among local governments offering concessions to attract inward FDI. Cumulative utilized FDI stock reached $395.4 billion and cumulative contracted FDI stock reached $745.1 billion by the end of 2001; FDI inflows further surged to $52.7 billion in 2002.

The PRC's policy of first attracting FDI to the eastern coastal area has resulted in the widening development gap between eastern coastal and western interior regions. This has led the government in recent years to launch a "Look West" strategy for inward FDI with the development of physical infrastructure and offer of various preferential incentives. Western region attractions include diminishing returns on investment in eastern coastal areas as land prices and production costs rise, abundant cheap labor, and government preferential policy. Disadvantages include inadequate infrastructure, particularly the higher cost of reaching ports for imports and exports, and relatively low availability of skills and entrepreneurship.[4]

Inward FDI raised annual GDP growth rates and per capita GDP and has had a positive impact on the balance of payments, created new jobs, upgraded skills, transferred technology, encouraged reform of Chinese domestic industries and raised total factor productivity. While the direct impact of inward FDI on total FAI and total employment generation in the PRC is admittedly small, it acted as a catalyst to foster additional reforms, productivity and innovations and served as a demonstration and business model for indigenous Chinese enterprises. The most obvious contribution of inward FDI is the rapid growth of globally competitive manufacturing and exports. The PRC has become a production base not only for labor-intensive manufactured goods, but also increasingly for technology-intensive products. Inward FDI accounted for over 50 per cent of Chinese exports of manufactured goods in recent years. The contribution of inward FDI to technological progress and managerial skill in the PRC has been significant, particularly in capital- and technology-intensive sectors.

However, Yu (2006) highlighted some negative impacts of inward FDI. First, preferential FDI policy and especially export-oriented FDI can create serious market distortions and resource misallocation. The preferential policy should be replaced by nondiscriminatory national treatment of both domestic and foreign enterprises. Second, over-reliance on the willingness of foreign MNCs to transfer technology may weaken

Chinese indigenous enterprises and their independent ability to conduct research and development. And some industries may be locked into a labor-intensive segment of the international production network. Third, FDI tends to have an asymmetrical income effect on the economy with a resultant widening income gap leading to serious social tensions. Fourth, with the growing stock of FDI, investment income outflows will accelerate rapidly, and together with FDI-related trade deficits, could weaken the PRC's balance of payments position.

Chinese outward direct investment (ODI) is a rapidly growing phenomenon in the past decade even though the PRC is still a developing economy with a relatively low per capita income. ODI flows were minimal until 2000 but have since accelerated to reach $57 billion in 2009. The GER has created investment opportunities for cash-rich Chinese enterprises to target foreign companies with falling asset values leading to the acquisition of companies and assets at much reduced cost. Chinese enterprises and rich Chinese individuals have also been snapping up real estate and properties in Hong Kong, China, as well as other Asian cities.

The rapid growth in the PRC's outward FDI has been largely the result of the Chinese government's "go-out" policy enunciated in 2000.[5] The policy objectives were intended to improve on the huge foreign exchange reserves earning low rates of return in foreign portfolio investments, secure supplies of energy and raw materials needed for economic growth and industrialization, and improve the global competitiveness of Chinese enterprises. The policy ramped up in 2005, as foreign reserves grew rapidly and SOEs found themselves in a better position to invest abroad. And as the need for energy and raw materials grew, the search for resources spread worldwide. In the wake of the GER and economic downturn, the various government agencies have further relaxed regulations allowing Chinese enterprises to invest abroad.

The PRC's outward FDI are largely undertaken by SOEs, with private enterprises playing a secondary role until recent years. Central government-affiliated SOEs are engaged in securing energy and raw materials required for Chinese industrialization. SOEs under provincial and local government administration also undertake outward FDI. Large SOEs enjoy the advantages of government support in access to finance and information and in networking and administrative support. The China Investment Corporation (CIC) is a sovereign wealth fund created in 2007 to invest part of the country's surging foreign exchange holdings and seeks partnerships with key SOEs in strategically important and commercially attractive investments. With extensive SOE reforms shrinking their presence in the economy, a growing number of private enterprises are investing overseas, many in building manufacturing facilities in ASEAN countries and investing in services in Hong Kong, China and Singapore. Some large private enterprises in the consumer goods sector, such as the Lenovo Group, Shanghai Automotive Industry, and Haier, have also been seeking outward FDI through mergers and acquisitions and acquiring international brand names and market shares.

The bulk of Chinese outward FDI has been in primary and tertiary sectors, with relatively little in manufacturing. Natural resource investments are to secure a stable resource supply to sustain economic growth. The PRC also invests abroad in oil and gas resources to boost its energy supplies. Overseas investments are often directed towards developing countries in Asia and Africa. At times, large SOEs have also targeted resources in developed countries such as Australia, Canada, and the US. The PRC has a huge domestic market and competitive production costs, so there is little incentive for outward FDI in manufacturing that is for markets or efficiency. Chinese outward FDI in advanced countries seeks advanced technology and international brand names to strengthen production at home. These are through technology transfers from foreign partners in joint ventures, acquiring stakes in foreign firms with advanced technologies, technology licensing and the purchase of advanced equipment through foreign affiliates. In services, much of the investment is aimed at facilitating Chinese exports.

Amid growing international tensions over control of natural resources and strategic assets, the PRC has defended its growing global commercial presence as a source of jobs, capital and technology, particularly in Africa. Tens of thousands of Chinese companies now operate throughout the developing world, often rejuvenating previously moribund economies with their investments, as well as development aid. Developing countries have generally welcomed Chinese investments. In many instances, Chinese SOEs are willing and able to take on projects that no MNCs find financially prudent. This economic outreach has been matched by offering a wide menu of trade and aid deals, infrastructure support, and educational and technical training opportunities. However, Chinese companies have also encountered resistance in a number of countries over their poor environmental and safety practices and labor policies that favor Chinese workers.

Rebalancing Economic Growth with Social Development and Environmental Sustainability

Before 1978, the PRC was an egalitarian society under the socialist model, but it has been experiencing growing income inequality after adopting the market-economy model. The Gini coefficient increased from 0.16 to 0.36

in urban areas and from 0.22 to 0.38 in rural areas from 1978 to 2007, while for the whole of the PRC the Gini rose from 0.30 in the early 1980s to 0.47 in 2007. The urban–rural income ratio of household income per capita rose from 1.8 in 1996 to 3.3 in 2007 (Li Shi 2010). There are also growing regional disparities between the eastern coastal and western interior regions. Failure to deal with domestic inequalities will threaten social stability in the next phase of growth and development.

Narrowing the income gap of households requires adequate employment opportunities; raising wages of low-wage workers; lowering the cost of and improving access to education, health care, and housing of low-income groups; and comprehensive coverage for pension benefits. Raising wages can only be sustainable in the long term if it is matched by improvements in labor productivity, hence the need for education and training for low-income households. Reforming the pension system involves de-linking pension benefits from SOEs and preferably the introduction of self-funded provident fund schemes. Farmers and SMEs should also be able to find easier access to credit from financial institutions. The rebalancing of public sector resources available to rural and urban areas is necessary so that improved physical and social infrastructure for the rural areas leads to improved rural productivity and quality of life. The problem with the existing social security system is its limited coverage to the urban formal sector, whereas the majority of Chinese workers are in the informal sector and in rural areas. Removing the household registration (*hukou*) system will improve the lot of migrant workers.

Growing development disparities between the eastern coastal and western interior regions, as well as reaching the Lewis turning point in the eastern coastal region, have occasioned a shift in policy emphasis towards development of the PRC's western interior. Massive infrastructure investments have taken place in the western interior, including the development of gateways to the sea that can facilitate exports and imports. Government policies have also encouraged private foreign investors to move westward. Likewise, as wages rise on the east coast and employers find increasing difficulties in recruiting "affordable" workers, industries dependent on low-wage labor may migrate westwards rather than relocate to neighboring countries with low-wage labor.[6]

The PRC's huge population, the growing number of automobiles and the country's role as "factory of the world" with its high consumption of energy and large emissions of pollutants are contributing to an emerging ecological disaster. Cities suffer from serious air pollution and continue to discharge untreated sewage and dump urban domestic waste. In rural areas the use of chemical fertilizers and pesticides and insecticides has left residues in the soil and groundwater. The consequences of pollution can also be seen in the increasing air pollution of cities and water pollution of rivers, lakes, and coastal waters. These will adversely impact economic growth and quality of life.

The PRC is still in the high-carbon phase of development, and it is in its national interest to take a more proactive role in carbon reduction. Although per capita income and emissions are lower in the PRC than in Western countries, the total impact of the pollution is huge. According to the Environmental Kuznets Curve (EKC), environmental degradation associated with economic growth increases most rapidly at low levels of per capita income; as income grows, the additional degradation due to economic gain slows until it eventually peaks; and as per capita income continues to grow, degradation eventually diminishes. It is possible to reduce pollution and improve the environment through policy changes and technological transfer and progress. The PRC recently has invested substantially in pollution control, but there is regional disparity in the extent of this investment, with provinces in eastern coastal regions of the PRC investing the most. To help cut carbon emissions per unit of GDP, the PRC is trying to develop renewable and nuclear energy with the goal of increasing the share of non-fossil fuels in total primary energy consumption from 7.8 per cent in 2009 to 15 per cent by 2020. In 2009 the PRC imposed a carbon tax on gasoline and it also imposed a value-added tax (VAT) on fossil-fuel heavy electricity at 17 per cent. Jiang Gaoming (2007) argued for several steps to be taken. First, the PRC must adopt the concept of "green GDP" in assessing and rewarding the performance of government officials. While in the past, government officials were assessed and rewarded for their role in economic growth, they should now be assessed and rewarded according to how they solve environmental problems. Second, the state must increase funding to protect the environment and improve environmental protection laws and implementation mechanisms. Third, the PRC needs to raise environmental education to better inform the public and enhance the role of environmental non-governmental organizations and the media on environmental awareness and protection.

THE PRC'S GROWTH PROSPECTS

Will the PRC's rapid growth continue? At one extreme, pessimists believe that problems such as the demographic transition, income inequality, corruption, and environmental concerns will seriously impair the PRC's growth sustainability. At the other extreme, optimists are convinced that the PRC will soon become the most important economic force in the

Table 11.4   Growth accounting, 1978–2020 (% change)

	1978–94	1995–2009	2010–15	2016–20
Potential GDP growth	9.9	9.6	8.4	7.0
Employment growth	3.3	1.0	0.2	−0.5
Labor productivity growth	6.4	8.6	8.2	7.5
from TFP growth	3.0	2.7	2.3	2.3
from higher H/L	0.5	0.3	0.5	0.6
from higher K/L ratio	2.9	5.5	5.4	4.6
Memorandum items (in per cent)				
Investment–GDP ratio (period average)	30.0	37.3	41.1	39.1

Source: Kuijs (2009).

world. On the demographic transition, the Chinese population is expected to begin to shrink around 2020 and that will affect the country's growth potential as it deals with a smaller labor force and a rising burden for health care and social security for a rapidly ageing population. The PRC may need to relax its stringent urban one-child policy to reduce the inter-generational burden on households, although it may be too late to reverse the behavior of urban couples toward having more children.

Kuijs (2009) developed a macroeconomic scenario of the PRC through 2020. The scenario analyzed the relationship between key macroeconomic variables in the recent past and developed assumptions about how these relationships might evolve in the coming decade. Using a growth accounting framework, the study discusses the likely trend growth through 2020. Issues of particular interest are how high can trend growth reasonably be, given the fundamentals; possible changes in the composition of demand and the structure of the economy as a result of rebalancing efforts after the global financial crisis; the impact of these factors on the external surplus; and the likely role of relative price changes (real exchange rate appreciation) as the PRC catches up. The study concludes (Tables 11.4 and 11.5) that with both working population and total factor productivity on course to decelerate, potential GDP growth is likely to moderate in the coming decade. With some rebalancing expected, the share of consumption is likely to bottom out and grow somewhat through 2015, while the share of investment edges down. With economic growth in the PRC likely to continue to be robust, import growth remains solid. Meanwhile, given the outlook for the world economy, exports are not expected to outgrow domestic activity from 2010 to 2015. With some further impact from relative prices, the export–GDP ratio should continue to diminish.

Table 11.5   Main growth forecasts

	2007	2008	2009	2010f	2011f	2012f	2013f	2014f	2015f
Per cent change:									
Real GDP	13.0	9.6	8.7	9.5	8.5	8.2	8.0	7.9	7.9
Domestic demand	10.8	9.4	13.8	9.6	8.5	8.3	8.2	8.1	8.0
Consumption	10.2	8.8	9.7	9.5	9.1	9.1	8.9	8.9	8.9
Gross capital formation	11.4	10.2	18.3	9.7	8.0	7.6	7.4	7.3	7.0
Contribution to GDP growth (ppp)									
Domestic demand	10.4	8.8	12.7	9.1	8.3	8.1	7.9	7.8	7.7
Net exports	2.6	0.8	−4.0	0.4	0.3	0.1	0.1	0.1	0.1
Contribution of net exports (ppp)	3.5	1.8	−4.8	0.4	0.3	0.1	0.1	0.1	0.1
Exports (goods and services)	20.0	8.6	−10.4	23.0	8.9	7.9	7.9	7.9	7.9
Imports (goods and services)	14.2	5.1	4.3	26.4	9.0	8.6	8.4	8.4	8.4
Potential GDP growth	10.4	10.1	10.0	9.3	8.8	8.5	8.2	8.0	7.8
Output gap (ppp)	2.4	1.9	0.5	0.7	0.5	0.2	0.0	0.0	0.1
External terms of trade	−0.9	−4.3	8.6	−6.4	−0.1	1.1	0.7	0.7	0.7
As % of GDP									
Gross national saving	54.1	52.0	51.4	51.1	50.9	50.8	50.4	50.0	49.6
Gross capital formation	43.1	42.5	45.4	46.4	46.2	45.9	45.6	45.3	44.9
Current account balance	11.0	9.4	6.1	4.7	4.7	4.9	4.8	4.7	4.7
$ billion									
Foreign exchange reserves	1529	1946	2400	2705	3028	3395	3798	4247	4745

Notes: GDP = Gross Domestic Product. PPP = Purchasing Power Parity.

Source: Kuijs (2009).

The current account surpluses would likely continue to grow in absolute amount, in large part because of rising earnings on the PRC's growing foreign reserves. By 2020 Chinese GDP per capita in terms of purchasing power parity would be one-quarter of the US level, and the PRC's total GDP would exceed that of the US. The pace of catch-up in current prices and market exchange rates will depend on the extent of the real exchange rate appreciation.

The 12th Five-Year Plan for 2011–15 approved in March 2011 seeks to rebalance the pattern of growth. While economic rebalancing has been a government priority for many years, the sharp decline in exports during the GER and international pressure underscored the necessity of moving to a more balanced growth structure.

Growth rate   GDP growth is set at a lower 7 per cent compared to 7.5 per cent for the 11th Plan. The lower growth target was meant to signal the central government's intention to shift away from GDP maximization and toward more socially inclusive and environmentally sustainable growth. Employment levels remain on target, as is the 2020 GDP per capita goal. The lower GDP growth rate will help rein in excessive spending by provincial governments and allow officials to reduce their focus on fixed asset investment (FAI) and increase their focus on policies to increase consumption. However, it should be noted that for 2005–10 the actual growth performance was 11.2 per cent, much higher than the planned 7 per cent, so it is highly probable that the PRC will also overshoot its 12th Plan growth target.

Policy direction   The 12th Plan's main policy directions include a better balance among investment, consumption, and exports; a larger role for services; a stronger emphasis on improving living standards and narrowing income inequalities; newly designated strategic industries to promote innovation; and plans to combat global warming and reduce carbon intensity, including ambitious emission-reduction targets, a carbon tax, new indicators for pollutants and carbon-trading programs. In order to enable consumption to grow quickly, the government plans to increase household disposable income, most likely through an increase in minimum wages and increased social safety nets, such as health care and social welfare payments. The seven strategic industries targeted for policy promotion through preferential fiscal and procurement policies include biotechnology, new energy, high-end equipment manufacturing, energy conservation and environment protection, clean energy vehicles, new materials, and next-generation information technology (IT). Critics might disapprove of the PRC's continuing industrial policy, but at least it is directed at developing new growth areas in IT and green technologies, and not in protecting noncompetitive sunset industries.

Inclusive growth   The 12th Plan will help increase income of the masses through higher minimum wages, the expansion of the government-funded social welfare and health care system, and the promotion of labor-intensive service industries. This improved income distribution is in turn expected to boost the consumption–GDP ratio. On the rural–urban divide, planned actions include increasing urbanization, in part by reforming the household registration system, and providing improved social safety nets for the rural population, such as basic health care coverage and improved land distribution. For more balanced regional development between the eastern coastal and western interior areas, the government will continue to grow the latter through preferential policies such as land credits, lower taxes and subsidies for manufacturers looking to locate inland.

Environmental sustainability   The 12th Plan will focus on reducing pollution, increasing energy efficiency, and ensuring a stable, reliable clean energy supply. The PRC's environmental goals will likely have a far-reaching effect as they will impact and shape a range of other industrial policies in numerous sectors. On energy conservation the 12th Plan is expected to contain preferential measures for developing energy-efficiency technology and mandatory energy emissions targets. On environmental quality, the 12th Plan has green indicators that will hold local government officials accountable for green development.

   Asian Development Outlook (2011) argues that implementing the 12th Plan will be a major challenge. Economic rebalancing was an objective in the 11th Plan (2006–10) and some progress was made, for example in curbing energy consumption and pollutants and expanding the coverage of urban and rural health care. Yet there was limited progress on major rebalancing targets. For example, consumption substantially lagged investment, with average contributions of 41 per cent for consumption and 54 per cent for investment to annual GDP growth in the past five years, and the services share of GDP remained relatively low at about 43 per cent. Furthermore, the implications of population aging threaten the sustainability of growth and complicate the reform agenda. Economic rebalancing is unlikely to occur without significant policy adjustments, including shifting the emphasis of public spending from investment to public services, liberalizing the finance sector, developing capital markets to help SMEs and the self-employed to access credit, and facilitating a greater role for private players in the economy.

CONCLUSION

The PRC's economic, social, and environmental challenges and their solutions are not only national issues but also issues of international concern because of their international impact and ramifications. As an emergent economic superpower, the PRC is also expected to play an active role in solving global problems and delivering on global public goods, such as international financial stability, climate, environment, and pandemics.

By undertaking domestic structural reforms to rebalance export and domestic demand and consumption and investment demand, and by removing factor market distortions, the PRC will achieve a more sustainable current account surplus. By accelerating its outward investments and greater awareness of host country sensitivities, the PRC will help channel its excess savings for development of developing economies in Africa, Asia, and Latin America. By undertaking environmental protection measures, including the development and use of green technologies, the PRC will help avert its own potential ecological disaster and slow down climate change globally.

While the PRC may not yield to external pressure with a "big bang" RMB revaluation, the current crawling appreciation is a disincentive to structural reforms and will not alleviate inflationary pressures. A more substantial RMB appreciation is called for.

NOTES

1. Fixed asset investment (FAI) is meant to measure investment in long-term assets, such as buildings and equipment, including land purchases, used facilities, equipment purchases, and mergers and acquisitions. Gross fixed capital formation (GFCF) measures how much of an economy's new output is invested, excluding purchases of land and other already owned assets. The extent of land purchases and merger-and-acquisition activity has pushed the PRC's overall level of investment using the FAI measure. However, the PRC's GFCF is still very high, as compared to other East Asian countries during their period of rapid growth.
2. There is also the relatively new phenomenon – the product of the PRC's one-child policy and the preference of parents for sons resulting in a scarcity of brides – that households now have to save to provide a "dowry" (usually home ownership) for the groom.
3. The advent of credit cards has changed consumption habits in many emerging Asian societies, particularly among members of the rapidly expanding middle class and young professionals.
4. In recent years the PRC has been focusing on political and economic relations with its southern neighbors in ASEAN, particularly the Mekong countries of Cambodia, the Lao People's Democratic Republic, Myanmar, Thailand, and Viet Nam. It is using the Mekong River to transport goods and is developing two ports in Myanmar to provide access to the Bay of Bengal.
5. See Chia (2010).
6. The traditional "flying geese" development in East Asia entailed the relocation of

industries from Japan (the head goose) to the Asian NIEs following the Plaza Accord in 1987 and from the Asian NIEs to the ASEAN countries following the rise in wage costs.

BIBLIOGRAPHY

Admas, C., H.Y. Jeong, and C.Y. Park (2010), 'Asia's contribution to global rebalancing', ADB Working Paper on Regional Economic Integration, No. 58.

Asian Development Bank, *Asian Development Outlook*, various years.

Beijing Review (2010), 'Aftermath of the PRC's stimulus plan', Web version, 3 December.

Bergsten, F. (2010), 'Correcting the Chinese exchange rate', Testimony before the Hearing on the PRC's Exchange Rate Policy, Committee on Ways and Means, US House of Representatives, 15 September.

Borst, N. (2011), 'How fast is the Renminbi appreciating', China Economic Watch, Peterson Institute for International Economics, 9 September.

Channel News Asia (2010), 'Abrupt yuan rise problematic for the PRC', 10 October.

Channel News Asia (2010), 'Wen says the PRC confident of keeping inflation in check', 26 December.

Chia, S.Y. (2010), 'Chinese direct investments in East Asia', Paper presented at the Roundtable on Chinese Overseas Investment, China Center for Economic Research, Beijing, 5 December.

Cline, W., and J. Williamson (2010), 'Currency wars?', Peterson Institute for International Economics Policy Brief, Washington, DC.

Garnaut, R. (2010), 'The turning period in Chinese development', East Asia Forum, 1 August.

Huang Yiping (2010), 'The PRC's great ascendancy and structural risks: consequences of asymmetric market liberalization', *Asia-Pacific Economic Literature.*

Huang Yiping, and T. Kunyu (2010), 'Causes and remedies of the PRC's external imbalances', China Center for Economic Research Working Paper No. 2010-02. February.

Jiang Gaoming (2007), 'The terrible cost of the PRC's growth', The PRC Dialogue, 12 January.

Kuijs, L. (2009), 'The PRC through 2020: a macroeconomic scenario', The PRC Office Research Working Paper No. 9, The World Bank, June.

Li Shi (2010), 'Issues and options for social security reform in the PRC', Paper presented at the Pacific Trade and Development Conference, Beijing, 7–9 December.

Ma, G., and Y. Wang (2010), 'The PRC's high saving rate: myth and reality', Bank for International Settlements (BIS) Working Paper No.312, June.

Plasschaert, S. (2011), 'Is the Renminbi undervalued? The myths of the PRC's trade surplus and global imbalances', European Centre for International Political Economy Working Paper No.02/2011.

Tao, K. (2010), 'The impact of the global financial crisis on the PRC's migrant workers', *East Asia Forum*, 8 February.

World Bank Office (2011), 'Quarterly update', Beijing, April.

Yu Yongding (2006), 'The experience of FDI recipients: the case of [the People's Republic of] China', in S. Urata, S.Y. Chia and F. Kimura (eds), *Multinationals and Economic Growth in East Asia: Foreign Direct Investment, Corporate Strategies and National Economic Development*, Routledge.

Yu Yongding (2008), 'Managing capital flows in the PRC', Asian Development Bank Institute, Manila, Philippines.

Yu Yongding (2009), 'The PRC's reactions to the global economic crisis', RIETI Report, **112**, 15.

Zheng, Y. (2011), 'The impact of the PRC's 12th Five Year Plan', *East Asia Forum*, 24 April.

12. Thailand

Bhanupong Nidhiprabha

INTRODUCTION

For a country to be able to continue to raise the standard of living of its citizens, its economy must grow continuously. It must achieve a high growth rate and avoid disruptions to long-term growth. Export-led growth policy can help sustain rapid growth provided that external factors are favorable. If the volume of world trade declines, countries that depend mainly on exports will bear the brunt of a worldwide recession. On the other hand, small countries that rely more on domestic markets will miss out on the opportunity to grow quickly when world trade expands. In order to exploit the benefits of the rapid expansion of world trade, an export-led country must maintain price stability that produces low interest rates and incentives to save and invest. Appropriate macroeconomic policy must provide a favorable environment that can sustain domestic demand in light of changing external conditions.

This chapter examines how Thailand managed to keep inflation low while maintaining rapid growth between 1961 and 1990. The impact of prudent macroeconomic policy employed during this period is discussed. The chapter examines Thailand's departure from its long-term growth path, which was disrupted by the Asian financial crisis (AFC) in 1997 and the global economic recession (GER) in 2007. It then investigates the overinvestment and underinvestment episodes that were related to the quantity and quality of investment. The chapter then looks at Thailand's macroeconomic management in response to shocks and highlights the role of exchange rate regimes that brought price stability and export competitiveness. The chapter also considers the role of financial factors contributing to capital formation and evaluates the impact on output of changes in aggregate demand components versus exports.

THE STABLE GROWTH PATH: 1961–90

The beginning of a new era of economic development in Thailand occurred from 1961 to 1968 (see Figure 12.1). The country's first economic development plan was implemented in 1961 and focused on building basic infrastructure. The share of investment to gross domestic product (GDP) rose from 15 per cent in 1961 to 25 per cent in 1968. The average GDP growth rate of 8.1 per cent and the average inflation rate of 2.2 per cent led to a substantial increase in the demand for deposits in commercial banks. Low inflation during this period implied that the real rate of return from bank deposits was positive. Until 1977, the tax exemptions on interest earned from saving and time deposits made bank deposits very attractive long-term investments.

From 1961 to 1990 real output moved in line with a trend of 7 per cent annual growth. There were some periods during which actual GDP was above the trend, as a new engine of growth emerged. On the other hand, actual GDP fell below the trend due to the 1973–74 and 1979–80 oil price shocks.

The slowdown in exports in the early 1980s as the result of the appreciation of the real exchange rate caused the output to grow at less than its expected potential. The 1984 currency devaluation restored international competitiveness, and the Thai economy resumed its pre-shock growth path rapidly after the exchange rate adjustments.

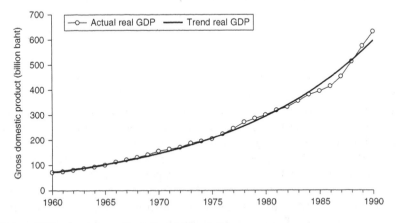

Note: GDP = gross domestic product (billion baht).

Source: International Monetary Fund, International Financial Statistics.

Figure 12.1   Stable growth path

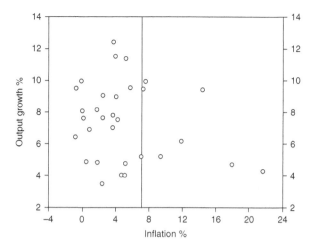

Source: Bank of Thailand.

Figure 12.2   Growth with price stability: 1961–90

From 1960 to 2000, the exponential growth rate of the population was
2.4 per cent, while the real GDP growth rate was 7 per cent. As a result,
real GDP per capita increased rapidly during this episode of high growth
and price stability. Double-digit inflation during this period was attributed to the oil price shocks in 1973–74 and 1979–80. The inflation rate
came down within a year after cost-push inflation put upward pressure
on consumer price levels. External shocks did not lead to runaway inflation, as the monetary growth rate was moderate. As Figure 12.2 indicates,
faster growth rates were achieved without accelerating inflation, except
for four years of double-digit inflation. There was no trade-off between
growth and price stability during this period. It is possible, therefore, to
grow without sacrificing price stability in the early stages of development.

The terms of trade were also favorable in 1973 when the first global oil
shock struck. During this period there was no single year that the economy
suffered from negative growth. In other words, the economy maintained
positive growth, albeit experiencing a slowdown during the shocks.

Figure 12.3 illustrates that growth was driven by investment. The share
of investment of GDP increased rapidly from below 15 per cent in 1960 to
25 per cent in 1980. Although imports rose sharply during the oil shocks,
both investment and imports were highly correlated. A large portion of
imports was capital goods. Imported capital goods contributed to productivity improvement in the manufacturing sector, which in turn gave rise to
competitiveness and enhanced export capacity.

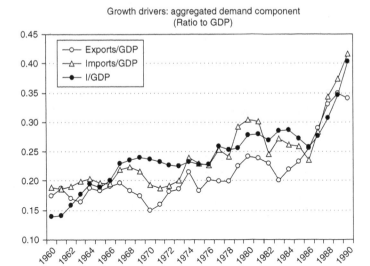

Note: GDP = gross domestic product.

Source: National Economic and Social Development Board (NESDB).

Figure 12.3   Investment as an engine of growth

As the consumption share of the GDP declined between 1960 and 1990, the impact of an increase in domestic demand on output growth was weakened. Fiscal policy would not be as powerful a force as in the early stages of development. Rising income levels also gave rise to a higher rate of saving. The share of foreign trade (the sum of the value of imports and exports) as a percentage of GDP increased from 35 per cent in 1960 to 75 per cent in 1990 (Figure 12.4). Openness in the trade sector was related to output growth. Exporters were able to exploit economies of scale and they were forced to improve their efficiency in order to compete in the world markets.[1]

In the first 10 years of implementation of Thailand's first economic development plan the trade deficit was insignificant. International trade expanded as the fixed exchange rate provided a conducive environment with no foreign exchange risk. As the trade deficit grew after 1978, the need for an exchange rate adjustment became apparent.

Exchange rate adjustments became more frequent as the trade balance widened. By 1990, the trade deficit deteriorated further as the baht appreciated, despite the existence of a fiscal budget surplus. Thus the widening trade deficit was due mainly to the growing investment–saving gap. The high growth rate did not generate savings high enough to close the

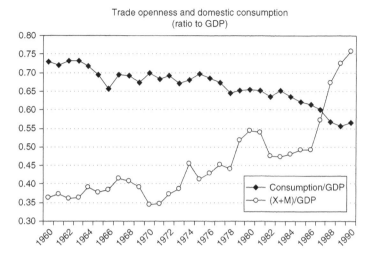

Trade openness and domestic consumption
(ratio to GDP)

Note: GDP = gross domestic product.

Source: National Economic and Social Development Board (NESDB).

Figure 12.4 Trade-biased growth

investment gap, which was financed through foreign borrowing. Despite the trade deficit and real appreciation of the currency, international reserves rose rapidly as the result of capital inflows. Dealing with excessive capital inflows has been a perennial problem for the Bank of Thailand (Figure 12.5).

In May 1981, the baht was devalued 1.1 per cent against the US dollar, followed by another devaluation of 8.7 per cent in July 1981. A major devaluation of 14.9 per cent was undertaken in November 1984, followed by another 1.9 per cent in December 1985. These devaluations were the policy response to the current account deficit tied to the loss of competitiveness caused by the baht appreciation against non-dollar currencies. The number of months of imports covered by international reserves declined steadily since the 1984 devaluation. Since the baht was pegged to the US dollar, the appreciation of the US dollar against other currencies implied that the baht was strengthened, resulting in the loss of competitiveness in non-US markets. These devaluations were undertaken as all other measures failed to correct the current account deficit. The ceiling on the issuance of letters of credit in 1983 and the 18 per cent ceiling on bank lending were imposed to avoid adverse political consequences caused by the large devaluations.

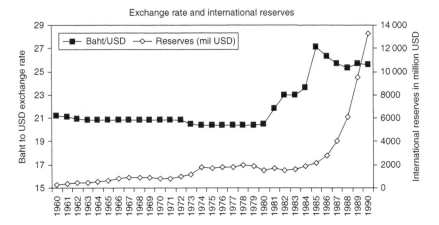

Sources: International Financial Statistics and Bank of Thailand.

Figure 12.5   The virtue of the fixed exchange rate

By using these indirect measures, the Bank of Thailand did not correct the root of the problem, which was the unrealistic exchange rate. Devaluations were quite successful as the level of international reserves increased sharply from $2 billion in 1985 to more than $12 billion in 1990. Both large devaluations did not lead to inflationary pressure. Nevertheless, the currency-basket exchange rate system in Thailand continued to provide the stability of the baht–dollar exchange rate, as the weight of the US dollar in the basket was more than two-thirds and had been rising over time. This practice led to the unsustainable current account deficit in the 1990s.

Export-biased growth tends to worsen a growing country's terms of trade. While export-biased growth patterns occur in developing countries, developed countries experience import-biased growth. There is a possibility that the terms of trade decline so much that the country is worse off than if they had not grown at all – thus immiserizing growth (Bhagwati 1958). This notion is not consistent with the case of Thailand (see Figure 12.6). One of the reasons is that Thailand's structure of exports has gradually changed from the export of primary commodities such as rice, rubber, teak, and tin to the export of manufactured products. Even if the terms of trade were unfavorable to agriculture, Thailand did not suffer much from deteriorating terms of trade between agriculture and manufactured products.

The terms of trade deteriorated marginally in the 1970s because when oil prices rose, export commodities such as rubber also fetched higher prices (see Figure 12.7). The first oil shock in 1973–74 was compensated by higher commodities prices. As a result, Thailand was not affected very

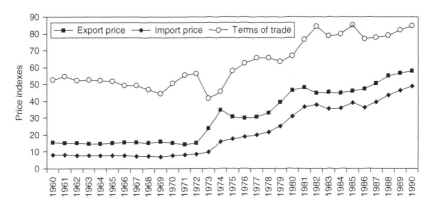

Source: Bank of Thailand.

Figure 12.6   Terms of trade the oil shocks

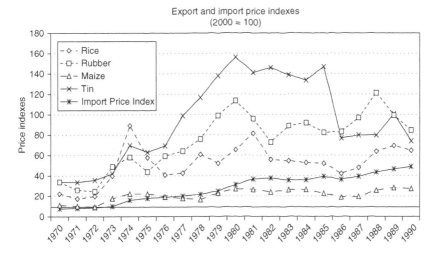

Source: Bank of Thailand.

Figure 12.7   Commodity booms

much by the oil shocks. In fact, the country experienced increases in export
prices of primary commodities between 1974 and 1990. During this period,
the importance of agricultural exports had declined, while manufacturing
exports became more dominant. The shift in the export structure protected
Thailand from the adverse effects of the declining terms of trade in agricultural commodities.

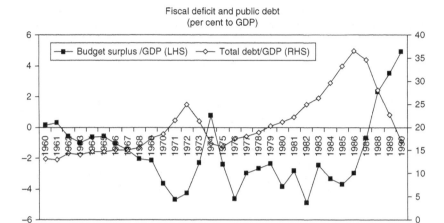

Fiscal deficit and public debt
(per cent to GDP)

Note: GDP = gross domestic product.

Source: Bank of Thailand.

Figure 12.8   Fiscal sustainability

The conservative fiscal policy of the Thai government in the early
stages of development is shown in Figure 12.8. The government adhered
to a balanced budget principle during the regime of the General Thamon
Kittikachorn administration (1964–74). The size of the budget deficit
was larger in the early 1970s, but the deficit turned into surplus in 1974
because of the increasing trade tax revenues. During the administration
of Prime Minister M.R. Kukrit Pramoj in 1975–76 the budget deficit
started growing due to his populist policies that injected money into
rural villages. The budget deficit was expanding during the administration of General Prem Tinsulanonda, which began in 1980. By 1989,
the strong growth of the Thai economy generated tax revenues and the
country experienced a substantial surplus budget, enabling the government to undertake a trade liberalization program through tariff
reduction.

Public debt is a mirror image of fiscal position. Figure 12.8 shows that
public debt increased gradually in the early 1960s, but the trend reversed
as the budget deficit was curtailed. That reversal was observed again when
the budget deficit grew and the share of public debt started climbing from
15 per cent of GDP in 1975 to more than 35 per cent in 1986. The ability
to cut the budget deficit led to a sharp decline in the ratio of debt to GDP
as a result of the turnaround in the fiscal position.

The fiscal discipline of the Thai government contributed to price stability. The budget deficit was not financed by printing money or borrowing from the Bank of Thailand. As debt declined, the government did not have a large burden of public debt to service and thus had sufficient capital spending for infrastructure development.

The stable long-term growth of the Thai economy was characterized by an average annual growth rate of 7 per cent between 1961 and 1990. The process of financial deepening led to price stability and strong economic growth. There are long-run relationships among real output, money supply, and bank credit. Trade openness led to rapid growth and transformed the output structure of the Thai economy. During this period, the Thai economy experienced two oil price shocks, causing the inflation rate to rise to double digits. Nevertheless, the economy regained price stability within a year. The problem with the current account deficit was dealt with by major currency devaluations in 1981 and 1984. This was a major policy change. Nevertheless, the benefits from exchange rate stability were considered greater than the associated costs. After adopting a basket-of-currencies system, the baht gradually returned to a fixed exchange rate system, in which the US dollar in the basket of currencies had gained more weight over the years. This practice paved the way for complications that became apparent in the following decade.

We can conclude that the principal drivers of growth were largely orthodox in the sense that the high growth rate was achieved with price stability and a sustainable current account deficit. The success of early development in Thailand can be attributed to prudent macroeconomic policy, an increasing degree of openness, the absence of political upheaval, and a predictable policy regime.

RESPONSES TO CRISES

The major deviation from the long-term trend in the Thai economy can be attributed to the premature liberalization of the capital account. The expansion of bank credit through massive inflows of cheap capital from abroad led to excessive and unsustainable growth. After the burst of the bubble, output contraction and exchange rate depreciation brought about the return to a stable growth path. The internal shock caused by the military coup in 2006 exacerbated by the global recession in 2007–09, once again pushed output growth below the long-term trend.

Economic literature on the effects of institutions on growth points to the relationship between sustained growth episodes on one hand and distributional conflict and weak domestic institutions that cannot handle

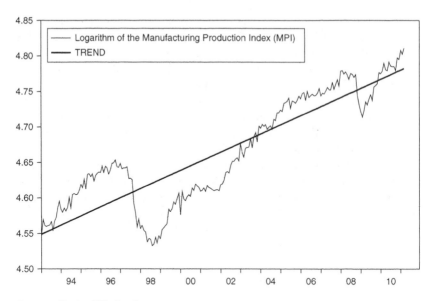

Source:　Bank of Thailand.

Figure 12.9　Actual and potential output (manufacturing output index)

shocks on the other hand (Berg and Sachs 1998; Rodrik et al. 2004). Poor institutions breed economic and political problems that make countries more crisis prone and growth more volatile.

To visualize how the Thai economy underwent upturns and downturns during periods of internal and external shocks, a stable output path is obtained by the Hodrick–Prescott (HP) filter. The data in Figure 12.9 are the monthly manufacturing production indexes from January 1993 to March 2011. By removing cyclical movements, we can observe the long-term trend of output in Thailand. This output path represents the trend of the total output of the country, with the share of agriculture in GDP at around 10 per cent and the manufacturing index covering agro-based industry. In addition, output from the service sector is highly correlated to the HP trend of manufacturing output. The stable output path is derived from the exponential growth rate of the monthly manufacturing production index.

The boom in the early 1990s can be attributed to the openness to trade and capital flows. Hausmann et al. (2005) argue that currency depreciation and political regime changes seem to be correlated with growth accelerations. Indeed, the return to democracy in the 1990s brought about a political environment that removed uncertainty about policy changes.

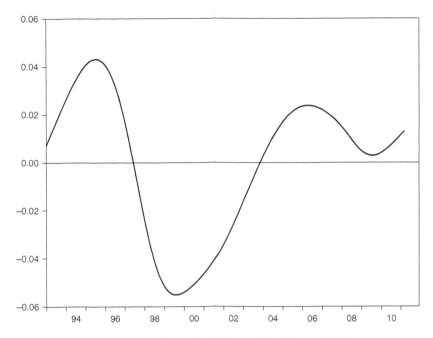

Note: Standardized deviation of actual level of output from its trend level.

Source: Calculation based on data in Figure 12.9.

Figure 12.10 *Climbing hills and falling off cliffs*

The period between growth acceleration and deceleration can be seen in Figure 12.10. The breakdown of growth duration was associated with an overvaluation of the exchange rate and the AFC. It took more than five years to return to the pre-shock growth path. As the economy was climbing the hill of rapid recovery, it was further shocked by internal conflict and political turmoil that triggered the deceleration of growth. Business sentiment and consumer confidence eroded because of risks and uncertainties.

Rodrik (1999) attributed the growth collapse to external shocks and social conflict. While internal shocks are homegrown, Thailand is vulnerable to external shocks due to a production and export structure that is related to openness. Global financial shocks and subsequent global economic recession in 2007 further dampened the growth rate. The growth collapse episode in Thailand is consistent with the observation that good political institutions help prolong growth spells. Growth decelerations are found to be associated with macroeconomic instability, conflict, and export collapses (Hausmann et al. 2006). The coup in September 2006 derailed the growth process in Thailand, confirming the hypothesis that growth is affected by democracy. Quality of institutions does affect economic performance.

The deviation from the steady growth path is associated with booms and busts in Thailand. We must understand how the booms started and how they collapsed. What factors shorten the growth periods? Development policy must minimize the amplitude of the deviation from the long-term growth path. In addition, it must sustain growth. Pritchett (2000) argued that the overriding characteristic of the development process of developing countries is the lack of persistence. The output path of developing countries is similar to mountains, cliffs, and plains rather than the steady "hills" observed in industrial countries. Berg et al. (2008) provide evidence that growth duration is positively related to the equality of income distribution, democratic institutions, and export orientation. Thailand has an elastic export supply of manufactured goods, openness to foreign direct investment (FDI) in manufactured goods, and macroeconomic stability. But problems remain with exchange rate undervaluation and democratic institutional reform.

Trade reform has been undertaken since the early 1970s by slowly dismantling tariff walls that protect domestic industries. Customs revenue as a percentage of the total value of imports declined to only 3 per cent by 2003. The surge in imports enhances revenue collections, although tariff rates have been reduced regularly in line with trade liberalization and the move to establish free trade areas with the member countries of the Association of Southeast Asian Nations (ASEAN). While trade integration has allowed the country to grow rapidly through the benefit of world trade expansion, it has created risk exposure through export dependency. The GER that began in 2007 did not hit Thai exports until 2009 (see Figure 12.11). The global food crisis in 2008 sustained high export growth because of favorable terms of trade in primary commodities. But when oil prices declined and food prices dropped sharply, along with a sharp fall in world trade in 2009, Thailand's exports took a severe hit in the global recession. Similarly, the Stock Exchange of Thailand (SET) Index fell precipitously below 400 points in 2009.

The sharp fall in exports prior to the 1997 AFC paled in comparison to the fall during the GER. It suggests that the substitution effect of the adverse impact of the exchange rate misalignment was not as strong as the output effect from the world recession. Exports declined by 6.7 per cent in 1998 when output contracted by 10.5 per cent (see Table 12.1). The recovery in the exports was rapid because the rest of the world was not in recession. The 32 per cent baht depreciation in 1998 helped stimulate exports by 7.4 per cent in 1999 and 19.5 per cent in 2000.

Source: Bank of Thailand.

Figure 12.11 Impact of the global economic crisis

Output increased by 4.4 per cent in 1999 and 4.8 per cent in 2000. It should be obvious from Table 12.1 that the major causes of output contraction were the decline in domestic demand. Investment fell by 22 per cent in 1997 and 51 per cent in 1998, ending the period of excessive boom in the property sector. Likewise, household consumption fell by 11.5 per cent at the trough of the recession in 1998. The major cause of the deep recession was the fall in domestic demand and not the export shortfall. Sustained recovery requires resumption of domestic demand growth from both investment and exports. Fiscal deficits occurred from 1997 to 2000. The size of the deficits ranged from 1.9 per cent to 2.8 per cent of GDP, reflecting an automatic fiscal stabilizer rather than fiscal stimulus. Inflation remained below 2 per cent during the recovery period, despite the currency depreciation. Core inflation dropped from 7 per cent in 1998 to 1.8 per cent in 1999 and 0.7 per cent in 2000. Thus the recovery trajectory in the aftermath of the 1997 currency crisis was smooth, posing no threat to price stability. The degree of openness had continued rising without disruption from the pre-crisis level of 69 per cent of GDP in 1996 to 106 per cent in 2000. The outward-oriented development strategy has been maintained.

GDP growth in 2006 and 2007 averaged 5 per cent, which was below the growth path from 1960 to 1990. The degree of openness continued rising from 123 per cent in 2006 to 144 per cent in 2010, with a temporary fall

Table 12.1   Recovery trajectories

	1996	1997	1998	1999	2000	2006	2007	2008	2009	2010
Real GDP growth	5.8	-1.4	-10.5	4.4	4.8	5.1	5.0	2.5	-2.3	7.8
Inflation (headline)	5.9	5.6	8.0	0.3	1.6	4.7	2.3	5.5	-0.9	3.3
Inflation core	5.1	4.6	7.1	1.8	0.7	2.3	1.1	2.4	0.3	1.0
Exchange rate (baht/US$)	25.3	31.4	41.4	37.8	40.2	37.93	34.56	33.36	34.34	31.87
% change	1.7	23.8	31.9	-8.5	6.1	-5.8	-8.9	-3.5	2.9	-7.2
Degree of openness (X+M) %GDP	69.0	78.2	83.6	85.1	106.3	123.2	117.4	128.9	107.1	144.1
Current account (%GDP)	-7.9	-2.0	12.7	10.2	7.6	1.1	5.7	0.6	8.2	5.5
Fiscal cash balance (%GDP)	2.3	-1.9	-2.4	-2.8	-2.4	0.1	-1.1	-0.3	-4.5	-2.0
Export growth (%)	-1.9	3.8	-6.7	7.4	19.5	16.9	18.2	15.8	-13.9	28.4
Investment (%)	5.2	-21.9	-50.9	8.5	11.3	-3.6	1.0	8.1	-25.2	–
Consumption (%)	5.8	-1.4	-11.5	4.3	5.2	3.2	1.8	2.9	-1.1	–

Note: GDP = gross domestic product.

Source: Bank of Thailand.

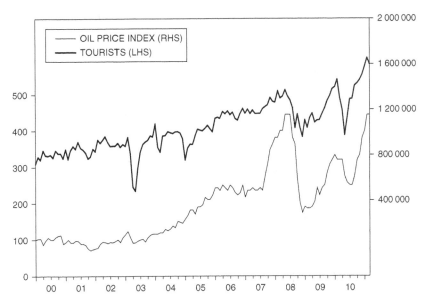

Note: RHS = right-hand scale; LHS = left-hand scale.

Source: Bank of Thailand.

Figure 12.12 External shocks, January 2000–March 2011

to 107 per cent of GDP in 2009, when GDP registered a negative growth rate of 2.3 per cent. Exports fell by 13.9 per cent in 2009, which was twice the percentage fall of exports in 1998. But output growth did not fall as much simply because the fall in investment was only 25 per cent compared to the 50 per cent fall in 1998 (Table 12.1). Consumption expenditures declined marginally by 1.1 per cent in 2009. The relatively small decline in domestic demand boded well for a mild recession in 2009. It was not the fall in exports that caused severe recession, but rather the contraction of aggregate demand. The contractionary impact on output of the export collapse was mitigated by the reduction of imported intermediate goods required to produce manufactured exports. The pattern of recovery in 2010 was consistent with the recovery in 1999. This time the sharp rebound was due to three growth drivers: exports, consumption, and investment. Fiscal stimulus, measured at 4.6 per cent of the public deficit, was much higher than during the AFC. With a low debt–GDP ratio, ample fiscal space permitted the government to stimulate domestic demand through stimulus packages. Headline inflation jumped from −0.9 per cent to 3.3 per cent in 2010. There will be an impact on price stability in the medium term, when some subsidies and price controls are phased out.[2] It is obvious that consumer price indexes increased due to energy and food prices. Since oil prices impact food prices through transportation costs, the Thai economy continues to be subject to external shocks. The global food crisis and a sharp rise in the oil prices in 2008 brought headline inflation to 5.5 per cent.

Figure 12.12 illustrates that both demand and supply side external shocks have become more common in terms of the volatility of the number of foreign tourists and oil prices. The political violence and unexpected events, such as the Thai tsunami and pandemic influenza, make the service sector vulnerable to a "constant shock syndrome." Thus relying on a domestic-demand led recovery is crucial in maintaining stable growth. The strong rebound of both exports and domestic demand was a key ingredient of the recovery in 2010. Despite the appreciation of the baht, exports earnings increased due to strong economic growth in Asia. Whether an export-led recovery is stronger than domestic-led growth is an issue that must be determined empirically.

OVERINVESTMENT AND UNDERINVESTMENT EPISODES

The growth of per capita income depends on physical capital deepening, human capital accumulation, and productivity growth. Other factors include trade integration and the quality of institutions.

Per capita income in Thailand has increased rapidly due to both capital accumulation between 1950 and 1990 and the fact that the steady increase

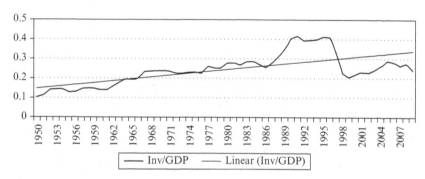

Note: GDP = gross domestic product.

Source: International Financial Statistics.

Figure 12.13   Overinvestment and underinvestment

in output was devoted to investment goods (Figure 12.13). The capital inflows in the early 1990s resulted in the investment boom, which was unsustainable. The collapse of investment after the 1997 AFC was captured by the considerable fall in the investment–output ratio. Financing investment was not a problem as interest rates were trending downward and there was plenty of excess liquidity in the banking system. There was a revival of investment, but it was not sustainable as business sentiment was affected by political uncertainty even before the Thaksin government was overthrown by a coup in 2006. The rising conflict within the nation dampened investor expectations of profitability.

The investment–output ratio increased steadily from 1950 to 1990. After capital account liberalization in the early 1990s, a surge in capital flows led to excessive credit expansion. Although investment increased to 40 per cent of GDP, the quality of investment was poor. Capital formation concentrated in the non-traded sector, which led to the erosion of international competitiveness. In 1997 the AFC reversed the trend of the investment–output ratio. The recovery in the early 2000s was temporary and did not climb back to the long-term trend of the previous three decades (Figure 12.14). The return to the steady state growth path was interrupted by the military coup in 2006. The Thai economy experienced a swing of investment from overinvestment to underinvestment, which has had a serious impact on productivity growth in the long run.

The erosion of business confidence was intensified by unstable governments, which disrupted public infrastructure investment that could have compensated for and encouraged private investment. As the economy slowed down, the virtuous cycle effect between growth and investment that the country enjoyed in the early stages of development disappeared.

During the time of high growth, the Thai government ran budget surpluses. Tax revenue increased faster than output growth. When the budget

Table 12.2   Investment–saving gap

	I/GDP	S/GDP	(I-S)/S	Credit growth	Prime rate
1980–96	34.3	29.0	19.3	21.1	14.1
1997	33.7	33.1	1.9	30.5	15.3
1998	20.4	31.8	–35.7	–7.9	11.8
1999–2006	25.4	29.3	–13.1	–0.2	7.0
2007–09	25.6	30.7	–16.7	6.3	6.6

Notes: GDP = gross domestic product; S = savings.

Source: National Economic and Development Board and Bank of Thailand.

deficit or surplus is small, the current account deficit is largely determined by the investment–savings gap. Investment that exceeds domestic savings must be financed from foreign sources, which adds to the trade deficit. Feldstein and Horioka (1980) suggested that the degree of capital mobility can be measured by examining the responsiveness of investment to changes in domestic savings. If capital mobility is high, the investment–GDP ratio should not be too dependent on the domestic saving rate. On the other hand, if capital mobility is low, investment must be subject to the availability of domestic savings.[3]

Table 12.2 shows investment and savings ratios in three episodes. During the economic boom from 1980 to 1996, investment on average was 19.3 per cent above savings. During the slump (1999–2006) investment fell below savings by 13.1 per cent. Growth and the investment–saving gap are intricately related. Causation can run both ways. The role of financial intermediaries is important in channeling household savings to investors via bank credit expansion.

On the average, during the boom period, credit grew by 21.1 per cent while the prime lending rate was 14.1 per cent. In 1997, bank credit grew by 30.5 per cent at the prime rate of 15.3 per cent. Both demonstrate the positive relationship between credit and the lending rate. Although the demand for credit is negatively related to the cost of borrowing, the rising cost of borrowing was not able to offset the rising demand for credit generated by rapid output growth and expected high rates of return from investment. In 1998 investment collapsed together with a credit contraction of 7.9 per cent. The prime lending rate declined from 15.3 per cent in 1997 to 11.7 per cent in 1998. For the first time, investment dropped below savings by almost 36 per cent. The current account went from deficit to surplus. Output adjustments, therefore, are very powerful but costly in terms of output losses.

As Thailand entered a period of recovery from 1999 to 2006, investment was 13 per cent below savings. This is the episode when credit growth was –0.2 per cent on average, while the prime rate was 7 per cent. Both the interest rate and the rate of credit expansion are pro-cyclical.

Since the average propensity to consume falls as income rises, the savings rate must be positively related to income growth rate. At the same time, the investment–income ratio should rise as growth accelerates, due to the accelerator impact of output changes on income. Figure 12.14 illustrates that the investment–savings gap became negative after the AFC and remained in negative territory until 2005. Nevertheless, as investment contracted in 2006 and 2007, the investment–saving gap was pulled down to the negative zone once again. Consequently, the current account surplus widened to 7.2 per cent of GDP, while the baht appreciated 8.8 per

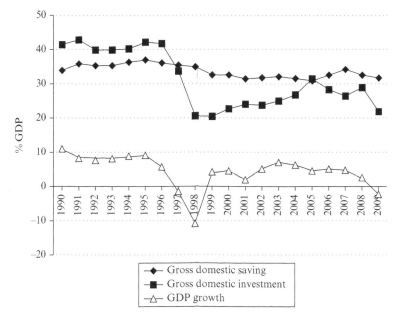

Source: National Economic and Development Board.

Figure 12.14   Investment-saving gap and growth

cent against the US dollar. The impact of the exchange rate adjustment is diminished by the fact that other Asian currencies also appreciated against the dollar.

Current account positions and GDP growth are related as growth has an indirect impact on the current account via investment–savings channels.[4] Whether growth can lead to a current account deficit or surplus depends on the net effect of growth on saving and investment. If domestic saving responds more to output growth than investment responds to growth, economic booms can lead to a current account surplus. If they respond less, it can lead to a current account deficit. The impact of growth on the current account is an empirical issue.

As Figure 12.14 illustrates, the excess of investment over savings was wiped out in 1997, but the severity of the recession was so intense that investment fell below savings by 37 per cent. Subsequently, the Thai economy has plunged into a downturn cycle with a low rate of capital formation. The saving rate gradually declined as GDP growth decelerated. Thailand experienced a current account surplus as investment remained consistently below saving. The problem during this slow growth episode

K/L (*1000 Bht/person)

Note: Bht = Thai baht.

Source: National Economic and Development Board.

Figure 12.15   Capital–labor ratios in various sectors

was excessive savings over domestic investment. Capital accumulation requires continuity and a slow buildup period. The investment rate began to pick up gradually between 2000 and 2005. Banks resumed lending and the investment gap became positive for a brief period in 2005. Then the investment rate began to fall again due to internal conflicts and political upheaval. The investment climate must be favorable for investors if capital formation is going to take place.

The rising capital–labor ratio in the manufacturing sector can be observed in Figure 12.15. The higher the capital–labor ratio is, the higher is labor productivity. It is evident that productivity growth in the agricultural sector is far below that of the manufacturing and service sectors. The output–labor ratio indicates that different rates of capital formation led to large differences in labor productivity in each sector.

The quality of investment can be gauged from the types of capital formation. It is clear that the excessive investment before the AFC was driven mainly by construction. Figure 12.16 shows the long-term decline in construction, while capital formation through equipment increased significantly in terms of its share in total investment, reaching 50 per cent in 2007. The share of imported capital goods remained stable below 20 per cent of total investment. An undervalued exchange rate can retard capital formation by discouraging the importation of capital goods.

The capital–labor ratio determines productivity of labor. Because the capital–labor ratio (K/L) in the manufacturing sector was highest among

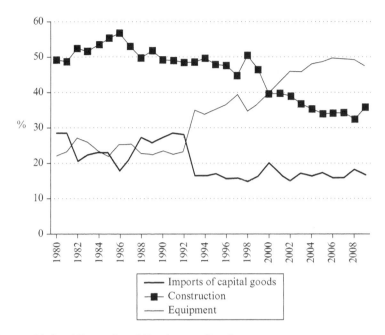

Source: National Economic and Development Board.

Figure 12.16   Distribution of capital formation

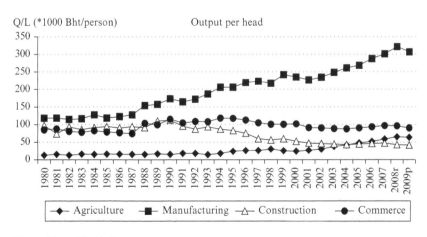

Note: Bht = Thai baht.

Source: National Economic and Development Board.

Figure 12.17   Productivity of labor

all sectors, productivity measured by output per head in this sector was therefore the highest (Figure 12.17). The productivity of the agriculture sector had been stagnant since 1980, but it rose rapidly in the early 2000s. Labor productivity in the construction sector declined sharply after the AFC. Overinvestment in the construction sector led to a property glut and a bust in the property sector. Overinvestment was related to the excessive quantity of building stock, which indicates the poor quality of investment during the boom years.

Quality investment requires more balanced capital formation. It requires narrowing productivity gaps; otherwise the country will have problems with unbalanced growth and income inequality. Productivity was low in the agricultural sector because of the unattractive rate of return and the protection of the sector through tariff walls and the restriction on FDI. The sectors that lag behind in productivity improvement have to pay higher wage rates because the flexibility of labor markets permits labor to move and seek higher wage rates in sectors that have rising productivity. Consequently, lagging productivity sectors come under the pressure of rising wage rates of the overall economy.

The continued increase in labor productivity in manufacturing was in stark contrast with the productivity in agriculture. Productivity in the non-traded sector was also stagnant due to the lack of capital investment. The quality of growth therefore depends on more balanced growth of productivity in all sectors. The low productivity in the agricultural sector makes it necessary for the majority of the labor force to remain in the agricultural sector. It is imperative that public infrastructure investment in rural areas be accelerated to boost farm productivity. Furthermore,

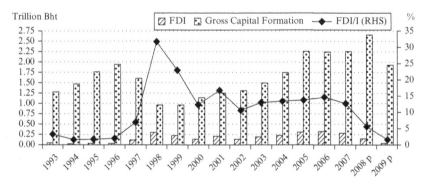

Source: National Economic and Development Board.

Figure 12.18   Foreign direct investment (FDI) and gross capital formation

productivity differentials are related to poverty and income inequality between urban and rural sectors. As such, public spending can enhance long-term growth and reduce regional income inequality.

The role of FDI also declined since the AFC. The sharp rise in the share of FDI in total investment can be attributed to an increase in the mergers and acquisitions of Thai banks that could have failed without foreign capital injection, as well as a large decline in total domestic investment (Figure 12.18). The declining trend of FDI in Thailand can be attributed to many factors: the increasing attractiveness of both giant economies and transitional economies in the region; the strength of the baht; rising real wage rates; political uncertainties; inconsistent policy regarding the openness of the capital market; and inefficient legal infrastructure.

MACROECONOMIC MANAGEMENT

The government responded to the economic shocks with expansionary fiscal and monetary policies. In 2006, before the GER, the government actually ran a budget surplus. The amount of public debt was well below

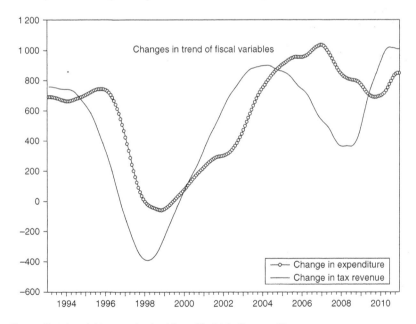

Note: Trend variables are obtained from Hodrick–Prescott filter.

Figure 12.19   Automatic fiscal stabilizers

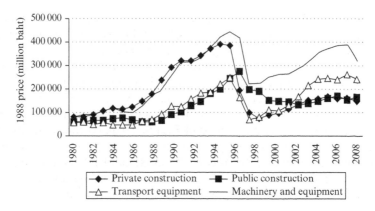

Source: National Economic and Social Development Board (NESDB).

Figure 12.20   Investment components

40 per cent, giving plenty of fiscal space to stimulate the economy to offset the shortfall in exports.

Because tax revenue is highly elastic with respect to output – while public spending is not – the fiscal deficit is partly explained by the reduction of tax revenue when GDP contracted. Discretionary fiscal policy was employed but largely on current expenditures rather than capital expenditures.

Figure 12.19 demonstrates the flexibility of Thailand's fiscal policy. The government was able to curtail expenditures after experiencing revenue shortfalls during the recessions in 1998 and 2008. On the other hand, fiscal spending increased when the economic recovery generated sufficient revenues. Automatic fiscal stabilizers and conservative budgetary rules provide fiscal soundness and enable the government to maintain price stability.

In 2009, investment declined by 25 per cent as a result of a reduction in expenditures for machinery and transport equipment (Figure 12.20). Public and private construction did not compensate for the fall in demand for investment goods. Because of the lag effect of the expansionary policy, the cut in interest rates in 2007 did not show the expansionary impact on investment until 2010. Figure 12.20 clearly shows that public investment was not counter-cyclical. Administrations no longer in power were unable to push forward the stimulus fiscal spending. Weak institutions impaired timely responses to shocks.

Unlike fiscal policy, the monetary policy instrument can be employed immediately by the central bank. However, there is a limitation to

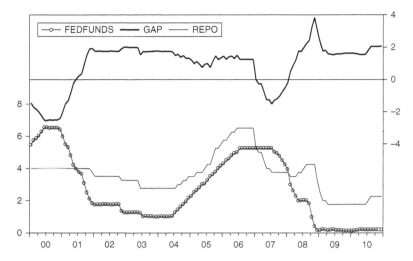

Source: International Monetary Fund, International Financial Statistics.

Figure 12.21   Monetary policy response

independent monetary policy. This is not due to the independence of the central bank, but rather the independence of monetary policy instruments. In Thailand, where capital mobility is high, the Bank of Thailand cannot change its key policy rate without considering the impact of capital flows on the exchange rate. When the gap between the repo rate and the federal funds rate grows larger, capital inflows cause the baht to appreciate against the US dollar. In general the gap is roughly 2 percentage points (Figure 12.21). Deviation from the norm would likely put pressure on the value of the baht. The Bank of Thailand has adjusted its key policy rate upward to fight inflation. There is a policy dilemma, however, since this encourages greater capital inflow just as the US dollar is depreciating.

The huge capital inflows and the accumulation of international reserves of $140 billion in 2010 indicates that there has been enormous intervention in the foreign exchange market to prevent the baht from appreciating. The main concern is fear that the strong baht might thwart exports, thereby reducing the growth rate.

One of the reasons why the increased flows have not generated upward pressure on price levels and asset price bubbles was the rather stable credit multiplier (Figure 12.22). Thus with growing monetary base, bank credit did not expand fast enough to generate asset bubbles. In fact the credit multiplier actually declined between 2000 and 2004 and has remained rather stable since then.

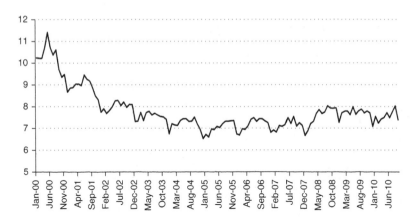

Source: Bank of Thailand.

Note: Ratio of bank credit to monetary base.

Figure 12.22   Credit multiplier

The threat of asset price bubbles was still low in 2010. However, these assets can serve as inflation hedges. Therefore rising inflation in 2010 led to the increase in demand for property. Speculative behavior cannot be ignored if bank credit growth accelerates to accommodate economic growth. Quantitative easing of the US Federal Reserve Board to stimulate the US economy lowered interest rates and pushed capital outflows to developing countries. Asset price bubbles were natural consequences of such measures. Capital inflows would lead to currency appreciation that may have an adverse impact on exchange rate movements.

EXCHANGE RATE REGIMES

The switch from a fixed regime to a managed float regime is illustrated in Figure 12.23. The value of the baht was allowed to move in a narrow band, providing time for the private sector to adjust to foreign exchange volatility. The Bank of Thailand did not fight the market. It prefers a smooth movement of the exchange rate. To neutralize the impact of growing money supply, it may try to sterilize capital inflow. However, the measures can be ineffective if the Bank of Thailand has to issue bonds with high interest rates to attract buyers. Sterilization is costly since its interest cost can outweigh the gain from sterilization.

As Table 12.3 indicates, the Bank of Thailand intervened less when the

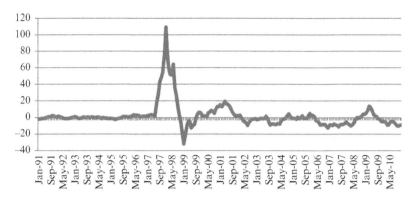

Source: Bank of Thailand.

Figure 12.23   *Baht–dollar exchange rate (% change yoy) January 1991–December 2010*

Table 12.3   *Exchange rate stability and intervention (average percentage change)*

	January 1991–June 1997	June 1997– December 1999	2000–10
Appreciation	−1.12	−11.93	−5.94
Depreciation	1.21	40.87	5.90
Overall	0.05	14.47	−0.02

Source: Calculation based on data from the Bank of Thailand.

baht depreciated and more when the baht appreciated. From January 1991 to June 1997, the baht moved in a range that depreciated against the US dollar by as much as 1.21 per cent and appreciated against the US dollar by as much as 1.12 per cent. As a result the baht maintained par with the US dollar during the period of the fixed exchange rate system. From June 1997 to December 1999, the baht depreciated 40.9 per cent on average, as compared with the 11.9 per cent rate of appreciation, on a monthly basis.

From 2000 to 2010, the average rate of appreciation was 5.94 per cent, while depreciation was 5.9 per cent. Indeed, Table 12.3 demonstrates that the Bank of Thailand intervenes regularly to maintain baht stability, despite the trend of US dollar depreciation against major currencies. Thus the behavior of the Bank of Thailand remained unchanged before and after the AFC.

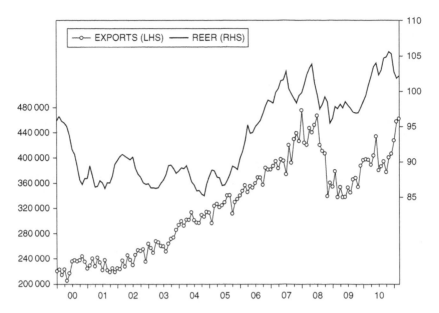

Notes: Exports in million baht, left-hand scale (LHS); Index of Real Effective Exchange Rate (REER), right-hand scale (RHS).

Source: Bank of Thailand.

Figure 12.24 Exports and real effective exchange rate

Figure 12.24 illustrates that exports continued their rising trend despite the appreciation of the real effective exchange rate between 2005 and the first half of 2008. The GER led to a steep decline in exports in the last quarter of 2008, which continued into 2009 before rebounding in 2010 as the global economy began to recover. During this period the real effective exchange rate also depreciated, partly as a result of price deflation and economic contraction in 2009. When the Thai economy experienced a V-shaped recovery in 2010, as a result of the revival of exports and consumption demand, inflation started to pick up and led to the appreciation of the real exchange rate. Since 2004, exports and the real effective exchange rate have been positively correlated. Hence the strength of the baht does not necessarily imply poor export performance.

Exports in the first quarter of 2011 grew by 27 per cent year on year because of high agricultural prices (rice and rubber) and strong export demand. Electronics and electrical appliances grew by 26 per cent and 17.7 per cent, respectively. Exports grew more than 20 per cent in the first quarter in all major markets, especially exports to Japan, which grew

32.3 per cent. Exports to the European Union increased by 25.8 per cent, to the People's Republic of China by 24.9 per cent, to the United States 21.3 per cent, and to five original members of ASEAN by 22.3 per cent. The strength of the baht in 2011 did not hurt Thai exports.

During the period of continued appreciation of the baht, the Bank of Thailand was under pressure to resist baht appreciation in order to protect exporters. It intervened less in the forward market and thus allowed the baht to appreciate against the US dollar to some extent. The Bank of Thailand has gradually raised its policy interest rate to curb inflationary pressure. There is a concern that the growing interest rate differential between the key policy rate and the federal funds rate would induce more capital inflows and further strengthen the baht.

In October 2010, the government revoked the 15 per cent withholding exemption on interest and capital gains earned by foreign investors. The policy was intended to prevent baht speculation as there was a surge in capital flows in the bond market. A tax instrument was employed to slow down the baht appreciation. But once again this policy instrument failed to reduce capital inflows.

A more flexible exchange rate system can insulate the economy from shocks originating in the goods market. The adverse impact of a fall in export demand can be partially offset by exchange rate depreciation. An oil price shock that causes stagflation and improves the current account can be offset by exchange rate appreciation. But it would be impossible for a flexible exchange rate system to cushion the financial shocks originating in the money market. Nor can the interest rate policy be used to target the value of the baht. Foreign exchange market intervention by the Bank of Thailand intensified as the baht appreciated against the US dollar from 2006 to 2009. Intervention in foreign exchange markets is costly and ineffective because the baht–dollar exchange rate is determined by movements of the US dollar against other currencies, as well as the short-term capital flows into the stock market. Accompanying sterilization is also costly and ineffective in the long run. When exchange rate adjustments are not allowed to work properly to equilibrate current account disequilibrium, adjustments have to take place through output growth.

FINANCING DEVELOPMENT AND GROWTH STRATEGY

Building an efficient and robust financial sector is essential to long-term economic development, in particular in the early stages of development when investors are constrained by limited financial resources. Investors in a bank-based economy such as Thailand can further relax their financial constraints through relying on capital inflows.

The Thai financial sector was vulnerable and weak in the late 1990s. With abundant capital funds, capital control relaxation in the early 1990s brought about premature capital liberalization because of the lack of prudential regulation of financial institutions. The large capital inflows that quickly ensued led to subsequent financial turmoil. Nevertheless, the Thai financial sector since then has emerged from the AFC and has become stronger and more resilient thanks to foreign capital injection, good governance, and strengthened financial rules. The rapid economic recovery provided an opportunity for banks to expand their credit and enjoy the benefit of rising interest rates. In addition, strong performance of the corporate sector enabled banks to reduce nonperforming loans further.

The large interest margin between lending and deposit rates bodes well for the monopoly rent of commercial banks, which also implies profitability and a high degree of solvency. Thai financial institutions and their regulators cannot resist the global trend of foreign penetration. By opening up the financial sector to foreign participation, the sector has become more efficient, reaping the benefit from competition and technology adaptation. With foreign capital injection, the monetary authorities can maintain system solvency while lessening the burden of financial bailouts.

Since the AFC, the Thai economy has been closely integrated with the world economy through international trade and capital flows. As such, it cannot completely shield itself from external shocks. The GER of 2007–09 led to an export collapse and output contraction in 2009. The crash of many global financial institutions and stock markets in 2008 had a negative impact on the Thai stock market. However, the adverse consequences for the Thai banking sector were minimal. Thai banks were able to profit during those difficult times. Most of them did not invest in collateralized debt obligations (CDOs) nor focus mainly on property lending. The level of nonperforming loans (NPLs) continued to decline, while banks enhanced capital strength and provided ample loan–loss provisions. The exploitation of economies of scale and scope improved efficiency in their operations. All of these factors are the result of financial reforms undertaken after the AFC. Thai banks were well prepared for the GER as they had learned valuable lessons about taking a conservative approach and obeying stringent rules and regulations.

The percentage of loans for real estate and for the manufacturing sector declined, while the percentage of personal loans increased when consumption started picking up (Figure 12.25). Low interest rates encouraged the purchase of durable consumer goods through consumer credit. The trend would reverse when the demand for loans from the business sector

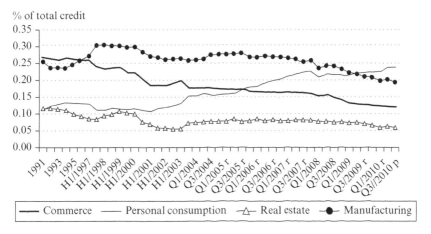

% of total credit

Source: Bank of Thailand.

Figure 12.25   Bank lending by top five sectors

increased in line with the recovery. The share of consumer loans would tend to decline. The consumer credit sector has a high rate of nonperforming loans, which implies that commercial banks will have to increase their loan–loss provision.

In 1998 the Thai economy experienced a severe recession, but it was able to recover within a few years. As noted by Bonin and Huang (2002), countries that had strong financial institutions and undertook more rapid restructuring of their banking systems were more successful in coping with the GER. The Thai banking sector had prepared well for the GER (see Nidhiprabha, 2011). GDP contracted by 2.3 per cent in 2009 as a result of the global recession. The decline in world trade volume in 2009 led to a sharp fall in exports. Moreover, political violence curtailed spending, which dampened business confidence. As the economy slowed down, the demand for loans was sluggish and lowered the quality of bank assets. As a result, risky assets increased, making it necessary for banks to raise capital funds and increase loan–loss provisions. Figure 12.26 illustrates that in Thai banks, both total and Tier 1 capital funds were raised above the requirement of the Bank for International Settlements.

The GER has not had a significant impact on the Thai economy, as its negative impact was limited to a mild recession in 2009. Business sentiment rebounded sharply in 2010 (Figure 12.26), leading to strong recovery in aggregate demand due to enhanced consumer confidence.

Figure 12.27 shows that consumer confidence and investor confidence declined from 2003 to 2008. Following the GER, investors regained their

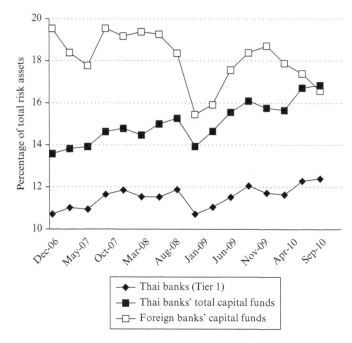

Source: Bank of Thailand.

Figure 12.26 Adequacy of bank capital during global financial crisis

confidence and there has been a sharp recovery in consumption and investment. The two sources of domestic demand, coupled with the export rebound, gave rise to the strong recovery in 2010. During the period when confidence was lower, the government could have spurred the economy through fiscal expansion.

The Thai government had difficulty implementing infrastructure development in the wake of domestic demand shortfall. The government had some fiscal space, but it had difficulty in making a rapid effort to undertake large-scale investment projects. Thus public consumption, such as transfer payments, seems to be the fastest way to increase domestic spending during a time of subdued investment and depressed private consumption. With uncertainties and rumors of military coups, the government employed populist policies and increased defense budgets to maintain its own stability rather than spending money for long-term investments.

The share of current expenditures in total public spending has increased gradually since 1998. The Ministry of Finance has imposed rules of fiscal sustainability, one of which requires that the proportion of capital

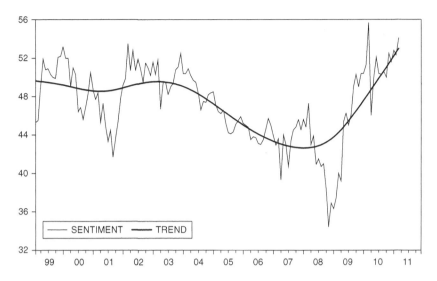

Source: Bank of Thailand.

Figure 12.27 Business Sentiment Index, 1993–2011

expenditures does not fall below 25 per cent of the total budget. It is obvious that this prudential rule was not strictly observed. By 2010, the share of capital expenditures was reduced to a mere 12 per cent.

Public spending on infrastructure can generate a crowding-in effect on private investment because public capital goods are complementary to private capital goods. It is possible that an increase in public investment has a spillover effect through raising the marginal productivity of private capital. Subdued private investment can be related to an insufficient level of public capital stock.

From 1970 to 1986, capital formation in the public sector increased more rapidly than in the private sector. The ratio of public to private capital stock petered out after 1987 (see Figure 12.28). It was easier to cut down capital expenditures than current expenditures. Fiscal stability was restored at the cost of a slowdown in long-term growth. The public capital stock in the transportation and communication sectors, which yields the highest rates of return, declined sharply relative to the private capital stock from 1987 to 1998. The ratio has increased slowly and remained stagnant in the late 2000s, which was in sharp contrast to the high growth in the 1970s and the early 1980s.

Nevertheless, public capital stock in the agricultural sector has continued to rise since 1970. This is consistent with the increasing trend of the

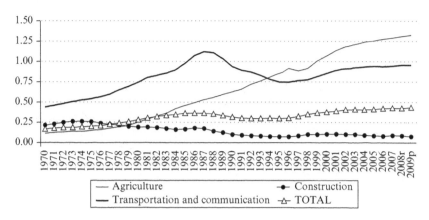

Source: National Economic and Social Development Board (NESDB).

Figure 12.28   Ratio of public to private capital stock, 1970–2009

productivity in the agricultural sector (see Figure 12.17). The agricultural sector achieved higher productivity than the construction sector, in which the share of public capital stock exhibits a long-term decline.

The breakdown of the rule of law after the most recent military coup inflicted considerable costs to the growth process. Fiscal spending has been diverted to defense at the expense of infrastructure development. With lower capital formation, the productivity of private capital stock and long-term growth have been adversely affected. The GER led to fiscal stimulus packages that are very difficult to phase out even after the economy experiences a V-shaped recovery. The temporary social safety net has become permanent government consumption, thereby creating a fiscal problem in the future. The GER in 2008 was an excuse for the incumbent government to implement pump-priming policies prior to the July 2011 general election.

DOMESTIC DEMAND VERSUS EXPORT-LED GROWTH

The contribution of exports to growth may not be the strongest growth driver because exports move together with imports of raw materials over the long run. The structure of Thailand's manufactured exports has shifted toward the importation and exportation of intermediate products along the value chain of fragmented production processes dictated by multinational corporations.

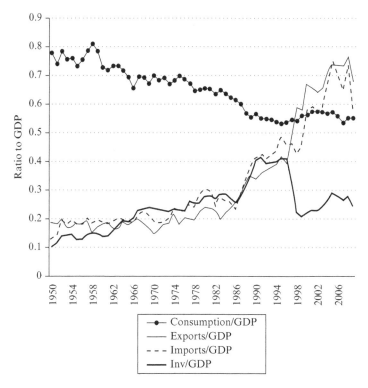

Notes: GDP = gross domestic product; INV = investments.

Source: International Monetary Fund, International Financial Statistics.

Figure 12.29 Domestic-led or export-led growth

Figure 12.29 shows that the shares of exports and imports increased and declined together. A decline in exports may not reduce net aggregate demand as much as the decline in consumption of the same magnitude. With the depressed investment climate, appreciating exchange rate, and pessimistic consumers, government spending was the only option to revive the economy.

To investigate the impact of policy responses to output and private investment, a vector autoregressive model has been employed. It uses monthly data from January 1993 to December 2010 to explore the impact of shocks to output and private investment. The model includes seven variables with the four-month lag length determined by the Akaike Information Criterion (AIC). The AIC variables are the manufacturing production index (OUTPUT), the private investment index (PII),

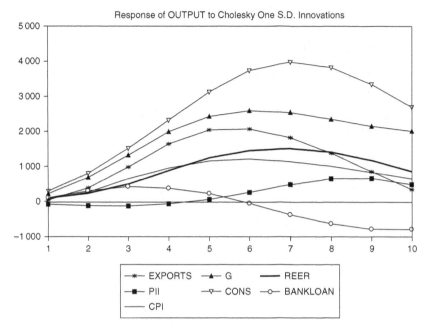

Notes: OUTPUT represents manufacturing output index; SD standard deviation; G
government expenditure; REER real effective exchange rate; PII private investment index;
CONS private consumption expenditure; BANKLOAN commercial banks' lending
volume; CPI Consumer Price Index.

Source: Data are obtained from the impulse response function derived from the
estimation of a Vector Auto Regressive (VAR) Model, based on the estimation of monthly
data from the Bank of Thailand.

Figure 12.30   Output adjustment to various shocks – a VAR model

government spending (G), the consumer price index (CPI), exports
(EXPORTS), consumption (CONS), the real effective exchange rate
(REER), and bank loans (BANKLOAN).

The results from the impulse response function indicate that consumption and public investment can stimulate output growth, with the strongest impact after six months and impact dying off slowly thereafter. As
previously discussed, the expansionary impact of export growth is smaller
than the stimulus in investment and consumption.

An increase in the price level also gives a boost to domestic output.
This can be interpreted as the positive supply response to price increases.
Controlling price levels in an attempt to suppress inflation may not result
in output expansion. Bank credit expansion can increase output in the

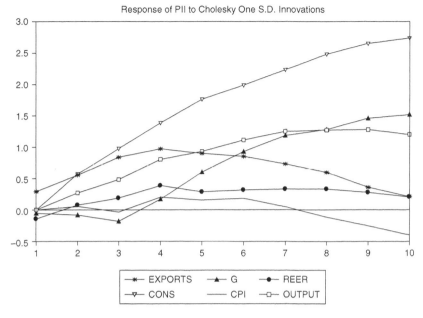

Notes: PII represents private investment index; SD represents standard deviation; G government expenditure; REER real effective exchange rate; CONS private consumption expenditure; BANKLOAN commercial banks' lending volume; CPI Consumer Price Index; OUTPUT manufacturing output index.

Source: Data are obtained from the impulse response function derived from the estimation of a Vector Auto Regressive (VAR) Model, based on the estimation of monthly data from the Bank of Thailand.

Figure 12.31   Impacts of various shocks on private investment

short run, but it does not have a long-lasting impact on output expansion. The implication is that monetary policy instruments can affect output only in the short run. An increase in investment can cause a temporary output contraction due to high imported capital goods, but it has an expansionary impact on long-term growth although it would not be able to help with short-run stabilization. It is interesting to note that real effective exchange rate appreciation does not lead to output contraction. Real exchange rate appreciation can lead to the importation of capital goods that would enhance productive capacity in the future.

Figure 12.31 indicates that this is indeed the case. Currency appreciation has a positive impact on private investment, therefore it can reduce the current account surplus indirectly through closing the saving–investment gap. Consumption and output growth can give rise to profitability and a better business environment. By improving business sentiment and enhancing consumer confidence, investment can rebound sharply when business and households resume their spending after experiencing political shocks.

CONCLUSIONS

The lessons learned from the AFC and GER that can be applied to development strategies are that both domestic-led growth and export-led growth can be employed simultaneously. There is no need to choose between them. But both fiscal and monetary policy instruments, including exchange rate policy, must be consistent and well coordinated when dealing with both internal and external shocks. If the exchange rate is not allowed to adjust to correct imbalances, the burden of the adjustment will fall on output and employment. The magnitude and duration of the departure from the steady growth path would be greater, thereby disrupting the growth process.

Reviving investment is one of the key elements in enhancing the long-term growth path. Both government spending and private consumption have the strongest effect on private investment. Since exports have a positive impact on private investment, export-led growth policy need not be inconsistent with a growth strategy led by domestic demand.

The overinvestment episode can be viewed as investments associated with an excessive quantity of capital stock that yielded diminishing rates of return. The low quality of investments was caused by speculation and created an unsustainable current account deficit. On the other hand, the underinvestment episode was related to the inability to make use of available savings to enhance long-term growth through the accumulation of capital stock.

The saving–investment gap remained high after the AFC because the government maintained a conservative fiscal policy. Moreover, the mechanism that leads to stability in fiscal position has remained the same: automatic fiscal stabilizers on the revenue side have been working remarkably well in maintaining price stability while the budgetary law put the ceiling on the level of public debt.

The level of investment is not constrained by savings but rather by risks and uncertainties. Because public investment goods are complementary to private investment, public infrastructure investment can boost growth in the long run. With ample fiscal space and a trend of currency appreciation, public investment would enhance growth through productivity improvement, particularly in the agricultural sector. The difficulty of using public spending in infrastructure during the period of economic slowdown was the result of frequent changes in the government after the 2006 coup. New administrations could not focus on long-term objectives, as they had to deal with immediate problems that threatened government stability.

Demand-led growth policy can be accomplished by creating an environment that nourishes investor sentiment and creates consumer confidence. All mechanisms that operated in the period before the GER are still operating, but the political turmoil and unstable governments destroyed business sentiment and depressed consumer confidence after 2006. Inefficient institutional factors prevented fiscal policy from employing capital spending during the global recession. Enhanced public investment during the economic downturn could have put the Thai economy on a higher growth trajectory over the long run.

NOTES

1. See Johnson (1955) for an early argument for using international trade to stimulate growth. Balassa (1978) provided early evidence of the impact of exports on economic growth in developing countries.
2. The inflation rate rose to 3.8 per cent in 2011, despite the impact of major flooding in the last quarter of 2011. The government has maintained subsidies and imposed price controls on certain key commodities.
3. Another method of capital mobility investigation involves an examination of the relationship between domestic and foreign interest rates. Willet et al. (2002) questioned whether capital mobility in developing countries is high.
4. A causality test, using monthly data between 2000 and 2008, indicates bidirectional causations: that GDP growth Granger causes current account deficits and vice versa.

REFERENCES

Balassa, B. (1978), 'Exports and economic growth: further evidence', *Journal of Development Economics*, **5**, 181–9.

Berg, A., and J.D. Sachs (1998), 'The debt crisis: structural explanations of country performance', *Journal of Development Economics*, **29**, 271–306. doi:10.1016/0304-3878(88)90046-6.

Berg, A., J.D. Ostry, and J. Zettlemeyer (2008), 'What makes growth sustained', International Monetary Fund Working Paper WP/08/59.

Bhagwati, J. (1958), 'Immiserizing growth: a geometric note', *Review of Economic Studies*, **25**, 201–5.

Bonin, J.P., and Y. Huang (2002), 'Foreign entry into Chinese banking: does WTO membership threaten domestic banks?', *World Economy*, **25**, 1077–93. doi:10.1111/1467-9701.00482.

Feldstein, M., and C. Horioka (1980), 'Domestic saving and international capital flows', *Economic Journal*, **90**, 314–29. doi:10.2307/2231790.

Hausmann, R., L. Pritchett, and D. Rodrik (2005), 'Growth accelerations', *Journal of Economic Growth*, **10**, 303–29. doi:10.1007/s10887-005-4712-0.

Hausmann, R., F. Rodriguez, and R. Wagner (2006), 'Growth collapses', Working Paper No. 136, Cambridge, MA: Center for International Development.

Johnson, H.G. (1995), 'Economic expansion and international trade', *The Manchester School*, **23**, 95–112.

Nidhiprabha, B. (2011), 'The global financial crisis and resilience of the Thai banking sector', *Asian Development Review*, **28**, 110–32.

Pritchett, L. (2000), 'Understanding patterns of economic growth: searching for hills among plateaus, mountains, and plains', *World Bank Economic Review*, 221–50.

Rodrik, D. (1999), 'Institutions for high-quality growth: what they are and how to acquire them', mimeo, Harvard University.

Rodrik, D., A. Subramanian, and F. Trebbi (2004), 'Institutions rule: the primacy of institutions over geography and integration in economic development', *Journal of Economic Growth*, **9**, 131–65.

Willett, T., M. Keil, and S. Young (2002), 'Capital mobility for developing countries may not be so high', *Japan and the World Economy*, **14**, 137–54.

13. Philippines

Desiree A. Desierto and Geoffrey M. Ducanes

INTRODUCTION

Unlike many Asian countries that have taken advantage of an increasingly globalized economy by pursuing export-led growth, the Philippines has relied mainly on strong domestic demand, particularly private and public consumption. The upshot is some insulation from the volatilities that occurred in world financial flows and global trade during the Asian financial crisis (AFC) and the more recent global economic recession (GER). The downside is missed growth opportunities due to limited access to global markets and the inevitably constrained growth of the domestic market. As domestic aggregate demand has come mostly in the form of consumption – and the contribution of investment has been low – domestic productivity growth has been slow and further expansion of the domestic market remains difficult.

This is true despite the large amount of remittances from overseas Filipinos that have boosted national savings. Remittances have exceeded 10 per cent of gross domestic product (GDP) since 2001 and have led to consistent current account surpluses since 2003. The failure to use these savings for investment in physical capital formation has constrained growth in domestic employment, potentially leading to the further loss of human capital to overseas employment.[1] It can be argued that this loss from labor export is an important reason why remittances have not contributed significantly to domestic productivity.[2] In contrast, trade and foreign direct investment (FDI) have been generally acknowledged to increase total factor productivity (TFP) through technological diffusion and economies-of-scale effects.

Of course, labor exports need not necessarily undermine growth in net exports. In fact, labor migration can facilitate trade between source and host countries by alleviating information asymmetries between them (Javorcik et al. 2010). Both can ideally go hand in hand to prop up the domestic economy and serve as a buffer in times of international crises and at the same time further increase growth by integrating into global markets.

In reality, however, this balanced approach is difficult to achieve. The political economy requirements of an export-led growth strategy can be daunting, and the danger is that the overreliance on domestic demand and labor exports can continue to mask and subsidize distortions and generate complacency in undertaking structural reforms.

Continued growth in exports requires sustained high-quality investments in both physical and human capital formation. Such investments, in turn, depend on sound macroeconomic and microeconomic environments that promote price stability, access to savings and credit, and a level playing field in which competitive pressures naturally allocate resources to the most productive endeavors. While the Philippines has gone a long way in instituting monetary and financial reforms, most notably flexible exchange rates and inflation targeting (Gochoco-Bautista and Canlas 2003; Gochoco-Bautista 1999), such efforts are undermined by structural rigidities in the labor and goods markets that prevent the efficient and productive use of investment. Thus, while there is potentially a greater supply of investment, investment demand is persistently low.

That investment demand is low is a product of deep-rooted institutional and political economy considerations. For instance, high industrial minimum wages and employment protection (Esguerra 2010; Nye 2011a) hamper factor mobility from the agricultural to the industrial sector. Such minimum wages, on the other hand, are not binding in the lower-productivity agricultural and services sectors (Nye 2011a). The failure of agrarian reform, the lack of property rights, and weak bureaucratic structures have also hindered growth in agricultural productivity (David 2003; Fabella 2009). While there have been amendments to the Foreign Investments Acts that limit participation of foreign equity in some manufacturing activities and services (Hill 2003; Abrenica and Llanto 2003; and Balisacan and Hill 2003), constitutional prohibitions still exist on the foreign ownership of land and there are limitations on foreign equity in corporations. Even trade liberalization has been skewed toward import-competing, rather than export-competing, industries (Bautista and Tecson 2003).

Instead of a level playing field, the overall business climate has been characterized by favoritism and cronyism, which induce corruption and rent-seeking behavior (De Dios and Hutchcroft 2003). Weak public sector institutions inhibit the proper alignment of incentives among civil servants and across the legislative, executive, and judicial branches, which constrains public goods provision and allows corruption to go unchecked (Human Development Network 2009).[3] The irony, however, is that deliberate efforts to expose and combat corruption may have contributed to greater political instability, with extra-constitutional turnovers, coup d'états, etc. that, we argue, have also contributed to the bad business climate and what

Pritchett (2003) has dubbed as "institutional uncertainty" in which economic actors cannot easily anticipate the rules of the game. Furthermore, one wonders whether the recent spate of suspensions and cancellations of foreign business contracts that are suspected to be anomalous will not undermine property rights for the sake of anticorruption efforts.

Thus, spurring investment demand is a formidable challenge that requires a comprehensive and integrated view of economic and institutional variables. One of the aims of this chapter is to quantify the contributions of such factors to investment growth, thereby identifying the most important opportunities and constraints. In this manner, we identify the challenges to an export-led growth strategy, which relies heavily on domestic and foreign investment.

More importantly, this chapter uses quantitative results to justify an analytical framework that shows how market reforms that foster greater competition and openness can better address the most significant barriers to investment and growth. Such reforms are what Nye (2011a) refers to as "first-order" reforms. Using a theoretical model, we show in particular that initial price distortions in a market can be aggravated when the government tries to limit the transactions in that market. This is essentially because in calculating the socially optimal level and price of transactions, the government takes into account all costs to society, including the losses to inefficient firms. The result is a higher price level that effectively subsidizes such losses. In contrast, opening up the market to greater competition drives out inefficient firms and pushes the price downward, thereby limiting the distortion.

The next section of this chapter provides recent time series data spanning at least two decades in the Philippines that show trends of subdued exports, investment, and productivity, amid some favorable macroeconomic conditions on the one hand, and some structural and institutional challenges on the other. It is followed by a section that statistically analyzes the data to identify the major constraints – and significant opportunities – in the sustained growth of high-quality investment. The section that follows finds that the more significant variables are structural and institutional factors that determine whether the overall business climate is more or less a stable and level playing field in which competition freely drives capital and labor toward their most efficient use. In that section, we find the effect of remittances on investment to be ambiguous at best. The final section proposes the need to prioritize first-order reforms that increase market competition and openness, and shows analytically how this can better achieve an efficient equilibrium, compared to government regulations that only address the manifestations of such distortions. That section is followed by a conclusion.

SUBDUED EXPORTS, INVESTMENT AND PRODUCTIVITY

On the expenditure side, GDP growth in the Philippines over the past two decades has been dominated by private consumption. Looking only at years since 1990 with positive GDP growth, private consumption has accounted on average for roughly four-fifths of total GDP growth (Figure 13.1). As a consequence, while private consumption's share in GDP has been on the rise (from 73.8 per cent of GDP in 1990 to 79 per cent in 2010), the shares of other sectors have been declining, especially capital formation (from 24 per cent in 1990 to 18.5 per cent in 2010).[4] As estimated in the income accounts, net exports have been positive in only two years in the past two decades, thus contributing negatively to GDP growth on average.

It is not surprising that the relative unimportance of exports to growth has limited the country's global exposure and vulnerability to international crises. As seen in Figure 13.2, the 1997 AFC and recent GER have had very short-lived – and relatively minor – impact on GDP and gross national product (GNP) growth, especially in comparison to other East Asian countries. In fact, Figure 13.2 shows that the political instability the country experienced in the early 1990s, as a result of repeated coup attempts, had a more severe and lingering effect on GDP growth.

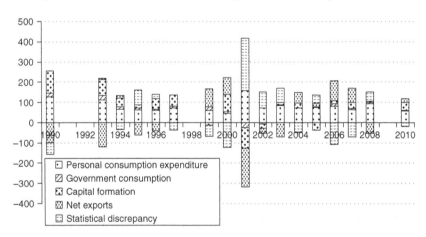

Note: Years when GDP growth was less than 1% or negative were excluded.

Source: Authors' computation based on National Income Accounts, National Statistical Coordination Board, Philippines.

Figure 13.1   Consumption-side sectoral contribution to GDP growth (shares of total growth, sum to 100%)

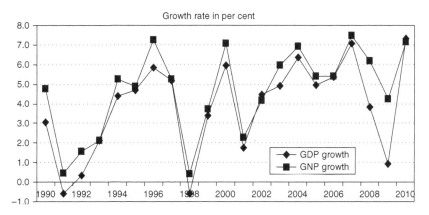

Growth rate in per cent

Note: GDP = gross domestic product; GNP = gross national product.

Source: National Income Accounts, National Statistical Coordination Board, Philippines.

Figure 13.2   GDP and GNP growth

Figure 13.2 also reveals the main reason for the resilience of consumption and consequently GDP growth: the strong inflow of remittances, reflected in GNP growth that is typically higher than GDP growth.[5] The Philippines is ranked fourth in the world in terms of foreign remittance receipts, following only third-ranked Mexico, second-ranked People's Republic of China (PRC), and first-ranked India. Figure 13.3 shows the surge in remittances by overseas foreign workers (OFWs), which have propped up balance of payment accounts and national savings in recent years. According to the World Bank's *World Development Indicators*, national savings has exceeded 30 per cent of GDP since 1999.[6] However, the investment rate has not kept pace with the rise in the savings rate, as Figure 13.4 shows.[7] The investment rate has been on a downward trend since the AFC, even as the current account surplus has been on an upward trend and the national savings rate has reached historical peaks. This clearly suggests that remittances are not translating to investments.

One could argue that the slow growth in investment might be due to the rise in the services sector relative to manufacturing, with services being less capital intensive than the manufacturing sector. Figure 13.5 lays out the relative contribution of agriculture, industry, and services to GDP growth in the last two decades and shows that services have accounted for more than half of total growth in the period. This is best exemplified by the business process outsourcing (BPO) sector, which has taken off in the last decade – growing more than 20 per cent per year – and is now second

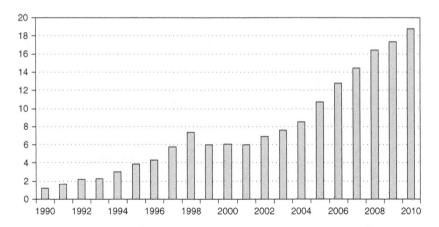

Source: Bangko Sentral ng Pilipinas.

Figure 13.3   Remittances inflow in US$ billion

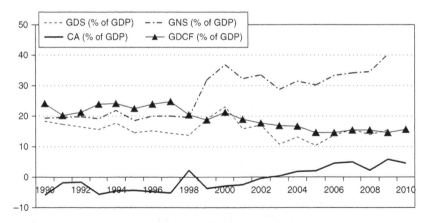

Notes: CA = current account; GDS = gross domestic savings; GNS = gross national savings; GDCF = gross domestic capital formation.

Source: World Development Indicators and Global Development Finance of the World Bank, Version 5, May 2011.

Figure 13.4   Philippine savings and investment rate

only to India's BPO sector in size and is expected to outpace the rate of growth of India's BPO sector growth in the coming years. Yet this raises the question of why industry lags behind, as previous studies have shown that it outperforms services and agriculture in terms of productivity.[8]

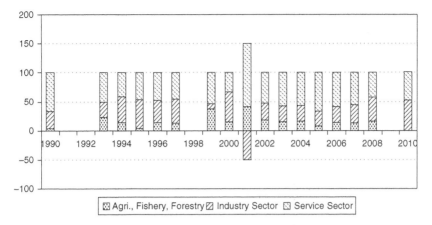

Note: Years when GDP growth was less than 1% or negative were excluded.

Source: Authors' computation based on National Income Accounts and National Statistical Coordination Board, Philippines.

Figure 13.5   *Production-side sectoral contribution to GDP growth (shares of total growth, sum to 100%)*

A possible reason might be that the industrial sector is constrained by high minimum wages, while minimum wages do not bind in the agricultural sector or much of the lower-productivity segment of the services sector (Nye 2011a; Esguerra 2010). From Nye: "According to Esguerra (2010) the Philippines had the 28th highest minimum wage in the world in 2007 at PPP (purchasing power parity) rates out of 130 countries and the 8th highest minimum wage out of a group of about 30 developing and transitional economies."

Even within the manufacturing industry, there exist some rigidities between export-generating and import-competing activities. Table 13.1 shows that the export-oriented segment has been constrained relative to the import-substituting segment. Such "import bias" in trade activities is a result of non-neutral trade liberalization policies (Bautista and Tecson 2003). Other factors such as high transport costs, red tape that slows down trade facilitation, and lack of infrastructure have also possibly undermined the competitiveness of exports. The Philippines ranked 85th out of 139 countries in the World Economic Forum *Global Competitiveness Index* ranking in 2010–11. It ranked poorly in almost all categories, but especially in institutions (125th), labor market efficiency (111th), innovation (111th), and infrastructure (104th). In the World Bank's *Ease of Doing Business* rankings, the Philippines ranked 148th out of 183 countries, and

Table 13.1   Distribution of manufacturing foreign direct investment,
1973–2000 (%)

Manufacturing industry	1973	1980	1985	1990	1995	2000
Import-substituting	69.9	73.8	78.4	72.9	52.4	87.5
Food	6.1	13.7	22.1	19.6	3.1	46.0
Chemicals and chemical products	9.3	29.2	26.5	27.0	10.7	34.4
Petroleum	41.8	4.6	6.2	5.2	12.9	0.0
Metal and metal products	3.5	15.8	13.1	10.8	6.9	3.3
Nonmetallic mineral products	3.2	2.1	2.6	3.1	3.1	0.0
Transport equipment	5.9	8.5	7.9	7.3	15.7	3.8
Export-oriented	15.4	11.6	10.1	14.8	43.1	10.9
Textiles and garments	12.7	5.6	4.4	5.1	3.7	0.3
Machinery, apparatus, appliances	2.7	6.0	5.7	9.8	39.3	10.5
Other	14.7	14.5	11.5	12.2	4.5	1.6
Total	100.0	100.0	100.0	100.0	100.0	100.0

Source: Bautista and Tecson (2003).

ranked especially poorly in Starting and Closing a Business (156th and 153rd, respectively), Protecting Investors (132nd), Getting Credit (128th), Paying Taxes (124th), and Enforcing Contracts (118th).

There are also various degrees of protection in all sectors due to institutional reasons, such as weak agrarian reform, subsidies including those from the National Food Authority (NFA), restrictions on foreign ownership, and tax breaks or particularistic concessions that have created distortions and have impeded the flow of investment to productive activities. The overall business climate is also characterized by corruption, rent-seeking, weak property rights, weak bureaucracy, red tape, and political instability (Figure 13.6).

It is thus no wonder that investment demand is low. Yet there are indicators that the supply of investment is relatively unconstrained. Figure 13.7 reflects the success of monetary and financial reforms that have lowered interest rates and inflation, thus contributing to overall macroeconomic stability since the establishment in 1993 of an independent central monetary authority, the Bangko Sentral ng Pilipinas (BSP). As recounted in Gochoco-Bautista and Canlas (2003), before 1993 members of the monetary board were mostly Cabinet secretaries, which made it easy to accommodate fiscal spending and created incentives to maintain a strong currency to help protected industries pay for imports. The monetary policy then was based on exchange rate targeting. The new BSP, however,

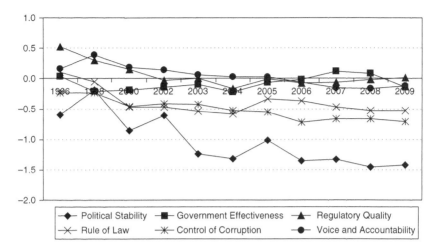

Source: World Bank Governance Indicators 2010.

Figure 13.6   Philippine governance indicators 1996–2009

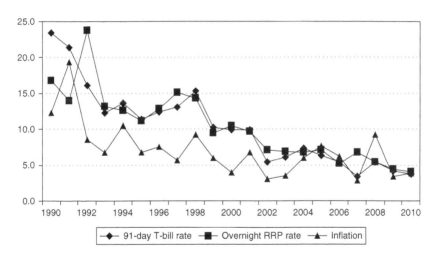

Source: Bangko Sentral ng Pilipinas and the National Statistics Office, Philippines.

Figure 13.7   Interest rates and inflation (%)

has moved toward inflation targeting and flexible exchange rates. While the financial sector has undergone greater liberalization, the BSP has also undertaken reform programs to strengthen banking regulation. Thus, it can be seen in Figure 13.8 that even during the AFC and the GER, the

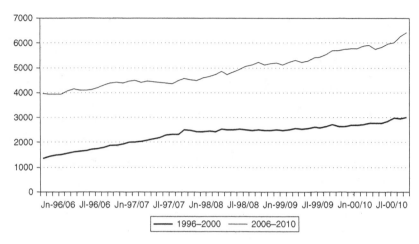

Source: Bangko Sentral ng Pilipinas.

*Figure 13.8   Total resources of universal and commercial banks (Php
              billion) 1996–2000 and 2006–2010*

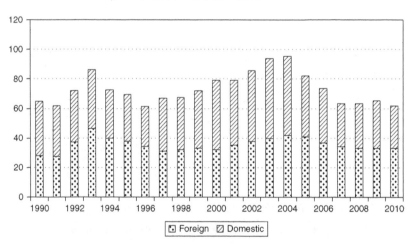

Source: Bureau of Treasury.

Figure 13.9   Philippine national government debt (% of GDP)

total financial resources of banks have more or less held up – more so after
the GER than AFC. Also, the debt–GDP ratio shows signs of lowering to
more modest levels in recent years (Figure 13.9).

    Thus, the constraints to investment growth seem largely determined by weak demand. In the next sections of this chapter, we show in particular that the most significant barriers that prevent the efficient use of investment flows are structural and institutional factors.

ESTIMATION

To the extent that both export-led growth and sustainable domestic demand-driven growth rely on sustained high-quality investments, we identify the significant constraints to investment in the Philippines. Our hypothesis is that the rate of investment is determined by institutional and governance factors, by the macroeconomic environment, and by the risk of default, among other factors. Using annual time series data from 1984 to 2006, we estimate the following equation:[9]

$$\Delta\left(\frac{I}{Y}\right)_t = \beta_0 + \beta_1\Delta\left(\frac{debt}{Y}\right)_{t-1} + \beta_2\Delta\left(\frac{def}{Y}\right)_{t-1} + \beta_3\Delta\left(\frac{fdi}{Y}\right)_{t-1}$$
$$- \beta_4\Delta\left(\frac{rem}{Y}\right)_{t-1} + \beta_5\Delta r_{t-1} + Inst_{t-1}\gamma - \varepsilon_i$$

where I is investment, Y is GDP, *debt* is government debt, *def* is government deficit, *fdi* is foreign direct investment, *rem* is remittances, r is the real interest rate, *Inst* is a vector of institutional measures (i.e. corruption, investment profile, bureaucratic quality, government stability), ε is the error term, and Δ denotes differenced values. We use differenced data to reduce the chance of getting a spurious relationship from the presence of unit roots, and we use lagged values of the explanatory variables to try to address simultaneity issues.[10]

We use data on fixed capital formation to proxy for the investment ratio, and we use the following data from Political Risk Services as proxies for institutional measures: (*BQ_prs*) for bureaucratic quality, (*Corrup*) for corruption, (*GS_prs*) for government stability, and (*InvProf*) for investment profile, which includes contract variability and expropriation risk.[11] We also have data on the government debt ratio (*Debt_pct*), the government budget deficit ratio (*Defct_pct*), the real interest rate (*RIntRate*), the FDI ratio to GDP (*FDI_pct*), and the remittance ratio to GDP (*Remit_pct*). Lastly, we include a dummy variable for the years 1998 and 1999 (*D1998_9*), which was the height of the AFC.

RESULTS

The regression results are presented in Table 13.2. There are three alternative models differing only in the subset of explanatory variables included in the regression.

Table 13.2   Determinants of fixed capital formation

Variable	Model 1		Model 2		Model 3	
	Coefficient	*p-value*	Coefficient	*p-value*	Coefficient	*p-value*
Constant	0.62	0.150	0.43	0.265	0.12	0.739
DBQ_prs_1	−1.77	0.228	–	–	–	–
DCorrup_1	2.85	0.003	2.69	0.003	2.96	0.002
DGS_prs_1	−0.17	0.626	–	–	–	–
DInvProf_1	2.91	0.003	2.30	0.006	1.50	0.026
DDebt_pct_1	−0.03	0.528	−0.05	0.280	−0.09	0.082
DDefct_pct_1	−0.39	0.115	−0.43	0.098	−0.40	0.149
DRIntRate_1	−0.06	0.483	−0.09	0.300	−0.05	0.570
DFDI_pct_1	0.10	0.754	0.19	0.585	0.40	0.271
DRemit_pct_1	−1.46	0.026	−0.97	0.085		
D1998_9	−4.86	0.008	−5.74	0.001	−5.76	0.002
R^2	0.803		0.730		0.651	
AIC	3.51		3.64		3.80	
No. of obs	21		21		21	

Notes:
BQ = Political Risk Services (PRS) measure of bureaucratic quality (1–4, with 4 as best score).
Corrup = PRS measure of corruption within the political system (1–6, with 6 as best score).
GS = PRS measure of government's ability to carry out its program and to stay in office (1–12, with 12 as best score).
InvProf = PRS measure of risk to investment including contract viability/expropriation (1–12, with 12 as best score).
Debt_pct = Government debt as a percentage of GDP.
Deft_pct = Government deficit as a percentage of GDP.
RIntRate = Real lending interest rate.
FDI_pct = Foreign direct investment as a percentage of GDP.
Remit_pct = Foreign remittances as a percentage of GDP.
D1998_9 = Dummy variable for 1998 and 1999 (Asian Financial Crisis).
(1) The dependent variable is the first-difference of fixed capital formation as percentage of GDP; (2) a D in front of a variable means a first-differenced value of the variable (e.g. $DBQt = BQt - BQt\text{-}1$, where t denotes time period) (3) an underscore followed by 1 (_1) means a one period lagged value of the variable.

Source: Authors' computations based on data from Political Risk Services, Bangko Sentral ng Pilipinas, The National Statistical Coordination Board and the Bureau of Treasury.

For Model 1, we regress fixed capital formation on bureaucratic quality (*BQ_prs*), control of corruption (*Corrup*), government stability (*GS_prs*), and investment profile (*InvProf*), as well as the government debt ratio (*Debt_pct*), the government budget deficit ratio (*Defct_pct*), the real interest rate (*RIntRate*), the FDI ratio to GDP (*FDI_pct*), and the remittance ratio to GDP (*Remit_pct*), as well as the AFC dummy variable (*D1998_9*). The results show that among the institutional variables, (lagged) *Corrup* and *InvProf* are strongly correlated with fixed capital formation and have the expected signs. In contrast, *BQ_prs* and *GS_prs* are insignificant.[12] All the other economic variables except for *Remit_pct* are insignificant but have the correct signs. *Remit_pct* is significant but negative, suggesting that increases in remittances have been associated with declines in the investment rate. D1998_9 is negative and highly significant, indicating an especially large decline in fixed capital formation during the AFC.

Model 2, which drops *BQ_prs* and *GS_prs*, shows roughly similar results (i.e. significant *Corrup*, *InvProf*, *Remit_pct*, *D1998_9*) except that *Defct_pct* is now also significant. As expected, a higher government deficit is associated with lower investments.

It can be argued that remittance figures may be misleading since the share of remittances that is being coursed through the formal financial system has been increasing over the years. This makes it difficult to disentangle the part of the rising remittances that is due to actual increases from the part that is merely due to better capture. If one takes out *Remit_pct* from Model 2, we get Model 3, which shows *Debt_pct* to be significant and to be of the expected sign, in addition to *Corrup*, *InvProf*, and *D1998_9*.

The results are consistent in showing that institutional variables, particularly corruption and contract enforcement, are crucial to raising capital formation in the country. Note, moreover, that such factors have the largest effects (apart from the AFC dummy variable) and that both of them are significant. This implies that measures to address one factor, e.g. corruption, cannot be as effective if they undermine contract enforcement at the same time. In this respect, the cancellation of contracts for the sake of anticorruption ideals might be detrimental to investment growth, since these anticorruption methods not only erode investors' property rights but also generate "institutional uncertainty." Pritchett argues that in some cases a corrupt environment can support rapid output growth if there is a steady system of contract enforcement that stabilizes investors' expectations. (See also Shleifer and Vishny 1993; Wei 1997; and Campos et al. 1999, which show that investment and growth can ensue as long as corruption is predictable.)

The results also indicate that government's fiscal standing, whether in terms of debt or deficit, is an important factor affecting capital formation.

However, what government debt or deficit actually proxies for cannot be easily disentangled, and the way in which it negatively affects investment is not clear. On one hand, it can be seen to affect investor confidence, or as a factor limiting investment supply. (Note that interest rates are insignificant, suggesting that fiscal standing might be a more important supply-side constraint.) This would be consistent with the low credit rating of the country's debt by different agencies, including Fitch Ratings, Moody's, and Standard & Poor's.

On the other hand, fiscal standing could be indicative of underlying demand-side factors, such as the lack of adequate public infrastructure or, more generally, government inefficiency in the use of funds, which depend on the capability of public institutions. Note precisely that in Model 2, *Defct_pct* becomes significant when *BQ_prs* and *GS_prs* are dropped, which suggests a strong correlation between these indicators of government performance. Thus, the fact that the government's fiscal standing matters could reflect the importance of bureaucratic efficiency. Indeed, the Human Development Network (HDN) elucidates the extent of public sector inefficiencies – from the fact that monetary and non-monetary incentives of civil servants and appointment processes prevent the government from attracting and hiring the most suitable candidates, to the loopholes in the budget process that skew the balance of powers of the executive and legislative branches, to the weak screening and selection processes in the judiciary that can compromise its independence.

Remittances seem to be perversely related to capital formation, although one could argue that brain-drain effects are so large as to deter investment. In any case, data issues render this result less than definitive. Finally, the results confirm that there has been an extraordinary decline in fixed capital formation as a result of the AFC.

COMPETITION AND OPENNESS: THE NEED FOR FIRST-ORDER POLICIES

The Philippine Development Plan 2011–2016, recently published by the National Economic Development Authority (NEDA 2011), points to the lack of investment as a crucial reason for low employment growth and low overall economic growth. The barriers to investment include the lack of infrastructure, especially in transportation and power supply; weak institutions and governance failures, particularly weak bureaucracy, red tape, corruption, and inadequate enforcement of law and contracts; and low competition measures. The latter is especially seen in the lack of competition in agriculture, maritime and air transport, power, cement, and banking, and is acknowledged to be due to "dominant firms exerting social influence and political clout," according to the Development Plan.

To address these problems, the Philippine Development Plan proposes to expand tax collection and participation of government (e.g. private-public partnerships), while putting in place policing and/or regulatory mechanisms to limit corruption and address institutional reforms.

While the plan is comprehensive in its acknowledgement of the various factors that hinder investment and growth, the proposed solutions are so broad and encompassing that the order of priorities is not clear. While it is laudable to attempt to address all issues, the reality is that resources are limited and that efforts in one area may have negative unintended consequences in other areas.

The previous section of this chapter similarly points to structural and institutional distortions as the main constraints to investment. However, we clarify that what makes such distortions important is that together they are symptomatic of the low level of competition and openness in the economy. Rent-seeking by elite groups is a feature of what North et al. (2009) refer to as "limited-access" societies. Although North et al. do not give exact recommendations as to how to transition from limited-access to open-access societies in which elite control is minimized and trade flourishes, they clearly point out that open access societies are characterized by competition and openness.

Thus, in this section, we stress the importance of prioritizing what Nye (2011a) calls first-order reforms that open up markets and increase competition, as opposed to second-order efforts that regulate against distortions, e.g. going after and punishing rent-seekers. We show that whenever underlying distortions are present, first-order market reforms are more efficient than government regulations that attempt to alleviate these distortions. That is, any economic activity or transaction that takes place amid existing distortions still attains its lowest price in a free market rather than in a regulated environment.

To illustrate this, consider a market with two firms or agents $i = 1, 2$ with corresponding marginal cost c_i who each choose price p_i to maximize its profit π_i from supplying at quantity q_i:

$$\text{Max}_{p_i}\pi_i = (p_i - c_i)q_i$$

Let total demand be equal to $Q = q_1 + q_2$, and assume that $c_1 < c_2$, such that Firm 1 is the relatively more efficient firm. If the firms can compete freely, each firm would try to undercut the other, since the firm with the higher price gets zero demand, while the lower-priced firm gets all Q (If both offer the same price, they each supply $\frac{Q}{2}$.) As a result of this

"Bertrand" competition, the (Nash) equilibrium price is the lowest possible price c_1, at which point the inefficient Firm 2 is driven out.

And yet even when there are underlying distortions such that the first-best price c_1 cannot be met, it can be shown that the second-best price under Bertrand competition is still lower than in a regulated environment – even with benign regulators who seek to cure the underlying distortion.

To see this, suppose there is some distortion ε that allows firms to bid prices above their marginal costs to the extent of ε and earn some positive profits. That is, let there be two competing price strategies: the lowest price $c_1 + \varepsilon$ below which not even Firm 1 wants to enter the market; and the highest possible price $c_2 + \varepsilon$ above which some other, even more inefficient, firms can start to enter. (That is, prices $c_1 + \varepsilon$ and $c_2 + \varepsilon$ restrict the model to a 2 × 2 game.) Then the payoffs from choosing price $c_1 + \varepsilon$ against $c_2 + \varepsilon$ are given by the following matrix:

	$c_1 + \varepsilon$	$c_2 + \varepsilon$
$c_1 + \varepsilon$	$\varepsilon\dfrac{Q}{2}, (c_1 + \varepsilon - c_2)\dfrac{Q}{2}$	$\varepsilon Q, 0$
$c_2 + \varepsilon$	$0, (c_1 + \varepsilon - c_1)Q$	$(c_2 + \varepsilon - c_1)\dfrac{Q}{2}, \varepsilon\dfrac{Q}{2}$

where the first (second) element in each pair of payoffs refers to the payoff/ profit from adopting row (column) strategy. Assuming that $\varepsilon > c_2 - c_1$, that is, that Firm 1 and Firm 2 are close enough competitors, then the unique Nash equilibrium of the game is $[(c_1 + \varepsilon), (c_1 + \varepsilon)]$.[13] That is, equilibrium price is bid down to the second-best price of $c_1 + \varepsilon$.

Consider the case in which instead of letting firms freely compete the government steps in to "enforce" against, or regulate, ε, by de facto choosing the socially optimal level of Q. Note that to the extent that firms could charge a premium ε, there would be a loss in social welfare W equal to εQ, which the government could limit by restricting Q at a level that internalizes society's negative externality from ε. Thus, the government, in weighing all the benefits and costs in society associated with the provision of Q, solves the following optimization problem:

$$Max_Q W = (p_G - c_1)q_1 + (p_G - c_2)q_2 - \varepsilon Q$$

where p_G is the de facto equilibrium price when government enforces the socially optimal level of Q. At the social optimum, this price is equal to

$$p_G = \varepsilon + c_1 + c_2$$

which is clearly greater than the equilibrium price under competition.[14]

The intuition is straightforward. When left on their own, profit-maximizing firms will take advantage of the distortion and bid at a premium, but forces of competition discipline firms to price close to the marginal cost of the efficient firm. Inefficient firms are driven out. But even a benign government regulator's objective is to optimize the benefits – and lessen the costs – to all sectors of society, including the welfare of less efficient ones since they are also part of society. In "balancing" the interest of all sectors, more efficient firms end up subsidizing the inefficiency of others for the initial failure or distortion ε. Thus, p_G has to cover all marginal costs on top of the cost of the initial distortion.

Furthermore, if there are other costs involved in enforcing the socially optimal level of Q, p_G will have to cover the additional marginal costs from these as well. These could include the actual costs of enforcement (e.g. regulatory bodies and bureaucratic processes, courts, and litigation) and "avoidance" costs which firms can incur in trying to avoid getting caught (e.g. bribes to officials: see Becker et al. 2006).

Thus, for reasons of pure efficiency, reforms that increase competition give better second-best outcomes than regulations that directly enforce against the distortions. While government might be well meaning in trying to combat distortions, regulation might end up creating more distortions – and unnecessarily increasing prices to higher levels.

Of course, the government might have different objectives, e.g. equity considerations, in choosing to regulate, such that subsidizing weaker segments of society is a desirable end on its own, especially with the government's thrust for "inclusive growth." Even then, however, it is not clear that more regulation is the best way to achieve this. Redistribution might be more efficiently addressed by non-distortionary taxes.[15] Simply put, the government can allow free competition to drive prices to $c_1 + \varepsilon$, and then impose a tax rate equal or close to ε

One might argue that marginal costs are difficult to infer, and that ε cannot be easily known. But determining the socially optimal way of regulating a good also requires some idea of the size of the distortion or externality, and the marginal costs not only of the most efficient firms, but of all other players as well. Note that one can easily generalize the model to include many firms or players, in which case competition still drives price close to the marginal cost of the most efficient players. But the regulated price entails covering the cost of the distortion and the marginal costs of all other players. Paradoxically, then, while free entry and competition even in an initially distorted environment can still approximate efficient outcomes, regulating more and more players – even in order to combat the distortion – can actually increase the overall distortionary effects.

Perhaps it is telling that throughout history, greater openness and competition have fuelled the rise of economies. Arguably, for instance, no country has reached developed-economy status by going after rent-seekers and corrupt agents. Instead, greater competition usually limits the scope of rent-seeking, which further strengthens the market and allows for greater increases in productivity.[16]

The danger is that in trying to address corruption directly, the government de facto can limit economic activity in order to limit the corruption. This is precisely the mechanism involved in the cancellation of anomalous contracts. It is not altogether clear that the result will even be socially optimal, let alone efficient, for the effort requires knowledge not only of the amount of corruption, but of the costs to all players involved – contracting parties and all third-party interests. And even if such information were perfectly known, it would be more efficient to let firms compete and transact freely. Even if such transactions involve some rent-seeking, the distortions would be limited for as long as there are ready entrants to step in; when rent-seeking becomes too high, the transaction would simply become unaffordable.

The key is that the market has to be truly open – not just from the supply side but also from the demand side. In centralized government transactions, for instance, the government is a monopsonist. The resulting price can be very high since there are no other buyers that could bid down the corruption rents or bribes, which would then lead suppliers to bid at even higher prices that include larger bribes in order to get the contract. If there were alternate buyers, e.g. decentralized and competing government units, then even corrupt buyers would decrease bribe requirements from suppliers in order to get the contract.[17]

Thus, that free market reforms seem not to have curbed corruption is not a failure of the market, but rather a failure to institute full market reforms and a tendency to compensate by adopting complicated and costly regulations. The enforcement and avoidance costs, including litigation, involved in anticorruption campaigns can be so large as to dissipate the net gains.[18]

There is the danger, then, of adopting a haphazard approach to reform in which competition is introduced, albeit incompletely, and regulation is added to try to address remaining distortions or to redistribute gains – or both. For instance, the Philippines' open-skies policy is supposed to encourage free entry and greater competition in the airline industry, but prohibitively high tax rates could undermine the entry of foreign competitors. Furthermore, other interests and parties, such as the competitiveness of airports, need to be considered as well. Note that anticorruption efforts have stalled the operations of the Ninoy Aquino International Airport

(NAIA) 3, which illustrates how second-order regulation can frustrate the first-order reform in opening up the airline industry.

More recently, the current administration's renegotiation and cancellation of public works contracts with foreign firms entered into by the previous administration, such as the Roll-On, Roll-Off (RORO) project with French company Eiffel-Matiere SAS Consortium and a dredging project with Belgian company Benelux, on suspicion of possible corruption or overpricing, has renewed concerns in some investors about the government's commitment to honor its contractual obligations (GlobalSource 2011).

Another example is the National Food Authority, which is difficult to justify either on efficiency or redistributive grounds. Given that there already exist distortions in agriculture, as in the failure of land reform and weakness of property rights (Fabella 2009), buying farmers' produce at uncompetitive rates only subsidizes the underlying distortions. Even for purely redistributive reasons, it is not altogether clear why such an arrangement would be more efficient than a straight transfer or subsidy to farmers. Lastly, in terms of ensuring a steady and stable supply of agricultural produce by importing and re-selling domestically, there seems to be no compelling reason to believe that government (NFA) as importer would be better at forecasting demand and holding adequate stock than would freely competing private importers.

Perhaps, then, it is not such a puzzle why the Philippine economy, despite many attempted reform efforts, still lags behind other economies and is constrained from taking off. Market reforms have simply not been deep and thorough enough. Without sustaining first-order reforms that promote real competition and openness, the temptation has been to rely on various regulatory efforts in the hope of addressing the issue of the day. The temptation for any government to overregulate, especially in weak economic environments, is understandable, but the danger is that this can perpetuate and create additional distortions even with the most benign governments.[19] To effectively destroy the layers of distortions, perhaps it is best to concentrate on the core competitive environment. This, though, is politically difficult as it would threaten the positions of incumbent elites, and the gains might not be immediately felt and therefore political leaders could not take credit for them.

CONCLUSION

Trade and investment are widely acknowledged to be drivers of sustained economic growth, but a debate now centers on how to increase and sustain them. The Philippines possesses some unique advantages in the growth of its labor exports and the establishment of important macroeconomic reforms, such as the creation of an independent central bank, increased financial liberalization, and prudent banking regulation, which have helped the country weather regional and global crises. However, the Philippines seems to miss out on opportunities to increase its productivity and gain export competitiveness. Corruption and rent-seeking remain unchallenged and the overall business climate remains weak because of the lack of complete and sustained microeconomic reforms that enable greater openness and competition. This deters investment and limits the growth potential of the country.

In this chapter, we have shown that the real barriers that the country faces are structural and institutional problems characteristic of limited-access societies, and that the most effective and efficient reforms are those that can address these barriers in a way that limits further distortions. Specifically, we have argued how prioritizing first-order market reforms that increase and open up competition produces better outcomes than overreliance on regulations that attempt to curb the distortions.

NOTES

1. Note that while evidence in some countries (e.g., Woodruff and Zenteno 2007) suggests that remittances increase investment in microenterprises, this does not seem to be the case in the Philippines.
2. This is not to discount the contribution of remittances to human capital when recipient households use them to increase education and health spending, among other things. But see Schiff and Ozden (2005) for estimates of the size and effects of migration and the brain drain phenomenon for a number of countries, including the Philippines.
3. Civil service morale is also low because of a number of external and internal inequities in the compensation system, the practice of creating *ad hoc* bodies whose jobs overlap with regular agencies, and the appointment of political advisers and consultants, among others (Human Development Network 2009). This has arguably affected the quality of people opting to join and stay in the bureaucracy.
4. More exactly, we only include years when GDP growth, exceeded 1 per cent, which excludes 1991, 1992, 1999, and 2009. Including 1992 and 2009, years of positive but marginal growth, would have increased further the share of private consumption.
5. Technically, the difference between GNP and GDP is net factor income from abroad, which in the case of the Philippines is comprised mainly of the estimated compensation of the millions of Filipino nationals working abroad and not remittances, per se. However, a strong link can be expected between income earned abroad and remittances.
6. These figures come from the World Bank *World Development Indicators*, which defines gross national savings as gross national income less consumption, plus net transfers. This may be overstated because some of net primary income will also be sent as remittances. But even if this is overstated, the current account surplus, another measure of the savings–investment gap, also indicates surplus savings in the country that in 2010 was equivalent to 4.5 per cent of GDP.
7. The investment rate and other figures are based on the 1985-based national income

account series. As of the 2nd quarter of 2011, the National Statistical Coordination Board has moved to a 2000-based series. In this new series, the investment ratio is higher by a few percentage points (for 2010, investment ratio was 20.5 per cent in the 2000 series compared to 15.6 per cent in the 1985 series). However, it appears some of this is simply due to a reclassification of what was formerly statistical discrepancy into the item 'change in inventory' without any good reason. Because of this, we used the 1985 series instead. See http://www.econ.upd.edu.ph/perse/?p=398.

8. See Table 1.3 of Balisacan and Hill (2003).
9. Clearly, the limited number of observations used in the regressions is an important caveat. The lack of an extended time series for institutional variables is the main constraint to increasing the number of observations used in the regressions.
10. The disadvantage, however, is the further loss of degrees of freedom.
11. We use the PRS measures of institutions and governance instead of the World Bank *World Governance Indicators* because they are available annually starting from 1984. The cross-country correlations for the two measures is typically very high, however. For 2006, for instance, the correlation between the PRS and the World Bank measure of corruption is 0.87.
12. This may also be partly because of correlations among the institutional variables.
13. If firm 2 is too inefficient such that $\varepsilon < c_2 - c_1$, then both $[(c_1 + \varepsilon), (c_1 + \varepsilon)]$ and $[(c_2 + \varepsilon), (c_2 + \varepsilon)]$ are the two pure Nash equilibria of the game. Note, however, that even price $(c_2 + \varepsilon)$ is still lower than the price under regulation. See subsequent exposition.
14. The first-order condition is given by $p_G - \varepsilon - c_1 - c_2 = 0$.
15. Becker et al. (2006), Weitzman (1974), and Miron (2008, 2004), for instance, precisely make the point that taxation of goods that produce negative externalities is more efficient than regulating such goods.
16. See, for instance, Mokyr and Nye (2007) and Nye (2009) for the example of Britain, and Nye (2011a, 2011b) for the PRC.
17. Beck and Maher (1986) and Lien (1986) show formally that with competitive bidding, the lowest-cost firm wins the contract and bribery is efficient. See also Pradhan (1997) for a review.
18. This point has been increasingly made in the literature since Tullock's (1967, 1971, 1975) and Krueger's (1974) seminal works on rent-seeking which show how resources can be wasted in trying to capture rents amid regulated environments.
19. In the case of anticorruption efforts, Bardhan (1997) notes that "too many rules rather than discretion may have the perverse effect of providing opportunities for corruption simply to circumvent mindless inflexibilities."

REFERENCES

Abrenica, M., and G.M. Llanto (2003), 'Services', in A. Balisacan and H. Hill (eds), *The Philippine Economy: Development, Policies and Challenges*, Quezon City, Philippines: Ateneo de Manila University Press.

Balisacan, A., and H. (Hill) (eds), (2003), *The Philippine Economy: Development, Policies and Challenges*, Quezon City, Philippines: Ateneo de Manila University Press.

Bardhan, P. (1997), 'Corruption and development: a review of issues', *Journal of Economic Literature*, **XXXV**, 1320–46.

Bautista, R., and G. Tecson (2003), 'International dimensions', in A. Balisacan and H. Hill (eds), *The Philippine Economy: Development, Policies and Challenges*, Quezon City, Philippines: Ateneo de Manila University Press.

Beck, P.J., and M.W. Maher (1986), 'A comparison of bribery and bidding in thin markets', *Economics Letters*, 20 1–5. doi:10.1016/0165-1765(86)90068-6.

Becker, G.S., K.M. Murphy, and M. Grossman (2006), 'The market for illegal goods: the case of drugs', *Journal of Political Economy*, **114**, 38–60. doi:10.1086/498918.

Campos, J.E., D. Lien, and S. Pradhan (1999), 'The impact of corruption on investment: predictability matters', *World Development*, **27**, 1059–67. doi:10.1016/S0305-750X(99)00040-6.

David, C.C. (2003), 'Agriculture', in A. Balisacan and H. Hill (eds), *The Philippine Economy: Development, Policies and Challenges*, Quezon City, Philippines: Ateneo de Manila University Press.

de Dios, E.S, and P.D. Hutchcroft. 2003, 'Political Economy,' in A. Balisacan and H. Hill (eds), *The Philippine Economy: Development, Policies and Challenges*, Quezon City, Philippines: Ateneo de Manila University Press.

Esguerra, E. (2010), 'Job creation: what's labor got to do with it?', University of the Philippines, unpublished.

Fabella, R. (2009), 'CARP without Coase: redistributing poverty in the Philippines', Working Paper, University of the Philippines School of Economics, Diliman, Quezon City, Philippines.

GlobalSource Partners (2011), 'Monthly report: a bet on PPP'. www.globalsourcepartners.com.

Gochoco-Bautista, M.S., and D. Canlas (2003), 'Monetary and exchange rate policy', in A. Balisacan and H. Hill (eds), *The Philippine Economy: Development, Policies and Challenges*, Quezon City, Philippines: Ateneo de Manila University Press.

Gochoco-Bautista, M.S. (1999), 'The past performance of the Philippine banking sector', in J. Lee (ed.), *Rising to the Challenge in Asia: A Study of Financial Markets*, Manila: Asian Development Bank.

Hill, H. (2003), 'Industry', in A. Balisacan and H. Hill (eds), *The Philippine Economy: Development, Policies and Challenges*, Quezon City, Philippines: Ateneo de Manila University Press.

Human Development Network (HDN) (2009), 'Philippine Human Development Report 2008/9'. http://hdn.org.ph/forthcoming-philippine-human-development-report-institutions-and-politics/.

Javorcik, B.S, C. Ozden, M. Spatareanu, and C. Neagu (2010), 'Migrant networks and foreign direct investment', *Journal of Development Economics*, **94**, 231–41.

Krueger, A.O. (1974), 'The political economy of the rent-seeking society', *American Economic Review*, **64**, 291–303.

Lien, D.H.D. (1986), 'A note on competitive bribery games', *Economics Letters*, **22**, 337–41. doi:10.1016/0165-1765(86)90093-5.

Miron, J.A. (2008). 'The budgetary implications of drug prohibition', Report for the Criminal Justice Policy Foundation and Law Enforcement Against Prohibition, Maryland.

Miron, J.A. (2004), *Drug War Crimes: The Consequences of Prohibition*, Oakland, California: Independent Institute.

Mokyr, J., and J.V.C. Nye (2007), 'Distributional coalitions, the Industrial Revolution, and the origins of economic growth in Britain', *Southern Economic Journal*, **74**, 50–70.

National Economic Development Authority (NEDA) (2011), *Philippine*

Development Plan 2011–2016. http://www.neda.gov.ph/PDP/2011-2016/default. asp.

North, D., J. Wallis, and B. Weingast (2009), *Violence and Social Orders*, Cambridge: Cambridge University Press.

Nye, J.V.C. (2011a), 'Taking institutions seriously: rethinking the political economy of development in the Philippines', *Asian Development Review*, **28**, 1–21.

Nye, J.V.C. (2011b), 'Why quantitative easing was good and should be better . . . and how the Philippines should benefit from it', Bangko Sentral ng Pilipinas (BSP) special lecture, 14 January. http://www.bsp.gov.ph/events/2011/Nye/nyetalk.pdf.

Nye, J.V.C. (2009), 'Why do elites permit reform?', in E. Chamlee-Wright (ed.), *The Annual Proceedings of the Wealth and Well-Being of Nations*, Beloit, Wisconsin: Beloit College.

Pritchett, L. (2003), 'A toy collection, a socialist star, and a democratic dud? (Growth theory, Vietnam and the Philippines)', in D. Rodrik (ed.), *In Search of Prosperity*, Princeton: Princeton University Press.

Schiff, M., and C. Ozden (eds) (2005), *International Migration, Remittances and the Brain Drain*, Washington DC and Basingstoke: World Bank and Palgrave Macmillan.

Shleifer, A., and R.W. Vishny (1993), 'Corruption', *Quarterly Journal of Economics*, **108**, 599–617. doi:10.2307/2118402.

Tullock, G. (1967), 'The welfare costs of tariffs, monopolies and theft', *Western Economic Journal*, **5**, 224–32.

Tullock, G. (1971), 'The cost of transfers', *Kyklos*, **24**, 629–43. doi:10.1111/j.1467-6435.1971.tb00624.x.

Tullock, G. (1975), 'Competing for aid', *Public Choice*, **21**, 41–51. doi:10.1007/BF01705944.

Wei, S.-J. 1997, 'Why is corruption so much more taxing than tax? Arbitrariness kills', National Bureau of Economic Research Working Paper No. 6255.

Weitzman, M.L. (1974), 'Prices vs. quantities', *Review of Economic Studies*, **41**, 477–91.

Woodruff, C., and R. Zenteno (2007), 'Migration networks and microenterprises in Mexico', *Journal of Development Economics*, **82**, 509–28. doi:10.1016/j.jdeveco.2006.03.006.

Index

Abiad, A. 165
accounting systems 156, 239
  growth accounting 85–8, 118, 338
Africa 13, 231, 335
Agénor, P. 80, 88
agglomeration, economics of 88
Aghion, P. 142, 300
aging populations 23, 24
  health services for 338
  savings/investments and 142, 143, 144, 145, 148, 151
agricultural sector 12, 20, 129; see also individual countries
Ahluwalia, M.S. 300
Akaike Information Criterion (AIC) 379
Ali Baba accommodations (Malaysia) 68
Allen, F. 156
Apergis, N. 149
Arab Spring, 2012 67
Argentina 124–5, 127, 129, 131
Aschauer, D. 85–6
Ascher, W. 95
ASEAN (Association of Southeast Asian Nations) 18, 41, 104, 184–210, 232, 318, 334–5
  as advisory 190
  Chiang Mai Initiative (CMI) 185
  economic integration 192, 193, 202
  FDI in 191–5, 196–200
  function 185, 196
  history 192
  internal disputes 187, 201, 202
  investment treaty regulation by 42, 184–204
  investments in 191–9
    definitions of 197, 200
  Japan and 185, 200
  Korea, Republic of and 185, 200
  membership 188, 195, 199, 202

most-favored nation status in 188, 189, 197, 200, 201
  national security issues 197–9, 202
  productivity levels in 232, 235
  structure 187, 191–5, 199
  trading partners 193, 194–5, 199–201
  see also individual countries
ASEAN Charter 42, 185, 191–5, 202–4
ASEAN Comprehensive Investment Agreement (ACIA), 2009 42, 195–9, 200
  dispute settlement under 201, 202
  restrictions enabled by 197–9
ASEAN Development Bank 104, 255–6, 341
ASEAN Economic Community (AEC) 42, 193–4
ASEAN Economic Ministers (AEM) 187, 188
ASEAN Free Trade Area (AFTA) 42, 194–5, 356
ASEAN Investment Area (AIA) Agreement, 1998 187–91, 193
  AIA Council 188, 90
  General Exceptions clause 188–9
ASEAN Investment Guarantee Agreement (IGA), 1987 185–7, 188, 189, 190, 191, 193, 195
  amendments to 187
ASEAN+3 185
ASEAN Summit 192
ASEAN Vision 2020 192, 203
ASEAN–PRC Investment Agreement, 2009 194, 200–201
Asian financial crisis (AFC), 1997–98 3, 4, 5, 12, 14–21, 30, 32, 34, 35, 37, 49, 51–2, 213
  effects of/response to 104–7, 154, 159, 175, 182, 185, 222, 246, 249, 252, 265, 267, 276, 278, 314, 345, 361, 389, 393–4

Asian values debate 53
Asia-Pacific Economic Cooperation
    (APEC) countries 203
Aswicahyono, H. 131
Australia, ASEAN and 193, 194–5,
    199–200, 201
automotive industry 20, 38, 214

Baek, C. 130
balance of payment protection 189–90
Banerjee, A. 93
Bangladesh 231
Bangko Sentral ng Pilipinas (BSP)
    392–4
bank failures/losses 31, 32, 163, 266
Bank Indonesia (BI) 20, 25, 247, 271,
    273–4, 281, 282–3
    risk-free securities (SBIs) 25, 247,
        265–7, 268, 271, 281, 283
bank lending 38, 154–5, 156, 157, 172,
    182, 265, 266–7, 270–80, 287, 296,
    319–20
bank regulation/reform 31–2, 247, 275,
    282, 283
bank rent 156
Bank of Thailand 350, 353, 369,
    370–71, 373
banking sector 30, 39
    central banks 19, 20, 35, 37, 40
    commercial banks 247
    as inefficient 267, 271, 281, 283
    international banks 31
    Islamic banking 228
    nationalization 287
    performance measurement in 163–70
    risk-taking in 265–6, 271, 273–4
    two-tier 31
    see also individual banks and
        countries
Barro, R. 52, 58, 89, 91
Basri, M.C. 20, 261
Beck, T. 146, 163
Benelux (Belgian company) 403
Berg, A. 356
Bergsten, F. 326
Bernanke, B.S. 91
Bhavani, A. 92
Blomstrom, M. 302
Bolivia 127
bond markets 30, 79, 85, 99, 154–5,

156, 163, 175–8, 247, 266; *see also*
    market structure
Bonin, J.P. 375
Bosworth, B. 299
brain drain 13, 232, 234–5, 242, 385–6;
    see also labor market
Brazil 127
bureaucracy, efficiency of 39, 40, 52,
    70, 240–41, 392, 398
business cycle theory 286, 303–4
    virtuous cycle effect 361

Caldéron, C. 86, 87, 88
Cambodia 188, 196, 199, 202
Campos, J.E. 397
Canning, D. 101
capacity utilization 276–7
capital accumulation/stock 4, 30, 91,
    137
    capital inflows 37–9
        see also foreign direct investment
    crony capitalism 30, 154, 386
    decline/stagnation in 104, 106–36,
        154, 155, 159
    in economic crises 106–36, 154
    growth model/measurement 108–15,
        157–70
    in offshore funds 38
    total factor productivity decline and
        106–36
        causes/impact of 116–31
    see also public goods; savings/
        investment
capital flight/outflows 18, 37, 137, 149
    home bias in 149
capital markets 150, 247, 275; *see also*
    market structure
Casacuberta, N. 130–31
central banks 19, 20, 37–8
    independence of 35, 37, 40
    see also individual banks
Chang, H.-J. 53
Chile 125, 127, 129
China, *see* People's Republic of China
    (PRC)
China Investment Corporation (CIC)
    334
civil liberties 52, 53, 54, 70
Collins, S.M. 299
Colombia 125–6, 127–8, 129

communications 86, 88, 90, 92, 95, 98,
231, 237, 261, 262–3, 264, 296–7
cost of 98
see also transport services
competition/competitiveness 85, 236,
237–41, 246, 263, 287, 345, 347,
349, 391, 398–403
in financial sector 31
competitive advantage 80
cooperation, *see* regional cooperation
corruption 14, 30, 34, 38, 52, 53, 232,
386–7, 392, 398, 403
control of 61, 67–8, 69–71, 386,
402
political instability and 54, 68, 69, 70
see also rents/rent seeking
cost–function methodology 88
Costa Rica 128
country studies, *see* individual
countries
credit arrangements 23, 143–4, 178–82,
266–74
consumption credit 267–8
domestic credit 157, 159, 178, 271
group financing 276, 277–8
investment credit 269–80, 282
public sector credit 157–8
securities market and 170–74
see also bank lending; savings/
investment
crony capitalism 30, 154, 386

de Long, J.B. 302
de Vries, G.J. 119, 124
debt 19, 27, 32–4
debt management 31
debt market 98
Deichmann, U. 80
Demetriades, P.O. 88
demographic bonus 12
demographic issues 12, 23
aging populations 23, 34, 142, 143,
144, 145, 148, 151, 338
population levels 4, 12, 76, 234,
336–7, 357
Demirgüç-Kunt, A. 146, 163
deregulation 29
free trade 30, 40, 194–5, 354
of labor market 287–8, 300
Dodd–Frank Act (US) 31

economic crises
Asian, *see* Asian financial crisis
capital accumulation in 106–36
causes of, *see* economic crisis, trigger
events
country outcomes 19–21
see also individual countries
effects of/response to 4, 5, 7–8, 12,
14–22, 30, 32, 34, 35, 37, 39–40,
42–3, 51–2, 104–6, 154
in Europe 3, 20, 41, 42–3
exogenous shocks 4, 51
in financial sector 30–31, 154–83
global, *see* global economic recession
in Latin America 12, 124–9
productivity levels in 106–36
recovery from 4, 5, 19, 77
patterns of 4
trigger events 18, 19, 30–31, 32–4,
154, 356
vulnerability indicators 18
economic growth 3, 6, 13, 19, 247
cost–function analysis of 88
evolutionary 13–14
financial sector and 156–70
growth accounting 85–8, 118, 338
measurement of 157–70
Economic Growth (Barro and
Sala-i-Martin) 52, 58
economic growth, in Asia 3–14, 42–3,
49, 154–7, 246–7, 315–19, 325–6
in Central Asia 49, 50
decline in 49–75
see also Asian financial crisis
dynamics of 4, 7–12
export-led 345, 350, 360, 378–82,
385, 386, 387, 388, 391
governance and 55–72
infrastructure and 76, 77–81, 85–95,
97–100
input growth 12
long-term 4
savings/investment and 148–51, 246,
302–6
in South Asia 49, 50
see also individual countries
economic integration 41
in ASEAN countries 192, 193, 202
Economic and Monetary Union
(EMU) 41

economic policies/reform 4, 5, 8,
    13–14, 18, 19–21, 30–42, 67–72
  on exchange rates, *see* exchange rates
  in financial sector 30–32, 37
  first-order reforms 387, 389, 403, 404
  fiscal 32–4, 39
  infrastructure reform 96–100
  institutional reform 39–40
  macroeconomic 20, 21, 32–9
  monetary 34–9
  on savings 23, 152
  see also individual countries
educational systems 13, 14, 231, 237,
    301, 331, 336
  investment in 80, 81, 95
Eiffel-Matiere SAS Consortium 403
electronics industry 20, 21; *see also*
    communications
energy supplies 77, 80, 85, 86, 88,
    90–91, 93, 94, 231, 264, 296–8,
    328, 329, 335, 337
  consumption levels 98
entrepreneurial activity 131, 274, 276,
    281–2
environmental issues 325, 327, 328–9,
    332, 336–7, 342
Environmental Kuznets Curve (EKC)
    337
Estache, A. 80
ethnic/racial issues 14, 52, 53, 68, 69,
    214, 235
European Union (EU) 41, 191, 373
  ASEAN and 200
  economic crises 3, 20, 41, 42–3
EU KLEMS Database 112
evolutionary economics 13–14
exchange rates 19, 20, 21, 26, 35, 37,
    38
  fixed 35, 38
  flexible 35–6, 37
  see also individual countries
exogenous shocks 4, 51
export-led growth 345, 350, 360,
    378–82, 385, 386, 387, 388,
    391; *see also* economic growth;
    international trade
exports, *see* international trade

family-owned firms 30
Fay, M. 80

Fazzari, S.M. 274, 278
Feldstein, M. 148–50, 362
Fernald, J. 87–8
financial crises, *see* economic crises
financial development, *see* savings/
    investment
financial regulation 19, 156
financial sector 10, 11, 19, 30–32, 37,
    154–8
  as competitive 31
  crises in 30–31, 154–83
  economic growth and 156–70
  growth measurement 157–70
  intermediation systems 155
  Islamic finance 228
  regression analysis of 161–2, 166–70,
    179–82
  as vulnerable 154
financial sector liberalization/reform
    154–6, 157, 159, 161, 164–5, 170,
    174
fiscal advisory councils 34
fiscal policies 32–4, 39, 85
  as cyclical 34, 306–9
  reform of 34
  revenue sharing 85
  see also economic policies/reform
Fisher, J.D.M. 304
food prices 36, 356
foreign direct investment (FDI) 5–6, 7,
    9, 37–9, 150
  in ASEAN area 191–5,
    196–200
  in infrastructure 99
  investment treaties and 184, 186–7,
    190–99
  see also savings/investment
Fukao, K. 130

G20 group 19, 40, 41
Gale, D. 156
Gandelman, N. 130–31
Gavin, M. 306
Germany 8, 9
Gerschenkron, A. 155
Glass–Steagall Act (US) 31
global economic recession (GER),
    2008–09 3–4, 5, 7, 8, 21, 32, 33, 35,
    37, 40, 41, 42, 49, 51–2, 164, 203–4,
    246, 251, 262, 264, 285, 294–6,

313, 318, 319–21, 345, 356, 372, 374, 375–6, 393–4
globalization, impact of 300, 325, 335, 378, 385
Gochoco-Bautista, M.S. 386, 392
governance 51–72, 79, 85
  economic growth and 55–72
  effectiveness measurement of 56, 66–72
  World Governance Indicators 67, 68, 233, 234
  see also institutional structure; political instability
Greenwood, J. 303, 304
gross domestic investment ratio 62–3
gross domestic product (GDP) 7, 14–18, 33, 59–61, 63–4, 108, 148, 157–60
  growth in 5, 6, 7, 9, 12, 21, 302
  measurement of 86, 90, 302
  projected trends in 145
  see also individual countries
gross national income (GN) 13; *see also* income levels
growth accounting 85–8, 118, 338
growth dynamics 4, 7–12; *see also* economic growth
Gurkaynak, R.S. 91

Hanushek, E. 95
Harrod-neutral production function 109, 114
Hausman specification tests 91
Hausmann, R.L. 354
health services 80, 81, 95, 240, 336, 338
  for aging populations 338
  medical tourism 231
  see also social welfare
Hellman, T.F. 156
Hercowitz, Z. 303, 304
Hill, H. 20, 261
Hong, K. 145
Hong Kong, China 8, 9, 81–3, 84, 120, 191, 335
  savings/investment 138–40, 141, 142, 146–7
Horioka, C.Y. 148–50, 362
household investment 286, 294, 295–7, 298, 303–6
housing shortages 304–6, 309

Huang Yiping, on market distortions 326–9, 375
Hubbard, G. 274
Hulten, C. 88
human capital 80, 91, 95, 98, 104; *see also* labor market
Human Development Network (HDN) 398
Huong, P.L. 44
Hurlin, C. 87

Iimi, A. 88
imports, *see* international trade
income levels 23, 77, 92, 145, 146, 213
  gross national (GNI) 13
  growth in 360–61
  infrastructure and 88, 92, 93–4, 95, 98
  middle-income economies, upgrading for 4, 12–14, 98
  see also poverty levels
Independent Commission on Banking (UK): Vickers Report 32
India 4, 285–312
  agricultural sector 287, 300, 301
  ASEAN and 193, 195
  banking sector 287, 289
  capital accumulation 286, 289, 292, 294, 298–9, 303
  see also household investment
  construction sector 296
  corporate sector 285–6, 287–8, 289–90, 299
  credit arrangements 288
  economic crises 285, 288–9, 294–5
  economic growth 4, 5–14, 285, 290–91
    dynamics of 7–12, 299–306
    literature survey 299–301
    regional differences 299–300
  economic policies/reform 8, 10, 32–4, 283, 285, 286, 287–90, 299, 300, 302–3, 310
    five-year plans 287, 304
    fiscal 292–3, 299, 306–9, 310
  educational system 231, 301
  exchange rates 35, 287, 288, 289
  external debt 27, 288, 292
  as a federation 299 300, 307, 309, 310

financial sector 286, 287, 288, 289–90, 293, 310
foreign direct investment (FDI) in 6, 9, 288–9
FDI by 191
GDP 5, 6, 9, 15, 18, 65–6, 285, 286, 291–3, 300, 307–9
governance 66, 68, 71, 72, 288, 290
housing policies 305–6, 310–11
housing shortages 304–6, 309
income levels 12, 299, 300, 304–6, 309
Indian migrant workers, remittances from 288, 389
industrial sector 287, 288, 290, 291, 299, 300
inflation rates 36, 285, 286, 290–91, 301, 310
infrastructure 10, 82, 84, 92, 285
infrastructure investment 296–8
institutional structure, *see* India, as a federation
interest rates 286, 289
international trade 6, 8, 9, 213, 285, 287, 288, 290, 291–2, 310
tariffs 288, 289
labor market 300, 301
skills base 300, 301
labor market regulation/liberalization 287–8, 300
legal/judicial system 286, 287–8, 289
manufacturing sector 299, 300–301
market structure 289–90
productivity levels 117, 120, 286, 299
total factor (TFP) 299
regulatory policies 287–8, 289–90
savings/investment 22–30, 65–6, 72, 138–40, 141, 146–7, 285, 287, 294–8, 302–6
household investment 286, 294, 295–7, 298, 302, 303–6, 311
services sector 291, 299, 300–301
business process outsourcing (BPO) 389–90
social structure 288, 290, 309, 310–11
state domestic product (SDP) 300
tax system 289

Indonesia 4, 246–84
agricultural sector 20, 248, 260, 261, 264, 265, 268
banking sector 20, 25, 247, 248, 265–80, 281
capital accumulation 247, 267, 272–3, 277, 283
competitiveness 236
construction sector 258, 259, 261, 264, 265, 268, 280
corruption in 234
credit arrangements 266–80
economic crises 5, 8, 10, 12, 19, 69, 104–7, 246, 247, 249, 251, 252, 262, 264, 265, 267, 276, 278
recovery from 20, 246, 252, 278, 279, 280–81
economic growth 5–14, 246, 248–9
dynamics of 7–12, 249–65
economic policies/reform 8, 10, 20, 32, 246, 247–9, 252
fiscal 248
ethnic/racial problems 69
exchange rates 35, 248, 263
external debt 27
financial sector 158–61, 163–70, 246–8, 264, 265–74
foreign direct investment (FDI) in 9, 256–7, 259, 275
GDP 9, 15, 18, 65–6, 248, 249–54, 256, 260, 261–2, 265, 276
governance 66, 68, 69, 71, 234, 247–8, 252, 254
health services 231
income levels 277–8
inflation rates 36, 271
infrastructure 10, 82, 84, 97, 248, 261, 262–3, 264
interest rates 259, 267, 272, 273–4, 275, 276, 281
international trade 9, 20, 248, 249, 251–2, 253, 256, 260, 264, 265, 268, 275–6
labor market 246, 252, 263
unemployment 246
legal/judicial system 248
decentralization law, 2001 252
manufacturing sector 258, 259, 261–2, 263–4, 265, 266, 267, 268, 277

machinery manufacture 258, 259, 264, 280
political instability 8, 19, 52, 252, 254, 268–9, 279
population levels 4
productivity levels 105–6, 129, 131–2, 235, 260–64
total factor (TFP) 105, 107, 116–26, 131, 132
property market 269
regulatory policies 248–9, 252, 260, 266, 275–6
savings/investment 10, 22–30, 65–6, 138–40, 141, 146–7, 247, 248, 249, 253, 254, 255–6, 256–81
investment behavior 274–80
services sector 264, 265
unemployment 246
see also labor market
industrial development 24, 53
industrial sectors 131, 172, 173–4
loans to 179–82
productivity levels 120–24, 127–31, 132
see also individual countries
inflation 35, 36–7, 38, 301
infrastructure 10, 11, 19, 76–103, 237
cost of 83, 85, 99
decision-making on 96–100
definition of 76, 78
demand for 78–83
economic growth and 76, 77–81, 85–95, 97–100
income levels and 88, 92, 93–4
as monopolistic 84, 97
poverty levels and 77, 78–9, 88, 92, 98
soft/hard 76, 97
spillover effects 76, 80
types of 76, 78
see also communications; energy supplies; transport services; urban services; water supplies
infrastructure investment 24, 25, 27–30, 34, 74, 76, 77, 78, 83–5, 96–100, 150, 285, 296–7
as inadequate 29–30
as long-term 79, 83, 97–100
opportunity costs 81
political issues in 83–5

private 30, 79, 85, 96–7, 98
productivity levels and 79–80, 85–8
in public goods 4, 29–30, 78–9, 86, 96–100
return on 96–100
types of 29, 30
see also individual countries
infrastructure performance 81–3, 96–100
innovation 97, 156
economic growth and 13, 14
intellectual property 333
technology transfer 80, 97, 156, 333–4, 335
innovation investment 14, 303–4, 332
institutional reform 39–40
institutional structure 49–75
banks, *see* banking system
central planning regimes 51, 53, 54
corruption in, *see* corruption
definition of 52
development of 13–14, 72, 163–70
economic performance and 52, 363–4
financial, *see* financial sector
formal/informal institutions 39, 52, 54
legal/judicial, *see* legal/judicial systems
open/closed regimes 51, 54
quality of 52, 66–72
social structure, *see* social structure
see also individual countries; infrastructure
intellectual property 333; *see also* innovation
International Monetary Fund (IMF) 19, 20, 21, 34, 106, 325
decline of trust in 26, 40, 41
IMF International Financial Statistics 157
International Road Federation (IRF) 91
international trade 3, 5–6, 7, 8, 9, 20–21, 192, 345
expansion/decline in 285, 345
import controls 288
import substitution 214, 287
import-biased 391
exports 3, 19, 20, 37, 99
see also import-led growth

free trade 30, 40, 194–5, 354
  importance of 76, 99, 246
  protectionism 3, 325
  tariffs 288, 289, 356
investment, *see* savings/investment
investment behavior 4, 24–5, 59–60, 61, 63–4, 274–80
investment law 190
investment treaties/agreements (IIAs) 41–2, 184–5
  FDI and 184, 186–7, 190–200
  UNCTAD survey of 223
  see also ASEAN
investment treaty regulation, by ASEAN 42, 185–204
  balance of payments protection 189–90
  regulatory administration 188
  treaty protection 190

Jalilian, H. 88
Japan 7, 8, 9, 33, 81, 82, 84, 191
  ASEAN and 185, 200
  economic crises 3, 42–3, 124–7, 130–31
  international trade 318, 372–3
  productivity levels 104–6, 117
    total factor (TFP) 105–6, 130–31
  savings/investment 23, 147, 149, 150
Jensen, R. 92
Jiang Gaoming 337
Jomo, K. 53
judicial systems, *see* legal/judicial systems

Kalirajan, K. 301
Kaminsky, G.M. 307
Karuppannan, S. 304
Kaufmann, D. 52, 67
Khan, M. 53
Kim, H. 149–50
Kochhar, K. 300–301
Korea, Republic of
  ASEAN and 185, 200
  economic crises 12, 104–7, 130–31
    recovery from 19
  economic growth 8, 9
    decline in 49, 174–5
  foreign direct investment (FDI) by 191

GDP 9, 17
  industrial sector 53
  infrastructure 81–3, 84
  market structure 175–8
  productivity levels 104–6, 117, 120, 132–3
    total factor (TFP) 12, 105–6, 130–31
  savings/investment 138–40, 141, 145–8
Krugman, Paul 19, 325
Krupp, C. 95
Kujis, L. 338–40
Kwon, H.U. 130

labor market 36, 116, 120–24, 129–30
  brain drain 13, 232, 234–5, 242, 385–6
  human capital 80, 91, 95, 98, 104
  migrant labor 229–30, 232, 235, 236
  skills base 13, 232, 234–5, 242, 300
  unemployment 36
  see also individual countries
labor market deregulation 287–8, 300
labor productivity, *see* productivity levels
Laeven, L. 124
Lal, D. 4
Lao, People's Democratic Republic 188, 195, 199, 202
Latin America 13, 129, 306
  economic crises 12, 124–9, 130–31
  productivity levels 107, 124–9, 130–31
Lee, J. 89, 91, 145
legal/judicial systems 39, 40, 52, 54, 58, 61, 65–6, 156, 189
  investment law 190
  international law 192
  see also corruption; individual countries
Lehman Brothers Holdings Inc. 225
Levine, R. 157
loans, *see* credit arrangements
Loke, W.H. 237

M2 measures 157–60, 175
McCawley, P. 98
McKinnon, R.I. 155, 156
Maddison, A. 6

Malaysia 4, 213–45
  accountancy services 239–40
  banking sector 222, 228, 231, 239
  capital accumulation 225–6
  competitiveness 235–7
  corruption in 232, 233, 241
  economic crises 5, 8, 11, 104–7, 213,
    215–16, 217, 218, 220–21, 222,
    227, 228, 230
  economic growth 5–14, 213, 214–26,
    241–3
    decline in 49, 213, 240
    dynamics of 7–12
  economic policies/reform 11, 14, 21,
    32–4, 220–25, 241
    Financial Master Plan, 2001 228
    fiscal 220–22, 239
    monetary 218
    New Economic Policy (NEP),
      1971 214–15, 241–2
    Vision 2020 213
  educational system 237
  ethnic/racial problems 14, 52, 68,
    214, 235
  exchange rates 35, 215, 219–20
  external debt 27, 214–15
  financial sector 158–61, 163–70, 228
    Islamic finance 228
  foreign direct investment (FDI) in
    9, 214–15, 241, 224, 225, 226,
    227–8
  FDI by 230–31, 241
  government-linked companies
    (GLCs) 228–9, 230–31
  GDP 9, 16, 18, 65–6, 215, 216,
    217–18
  governance 66, 68, 233, 234
  health services 240
  income levels 12, 213, 215, 226–7
  industrial sector 214, 217–18, 223
  inflation rates 36, 215, 218, 218, 219
  infrastructure 11, 82, 84, 231, 237,
    239–40
  institutional structure 232, 239–40
  interest rates 32
  international trade 9, 20–21, 213,
    214–15, 216, 217, 223
  labor market 229, 232, 234–5, 241
    migrant labor 229–30, 232, 235,
      236

    outflow of skilled labor 232,
      234–5, 242
    unemployment 215, 218, 230
  legal/judicial system 233, 239
  manufacturing sector 213, 214, 215,
    217–18, 223, 227–8, 229–31,
    235–7, 242
  as a middle-income economy 4,
    12–13, 14, 227
  natural resources 20, 213, 214, 217
  political instability 14, 52, 68
  prices/price stability 218, 223
  productivity levels 105–6, 117, 122,
    213, 214, 215, 217–18, 223, 227,
    232, 234–5, 242
    total factor (TFP) 216–17
  regulatory policies 233, 237–8,
    240–41
  savings/investment 11, 22–30, 65–6,
    138–40, 141, 146–7, 216, 223–41
  services sector 214–15, 218, 228,
    230–31, 238, 242–3
    entry barriers 237–41
  social welfare 218–19
  unemployment 215, 218, 230
    see also labor market
Mamuneas, T. 88
market confidence 252
market distortions 326–9
market entry 237–41, 288
market failure 131, 156
market integration 80
market structure 14, 32, 79, 335
  bonds 30, 79, 85, 99, 154–5, 156,
    163, 175–8, 247, 266
  capital 150, 247
  commodities 41
  debts 98
  government procurement 237
  loans 170
    see also bank lending
  open 155, 157
  protectionism 237
  securities 170–74
    risk-free 25, 247, 265–7, 268, 271,
      281
  stocks/shares 31, 32, 154–5, 156, 157,
    163, 175–6, 182, 247, 289–90
Mendoza, A.M. 97
Menon, J. 88

Mexico 126, 128, 129, 389
middle-income economies 4, 12–14, 98
migrant workers, remittances sent
    home by 288, 385, 388, 389, 390,
    397, 398
Mishkin, F.S. 36, 37
monetary policies 34–9
  on exchange rates 19, 20, 21, 26, 35,
    37, 38, 373
  quantitative easing 40–41
  see also economic policies/reform
Mongolia 49, 50, 65, 82, 84
monopolies 84, 97
moral hazard concept 31, 97, 156
Moreno-Dodson, B. 80, 88
Myanmar 188, 196, 199, 202
Myint, H. 4

National Food Authority (NFA),
    Philippines 392, 403
national security issues 197–9, 202
natural resources 20, 213, 214, 217, 335
Nelson, Richard, on evolutionary
    economics 13–14
New Zealand, ASEAN and 193, 194–5,
    199–200, 201
newly industrialized economies (NIEs)
    24
North, D. 52, 53, 399
Nye, J.V.C. 387, 391, 399

Obstfeld, M. 149
Oceania 49, 50
OECD (Organisation for Economic
    Cooperation and Development)
    countries 32, 34, 36, 40, 87, 235
  infrastructure 81, 83
  savings/investment 148–9
oil prices 248, 288, 328, 346, 347,
    350–51, 353, 356, 360
Orazio, P.A. 302

Pakistan 49, 50, 82, 84, 92, 231
  savings/investment 138–40, 141, 142,
    145–8
Park, C.Y. 149–50
patronage 68
Pedroni, P. 101
Penn World Tables (PWT) 90, 91, 141,
    302

pensions, *see* social welfare
People's Bank of China (PBC) 319
People's Republic of China (PRC) 4,
    313–44
  agricultural sector 313, 314, 315, 320
  ASEAN and 185, 193, 194, 200–201,
    334–5
  banking sector 319–20, 327–8, 332
  capital accumulation 313, 315, 318,
    320, 323
    gross domestic (GDCF) 318
  Chinese migrant workers,
    remittances from 389
  competitiveness 236, 237, 263
  construction industry 334–5
  consumption levels 322, 323–4,
    331–2
  corruption in 70, 232, 254
  economic crises 10, 313, 314, 318,
    319–21
  economic growth 5, 5–14, 54,
    299–300, 315–18, 320–21,
    330–37
    dynamics of 7–12, 313–14
    economic policies/reform 8, 10,
    52–4, 313–15, 319–21, 327,
    340–41
    as export-led 315–19, 325–7,
    330–31
    fiscal 319–21, 332
    five-year plans 313, 340
    future of 337–42
    imbalances in 321–30
    monetary 319–20, 321
    open-door 313, 314, 315
  economic/political importance
    145–8, 337–42
  educational system 231, 331, 336
  energy supplies 328, 329, 335, 337
  environmental issues 325, 327,
    328–9, 332, 336–7, 342
  exchange rates 35, 36, 324–6, 327,
    328, 330–31, 342
  external debt 27
  financial sector 158–61, 163–70,
    327–8
  foreign direct investment (FDI) in
    5–6, 7, 9, 289, 299, 318, 325,
    328, 329, 332–5
    Look West strategy 333

FDI by 318, 328, 332–5, 342
GDP 5, 6, 7, 9, 15, 18, 65–6, 314,
    315–18, 319, 320, 333, 338, 339,
    340, 341
governance 65–6, 68, 70, 72, 234,
    337
  regional 319, 320, 321, 324, 333,
    336
health services 336, 338
housing policies 319, 320, 336
income levels 12, 320, 327, 332,
    335–6
  gross national (GNI) 314, 315
  minimum wage 320
  see also poverty levels
industrial sector 299, 313, 315
  strategic industries 340–41
inflation rates 36, 320, 327
infrastructure 10, 81–3, 84, 92, 93,
    236
  see also energy supplies
infrastructure investment 319,
    320–21, 336
innovation in 333–4, 335
international trade 5–6, 7, 9, 20, 213,
    299, 315–18, 324–5, 373
  export-led growth 315–19, 325–6
  friction in 325–6
  liberalization 314, 318
  tariffs 314
labor market 315, 320, 325, 327, 329,
    333, 334, 336, 338
  migrant labor 319, 327, 336
  unemployment 314, 319
land ownership 328
legal/judicial system 332
manufacturing sector 263, 320, 324,
    333
market structure 314, 329
  free market 314–15
  Special Economic Zones (SEZs)
    314
natural disasters 319
political instability 70
population levels 12, 336–7, 338
  aging population 338
poverty levels 314, 336
  see also income levels
prices/price stability 314, 320, 327,
    329

productivity levels 117, 336
  total factor (TFP) 299
processing sector 318, 325, 327
regulatory policies 318, 333
savings/investment 10, 22–30, 49, 50,
    65–6, 72, 138–40, 141–2, 143–8,
    150, 154, 314, 318, 322–4, 331–2
  decline in 319
  household savings 322–3, 331
  trade-related investment measures
    (TRIMS) 333
social structure 335–6
social welfare 320, 322–3, 331, 336
state-owned enterprises (SOEs) 314,
    323, 327–8, 332, 334–5, 336
tax system 329, 331, 332, 337
unemployment 314, 319
  see also labor market
US and 325–6
  see also Hong Kong, China;
    Taipei,China
Perotti, R. 306
Peru 128
Peterson Institute (US) 325, 326
Philippines 4, 385–407
  agricultural sector 386, 389, 390,
    391, 392, 403
  airline industry 402–3
  ASEAN and 201
  banking sector 392–4
  competitiveness 236, 287, 391,
    398–403
  corruption in 234, 386–7, 392, 398,
    402–3
  domestic demand/consumption 385,
    388–9
  economic crises 8, 11, 19, 104–7,
    385, 389, 393–4
    recovery from 21–2
  economic growth 5–14
    decline in 49
    dynamics of 7–12, 385
    export-led 385, 386, 387, 388,
      391
    time-series analysis if 387–98
  economic policies/reform 8, 11,
    32–4, 385, 387, 398–404
    Development Plan 2011–16 398–9
    fiscal 386, 392, 397 8
    monetary 386, 392–3

exchange rates 35, 386, 392–3
external debt 27, 294, 397–8
Filipino migrant workers,
    remittances from 385, 388, 389,
    390, 397, 398
financial sector 158–61, 163–70, 392
foreign direct investment (FDI) in 9,
    385, 392
GDP 9, 16, 18, 65–6, 385, 388–9
governance 65–6, 68, 69–70, 234,
    395–403
income levels 12, 386, 391
industrial sector 386, 389, 391, 392,
    403
inflation rates 36, 386, 392, 393
infrastructure 11, 82, 84, 97, 391,
    398
institutional structure 386, 391, 392,
    395–8, 404
interest rates 392
international trade 8, 9, 385, 387–95
    export-led growth 385, 386, 387,
        388, 391
    import bias 391
    liberalization 386
labor market 385, 386, 391
    outflow of skilled labor 385–6
labor protection 386
legal/judicial system 386, 398, 402,
    403
    land ownership 386, 392, 403
manufacturing sector 389, 391, 392
market structure 401–3
as a middle-income economy 4
political instability 8, 19, 69–70,
    386–7, 388, 392
prices/price stability 386, 387,
    399–401, 403
productivity levels 105–6, 121, 235,
    385, 387–95
    total factor (TFP) 106, 116–17,
        121, 385
public works contracts 403
regulatory policies 387, 392, 403
savings/investment 11, 22–30, 65–6,
    69–70, 138–40, 141, 145–8, 385,
    386–95, 403–4
services sector 389, 390
    business process outsourcing
        (BPO) 389–90

tax system 402
technology transfer to 385–6
Pill, H. 156
Plasschaert, S. 325
political instability 8, 14, 19–20, 30, 52,
    54, 69, 70, 97
    corruption and 54, 58, 69, 70
    see also governance; individual
        countries
population levels 4, 76; *see also*
    demographic issues
poverty levels 3, 41, 54, 76–7, 213, 314,
    331–2
    housing policy and 304–6
    infrastructure for the poor 77, 78–9,
        88, 92, 98
    slum dwellers 77
    see also social welfare
prices/price stability 37, 41, 248, 345,
    350, 387
    of food 36, 356
    of infrastructure services 85
    of oil 248, 288, 328, 346, 347,
        350–51, 353, 356, 360
Pritchett, L. 356, 387
productivity levels 12, 37, 302
    decline in 104–7
        capital accumulation and 106–36,
            154
        causes of 116–31
    in economic crises 106–36
    GDP, *see* gross domestic product
    growth model of 108–15
    household investment and 304
    infrastructure investment and 79–80,
        85–8
    labor migration and 116
    resource allocation and 116–30, 131,
        132
    by sector 120–24, 127–31, 132
    total factor (TFP), *see* total factor
        productivity
    see also individual countries
protectionism 3, 41, 53
public goods, provision of 4, 29–34,
    40–41, 78–9, 96–100, 237, 261, 385
    contracts for 403
    difficulties of 29–30
    state-owned enterprises (SOEs) 29,
        314, 323, 327–8, 332, 334–5, 336

public–private partnerships (PPPs) 30, 79, 85, 96–7, 98
  divestment/buy-outs 97

quantitative easing policies 40–41
Quibria, M. 56

racial issues, *see* ethnic/racial issues
regime legitimacy, *see* political instability
regional cooperation 40–42, 99
  G20 group 19, 40, 41
  investment agreements 41–2
  see also ASEAN
regulatory policies 31–2, 40, 98
  as barriers to market entry 237–8, 240–41
  ethnic/racial issues and 14, 52, 68, 214, 235
  investment treaty regulation 42, 185–204
  quality of 67, 68
Reinhart, C.M. 32
rents/rent-seeking behavior 30, 53, 54, 86, 248, 252, 386, 392, 399; *see also* corruption
Republic of Korea, *see* Korea, Republic of
research and development (R&D), *see* innovation
Reserve Bank of India (RBI) 289
Reside, R.E. 97
resource allocation 155–6, 287
  productivity levels and 116–30, 131, 132
risk/risk-sharing 79, 96–7, 98, 274, 276, 282, 395
  in banking sector 265–6, 271, 273–4
Roberts, M. 80
Rodrik, D. 299, 355
Rogoff, K.S. 32, 149
Roland-Holst, D. 79
Rybczynski theorem 130

Sala-i-Martin, X. 52, 58
Sandleris, G. 131
sanitation, *see* water supplies/ sanitation
Saudi Arabia 231

savings/investment 3, 4, 10, 11, 12, 21–30, 104, 137–53, 345
  aging populations and 142, 143, 144, 145, 148, 151
  capital accumulation, *see* capital accumulation
  convergence effect 150
  corporate savings 145
  credit arrangements, *see* credit arrangements
  current account deficits 21
  definitions of 197, 300
  economic growth and 149–51, 246, 302–6
  equipment investment 302
  foreign direct investment 5–6, 7, 9, 37–9, 99, 150, 184, 186–7, 190–200
  future trends 145–8, 150–52
  gross domestic investment ratio 62–3
  historical trends 137–42, 151
  household investment 286, 294, 295–7, 298, 303–6
  imbalances in 21–2, 25–7
  infrastructure investment, *see* infrastructure investment
  innovation investment 14, 303–4, 332
  investment behavior 4, 24–5, 59–60, 61, 63–4, 274–80
  investment law 190
  investment quality 256–8, 279–80
  investment treaties/agreements 41–2, 184–5, 186–7, 190–200, 203
  levels of 14, 23, 24–5, 33–4, 302
    decline in 49–75, 147–8, 150–51, 155
    measurement of 141, 142–8
    nominal/real savings rates 138–9, 141–2, 152
    over/under investment 22, 32, 345, 360–67
  literature survey of 149
  mandatory savings 22, 34
  neo-classical model 247
  policies on 23, 152
  see also individual countries
Securities and Exchange Board of India (SEBI) 289–90
securities market 170–74

private 171, 172–4
public 170–71, 172
risk-free 25, 247, 265–7, 268, 271,
	281, 283
Seethepalli, K. 86
Servén, L. 86, 88
services sector 129, 299, 300
	business process outsourcing (BPO)
		289–90
Shaw, E.S. 155
Shioji, E. 142, 150
shocks, *see* economic crises
Singapore
	competitiveness 235, 236, 237
	corruption in 232, 234
	economic growth 8, 9
		decline in 49
	economic policies/reform 27, 33
	exchange rates 35
	financial sector 158–61, 163–70
	foreign direct investment (FDI) in
		335
	governance 234
	GDP 16, 33
	inflation rates 36
	infrastructure 81–3, 84
	productivity levels 121, 122, 232, 235
	savings/investment 22, 24, 25,
		138–40, 141, 145–8
	services sector 335
Singh, K. 301
Sivam, A. 304
social structure/stability 53–4, 69
	limited-access societies 399
	legal/judicial systems 39, 40, 52, 54,
		58, 61, 65–6, 156, 189, 192
	see also corruption
social welfare 18, 19, 23, 32, 34, 36, 39,
		80, 145, 152, 320, 331
	health services 80, 81, 95, 231, 240,
		336, 338
Sri Lanka 49, 50
Srinivasan, T.N. 299
state-owned enterprises (SOEs) 29,
		314, 323, 327–8, 332, 334–5, 336
Stiglitz, J. 156
stock/shares market 31, 32, 154–5, 156,
		157, 163, 175, 247, 289–90
	capitalization of 163–70, 175–6, 180
Straub, S. 87, 88

Subramanian, A. 299
Summers, L.M. 302

Taipei,China 13, 65, 81, 82, 84, 117,
		121
	foreign direct investment by 191
	savings/investment 138–40, 141,
		146–7
Talvi, E. 306
tax cuts 34, 329, 332
tax systems 70, 81, 329, 331
	VAT 337
technology transfer 80, 97, 156, 333–4,
		335, 385–6; *see also* innovation
telecommunications, *see*
	communications
Telekom Malaysia Berhad (TMB)
		231
Tenaga Nasional Berhad (Malaysia)
		231
Tendulkar, S.R. 299
Terada-Hagiwara, A. 87
Thailand 4, 345–84
	agricultural sector 350, 351, 354,
		372, 377–8
	ASEAN and 201
	banking sector 346, 361, 362, 369,
		374, 375, 380–81
	capital accumulation 348–9, 350,
		360–61, 364, 369, 377–8
	competitiveness 236, 237, 345, 347,
		349
	corruption in 234
	economic crises 5, 8, 11, 12, 18,
		69, 104–7, 154, 246, 347, 361,
		363–4, 372, 374, 375–6
		recovery from 20–21, 353–60
	economic growth 5, 14, 345–53
		decline in 49
		dynamics of 7–12, 354–5, 356
		as export-led 345, 350, 360,
			378–82
		vector autoregressive model of
			379–82
	economic policies/reform 11, 32–4,
		349, 352, 353
		development plans 346, 348
		fiscal 348, 352–3, 357, 367–8,
			376–7
		monetary 368–70, 381

exchange rates 35, 345, 346, 348–9,
  353, 354, 356, 369, 370–73, 381
external debt 27
financial sector 32, 155, 158–61,
  163–74, 179–82, 345, 373–8
foreign direct investment (FDI) in 9,
  356, 366, 367, 374
GDP 9, 17, 18, 65–6, 346, 347, 348,
  354, 357, 358, 359, 361, 363,
  375
governance 66, 68–9
income levels 12, 348, 356, 360–61,
  362–3
inflation rates 36, 345, 346, 347, 357,
  358, 370
infrastructure 11, 82, 84, 92, 346
institutional structure 353–4, 356
interest rates 374
international trade 9, 20–21, 345,
  347, 348–52, 353, 356, 359,
  372–3, 374
  export-led growth 345, 350, 360,
    378–82
labor market 364
manufacturing sector 347, 350, 351,
  354, 364, 365, 366, 378
market structure 170–74
as a middle-income economy 4, 350
political instability 8, 20, 52, 69, 353,
  354, 355–6, 360, 361, 375
population levels 12, 234, 357
prices/price stability 345, 360, 372,
  380, 381
  of food 356
  of oil 346, 347, 350–51, 353, 356,
    360
productivity levels 105–6, 129,
  131–2, 235, 346, 347, 357,
  360–61, 364, 365, 366, 382
  total factor (TFP) 106, 107,
    116–26, 130, 132
property market 374–5
public debt 350–51, 353, 357
regulatory policies 356, 374
savings/investment 11, 22–30, 65–6,
  138–40, 141–2, 146–8, 346,
  347–9, 357, 373–4, 381, 382
  over/under investment 345, 360–67
tax system 346, 361–2, 368, 373
Tham, S.Y. 237

Timmer, M.P. 119, 124
total factor productivity (TFP) 12, 80,
  87, 104, 105–6
  decline in 105–7
  impact of 116–31
  in industrial sectors 130–31
  measurement of 12
  see also productivity levels
trade, *see* international trade
trade treaties/agreements 185–204
  Model Bilateral (Model BITs)
    196
Transparency International Corruption
  Perception Index 232
transport services 77, 80, 85, 90, 92–3,
  261, 296–7
  air 90, 92–3, 402–3
  low carbon 99
  rail 90, 92, 94, 98
  roads 86, 87–8, 90, 92, 94, 98, 297
  see also communications
Tsoumas, C. 149

unemployment 36; *see also* individual
  countries; labor market
United Kingdom (UK) 20
United Nations (UN) 145
UN Conference on Trade and
  Development (UNCTAD) 184,
  203
  World Investment Report 184
UN Industrial Development
  Organization (UNIDO)
  Comparative Industrial
  Performance Index 235, 236, 237
United States (US) 9, 31, 52
  ASEAN and 193, 195
  People's Republic of China and
    325–6
  economic crises 18, 20, 37, 42–3,
    222
    recovery from 19
  exchange rates 326
  foreign direct investment (FDI) by
    191
  infrastructure 87–8
  international trade 373
US Congressional Budget Office 34
urban infrastructure/urbanization 77,
  98–9

Uruguay 130–31
utilities, *see* energy supplies; water
  supplies/sanitation

Valencia, F. 124
Vegh, C.A. 306
Venezuela 128
Vial, V. 131
Viet Nam 44
  ASEAN and 188, 196, 199,
    202
  corruption in 71
  economic crises 10, 21
  economic growth 5, 7
  economic policies/reform 8, 10,
    33
  exchange rates 35
  external debt 27
  financial sector 158–61
  foreign direct investment (FDI) in
    196
  GDP 7, 10, 17, 18, 33, 65–6
  governance 65–6, 68, 71, 72
  income levels 12
  inflation rates 36
  infrastructure 10, 82, 84
  international trade 213
  productivity levels 235
  savings/investment 10, 22, 23, 24, 25,
    26, 49, 50, 65–6, 71, 72, 138–40,
    141, 146–7, 154
Volcker, Paul 31
Vu, T.K. 142, 150

Warr, P. 88
water supplies/sanitation 77, 85, 88, 95,
  264, 296–8
Weiss, J. 88
Wells, R. 19
Woo, J. 307
World Bank
  Ease of Doing Business 237, 240–41,
    391–2
  Global Development Finance 163
  on income groups 13, 92, 145
  in investment behavior 24
  on skill shortages 232, 235, 242
World Bank Enterprise Surveys 80
World Bank Logistics Performance
  Index (LPI) 81
World Bank Private Participation in
  Infrastructure (PPI) Project 95
World Databank 90
World Development Indicators (WDI)
  (World Bank) 90, 141, 389
World Economic Forum Global
  Competitiveness Report/Index
  (GCR) 81, 391
World Trade Organization (WTO) 237,
  314, 318, 332
Wößmann, L. 95
Wright, M.L.J. 131

Yu Yongding 320, 325, 333–4

Zainal, A.Y. 214
Zervas, S. 157